THE DAY IS NOW FAR SPENT

Robert Cardinal Sarah
with Nicolas Diat

The Day Is Now
Far Spent

Translated by Michael J. Miller

IGNATIUS PRESS   SAN FRANCISCO

Original French edition:
Le soir approche et déjà le jour baisse
© 2019 by Librairie Arthème Fayard, Paris, France

Cover art: © 2019 Rights Reserved

Cover design by John Herreid

ISBN 978-1-62164-324-1
Library of Congress Catalogue number 2019937031
Printed in the United States of America ∞

*For Benedict XVI, peerless architect of
the rebuilding of the Church.*

*For Francis, faithful and devoted son of
Saint Ignatius.*

*For the priests throughout the world,
in thanksgiving on the occasion of my
Golden Jubilee of priesthood.*

If God is for us, who is against us?

—Letter of Saint Paul
to the Romans

CONTENTS

Part IV

Rediscovering Hope:
The Practice of the Christian Virtues

ALAS, JUDAS ISCARIOT

If these were silent, the very stones would cry out.

—Luke 19:40

A traitor ... is one that swears and lies.

—William Shakespeare, *Macbeth*

Why speak up once more? In my last book, I invited you to silence. However, I can no longer be silent. I must no longer remain silent. Christians are disoriented. Every day from all sides, I receive calls for help from those who no longer know what to believe. Every day I meet in Rome with priests who are discouraged and wounded. The Church is experiencing the dark night of the soul. The mystery of iniquity is enveloping and blinding her.

Every day the most terrifying news reports reach us. Not a week goes by without the revelation of a case of sexual abuse. Each one of these revelations comes to rend our hearts as children of the Church. As Saint Paul VI used to say, we are being invaded by the smoke of Satan. The Church, which ought to be a place of light, has become a dwelling place of darkness. It ought to be a secure, peaceful family home, but look: it has become a den of thieves! How can we tolerate the fact that predators have entered among us, into our ranks? Many faithful priests behave every day as attentive shepherds, kindly fathers, and sure guides. But some men of God have become agents of the Evil One. They have sought to defile the pure souls of the littlest ones. They have humiliated the image of Christ that is present in every child.

Priests throughout the world have felt humiliated and betrayed by so many abominations. Following Jesus, the Church is experiencing the mystery of the scourging. Her body is lacerated. Who is inflicting the lashes? The very ones who ought to love and protect her! Yes, I make so bold as to borrow the words of Pope Francis: the mystery of Judas hangs over our time. The mystery of betrayal oozes from the walls of the Church. The acts of abuse committed against minors reveal this in the most abominable way possible. But we must have the courage to look our sin in the face: this betrayal was prepared and caused by many other less visible, more subtle ones that, nevertheless, were just as profound. For a long time, we have been experiencing the mystery of Judas. What is now appearing in broad daylight has deep-seated causes that we must have the courage to denounce clearly. At its root, the crisis through which the clergy, the Church, and the world are going is a spiritual crisis, a crisis of faith. We are experiencing the mystery of iniquity, the mystery of betrayal, the mystery of Judas.

Allow me to meditate with you on the figure of Judas. Jesus had called him, like all the other apostles. Jesus loved him! He had sent him to proclaim the Good News. But little by little, doubt had taken hold of Judas' heart. Imperceptibly, he started to judge the teaching of Jesus. He told himself: This Jesus is too demanding, not very effective. Judas wanted to make the Kingdom of God come to earth right away, by human means and according to his personal plans. However, he had heard Jesus tell him: "Your thoughts are not my thoughts, your ways are not my ways" (see Is 55:8). Despite everything, Judas distanced himself. He no longer listened to Christ. He no longer accompanied him during those long nights of silence and prayer. Judas took refuge in worldly affairs. He busied himself with the purse, money, and commerce. The liar continued to follow Christ, but he no longer believed. He murmured. On Holy Thursday, the Master washed his feet. His heart must have been quite hardened, for he was not moved. The Lord was there in front of him, on his knees, a humbled servant, washing the feet of the one who was to hand him over. Jesus looked at him one last time, his eyes full of kindness and mercy. But the devil had already entered into Judas' heart. He did not lower his eyes. Interiorly he must have pronounced the ancient words of rebellion: *Non serviam,* "I will not serve." During the Last Supper, he took Communion even though his plan was set. This was the first sacrilegious Communion in history. And he betrayed him.

Judas is for all eternity the traitor's name, and his shadow hangs over us today. Yes, like him, we have betrayed! We have abandoned prayer. The evil of efficient activism has infiltrated everywhere. We seek to imitate the organization of big businesses. We forget that prayer alone is the blood that can course through the heart of the Church. We say that we have no time to waste. We want to use this time for useful social works. Someone who no longer prays has already betrayed. Already he is willing to make all sorts of compromises with the world. He is walking on the path of Judas.

All sorts of things are challenged, and we tolerate it. Catholic doctrine is called into question. In the name of so-called intellectual positions, theologians amuse themselves by deconstructing dogmas and emptying morality of its profound meaning. Relativism is the mask of Judas disguised as an intellectual. How then can we be surprised to hear that so many priests break their commitments? We relativize the meaning of celibacy; we claim the right to have a private life, which is contrary to the priest's mission. Some go so far as to claim the right to perform homosexual acts. Scandals follow one another, among priests and among bishops.

The mystery of Judas is spreading. Therefore, I want to say to all priests: stay strong and upright. Certainly, because of a few ministers, you will all be labeled as homosexuals. They will drag the Catholic Church through the mud. They will present her as though she were made up entirely of hypocritical, power-hungry priests. Let not your heart be troubled. On Good Friday, Jesus was charged with all the crimes in the world, and Jerusalem shouted: "Crucify him! Crucify him!" Notwithstanding the tendentious investigations that show you the disastrous situation of irresponsible churchmen who have an anemic interior life yet are in command of the very government of the Church, remain calm and confident like the Virgin and Saint John at the foot of the Cross. The immoral priests, bishops, and cardinals will in no way tarnish the luminous testimony of more than four hundred thousand priests throughout the world who, every day and faithfully, serve the Lord in holiness and joy. Despite the violence of the attacks that she may suffer, the Church will not die. This is the Lord's promise, and his word is infallible.

Christians are trembling, wavering, doubting. I want this book to be for them. To tell them: do not doubt! Hold fast to doctrine! Hold fast to prayer! I want this book to strengthen faithful Christians and priests.

The mystery of Judas, the mystery of betrayal, is a subtle poison. The devil seeks to make us doubt the Church. He wants us to regard her as a human organization in crisis. However, she is so much more than that: she is the continuation of Christ. The devil drives us to division and schism. He wants to make us believe that the Church has betrayed us. But the Church does not betray. The Church, full of sinners, is herself without sin! There will always be enough light in her for those who seek God. Do not be tempted by hatred, division, manipulation. It is not a matter of believing a party, of rising up against each other: "The Master warned us against these dangers to the point of reassuring the people, even with regard to the bad shepherds: one must not abandon the Church, that seat of truth, because of them.... Therefore let us not become lost in the evil of division because of those who are wicked", Saint Augustine said (Letter 105).

The Church is suffering; she is trampled on, and her enemies are within. Let us not abandon her. All pastors are sinful men, but they bear within themselves the mystery of Christ.

What is to be done, then? It is not a matter of organizing and implementing strategies. How could anyone think that we could improve things by ourselves? That would be to enter again into the lethal illusion of Judas.

Given the surge of sins in the ranks of the Church, we are tempted to try to take things into our own hands. We are tempted to try to purify the Church by our own strength. That would be a mistake. What would we do? Form a party? A movement? That is the most serious temptation: the showy disguise of division. Under the pretext of doing good, people become divided, they criticize each other, they tear each other apart. And the devil snickers. He has succeeded in tempting good people under the appearance of good. We do not reform the Church by division and hatred. We reform the Church when we start by changing ourselves! Let us not hesitate, each one in his place, to denounce sin, starting with our own.

I tremble at the thought that Christ's seamless garment is in danger of being torn again. Jesus suffered agony when he saw in advance the divisions of Christians. Let us not crucify him again! His heart begs us: he thirsts for unity! The devil is afraid of being called by his name. He likes to drape himself in the fog of ambiguity. Let us be clear about one thing. "To call things by the wrong name is to add to the world's misfortune", Albert Camus said.

In this book, I will not hesitate to use forceful language. With the help of the author and essayist Nicolas Diat, without whom little would have been possible and who has been unfailingly faithful since the writing of *God or Nothing*, I intend to take my inspiration from the Word of God, which is like a two-edged sword. Let us not be afraid to say that the Church needs profound reform and that this happens through our conversion.

Forgive me if some of my words shock you. I do not want to put you to sleep with soothing, lying talk. I seek neither success nor popularity. This book is the cry of my soul! It is a cry of love for God and for my brethren. I owe to you, to you Christians, the only truth that saves. The Church is dying because her pastors are afraid to speak in all truth and clarity. We are afraid of the media, afraid of public opinion, afraid of our own brethren! The good shepherd gives his life for his sheep.

Today, in these pages, I offer you what is at the heart of my life: faith in God. In a little while I will appear before the eternal Judge. If I do not hand on to you the truth that I received, what will I say to him then? We bishops ought to tremble at the thought of our guilty silences, our complicit silences, our over-indulgent silences in dealing with the world.

People often ask me: What should we do? When division threatens, it is necessary to strengthen unity. This has nothing to do with a team spirit as it exists in the world. The unity of the Church has its source in the heart of Jesus Christ. We must stay close to it, in it. This heart that was pierced by the lance so that we might be able to take refuge there will be our house. The unity of the Church rests on four columns. Prayer, Catholic doctrine, love for Peter, and mutual charity must become the priorities of our soul and of all our activities.

Prayer

Without union with God, every attempt to strengthen the Church and the faith will be in vain. Without prayer, we will be clanging cymbals. We will sink to the level of media hypesters who make a lot of noise and produce nothing but wind. Prayer must become our innermost respiration. It brings us face to face with God. Do we have some other purpose? Do we Christians, priests, bishops have some reason for existing other than to stand before God and to lead others to him? It is time to teach this! It is time to put it into practice! The one who prays is saved, the one who does not pray is damned, Saint Alphonsus said. I want to insist on this point, because a church that does not have prayer as its most precious treasure is headed for ruin. If we do not rediscover the meaning of long, patient vigils with the Lord, we will betray him. The apostles did this: Do we think we are better than they were? Priests in particular absolutely must have a soul of prayer. Without it, the most effective of social actions would become useless and even harmful. It would give us the illusion of serving God while we were only doing the work of the Evil One. This is not a matter of multiplying our devotions. It is a matter of being silent and adoring. It is a matter of getting on our knees. It is a matter of entering into the liturgy with fear and respect. It is God's work. It is not a theater.

I would like my brother bishops never to forget their serious responsibilities. Dear friends, you wish to lift up the Church? Get down on your knees! That is the only way! If you proceed otherwise, what you do will not be from God. Only God can save us. He will do so only if we pray to him. How I wish that a profound, uninterrupted prayer would rise up from the whole world: adoring praise and supplication. On the day when this silent song echoes in hearts, the Lord finally will be able to make himself heard and to act through his children. Until then, we create a barrier to him by our agitation and our chattering. Unless we place our head on the heart of Christ, like Saint John, we will not have the strength to follow him to the Cross. If we do not take the time to listen to the heartbeats of our God, we will abandon him, we will betray him as the apostles themselves did.

Catholic doctrine

We do not have to invent and build the unity of the Church. The source of our unity precedes us and is offered to us. It is the revelation that we receive. If everyone defends his opinion, his novelty, then division will spread everywhere. It wounds me to see so many pastors selling off Catholic doctrine and sowing division among the faithful. We owe the Christian people clear, firm, stable teaching. How can we accept bishops' conferences that contradict each other? Where confusion reigns, God cannot dwell!

The unity of the faith presupposes the unity of the Magisterium in time and space. When a new teaching is given to us, it must always be interpreted in a way consistent with the earlier teaching. If we introduce ruptures and revolutions, we break the unity that rules Holy Church over the course of the centuries. This does not mean that we are doomed to repeat fixed formulas. But any development must be a better understanding and a more in-depth version of past teaching. The hermeneutic of reform in continuity that Benedict XVI taught so clearly is an indispensable condition of unity. Those who make sensational announcements of change and rupture are false prophets. They do not seek the good of the flock. They are mercenaries who have been smuggled into the sheepfold. Our unity will be forged around the truth of Catholic doctrine. There are no other means. Trying to win popularity with the media at the expense of the truth amounts to doing the work of Judas.

Let us not be afraid! What more wonderful gift is there to offer to mankind than the truth of the Gospel? Certainly, Jesus is demanding. Yes, following him requires carrying his Cross each day! The temptation to cowardice is everywhere. It lies in wait for pastors in particular. Jesus' teaching appears too harsh. How many among us are tempted to think: "This is a hard saying; who can listen to it?" (Jn 6:60). The Lord turns then to those whom he has chosen, to

us priests and bishops, and again asks us: "Will you also go away?"
(Jn 6:67). He looks us right in the eye and asks each one of us: Will
you abandon me? Will you give up teaching the faith in all its fullness? Will you have the courage to preach my Real Presence in the
Eucharist? Will you have the courage to call these young people to
the consecrated life? Will you have the strength to say that, without
regular confession, sacramental Communion is in danger of losing its
meaning? Will you have the audacity to recall the truth of the indis-
solubility of marriage? Will you have the charity to do so even for
those who might blame you for it? Will you have the courage kindly
to invite divorced persons who have entered into a new union to
change their lives? Do you prefer success, or do you want to follow
me? May it please God that with Saint Peter we, filled with love and
humility, might answer him: "Lord, to whom shall we go? You have
the words of eternal life" (Jn 6:68).

Peter's love

The pope is the bearer of the mystery of Simon Peter, to whom
Christ said: "You are Peter, and on this rock I will build my Church"
(Mt 16:18). The mystery of Peter is a mystery of faith. Jesus willed to
hand his Church over to a man. To remind us of this more strikingly,
he allowed that man to betray him three times in front of everyone
before handing over to him the keys of his Church. We know that
the barque of the Church is not entrusted to a man because of his
extraordinary abilities. We believe, nevertheless, that this man will
always be assisted by the Divine Shepherd so as to hold fast the rule
of the faith.

Let us not be afraid! Let us listen to Jesus: "You are Simon....
You shall be called Peter" (Jn 1:42). From those first hours, the fabric of Church history has been woven with the golden thread of
the infallible decisions of the pontiffs, the successors of Peter, and the
black thread of the human, imperfect acts of the popes, successors of
Simon. In this incomprehensible overlapping of intertwined threads,
we sense the little needle guided by the invisible hand of God, intent
on tracing onto the fabric the only name by which we can be saved,
the name of Jesus Christ!

Dear friends, your pastors are full of faults and imperfections. But despising them is not the way to build Church unity. Do not be afraid to demand of them the Catholic faith, the sacraments of divine life. Remember the words of Saint Augustine: "Let Peter baptize, this is the one [Jesus] who baptizes; . . . Let Judas baptize, this is the one who baptizes!"[1] The most unworthy priest of all is still the instrument of divine grace when he celebrates the sacraments. See how much God loves us! He consents to handing over his Eucharistic Body into the sacrilegious hands of miserable priests. If you think that your priests and bishops are not saints, then be one for them. Do penance, fast to make reparation for their defects and their cowardice. That is the only way that anyone can bear another's burden.

Fraternal charity

Let us recall the words of Vatican Council II: "The Church is in Christ like a sacrament . . . of the unity of the whole human race."[2] However, so much hatred and division disfigure her. It is time to rediscover a little kindness among us. It is time to declare an end to suspicion! For us Catholics, it is time to come "to an interior reconciliation", as Benedict XVI put it.[3]

I write these words from my office, from which I have a view of Saint Peter's Square. It opens its arms wide so as to embrace all mankind better. For the Church is a mother; she opens her arms to us! Let us run to snuggle up there, to stand close together there, side by side! Within her, nothing threatens us! Christ extended his arms once for all on the Cross so that from then on the Church could open hers and reconcile us in her, with God and with one another. To all who are tempted by betrayal, dissension, manipulation, the Lord again says these words: "Why do you persecute me? . . . I am Jesus, whom you

---

[1] St. Augustine of Hippo, Homily 6, 7, trans. Edmund Hill, O.P., in *The Works of Saint Augustine*, vol. 3, 20, *Homilies on the Gospel of John 1–40* (New York: New City Press, 1990), 127.

[2] Vatican Council II, Dogmatic Constitution on the Church *Lumen Gentium* (November 21, 1964; hereafter cited as *LG*), no. 1.

[3] Pope Benedict XVI, Letter accompanying the Motu Proprio *Summorum Pontificum* (July 7, 2004).

are persecuting" (Acts 9:4–5): when we quarrel, when we hate each other, Jesus is the one whom we are persecuting!

Let us pray for a moment together at the large fresco by Michelangelo in the Sistine Chapel. There he depicted the Last Judgment. Let us kneel down before the Divine Majesty portrayed here. The whole heavenly court surrounds him. The saints are there; they carry the instruments of their martyrdom. Here are the apostles, the virgins, the unknown, the saints who are the secret of God's heart. They all sing his glory and praise. At their feet, the damned of hell shout their hatred of God. And all of a sudden, we are aware of our littleness, of our nothingness. All of a sudden, we, who thought that we had so many important ideas and necessary projects, we fall silent, over-whelmed by the grandeur and transcendence of God. Full of filial fear, we lift our eyes toward the glorious Christ, while he asks each one of us: "Do you love me?" Let us allow his question to resound. Let us not hurry to answer.

Do we truly love him? Do we love him enough to die for love? If we can answer humbly, simply: "Lord, you know everything, you know that I love you", then he will smile at us, then Mary and the saints in heaven will smile at us, and to each Christian they will say, as once to Francis of Assisi: "Go and repair my Church!" Go, repair by your faith, by your hope and your charity. Go and repair by your prayer and your fidelity. Thanks to you, my Church will again become my house.

Robert Cardinal Sarah
Rome, Friday, February 22, 2019

PART I

Spiritual and Religious Collapse

When the Son of man comes, will he find faith on earth?

—Luke 18:8

I

THE CRISIS OF FAITH

NICOLAS DIAT: Do you think that our age is going through a crisis of faith?

ROBERT CARDINAL SARAH: Allow me to reply to you with an analogy. I think that the attitude of the modern world resembles the cowardice of Saint Peter during the Passion, as it is described for us in the Gospels. Jesus has just been arrested. Peter, who followed him at a distance, enters right into the courtyard of the high priest (Mk 14:54), no doubt profoundly distressed.

> And as Peter was below in the courtyard, one of the maids of the high priest came; and seeing Peter warming himself, she looked at him, and said, "You also were with the Nazarene, Jesus." But he denied it, saying, "I neither know nor understand what you mean." And he went out into the gateway [and the cock crowed]. And the maid saw him, and began again to say to the bystanders, "This man is one of them." But again he denied it. And after a little while again the bystanders said to Peter, "Certainly you are one of them; for you are a Galilean." But he began to invoke a curse on himself and to swear, "I do not know this man of whom you speak." (Mk 14:66–71)

Like Peter, the modern world has denied Christ. Contemporary man is afraid of God, afraid of becoming his disciple. He has said: "I do not want to know God." He feared what others might think. They asked him whether he knew Christ, and he replied: "I do not know this man." He was ashamed of himself, and he swore: "God? I don't know who that is!" We wanted to shine in the world's sight, and, three times, we denied our God. We declared: I am not sure about him, about the Gospels, about dogmas, about Christian morality. We were ashamed of the saints and the martyrs; we were embarrassed

23

by God, his Church, and her liturgy and trembled in the presence of the world and its servants. Jesus looked at Peter when he had just betrayed him. What love and mercy, but also what reproaches and how much justice in that look! Peter wept bitterly. He was able to ask forgiveness.

Will we agree to look back at Christ? I think that the modern world averts its eyes: it is afraid. It does not want to see its image reflected in the kindly eyes of Jesus. It shuts itself in. But if it refuses to let him look at it, it will end as Judas did, in despair. This is the meaning of the contemporary crisis of faith. We do not want to look at the One whom we have crucified. And so we rush toward suicide. This book is an appeal to the modern world to agree to look back at God and to be able finally to weep.

How can faith be defined? What does it mean to believe?

These are questions that ought to haunt us constantly. We should ask ourselves about the meaning of our belief so as to avoid living on the periphery of ourselves, in superficiality, routine, or indifference. There are some realities that are experienced but difficult to define, such as love or the experience of interior intimacy with God. These realities grip and seize all of life, disrupt it, and transform it from within. If we want to try to stammer something about faith, I would say that, for a Christian, faith is man's total and absolute confidence in a God whom he has encountered personally. Some people declare that they are unbelievers, atheists, or agnostics. For them, the human mind is in complete ignorance about the intrinsic nature, origin, and destiny of things. These persons are profoundly unhappy. They resemble immense rivers with no sources whatsoever to nourish their life. They resemble trees that, having inexorably cut themselves off from their roots, are doomed to perish. Sooner or later, they dry up and die. People who have no faith are like those who have neither father nor mother to engender them and renew them in their perception of their own mystery. Now the faith is a true mother. In the *Acts of the Martyrs*, the Roman prefect Rusticus asks the Christian Hierax: "Where are your parents?" The latter replies: "Our true father is Christ, and our mother: faith in Him." It is a great misfortune not to believe in God and to be deprived of one's mother.

Fortunately, there are many men and women who say they are believers. Many people assign a capital importance to faith in a transcendent being. Some have their gods, who are often presented in the form of more or less personified powers that rule over men. They inspire terror and fear, dread and anxiety. Hence the temptation to magic and idolatry. It is imagined that they demand bloody sacrifices in order to attract their benevolence or to appease their wrath.

In the history of mankind, one man, Abraham, was able to turn things around totally by discovering faith as an essentially personal relationship with a unique God. This relationship had been initiated by his unreserved confidence in God's word. Abraham hears a word and a call; he obeys immediately. He is asked, in an imperative, radical way, to leave his country, his relatives, and his father's house and to go "to the land that I will show you" (Gen 12:1).

Faith is therefore a Yes to God. It requires a person to leave his gods, his culture, all human assurances, and riches in order to enter the land, the culture, and the inheritance of God. Faith consists of letting oneself be guided by God. He becomes our only wealth, our present and our future. He becomes our strength, our support, our security, our unshakable rock on which we can rely. Faith is experienced by building the house of our life on the rock that is God (Mt 7:24). Thus he can say to man: "If you will not believe, surely you shall not be established" (Is 7:9).

Abraham's faith develops, takes root, and is strengthened in an interpersonal covenant made up of indestructible bonds with his God. Faith implies and requires fidelity. The latter puts into action and expresses an unfailing commitment to devote ourselves to God alone. The fidelity is first of all that of the God who is always faithful to his promises, never forsaking those who seek him (cf. Ps 9:10). "I will make with them an everlasting covenant, that I will not turn away from doing good to them; and I will put the fear of me in their hearts, that they may not turn from me" (Jer 32:40; cf. Is 61:8; Is 55:3).

Faith is contagious. If it is not, that is because it has become insipid. Faith is like the sun: it shines, lights up, radiates, and warms everything that gravitates around it. By the strength of his faith, Abraham draws his whole family and his descendents into a personal relationship with God. Certainly, faith is an intimately personal act, but it must also be professed and lived out in the family, in the Church, in ecclesial communion. My faith is the faith of the Church. So it is that God will call himself the God of Abraham, of Isaac, and of Jacob (Ex 3:6), the God of the fathers of the people Israel.

Faith is truly a strong relationship between God and his people Israel. At first, God takes the initiative in everything. But man must respond to this divine initiative by faith. Faith is always a loving response to a loving, covenantal initiative.

Faith grows in an intense life of prayer and contemplative silence. It is nourished and strengthened in a daily face-to-face meeting with God and in an attitude of adoration and silent contemplation. It is professed in the Creed, celebrated in the liturgy, lived out in keeping the Commandments. It achieves its growth through an interior life of adoration and prayer. Faith is nourished by the liturgy, by Catholic doctrine, and by the Church's tradition as a whole. Its principal sources are Sacred Scripture, the Fathers of the Church, and the Magisterium.

Although knowing God and forming a personal and intimate relationship with him is arduous, difficult work, we really can see him, hear him, touch him, and contemplate him through his Word and the sacraments. By being sincerely open to the truth and beauty of Creation, but also through our ability to perceive the meaning of moral good and by paying attention to the voice of our conscience, because we carry within us this aspiring desire for an unending life, we put ourselves into the right circumstances to enter into contact with God: "Question the beauty of the earth," Saint Augustine says, "question the beauty of the sea, question the beauty of the air amply spread around everywhere, question the beauty of the sky ... question all these things. They all answer you: 'Here we are, look; we're beautiful.' Their beauty is their confession. Who made these beautiful, changeable things, if not one who is beautiful and unchangeable?"[1]

In the view of many of our contemporaries, faith was sufficient light for societies in antiquity. But for modern times, the era of science and technology, it is an illusory light that would prevent man from cultivating the boldness of knowledge. It would even be a restriction on his freedom and would keep man in ignorance and fear.

---

[1] St. Augustine of Hippo, Sermon 241, 2, trans. Edmund Hill, O.P., in *The Works of Saint Augustine*, vol. 3, 7, *Sermons 230–272* (New York: New City Press, 1995), 70.

To this contemporary mentality, Pope Francis responds brilliantly:

The light of faith is unique, since it is capable of illuminating *every aspect* of human existence. A light this powerful cannot come from ourselves but from a more primordial source: in a word, it must come from God. Faith is born of an encounter with the living God who calls us and reveals his love, a love which precedes us and upon which we can lean for security and for building our lives. Transformed by this love, we gain fresh vision, new eyes to see; we realize that it contains a great promise of fulfilment, and that a vision of the future opens up before us. Faith, received from God as a supernatural gift, becomes a light for our way, guiding our journey through time.... We come to see that faith does not dwell in shadow and gloom; it is a light for our darkness.[2]

A man deprived of the light of faith resembles an orphan, or, as we said earlier, he resembles someone who never knew either his father or his mother. It is sad and dehumanizing to have neither father nor mother. For the first Christians, the faith, being an encounter with the living God manifested in Christ Jesus, was a "mother" because it brought them to the light, it engendered in them the divine life, a new experience, a luminous vision of life for which one had to be ready to give public witness even to the shedding of one's blood, even to death.

But it is necessary to stress with sufficient insistence that faith is inseparably connected with conversion. It is a break with our life of sin, with the idols and all the "golden calves" of our own making so as to return to the living, true God through an encounter that throws us from our horse and turns us completely upside down. The encounter with God is terrifying and pacifying at the same time. To believe means to entrust oneself to God and to his merciful love, a love that always welcomes and forgives, sustains and orients life, and proves powerful in its ability to straighten out the distortions in our story. Faith consists of the willingness to let ourselves be transformed again and again by the call of this God, who constantly repeats these words to us: " 'Return to me with all your heart, with fasting, with weeping,

[2] Pope Francis, Encyclical Letter *Lumen fidei* on Faith (June 29, 2013; hereafter cited as *LF*), no. 4.

and with mourning; and tear your hearts and not your garments.'
Return to the LORD, your God, for he is gracious and merciful" (Joel
2:12–13). But our return to the Lord, our genuine conversion by a
loving response, for a new covenant with him must be made in truth
and in an incarnate way and not just theoretically or by theological
or canonical subtleties. We are not that different from the people of
the First Covenant. Often struck by God's hand for its adulteries and
infidelities, Israel thought that it could find its return to grace and
its deliverance in a repentance with no tomorrow and without deep
roots. The prophets vigorously reject such superficial, sentimental
repentance with no real break with sin, without a true abandonment
of one's state of sin and of the idols that have monopolized one's heart.
Only repentance that comes from the depths of the heart can obtain
God's forgiveness and mercy.

Faith is also and above all an ecclesial reality. God is the one who
gives us faith through our Holy Mother Church. Thus the faith of
each individual fits into the faith of the community, into the ecclesial
"we". The light of faith is an incarnate light proceeding from the
luminous life of Jesus.

> The light of Christ shines, as in a mirror, upon the face of Christians;
> as it spreads, it comes down to us, so that we too can share in that
> vision and reflect that light to others, in the same way that, in the
> Easter liturgy, the light of the paschal candle lights countless other
> candles. Faith is passed on, we might say, by contact, from one person
> to another, just as one candle is lighted from another. Christians, in
> their poverty, plant a seed so rich that it becomes a great tree, capable
> of filling the world with its fruit.[3]

It is impossible to believe alone, just as it is impossible to be born
by oneself or to engender oneself ... Faith is not just an individual
decision that the believer makes interiorly; it is not an isolated relation between the I of the faithful and the divine Thou, between
the autonomous subject and God. Some people today would like to
reduce faith to a subjective, private experience. Nevertheless, faith
always comes about in the community of the Church, because that is

[3] Ibid., 37.

where God reveals himself fully and allows himself to be encountered as he is in reality.

In his dialogue with priests on Saint Peter's Square at the conclusion of the Year for Priests (June 10, 2010), Pope Benedict XVI said: "There is no majority against the majority of the Saints. Saints are the true majority in the Church and we must orient ourselves by the Saints!" In what way does this priority given to sanctity have a particular resonance today?

Some people would like the Church to be transformed after the model of modern democracies. In it the government would be entrusted to the majority. But that would amount to making the Church a human society and not the family founded by God.

In the history of the Church, the "little remnant" is what has saved the faith. A few believers who remained faithful to God and to his covenant. They are the stump that will always revive so that the tree does not die. However destitute it may be, a little flock will always exist, a model for the Church and the world. The saints found God. These men and women found what is essential. They are the cornerstone of mankind. The earth is reborn and is renewed by the saints and their unfailing attachment to God and to men, whom they want to lead to eternal salvation.

No human effort, however talented or generous it may be, can transform a soul and give it the life of Christ. Only the grace and the Cross of Jesus can save and sanctify souls and make the Church grow. Multiplying human efforts, believing that methods and strategies have any efficacy in themselves, will always be a waste of time. Christ alone can give his life to souls; he gives it in the measure in which he himself lives in us and has completely taken hold of us. So it is with the saints. Jesus lives in their whole lives, in all their actions, in all their desires. The apostolic value of an apostle is measured solely by his sanctity and by the intensity of his prayer life.

Every day we see an unprecedented quantity of works, of time and effort spent ardently and generously but with no result. Now the whole history of the Church shows that one saint is enough to transform thousands of souls. Let us look, for example, at the Curé of Ars. Without doing anything but being holy and spending hours in front of the tabernacle, he attracted crowds from all parts of the world to a little unknown village. Saint Thérèse of the Child Jesus, who died of tuberculosis after spending several years in a provincial Carmel, did nothing but be holy and love Jesus alone; by now she has transformed millions of souls. The chief preoccupation of all the disciples of Jesus must be their sanctification. The first place in their lives must be given to prayer, to silent contemplation, and to the Eucharist, without which all the rest would be vain agitation. The saints love and live in the truth and are concerned about leading sinners to the truth of Christ. They could never remain silent about this truth or display the least indulgence toward sin or error. Love for sinners and for those who are in error requires that we fight relentlessly against their sins and errors.

The saints are often hidden from the eyes of their contemporaries. How many saints in monasteries will never be known by the world?

I deplore the fact that a good many bishops and priests neglect their essential mission, which is their own sanctification and the proclamation of the Gospel of Jesus, in order to get involved with sociopolitical issues like the environment, migrants, or the homeless. Taking an interest in these debates shows praiseworthy commitment. But if they neglect evangelization and their own sanctification, their advocacy is in vain. The Church is not a democracy in which the majority ends up making the decisions. The Church is God's holy people. In the Old Testament, a little nation that was always persecuted ceaselessly renewed the holy covenant by the holiness of its everyday life. In the early Church, Christians were called the "saints" because their whole lives were imbued with the presence of Christ and with the light of his Gospel. They were in the minority, but they transformed the world. Christ never promised his faithful that they would be in the majority.

Despite the greatest missionary efforts, the Church has never dominated the world.

For the Church's mission is a mission of love, and love does not dominate. Love is there to serve and to die, so that man might have life, and have it abundantly. John Paul II was right when he used to say that we are only just starting to evangelize.

A Christian's strength comes from his relation to God. He must embody the holiness of God in himself and put on the armor of light (Rom 13:12), "having fastened the belt of truth around your waist, and having put on the breastplate of righteousness, and having shod your feet with the equipment of the gospel of peace; besides all these,

taking the shield of faith" (Eph 6:14–16). This armor equips us pow-
erfully for the great battle of the saints, the battle of prayer. It is a
struggle: "I appeal to you," Saint Paul writes to the Romans, "by our
Lord Jesus Christ and by the love of the Spirit, to strive together with
me in your prayers to God on my behalf" (Rom 15:30). "Epaphras,
who is one of yourselves, a servant of Christ Jesus, greets you, always
remembering you earnestly in his prayers, that you may stand mature
and fully assured in all the will of God" (Col 4:12).

The Book of Genesis relates a mysterious event: the physical combat between Jacob and God. We are impressed by Jacob, who dares
to come to blows with God. The combat lasts the whole night. Jacob
appears at first to win, but his mysterious adversary strikes him at
the hollow of his thigh, and it is put out of joint while he is fighting with him. Jacob would always bear the injury of that nocturnal
struggle and from that day on would become the eponym of the
people of God: "Your name shall no more be called Jacob, but Israel,
for you have striven with God and with men, and have prevailed"
(Gen 32:28). Without revealing his own name, God blesses Jacob and
gives him a new name. This scene became the image for the spiritual
combat and the efficacy of prayer. At night, in silence and solitude,
we struggle with God in prayer.

The saints are people who struggle with God the whole night until
the dawn. This struggle increases our standing; it makes us attain our
true stature as human beings and children of God, because "the God
and Father of our Lord Jesus Christ ... chose us in him before the
foundation of the world, that we should be holy and blameless before
him. He destined us in love" (Eph 1:3–4).

God chose us to adore him. Nevertheless, man does not want to
kneel down. Adoration consists of placing ourselves in the presence
of God in an attitude of humility and love. This is not a purely ritual
act, but a gesture of acknowledging the Divine Majesty. It expresses
a filial gratitude. We must not ask for anything. It is of fundamental
importance to remain in a spirit of gratuitousness.

*For Joseph Ratzinger, later Benedict XVI, the crisis in the Church was essen-
tially a crisis of faith.*

In a speech to the Roman Curia on December 22, 2011, Benedict
XVI reflected that "The essence of the crisis of the Church in Europe

is the crisis of faith. If we find no answer to this ..., then all other reforms will remain ineffective." When Joseph Ratzinger speaks about a "crisis of faith", we should understand that he is not talking in the first place about an intellectual or theological problem in the academic sense of the word. He means a "living faith", a faith that imbues and transforms life. "If faith does not take on new life, deep conviction and real strength from the encounter with Jesus Christ," Benedict XVI added that day, "then all other reforms will remain ineffective." This loss of the sense of faith is the deep root of the crisis of civilization that we are experiencing. As in the first centuries of Christianity, when the Roman Empire was collapsing, all human institutions today seem to be on the path of decadence. Relations between people, whether political, social, economic, or cultural, are becoming difficult. In losing the sense of God, we have undermined the foundation of all human civilization and opened the door to totalitarian barbarity.

Benedict XVI explained this idea perfectly in a catechesis on November 14, 2012:

> Human beings, separated from God, are reduced to a single dimension—the horizontal—and this reductionism itself is one of the fundamental causes of the various forms of totalitarianism that have had tragic consequences in the past century, as well as of the crisis of values that we see in the current situation. By obscuring the reference to God the ethical horizon has also been obscured, to leave room for relativism and for an ambiguous conception of freedom which, instead of being liberating, ends by binding human beings to idols. The temptations that Jesus faced in the wilderness before his public ministry vividly symbolize which "idols" entice human beings when they do not go beyond themselves. Were God to lose his centrality man would lose his rightful place, he would no longer fit into creation, into relations with others.

I would like to insist on this idea. Refusing to let God enter into all aspects of human life amounts to condemning man to solitude. He is no longer anything but an isolated individual, without origin or destiny. He finds himself condemned to wander through the world like a nomadic barbarian, without knowing that he is the son and heir of a Father who created him through love and calls him to share his eternal happiness. It is a profound error to think that God came to limit and frustrate our freedom. On the contrary, God comes to free us from solitude and to give meaning to our freedom. Modern man has made himself the prisoner of reason that is so autonomous that it has become solitary and autistic. The theologian Joseph Ratzinger wrote in "La Théologie, un état des lieux" (Theology, a status report):

> Revelation is the break-in of the living, true God into our world; it liberates us from the jails of our theories, the bars of which try to protect us against the irruption of God into our life.... The poverty of philosophy, that is, the poverty into which positivist reason has thrown itself, has become the poverty of our faith. The latter cannot be liberated unless reason becomes open to what is new. If the door of metaphysical knowledge remains shut, if the boundaries of human knowledge as they were set by Kant cannot be crossed, then the faith can only waste away: it is short of breath.[4]

This discontent in civilization goes way back. It reached a critical moment at the end of World War II. The confrontation of the Church with modernity created suffering and doubt among many priests and Christians in the West. In 1966, in the conference that he presented at the *Katholikentag* in Bamberg, Joseph Ratzinger was especially explicit. To illustrate the situation of the Church in the contemporary world, he evoked the image of the neo-Gothic cathedral in New York City, surrounded and dwarfed by iron giants, the skyscrapers. Nascent modernity despised the Church. Intellectuals no longer understood her teaching. People had the impression of a misunderstanding that could never be cleared up. Hence the desire, which was found especially in the youth movements, to be free from some outdated, outmoded external details. The heart of Christian life was becoming incomprehensible for many, who ended up looking only at these secondary details. Joseph Ratzinger gives as an example the obsolete style of some pre-Vatican-II theological documents, the external trappings of the Roman Curia, or the exaggerated display of ceremonies in the Baroque pontifical liturgies. It was necessary to

---

[4]Joseph Cardinal Ratzinger, "La Théologie, un état des lieux", *Communio*, French ed., 22, 1 (February 1997).

remove these causes of misunderstandings and of useless scandals. It was urgent to express the heart of the Gospel in a language that modern men could understand.

During the Second Vatican Council, the Pastoral Constitution on the Church in the Modern World, *Gaudium et spes*, tried to dust off the heritage so as to utilize it better. Nevertheless, when it came to describing in new terms the relation of the Church with the modern world, it was realized that there were many problems at stake that were quite different from the mere pruning of forms from another era.

It is legitimate to find new forms of evangelization that the modern world can understand and to which it can be receptive, but it is naïve and superficial to try at all costs to reconcile it with the Church. It is even the sign of a theological blindness. "In our time, too," Benedict XVI declared in his speech to the Roman Curia when he offered them his Christmas greetings in December 2005,

> the Church remains a "sign that will be opposed" (Lk 2:34)—not without reason did Pope John Paul II, then still a Cardinal, give this title to the theme for the Spiritual Exercises he preached in 1976 to Pope Paul VI and the Roman Curia. The Council could not have intended to abolish the Gospel's opposition to human dangers and errors. On the contrary, it was certainly the Council's intention to overcome erroneous or superfluous contradictions in order to present to our world the requirement of the Gospel in its full greatness and purity. The steps the Council took towards the modern era which had rather vaguely been presented as "openness to the world", belong in short to the perennial problem of the relationship between faith and reason that is re-emerging in ever new forms.

Indeed, some relied on the notion of incarnation to affirm that God had come to meet the world and had sanctified it. Hence, in their view, the world and the Church had to be reconciled. They naïvely thought that being Christian could be summed up as a joyous immersion in the world. Countering this adolescent irenicism, Cardinal Ratzinger points out[5] that the Incarnation can be understood in the New Testament only in light of the Passion and the Resurrection. In the preaching of the apostles, the proclamation of the

---

[5] In a speech given in Bamberg at the 1966 *Katholikentag*.

Resurrection, which itself is inseparable from the Cross, occupies a central place. In the same speech, he declared:

> There is one thing, however, that we can say, and that is that an orientation of the Church toward the world that would mean a turning away from the Cross would lead, not to a renewal of the Church, but to her decline and eventual decay. The purpose of such an orientation on the part of the Church can never be the removal of the scandal of the Cross but the revealing of it in all its naked truth, shorn of all secondary scandals that obscure it and that often conceal the folly of God's love behind the folly of man's own self-love. To put it another way, the Christian faith is a scandal for men of all ages: to believe that the eternal God knows us and has a loving care for us; that he whom it is beyond our comprehension to understand has presented himself to our minds in the person of the man Jesus; that the immortal God has suffered on the Cross and that we mortals have been promised resurrection and everlasting life—all this is something that makes tremendous demands on our human faith. The Council could not remove this Christian scandal and had no intention of trying to do so. At the same time, we must recognize that this primary scandal, which could not be removed without the destruction of Christianity itself, has often during the course of history been overshadowed by the secondary scandal of the teachers of the faith, which is not at all essential to Christianity but which can easily be made to appear inseparable from the primary scandal. These people like to affect a pose of martyrdom when in reality they are only victims of their own narrowmindedness.

I wish to insist on this essential point: Jesus Christ is the unique source of salvation and of grace through the Cross. By offering his death and triumphing over sin, he restores supernatural life to us, the life of friendship with him that will be completed in eternal life. In order to find in Jesus Christ the life of God that is given to us, there is no other way than the Cross, which the Church calls *spes unica*, our "sole hope". The Cross about which Saint Paul says: "But far be it from me to glory except in the cross of our Lord Jesus Christ, by which the world has been crucified to me, and I to the world" (Gal 6:14). Saint Paul is forthright: in his preaching he wants to know nothing but "Jesus Christ and him crucified" (1 Cor 2:2). In order to make amends for Adam's disobedience and pride, it was necessary for Jesus, out of love, to humble himself, becoming "obedient unto death, even death on a cross. Therefore God has highly exalted him and bestowed on him the name which is above every name" (Phil 2:8–9). With these words, which are fundamental for Christianity, Saint Paul explains that the triumph of God is born of the Cross. Human nature, wounded by the sin of our first parents, who had rejected God's life out of self-indulgence, is repaired by the Cross. It was necessary for our nature, assumed by Christ, to become the instrument of an immolation, of a total renunciation through the acceptance of death in loving obedience.

Because of this, the Church's orientation toward the world cannot mean a departure from the Cross, a renunciation of the scandal of the Cross. The Church unceasingly seeks to reform herself, in other words, to remove from her life all the scandals caused by sinful men. Yet she does this so as to bring out more clearly the first and irreplaceable scandal of the Cross, the scandal of God walking ahead of the Cross out of love for mankind. How can anyone not be saddened by the avalanche of scandals that are caused today by men of the Church? Not only do they wound the hearts of the little ones, but, more seriously, they cover Christ's glorious Cross with a black veil. The sins of Christians prevent our contemporaries from confronting the Cross. Yes, a true reform is necessary in the Church, which must make the Cross central again! We do not have to make the Church acceptable according to the world's criteria. We have to purify her so that she presents to the world the Cross in all its nakedness.

In your mind is there a connection between the loss of the sense of God and the loss of the sense of adoration and of the divine absolute?

The loss of the sense of God is at the origin of all crises. Adoration is an act of love, of respectful veneration, of filial abandonment and humility before the terrifying majesty and holiness of God. Like Isaiah, man finds himself before this imposing Presence, in whose sight the seraphim cry out to each other these words: "Holy, holy, holy is the LORD of hosts; the whole earth is full of his glory" (Is 6:3). So we exclaim with the prophet: "Woe is me! For I am lost; for I am a man of unclean lips, and ... my eyes have seen the King, the LORD of hosts!" (Is 6:5).

In the presence of God, Isaiah falls to his knees and prostrates himself so as to adore him and to ask him to be cleansed of his sin. Indeed, how can we prostrate ourselves and adore if we are full of sins? How can we stand before the holiness of God if we cling to our sin? Adoration is the greatest mark of man's nobility. It is an acknowledgment of the benevolent closeness of God and the human expression of man's astonishing intimacy with God. Man remains prostrate, literally crushed by the immense love that God has for him. To adore is to let oneself be burned by the divine love. One is always kneeling in the presence of love. The Father alone can show us the way to adore and to behave in the presence of love.

Thus we must understand that the liturgy is a human act inspired by God by which we respond to God, who loves us and comes to us with so much benevolence.

But we have a shortage of adorers. In order for the people of God to adore, the priests and the bishops must be the first adorers. They are called to be constantly in the presence of God. Their life is supposed to become an unceasing, persevering prayer, a permanent liturgy. They are like the first in a group of mountain climbers roped to each other. Adoration is a personal act, a heart-to-heart conversation with God, which we need to learn. Recall Moses, who taught the Jewish people to be a nation of adorers, to be childlike in God's presence. And God himself is the one who appoints Aaron as priest. The latter together with his sons will carry on the priesthood of God. The Hebrews know that, through their celebration of the Passover, they must preserve the memory of their exodus from Egypt, God's great act of love for his people, Israel.

Focused on themselves and their activities, preoccupied by the human results of their ministry, it is not uncommon for bishops and priests to neglect adoration. They find no time for God because they have lost the sense of God. There is not much room left for God in their lives. Nevertheless, the primacy of God ought to mean the centrality of God in our lives, our actions, and our thoughts. If man forgets God, he ends up celebrating himself. He then becomes his own god and sets himself up plainly in opposition to God. He acts as though the world were his own private domain. God no longer has anything to do with the Creation that has become human property, from which it is necessary to profit.

Under the pretext of "keeping the supernatural pure", we forbid God to enter into our lives; we reject the Incarnation. We reject the idea that God speaks about himself through Scripture, and therefore we try to purge it of all the myths that it supposedly contains. We reject the possibility of speaking about God through theology, under the pretext of maintaining his transcendence. We reject piety, religiosity, and the sacred, under the pretext of not introducing human elements into our relation with God. Cardinal Ratzinger wrote in *The Spirit of the Liturgy*:

> Our current form of sensibility, which can no longer apprehend the transparency of the spirit in the senses, almost inevitably brings with it a flight into a purely "negative" (apophatic) theology. God is beyond all thought, and therefore all propositions about him and every kind of image of God are in equal proportions valid and invalid. What seems like the highest humility toward God turns into pride, allowing God no word and permitting him no real entry into history.[6]

By dint of trying to "keep the supernatural pure", we isolate it from nature, and the world is then organized without God, in a profane manner.

In a 1942 conference, Henri de Lubac, too, had considered that

> Now, as a result of the dualism into which, in the recent past, we have too often allowed ourselves to be led, men, taking us at our word, have brushed aside all the supernatural, that is, in practice, all the sacred.... They relegated this supernatural to some distant corner where it could only remain sterile. They exiled it to a separate province, which they willingly abandoned to us, leaving it to die little by little under our care. And during this time, they set about to organize the world, this world that was for them the only truly real one, the only living world, the world of things and men, the world of nature and the world of business, the world of culture and that of the city. They explored it, or they built it, outside any Christian influence, in a wholly secular spirit.... Through a tragic misunderstanding, we more or less fell in with this game. There was, as it were, an unconscious conspiracy between the

---

[6] Joseph Cardinal Ratzinger, *The Spirit of the Liturgy*, trans. John Saward (San Francisco: Ignatius Press, 2000), 124.

movement that led to laicism and a certain theology, and while the supernatural found itself exiled and proscribed, it happened that some among us thought that the supernatural was placed beyond the reach of nature, in the domain where it was to reign.[7]

At the root of this attitude, there is a theology of a Protestant stripe that aims to pit the "faith" against religiosity. The sacred attitude and religious fear are allegedly profane, pagan elements, and the Christian faith must be refined to eliminate them. They would like to make Christianity an altogether interior contact with God, without any concrete expression in life. Christianity becomes a form of gnosis. The effect of this movement is to abandon all human realities to themselves, to their profane side, which is closed off from God. This gnosis turns into "Pelagianism" and practical atheism.

Why do you say so often that service to one's neighbor must be understood only in terms of service to Christ?

Man wounded by original sin often proves to be egocentric, individualistic, and selfish. Inspired by Christ, he serves his neighbor. Without Christ, he knows only his own interest. Mother Teresa stated that without the intense, burning presence of God in our hearts, without lives of profound, intense intimacy with Jesus, we are too poor to take care of the poor. Jesus present in us is the one who presses us toward the poor. Without him, we can do nothing. We are rarely capable of making the gift of ourselves to others. Christians are not called to be involved only in humanitarian activities. Charity goes far beyond that. Often the activity of humanitarian non-governmental organizations that I have been able to observe in Africa or elsewhere is useful. But it always has a tendency to become a kind of commerce in which grasping interests are mixed with generosity.

True charity is gratuitous. It expects nothing in return. True gratuitousness comes from the One who gave his life freely for us. Charity

---

[7] From a conference given by Henri de Lubac at the École Uriage in 1942, "Causes internes de l'atténuation et de la disparition du sens du sacré" (Internal causes of the weakening and disappearance of the sense of the sacred), later included in *Paradoxes*, Oeuvres Complètes 31 (Paris: Cerf, 1999), 328–29.

is a participation in the very love of the heart of Jesus for mankind. Without Christ, charity is a masquerade. When Mother Teresa's nuns arrive in a country, they ask for nothing. They desire nothing but to serve the most obscure shantytowns, humbly, with a smile, after spending much time contemplating the Lord. They simply want a priest to come celebrate Mass each day in their house. These women know that it is impossible for them to bring charitable work to a successful conclusion without the Son of God, because God is the source of love. Our model is Christ, who said: "[I] came not to be served but to serve" (Mt 20:28). In him and through him, all service is possible for us. As Saint Paul says, "[we remember] before our God and Father your work of faith and labor of love and steadfastness of hope in our Lord Jesus Christ" (1 Thess 1:3).

I am convinced that Catholic charitable organizations cannot be NGOs alongside others. They are the expression of a radiant faith in Jesus Christ. All the great saints who served the poor founded their charitable work on the love of God.

The words pronounced by Francis on this subject during his homily in the Sistine Chapel on March 14, 2013, are particularly eloquent:

> We can walk as much as we want, we can build many things, but if we do not profess Jesus Christ, things go wrong. We may become a charitable NGO, but not the Church, the Bride of the Lord. When we are not walking, we stop moving. When we are not building on the stones, what happens? The same thing that happens to children on the beach when they build sandcastles: everything is swept away, there is no solidity.

Do you get the feeling that the act of faith nowadays is placed at the service of human development alone?

In fact, we too often work in the service of human well-being exclusively. But economic development, health care, and quality of life are important, indispensable things. Welcoming refugees who have lost everything at the end of their long, exhausting journeys is a humane act of solidarity. To come to the material aid of someone in need is a fraternal act of great value: when we take care of a mistreated person, we take care of Christ himself.

Saint John Chrysostom vigorously reminds us of this. He protested at the same time against the social scourges of luxury and greed. He recalled the dignity of man, even if poor, and the limits of property. His words are biting: "Mules carry fortunes, while Christ is dying of hunger in front of your door." He shows Christ in the poor man and has him say: "I could feed myself, but I prefer to wander about begging, holding out my hand in front of your door, so as to be fed by you. It is for love of you that I act in this way." He protests against slavery and the alienation that it involves: "What I am about to say to you is horrible, but it is necessary for me to say it to you: Put God at the same level as your slaves. Liberate Christ from hunger, from want, from prisons, from nakedness. Ah! You tremble."

How do we nourish our love for the Son of God? What are the marks of our love? The poor whom we serve must know in whose name we love them. The poor must know the source of our generosity. We love because we love Christ. We love because we have been loved by the One who is Love and handed his Son over to death.

Although we personally are poor, God acts through us. Generosity without love for God is a sterile act. It is not proselytizing to speak to a poor person about God.

Thus Benedict XVI could write in *Deus caritas est*:

Charity, furthermore, cannot be used as a means of engaging in what is nowadays considered proselytism. Love is free; it is not practised as a way of achieving other ends. But this does not mean that charitable activity must somehow leave God and Christ aside. For it is always concerned with the whole man. Often the deepest cause of suffering is the very absence of God. Those who practise charity in the Church's name will never seek to impose the Church's faith upon others. They realize that a pure and generous love is the best witness to the God in whom we believe and by whom we are driven to love. A Christian knows when it is time to speak of God and when it is better to say nothing and to let love alone speak. He knows that God is love (cf. 1 Jn 4:8) and that God's presence is felt at the very time when the only thing we do is to love. He knows ... that disdain for love is disdain for God and man alike; it is an attempt to do without God.[8]

---

[8] Pope Benedict XVI, Encyclical Letter *Deus caritas est* on Christian Love (December 25, 2005; hereafter cited as *DCE*), no. 31c.

Do you think therefore that man must not confine God to his own little desires?

Even if man wanted to, he would never succeed in confining God. He must instead love, listen to, and adore God and follow Christ. In our materialistic civilization, man thinks almost exclusively of his own narrow interests. He sees God as the one who ought to provide him with what consumption does not give him. God is utilized to satisfy selfish demands. If he does not answer prayer, they abandon him. Some even go so far as to blaspheme his holy name. The religion that ought to connect heaven and earth then runs the risk of becoming a purely narcissistic space. Some evangelical sects excel in this commerce. They transform God into a pagan idol that is supposed to assure them of health, happiness, and prosperity and to grant every human whim. They command miracles, and he is supposed to shower us with them immediately. This is how the sects ridicule God and mock the credulous persons who have neither intelligence nor faith.

I do not mean to condemn the requests that people may make to implore divine aid. The beautiful votive offerings in chapels, churches, and cathedrals show how much God has been able to intervene to help men. But the prayer of petition is based on trust in God's will; the rest will be given to us in addition. If we love God, if we are careful to carry out his holy will joyfully, if we first and most importantly desire his light, that is, the law of God in the depths of our hearts so as to enlighten our paths (Ps 40:8; Heb 10:5–9), then he will naturally help us in our difficulties.

Religion is not a market regulated by supply and demand. It is not a comfortable cocoon. The base of Christianity rests on the love of a God who does not abandon his children. It is not a matter of requesting but of hoping and of placing trust in a God whose love is inexhaustible and who pours out on us his mercy by pardoning what troubles our consciences and by giving us more than we dare to ask for (Collect for the Twenty-Seventh Sunday in Ordinary Time). God is our Father. We are his children. Christianity invites us to rediscover the spirit of childhood. Our religion is a surge of the Son toward the Father and of the Father toward the Son. Simplicity, confidence, self-abandonment in God's hands: that is our path to God. Christian life is a conspiracy of charity.

Have we lost the sense of God's transcendence?

In the Catholic faith, transcendence is expressed and symbolized by the altar. What does it signify? In his book *Meditations before Mass*, Romano Guardini explains it marvelously:

> Its meaning is probably most clearly suggested by two images: it is threshold and it is table. Threshold is door, and it has a double significance: border and crossing over. It indicates where one thing ends and another begins. The border, which marks the end of the old, makes possible entry into the new. As a threshold, the altar creates first the border between the realm of the world and the realm of God. The altar reminds us of the remoteness in which he lives "beyond the altar," as we might say, meaning divine distance; or "above the altar," meaning divine loftiness—both to be understood of course not spatially but spiritually. They mean that God is the Intangible One, far removed from all approaching, from all grasping; that he is the all-powerful, Majestic One immeasurably exalted above earthly things and earthly striving. Such breadth and height are founded not on measure, but on God's essence: his holiness, to which man of himself has no access.
>
> On the other hand, this is not to be understood merely spiritually, or rather, merely intellectually. In the liturgy everything is symbolical.... The altar is not an allegory, but a symbol. The thoughtful believer does not have to be taught that it is a border, that "above it" stretch inaccessible heights and "beyond it" the reaches of divine remoteness; somehow he is aware of this. [That is why it is not fitting for the priest celebrant to stand "on the other side of the altar", as though he were taking God's place. In doing so, he is like a screen that hides the Transcendence of God. He is a veil that hides the majesty of God. Thus, instead of looking at God, the faithful look at the priest. And he, by his movements, gestures, and many words, muddles the mystery, hides the divine Transcendence.]
>
> To grasp the mystery all that is necessary on the part of the believer is intrinsic readiness and calm reflection; then his heart will respond with reverence. In a vital hour he may even have an experience somewhat similar to that of Moses when he guarded his flocks in the loneliness of Mount Horeb. Suddenly "The Lord appeared to him in a flame of fire out of the midst of a bush: and he saw that the bush was on fire and was not burnt. And Moses said: 'I will go and see this great sight, why the bush is not burnt.' And when the Lord saw that

he went forward to see, he called to him out of the midst of the bush, and said: 'Moses, Moses.' And he answered: 'Here I am.' And he said: 'Come not nigh hither. Put off the shoes from thy feet: for the place whereon thou standest is holy ground'" (Ex 3:2–5).[9]

Do we really understand what the altar represents? Does the priest who climbs the steps to it realize that he is in the presence of the burning bush, the Divine Majesty, and transcendence? Does he realize that all of Christian civilization is born from the altar as from its source? The altar is the heart of our cities. Literally, our towns are built around the altar, huddled around the church that protects them. The loss of the sense of God's grandeur is a dreadful regression toward savagery. The sense of the sacred is indeed the heart of all human civilization. The presence of a sacred reality gives rise to sentiments of respect, gestures of veneration. Religious rites are the mold that shapes all attitudes of human politeness and courtesy. Indeed, if every person is respectable, it is fundamentally because he is made in the image and likeness of God. Man's dignity is an echo of God's transcendence. But if we no longer tremble with a joyful, reverential fear before the greatness of God, how could man be for us a mystery worthy of respect? He no longer has this divine nobility. He becomes a piece of merchandise, a laboratory specimen. Without the sense of the adoration of God, human relations become tinged with vulgarity and aggressiveness. The more deference we show to God at the altar, the more tactful and courteous we will be toward our brethren.

We will rediscover the sense of human greatness if we agree to acknowledge God's transcendence. Man is great and attains his loftiest nobility only when he gets down on his knees before God. The great man is humble, and the humble man kneels. If, like Jesus, we humble ourselves in the presence of God and become obedient even unto death, he will exalt us regally and will bestow on us a name that is above all other names (Phil 2:8–9). We do not kneel before God's majesty and holiness like slaves. Rather, we are lovers in the company of the seraphim, dazzled by the splendor of God, who

---

[9] Romano Guardini, *Meditations before Mass*, trans. Elinor Castendyk Briefs (1956; Notre Dame, Ind.: Ave Maria Press, 2014), 41–43.

fills the temple of our heart with his presence. We are overwhelmed by God, not so that he can catch us, but rather so as to make us grow. The transcendence of God is a call to the transcendence of man. For God's mystery and man's are closely connected.

Roman Guardini also wrote in the same book:

> It is essential for every one of us to experience at some time or another the fear of the Lord, to be repelled by him from the sacred place, that we may know with all our being that God is God, and we are but man. Trust in God, nearness to him and security in him remain thin and feeble when personal knowledge of God's exclusive majesty and awful sanctity do not counterbalance them. We do well to pray God for this experience, and the place where it is most likely to be granted us is before his altar.[10]

The altar is a place of transcendence and a burning bush and a holy place where God's majesty and holiness are manifested.

In Rome, over the door to the Church of Santa Maria in Campitelli, an inscription recalls the disposition of soul with which we ought to enter a sacred place. The visitor can see there in black letters on a gold background these words of the Psalmist: *Introibo in domum tuam, Domine. Adorabo ad templum sanctum tuum in timore tuo.* "I will enter your house, O Lord. I will worship toward your holy temple in the fear of you" [Ps 5:7]. I think that all of us should remember these words when entering a church. Priests in particular ought to carry them in their heart when they climb the steps to the altar. They must remember that at the altar they are facing God. At Mass, the priest is not a professor who gives a lecture while using the altar as a podium centered on the microphone instead of the Cross. The altar is the sacred threshold par excellence, the place of the face-to-face encounter with God.

How should we respond to this temptation to make a transition to the world?

We sometimes have the feeling of being prisoners of a sort of detention that prevents us from looking at the heavenly realities. We could

---

[10] Ibid., 43–44.

speak about quicksand. How can I drag myself away from the world? How can anyone escape the noise? How can we get out of this dark night that oppresses us and obstructs our path to heaven, that dazes us and makes us forget the essential thing? God created us to be and to live with him. God, who willed everything, did not create nature for its own sake. God did not create us for a merely natural perfection. God had an infinitely higher purpose than the perfection of nature alone: the supernatural order, the gift of pure love that we call grace, which makes us participate in his own divine nature, the communication of his own life that makes us his children, capable of knowing him and loving him in all his intimacy, as he knows and loves himself. We were created to get out of the world and to live fully with God's own life. We were created to know and to love God in his full reality as God. Man by himself is absolutely incapable of this supernatural life, from which he is separated by an infinite abyss; it is a gratuitous gift of God. But we are made to live with God and to reach our perfection in God. When Christ explains to men what their goal should be, he does not say to them: "Be fully and perfectly human beings, flourish and attain the perfection of your human nature", but rather: "Be perfect as your heavenly Father is perfect", in other words, with God's own perfection.

Although God created us in order to give us his own life, he does not give it to us in spite of us. We must respond to his gift of love with a free gift of love. It is up to us to accept freely the gift of his own life that God has given us. One consequence of this is man's terrible power to refuse to give himself in return but, instead, to despise the gift of God's infinite love. This refusal, this contempt, is sin. Sin deprives us of divine life. It enchains us and rivets us to earthly things. On the other hand, through prayer, which is a personal, real contact with God, we can get out of the world.

Oddly, while God is inviting us to a boundless, never-ending happiness in him, we let ourselves become fascinated by limited, superficial pleasures. Science and technology hypnotize us to the point where we act as if nothing existed beyond matter. We know that everything on earth is perishable, but we continue to prefer the fleeting to the eternal. It must be said, in season and out of season, that God alone fits the measure of our hearts. He alone can bring us the fullness to which we aspire.

Christians must ceaselessly explain to people the sort of happiness to which they are called. They have the obligation to tell the world that technological advances are nothing compared to God's love. Man bears in himself the image of God, and his soul is immortal. How can we not take into account this imprint of God in ourselves? Why does man look only at the earth? He no longer raises his head, bent over like a slave of this world. Nevertheless, the earth is only a door leading to heaven. I am not telling anyone to neglect earthly realities. This world was willed by God, loved by God, and fashioned tenderly by the heart of God. We must respect it and love it passionately. But one day we will leave it. Heaven is our eternal homeland. Our fatherland and our true dwelling place are in God.

Unquestionably, the loss of the sense of salvation in God is a mark of our times.

Man does not feel that he is in danger. Many in the Church no longer dare to teach the reality of salvation and eternal life. In homilies there is a strange silence concerning the last things. Preachers avoid speaking about original sin. That appears to be archaic. The sense of sin seems to have disappeared. Good and evil no longer exist. Relativism, that terribly effective bleach, has wiped out everything in its path. Doctrinal and moral confusion is reaching its height. Evil is good, good is evil. Man no longer feels any need to be saved. The loss of the sense of salvation is the consequence of the loss of the transcendence of God.

We do not seem to be worried about what will happen to us when we have left this earth. From this perspective, we prefer to think that the devil no longer exists. Some bishops even say that he is only a symbolic image. Jesus Christ is supposedly lying, therefore, when he claims that he is quite real, that he was tempted several times by him, the Prince of this world!

In his *De Lubac: A Theologian Speaks*, Henri de Lubac accurately wrote that

[Modernity can be used] as the signpost for a general attitude adopted by many of our intellectuals. This attitude is the result of the extraordinary conquests of modern science and the equally great disillusions that follow upon great dreams of progress and man's self-deification. In this case, one can say that the ultimate origin of "modernity" is the refusal of all faith, which follows the refusal of mystery. Modernity refuses mystery. It will always know more, *explain* more. But it will not really *understand* anything anymore, because it has refused mystery.[11]

The theologian continued:

[Modern thinkers] all share the same presupposition (though it isn't always clear from the outset): The heart of what the Bible, the Church and Tradition have to say is not faith in a transcendent God, but the true discovery of man. In their eyes, the mysteries of Christianity are nothing but a superficial covering, pure superstition so long as one hasn't penetrated into the gnosis that they, the initiates, obligingly translate for weaker minds.

This attitude is really the subtlest and most profound kind of atheism. It is the opposite of the attitude that suits the logic of the Incarnation, which is humility. As Augustine observes: You have to be humble to admit the Incarnation of the Word.[12]

Our pride as modern men sometimes leads us to a ridiculous blindness. Yes, it is a beautiful, great thing to tremble about our salvation. Certainly not with a pathological fear of a terrible god who would relentlessly damn souls for the fun of it. But how could we ever be saved by God if we do not have the radical humility to receive salvation as a gratuitous grace? Are we going to stand before God asserting our right to it? Is it not urgently necessary to receive the mysteries of the faith and of salvation with the heart of a poor person? The wealth of modern societies no longer teaches us to receive gratuitously. This is a great misfortune. We resemble those spoiled children who can no longer rejoice when they receive presents from their parents. They complain of not having enough. Though still young, they are already embittered and sad like senile old men. With respect to God, we are fundamentally children, poor beggars who have to receive everything. Well then, yes, let us tremble about our salvation! Not because

[11] Henri de Lubac, *A Theologian Speaks*, trans. Stephen Maddux (Los Angeles: Twin Circle, 1985), 25.
[12] Ibid., 28–29.

we are afraid of God, but because we measure our littleness by the gift that he gives us. It is possible to tremble with confidence and love; this sentiment has a name. It is the holy fear of God, which is a gift of the Holy Spirit. Yes, let us fear, out of love, that we might not be able to abandon ourselves to his mercy.

Can we say that we are going through a time of deliberate confusion between the natural and the supernatural?

Do priests busy themselves with Christ and the evangelization of the world or with the earthly well-being of men? The supernatural seems to be absorbed and engulfed in the natural. The supernatural is swallowed up in the desert of the natural. We become deaf, autistic, and blind to the things of God. We forget that heaven exists. We no longer see heaven, and we no longer see God, either. Man is bewitched by what is tangible.

The Western world no longer has any experience of the supernatural. It is necessary to restore our ties with heaven. Man's eyes have been closed, and he no longer knows how to look into the depths of the abyss. Supernatural language has become impenetrable to him. He is used to explaining everything, understanding everything, proving everything. But the knowledge of divine things will always be based on mystery and the relation with the One who revealed the Father to us: the Eternal Son made man. In order to hear God's language, we need to let him speak to us through the Gospel and the liturgy. Our pride refuses to let God speak to us in human words. We cannot accept the fact that God should make himself so close by being an infant. We cannot bring ourselves to accept the fact that God wants to give himself through the Church by means of the sacraments. Louis Bouyer already emphasized this in his book *Le Métier de théologien* [The theologian's trade]:

> This is the outcome of a tendency that Péguy had stigmatized in speaking about people who want so much to have clean hands that finally they no longer have hands. They want to have a Christianity so purified of its simply human elements that the divine element, no longer having something on which to rest and through which to express itself, is then completely eliminated.

For this great theologian of Vatican Council II,

> False Gnosis, thinking that it can surpass the word of God as well as myth, in fact reduces this word to a completely self-enclosed myth. Man believes that he can be affirmed by himself and be divinized by brute strength, without recourse to God, without receiving grace; in fact he becomes the slave of the demonic power, of the power of Satan.

Henri de Lubac said nothing different in his *Paradoxes*. He sought to identify the fundamental rejection on which modernity is constructed:

> We do not want a mysterious God. Neither do we want a God who is Some One. Nothing is more feared than this mystery God who is Some One. We would rather not be some one ourselves, than meet that Some One!... The total submission of the [mind] to Revelation is a fertilizing submission, because it is submission to Mystery. But the total submission of the [mind] to any human system whatever is a *sterilizing* submission.[13]

Is conversion a radical break with the world?

Saint John provides us with a precise elucidation of this question:

> I am writing to you, little children, because your sins are forgiven for his sake. I am writing to you, fathers, because you know him who is from the beginning. I am writing to you, young men, because you have overcome the Evil One.... I write to you, young men, because you are strong, and the word of God abides in you, and you have overcome the Evil One. Do not love the world or the things in the world. (1 Jn 2:12–15)

What is this world that we must not love? I tried to answer this question in my homily during the pilgrimage to Chartres, on May 21, 2018:

---

[13] Henri de Lubac, *Paradoxes of Faith*, trans. Paule Simon et al. (San Francisco: Ignatius Press, 1987), 214, 223.

The world that we must not love and to which we must not conform is not, as we know very well, the world that was created and loved by God; it is not the persons of the world to whom, on the contrary, we must always go, especially to the poor and the poorest of the poor, so as to love and serve them humbly.... No! The world that should not be loved is another world, namely, the world as it has become under the dominion of Satan and of sin. The world of ideologies that deny human nature and destroy the family.... The U.N. structures, which impose a new world ethic, play a decisive role and have become today a crushing power that propagates itself over the airwaves through the unlimited possibilities of technology. In many Western countries, it is a crime today to refuse to submit to these horrible ideologies. This is what we call adaptation to the spirit of the age, conformism. A great British poet of the last century, Thomas Stearns Eliot, wrote three lines that say more about this than whole books do: "In a world of fugitives, the person taking the opposite direction will appear to run away."[14] Dear young Christians, if it is permissible for an old man, like Saint John was, to speak to you directly, then I too exhort you, and I tell you: you have overcome the Evil One! Fight any law against nature that they try to impose on you, oppose any law against life, against the family. Be one of those who take the opposite direction! For us Christians, the opposite direction is not a place; it is a Person, it is Jesus Christ, our Friend and our Redeemer. One task in particular is entrusted to you: to save human love from the tragic drift into which it has fallen: love that is no longer the gift of oneself but only the possession of the other—a possession that is often violent, tyrannical. On the Cross God revealed himself as "*agape*", that is, as the love that gives itself even unto death. To love truly is to die for the other. Like this young policeman, Colonel Arnaud Beltrame!

It is necessary and urgent for us to convert. It is necessary and urgent to change direction.

Conversion is a personal commitment, but it cannot be done without the help of God and of his grace. From an etymological perspective, to convert is to turn around and look in a different direction.

The path that we set out on now is not a place. It is a person. It is Jesus Christ, our Savior and our God. We leave behind a wicked

---

[14] T.S. Eliot, *The Family Reunion* (1939; San Diego, New York, and London: Harcourt Brace, 1967), 110.

life, a life of error, so as to find love. Saint Paul's conversion on the road to Damascus perfectly illustrates the sense of a break that is truly rooted in Christ.

Conversion is a break with the past. We take the direction of Christ.

Certainly, the crisis of faith is part and parcel of a secularized society that is cut off from God and from supernatural realities. John Paul II denounced on several occasions the apostasy of the Western world and the enormous danger that it will paganize all the other nations and cultures of the world by its powerful media and its capacity for economic corruption.

But the Church has her own responsibility. Priests are called to nourish and to strengthen the people's faith. How could anyone imagine that this crisis will not extend its empire when we observe that the faith of priests is wilting?

The crisis of faith is deep, serious, and quite old.

2

THE CRISIS OF THE PRIESTHOOD

NICOLAS DIAT: Do you think that we are going through a crisis of the priesthood?

ROBERT CARDINAL SARAH: How could anyone doubt it? I have already mentioned the very painful crisis of pedophilia. This one is the tragic, unbearable symptom of a much deeper and more radical crisis. The Church today is running a great risk, because the profound meaning of the priesthood is unraveling. Pope Francis spoke forcefully and uncompromisingly about this subject on December 21, 2018:

> Today too, there are consecrated men, "the Lord's anointed", who abuse the vulnerable, taking advantage of their position and their power of persuasion. They perform abominable acts yet continue to exercise their ministry as if nothing had happened. They have no fear of God or his judgement, but only of being found out and unmasked. Ministers who rend the ecclesial body, creating scandals and discrediting the Church's saving mission and the sacrifices of so many of their confrères.[1]

I think that the pope was not speaking only about pedophile criminals. His words were aimed at all those who divert the priestly anointing to put it at the service of a power that does not come from God. Using one's authority to preach a human doctrine and not the Catholic faith, giving up the fight to remain faithful to one's commitment

---

[1] Christmas Greetings to the Roman Curia, Address of His Holiness Pope Francis, December 21, 2018.

to chastity, or simply giving up the resolution to put God in first place—these are so many behaviors that deny the profound truth of the priesthood and endanger the salvation of the faithful.

The light of the priesthood has been darkened. It pains me even more to say this because I know that there are many faithful priests. These priests devote themselves tirelessly to their mission. I think that we bishops bear a heavy responsibility. We must undergo an examination of conscience. Have we loved and accompanied our priests as good fathers of a family? Do we do all that we can to know them, to support them, and to help them? Very often dioceses turn into administrative structures, whereas each one ought to function like a big family.

A father must love, correct, punish, and put his children back on the right road. We have too often been permissive, closed our eyes, and delegated to others our primary duty under the pretext of a lack of time. Today we are facing the costly consequences of that. Perhaps we were the first to have given a bad example. The bishop ought to be the model of the priesthood in his diocese. He ought to be the model of the life of prayer. Now we are far from being the first to pray in silence and to recite the office in our cathedrals. I fear that we have lost our way in worldly, secondary responsibilities.

You often say that a priest is a man who prays and not a social worker. Why this insistence?

It is essential for every priest to be fully aware that he is first of all a man of God and a man of prayer. A priest exists exclusively for God and for divine worship. He must not let himself be taken in by the world, as though the time dedicated to Christ in intimate, silent prayer were wasted time. The most wonderful fruits of our ministry are born in silent prayer in front of the tabernacle.

Often discouragement lies in wait for us. Prayer requires an effort and a break with the world. We sometimes get the disconcerting impression that Jesus is silent. He is silent, but he is at work. Jesus himself often withdrew to the silence of the desert; he found it indispensable to leave the world of men so as to be with the Father, one on one. One day this moment of silent prayer happened to be painful and sorrowful. What did he do then? "[H]e prayed more earnestly;

and his sweat became like great drops of blood falling down upon the ground" (Lk 22:44).

Prayer can be exhausting and apparently sterile. In a world of noise, aberrations, and agitation, in a world that is anxious to produce more and more, priests must find the time to hide themselves in silent adoration. Their priestly identity is at stake there. They will have a priestly soul only if they set their hearts on being diligent in prayer while teaching the faithful to meet the Eucharistic Jesus in silence and adoration.

Certainly, the priest is faced with multiple obligations; often he must work in several parishes, conduct numerous meetings, and spend time with his parishioners. A good pastor is accessible to all, but he knows in the depths of his soul that the top priority of priestly life is to be with the Lord. Saint Charles Borromeo always used to say: "You will not be able to care for the souls of others if you let your own wither away. Ultimately you will no longer accomplish anything, not even for the others. You must have time for yourself so as to be with God."

However many commitments pile up, whatever pastoral emergencies there may be, it is a real priority to find the time for prayer, the Divine Office, spiritual reading, adoration, and the celebration of the Eucharist. In everyday life, the priest is often torn between the many urgent pleas of the faithful and the silent call of God. The priest sometimes gets the impression that he must make two lives coexist in his life. But deep down that is not how the reality presents itself. I would like to say to priests that their life is profoundly one. Its sole and unifying principle lies in union with God, in the worship of God. The works of his ministry must follow from that. When we visit the sick, when we hear confessions, when we console the afflicted, when we teach catechism and bring the Good News to everyone, we must remain united with God. These moments must not be digressions in our life of adoration. On the contrary, they must be full of this union with God that we have drawn from the well of silence. They are like an echo of this silence. Through the gift of ourselves to others in the ministry, we continue to adore God himself. At the very heart of the ministry, our soul murmurs its adoration of God, present in the persons whom we serve. Prayer gives life to the ministry. And the ministry gives us a hunger for God. It leads us to prayer. How could a priest not deposit in the Teacher's heart all the secrets that he has heard in the confessional? How could our ministry remain the continuation of the work of Jesus himself if it did not begin and end in loving adoration?

Without prayer, the priest wears and empties himself out and quickly becomes a machine that makes a lot of useless noise.

Priests must dedicate the important times of their days to prayer. They must ruminate on the Word of God. I think that it is vital to withdraw often to the desert or to Horeb, the mountain of God, like Moses, Elijah, and Jesus himself. For thirty years Jesus hid beneath the veil of our humanity, learning to work in silence and contemplative prayer. *Ora et labora* (pray and work), that was his daily life. He constantly remained in conversation with his Father. These moments of intimacy, one on one with God for long hours and whole nights, were indispensable moments of communion and of intra-Trinitarian intimacy.

Unless the priest imitates Jesus in his life of intimacy with the Father, he is lost. Christ did not hesitate to flee, to go far away from the crowd that harried him, so as to find the Father in solitude, prayer, contemplation, and silence. In order to help others, the priest must first ask for help from the Lord.

Today it is imperative for us to return to the root of our priesthood. This root, as we know, is unique: it is Jesus Christ. He is the one whom the Father sent, he is the cornerstone. In him, in the mystery of his death and Resurrection, the Kingdom of God comes and the salvation of the human race is accomplished. He has nothing that belongs to him personally; everything belongs entirely to the Father and is for the Father. And so the Jews were amazed by the extent of Jesus' knowledge: "How is it that this man has learning, when he has never studied?" (Jn 7:15). Jesus replies: "My teaching is not mine, but his who sent me; if any man's will is to do his will, he shall know whether the teaching is from God or whether I am speaking on my own authority" (Jn 7:16–17).

The Son alone can do nothing. Jesus told them this in these terms: "Truly, truly, I say to you, the Son can do nothing of his own accord, but only what he sees the Father doing; for whatever he does, that the Son does likewise" (Jn 5:19). And he added: "I can do nothing on my own authority; as I hear, I judge; and my judgment is just, because I seek not my own will but the will of him who sent me" (Jn 5:30).

This is the true nature of the priesthood. Everything that is essential to our ministry cannot be the product of our personal abilities. This applies to the administration of the sacraments, but also to the ministry of the Word. We are sent, not to talk about our personal opinions, but to proclaim the mystery of Christ. We are not commissioned to speak about our feelings, but to be the bearers of a single "word" who is the Word of God made flesh for our salvation: "My teaching is not mine, but his who sent me" (Jn 7:16).

The Lord Jesus calls us his friends. Despite our unworthiness and our many sins, he hands himself over to us totally. He entrusts to us his Body and Blood in the Eucharist. He entrusts his Church to us. What an awesome task! What a frightening responsibility: "You are my friends if you do what I command you" (Jn 15:14).

What do the people of God demand of their priests? They want one thing only: "We wish to see Jesus" (Jn 12:21). They want priests to lead them to Jesus, to put them in touch with him. The baptized want to know Christ personally. They want to see him through their priests. They want to hear his Word. They want to see God. A priest who does not have Jesus in his heart can give nothing. No one can offer what he does not possess. How can a priest lead community prayer if he does not remain constantly in deep, intimate contact with the Lord by taking the time to live an intense prayer life: the Liturgy of the Hours, daily prayer, that face-to-face encounter with God? If the priest does not pray, then his offering is an empty shell, a social, worldly act. Little by little, the faithful go away because the well in which they hoped to find water has run dry.

Christ was the great man of prayer. I advise all priests who, consciously or not, are drifting toward activism not to forget Mother Teresa of Calcutta. Jesus always held the first place in her day. Before meeting the poor, she would meet God. Before taking the poor and the dying into her arms, she had spent long hours in the arms of Jesus. She had contemplated and loved him for a long time. From this source of love, she drew the energy she needed in order to give herself totally to the most abandoned persons on earth. Silence with the Father prepares us to find the other. It is necessary to approach mankind with the eyes of God.

In his *Spiritual Canticle*, Saint John of the Cross invites us to reflect on the place occupied by prayer and supplication with regard to our missionary activities. He urges us to combine contemplation and action and to keep ourselves constantly in the presence of God, instead of scattering ourselves in external things and activism:

> Let those, then, who are singularly active, who think they can win the world with their preaching and exterior works, observe here that they would profit the Church and please God much more, not to mention the good example they would give, were they to spend at least half of this time with God in prayer, even though they might not have reached a prayer as sublime as this. They would then certainly accomplish more, and with less labor, by one work than they otherwise would by a thousand. For through their prayer they would merit this result, and themselves be spiritually strengthened. Without prayer they would do a great deal of hammering but accomplish little, and sometimes nothing, and even at times cause harm. God forbid that the salt should begin to lose its savor [Mt. 5:13]. However much they may appear to achieve externally, they will in substance be accomplishing nothing; it is beyond doubt that good works can be performed only by the power of God.[2]

How would you define precisely the temptation to worldliness and activism?

Some priests have a fear of appearing like strangers to the world. They are worried about being open to the world and understanding it. They are immersed in the world and end up drowning in it. Nevertheless, the priestly vocation is a call to follow Jesus by leaving the world. We see this in the Gospel. The apostles leave their boats, their occupations, their friends. To follow Christ is to renounce the world, its criteria, and its approval. In the world's eyes, the priest will always be a sign of contradiction. Jesus was rejected and crucified, and priests should aspire to be popular? On the contrary, I would like to tell them: my brothers, let us be uneasy if we meet with nothing but success, approval, and applause! Maybe that is the sign that we are no longer walking in the footsteps of Jesus, which can lead only to the Cross.

---

[2] St. John of the Cross, *Spiritual Canticle*, 29, 3, in *The Collected Works of St. John of the Cross*, trans. Kieran Kavanaugh, O.C.D., and Otilio Rodriguez, O.C.D. (Washington, D.C.: Institute of Carmelite Studies, 2017), 588.

How could anyone imagine a priesthood that kept accounting books and made a profit? Some priests want their actions to be efficient, assessed and recorded on a ledger in a worldly way. But the only action that should be necessary to quantify is prayer. A priest's work finds its sole measure in God. To be a priest is not primarily an office, it is a participation in the life of Christ crucified.

A priest must not be preoccupied with knowing whether he is appreciated by the faithful. He must simply ask himself whether he proclaims God's Word, whether the doctrine that he teaches is God's, whether he fully carries out God's will. The invisible things are the most important ones. Certainly, he must satisfy completely the expectations of the faithful. But the faithful ask nothing of him but to see Jesus, to hear his Word, and to experience his love in the Sacrament of Reconciliation and the beautiful Eucharistic liturgy.

The priest who ceaselessly runs from one parish to another, without bearing in his flesh the Paschal Mystery that he proclaims, is a dying man. Activism atrophies the priest's soul and prevents him from leaving room within himself for Christ.

Dear brother priests, allow me to address you directly. Christ left to us a terrible, magnificent responsibility. We continue his presence on earth. He decided to have need of us! Our hands, consecrated by the sacred chrism, are no longer our own. They are his for the purpose of blessing, forgiving, and consoling. They must be pierced, like his, so as to keep and hold nothing greedily. The dramatic, terrifying words of Charles Péguy in his *Éthique sans compromis* (Uncompromising ethics) come to mind:

Parish priests believe in nothing, no longer believe in anything—that is the common remark nowadays, the formula generally adopted, and unfortunately it is unfair to only a few.... They say, "This is the misfortune of our times...." There is no misfortune of our times. There is the misfortune of the clerics. All times belong to God. All clerics, unfortunately, do not belong to him. One is terrified by the enormous responsibilities that they will have to bear; and perhaps the ones who are involved in the extreme responsibilities are the only ones who will have any burden to bear. This is what they do not want to see.... It is an open secret, and even in the classroom it can no longer be concealed, except perhaps in seminary classrooms, that all this de-Christianization [in France], all de-Christianization in general has come from the clergy. All the withering of the trunk, the drying up of the spiritual city, does not come from the laity at all. It comes solely from the clergy.

Péguy concluded: "They want to have Christianity make progress. Let them be careful, let them beware! They want to have Christianity make progress that could cost them, that could cost them dearly. Christianity is in no way and by no means a religion-in-progress: nor (perhaps even less so, if that is possible) is it a religion of progress. It is the religion of salvation."

These words are harsh, pitiless, hyperbolic, and provocative. But the writer expresses himself in these terms because he wants to reawaken our sense of responsibility as pastors. Lay people expect us priests to tell them—clearly, firmly, and with paternal concern—not our opinions, but God's doctrine. They expect us to be "examples to the flock" (1 Pet 5:3), attentive to the whole flock for which the Holy Spirit has appointed us guardians to feed the Church of the Lord, which he obtained by the blood of his own Son (Acts 20:28).

When the faith of the clergy grows weak, something like an eclipse takes place: the world is plunged into dark shadows.

Pope Pius X, on May 27, 1914, already deplored this loss of faith among those responsible for the Church:

> We are, alas! in a time when men are welcoming and adopting with great facility certain ideas of conciliation of the faith with the modern spirit, ideas that lead farther than one thinks, not only to the weakening but even to the total loss of the faith. It is not unheard of to meet persons who express doubts and uncertainties about the truths of the faith and even stubbornly affirm manifest errors that have been condemned a hundred times and who despite that convince themselves that they have never left the Church because sometimes they have followed her Christian practices. Oh! how many navigators, how many pilots, and—God forbid!—how many captains, trusting in profane novelties and in the deceitful science of the age, have been shipwrecked instead of reaching the port!

How could anyone fail to apply these words to our times? Some clerics conspicuously indulge in tolerance of extremely uncertain theological theories. It leads them to despise the faith of little ones and of simple souls. In the name of an altogether academic theological science, they relativize the very heart of revelation. One wonders whether there is not a kind of intellectual snobbery here rather than a sincere search for God. So it happens that Sunday preaching becomes a moment to deconstruct the truths of the faith. Here we see a very serious abuse of authority, which Pope Francis untiringly denounces. A priest cannot take advantage of his authority over the people of God to set forth his personal ideas. His word does not belong to him! He is only the echo of the Eternal Word.

I recall on this subject the severe, disturbing words of Hans Urs von Balthasar, who dared to write in *A Short Primer for Unsettled Laymen* that the confusion within the Church had its origin in the preaching of "the secularized clergy (always including a large number of religious)".[3] This theologian saw this as one reason for the almost total abandonment of the Sacrament of Penance—and above all for the crisis "in the sphere of faith, where a small or large question mark was placed behind almost every article of the Creed."[4] The people of God suffered the consequences of this uncertainty of the pastors:

> A great number of laymen distance[d] themselves from the life of the Church, alienated by the spectacular identity crisis of clerics or religious.... Those who behaved so theatrically before them did not in any case correspond to the clear image of a priest [*Geistlichen*], someone who has been seized and illumined by the Spirit [*Geist*] of God, someone to whom a layman can turn and upon whom he can rely as a leader on the way to God. For the layman, the priest is still the man who gives visible expression to the hidden nature of the Church and to the demands made by Christ in the gospel, the man who according to Paul is a *typos*, a pattern by which one can orient oneself.[5]

Do some priests therefore take on nowadays the role of a social worker, which does not belong to them?

The mission of the priest is threefold: to sanctify, to evangelize, and to guide the people of God.

---

[3] Hans Urs von Balthasar, *A Short Primer for Unsettled Laymen*, trans. Michael Waldstein (San Francisco: Ignatius Press, 1985), 13.

[4] Ibid.

[5] Ibid., 14.

First, he is the steward of the mysteries of God. He is essentially commissioned to celebrate the Paschal Mystery, the Eucharist, and to reconcile sinners with God in the Sacrament of Reconciliation. We will never be able to delegate a layman to perform these ministries. It is necessary to have received the Sacrament of Holy Orders to act *in persona Christi capitis*—in the name of Christ the Head. Like Jesus, he must incarnate the presence of God, a presence that is supposed to convert, heal, and save souls.

Next, he has the obligation to proclaim the Good News of the Gospel, in other words, to make Jesus Christ known and to work to put those who wish to know him into a true, intimate relationship with him. He must also watch to make sure that the faith remains authentic, faithful, that it does not fail, that it is neither altered nor ossified. His mission is to make all Christians disciples and missionaries who are willing to die for Christ and his Gospel. It is his responsibility to give substantial spiritual nourishment that strengthens faith and the interior life.

Finally, the priest is guide and pastor. He must build and maintain communion among the Christians in the parish community that is entrusted to him. In a filial bond with the successor of Peter, and with his bishop, the priest has the responsibility to lead the people of God within his parochial territory where the Holy Spirit has set him.

A priest is a good shepherd. He is not there to invest his time primarily in advocacy of social justice, democracy, ecology, or human rights. These diversions turn the priest into an expert in areas that are far removed from the priestly identity intended by Christ.

The missionaries employed all their energy for the cause of evangelization, human and intellectual formation, and the physical and spiritual health of the people of God. They sought the right balance between the spiritual life and human flourishing. But they knew that they had to devote themselves first to prayer in order to lead men to God. Their hearts were set on making their lives a spiritual offering.

How can anyone successfully take care of material poverty if he does not combat spiritual poverty? How can anyone fight against corruption, violence, injustices, and all the violations of human life and dignity if the light of the Gospel is not proposed first to human consciences, if God is rejected as being far from humanitarian, political, or economic concerns?

It should hardly be surprising that the work of evangelization is weak. The level of catechetical life is sometimes not what it should be, to the point where Christians no longer know the basics of their own faith. Ongoing formation for believers is of fundamental importance. How can the faithful be fed if they hear only a brief ten-minute sermon each week? It is a lie to pretend that after ten minutes people no longer listen: If their attention span is so short, how do they manage to spend hours in front of the television? We write a lot about the new evangelization. It is urgent that each priest, each bishop, make an examination of his conscience and clarify where he stands with God on his teaching and his catechetical commitment. We do too many things, we run from one meeting to another. We make many journeys and visits, and we neglect the essential thing: prayer, our duty to teach, to sanctify, and to lead to God the Christian people and all who seek the Lord. Recall this passage which ought to make a profound impression on our priestly lives: "And the Twelve summoned the body of the disciples and said, 'It is not right that we should give up preaching the word of God to serve tables. Therefore, brethren, pick out from among you seven men of good repute, full of the Spirit and of wisdom, whom we may appoint to this duty. But we will devote ourselves to prayer and to the ministry of the word'" (Acts 6:2–4).

The bishops are the successors of the apostles. We ought to follow in their footsteps and preach as they had the courage to do. We are not administrators or ecclesiastical officials. We are the bearers and the guardians of the Word of God. Bishops should take inspiration from the letters that Saint Paul wrote to the first Christians. Would we have the courage to speak with such fire? God grant that our love for his Word may not grow lukewarm under the weight of procedures and meetings. In the Church, the heavier the administrative apparatus, the less room there is for the Holy Spirit! Woe to me if I do not evangelize!

How would you describe the close relation between priestly celibacy and the divine absolute?

I often hear people say that this is only a question of historical discipline. I think that that is wrong. Celibacy reveals the very essence of the Christian priesthood. To speak about it as a secondary reality is hurtful to all the priests of the world. Deep down I am persuaded that relativizing the law of priestly celibacy is tantamount to reducing the priesthood to a simple office. Now, the priesthood is not an office but a state of life. Priesthood in the first place is not doing; it is being.

Jesus Christ is priest. His whole being is priestly, in other words, given, handed over, and offered. Before he came, priests offered animals as a sacrifice to God. He revealed to us the fact that the true priest offers himself as a sacrifice. To be a priest is to enter ontologically into this offering of self to the Father for the Church that Jesus exemplified throughout his life. It is to adopt the sacrifice of the Cross as the form of one's whole life. The priesthood is an ontological participation in Christ's self-deprivation in this way. This gift takes the form of a spousal sacrifice. Christ is truly the Bridegroom of the Church. The ordained minister sacramentally represents Christ the Priest. The sacramental character configures him to Christ the Bridegroom. The priest is called to make of himself a complete, unlimited gift. He makes Christ the Bridegroom present sacramentally. Celibacy manifests this spousal gift; it is the concrete and vital sign of it. Celibacy is the seal of the Cross on our lives as priests. It is a cry of the priestly soul that proclaims its love for the Father and the gift of self to the Church. The wish to relativize celibacy amounts to disdain for this radical gift that so many faithful priests have lived out since their ordination.

By his celibacy, a priest renounces the human fulfillment of his ability to be a spouse and father according to the flesh. Out of love, he chooses to give that up in order to live exclusively as the spouse of the Church, offered entirely to the Father. I wish to proclaim with many of my brother priests the profound suffering that disdain for priestly celibacy causes me! This treasure cannot be relativized. Celibacy is the sign and the instrument of our entrance into the priestly being of Jesus. It takes on a value that we could describe analogously as sacramental. In 1992, John Paul II explained this idea in his apostolic exhortation *Pastores dabo vobis*:

> But the will of the Church [with regard to priestly celibacy] finds its ultimate motivation in the link between celibacy and sacred ordination, which configures the priest to Jesus Christ the head and spouse

of the Church. The Church, as the spouse of Jesus Christ, wishes to be loved by the priest in the total and exclusive manner in which Jesus Christ her head and spouse loved her. Priestly celibacy, then, is the gift of self in and with Christ to his Church and expresses the priest's service to the Church in and with the Lord.[6]

With this magisterial statement, Saint John Paul II expressed the doctrine of Vatican Council II about the priesthood. He affirms authoritatively that priestly celibacy is not a mere ecclesiastical discipline, but a manifestation of the sacramental representation of Christ the Priest. This document makes it difficult to derogate from the law of priestly celibacy, even for a limited region. On the contrary, it paves the way for a rediscovery by the Eastern Churches of the profound and radical ontological suitability of celibacy for the priestly state.

In 2007, in his apostolic exhortation *Sacramentum caritatis*, Pope Benedict XVI reminded us that priestly celibacy

> expresses in a special way the dedication which conforms [the priest] to Christ and his exclusive offering of himself for the Kingdom of God. The fact that Christ himself, the eternal priest, lived his mission even to the sacrifice of the Cross in the state of virginity constitutes the sure point of reference for understanding the meaning of the tradition of the Latin Church. It is not sufficient to understand priestly celibacy in purely functional terms. Celibacy is really a special way of conforming oneself to Christ's own way of life. This choice has first and foremost a nuptial meaning; it is a profound identification with the heart of Christ the Bridegroom who gives his life for his Bride.[7]

If the priest manifests and signals to the world by his celibacy that he intends to marry the Church, what meaning can be assigned to the life of married priests? Would they be less dedicated to the Church? How could they live out the fullness of their responsibility as husbands and fathers of families if they are above all spouses of the Church and

---

[6] Pope Saint John Paul II, Post-Synodal Apostolic Exhortation *Pastores dabo vobis* on the Formation of Priests in the Circumstances of the Present Day (March 25, 1992), no. 29.

[7] Pope Benedict XVI, Post-Synodal Apostolic Exhortation *Sacramentum caritatis* on the Eucharist as the Source and Summit of the Church's Life and Mission (February 22, 2007), no. 24.

fathers of Christians? Renouncing priestly celibacy would therefore amount to creating a real confusion of signs.

From this perspective, it is difficult to see how the priestly identity could be encouraged and protected if Rome abolished, even just for one region or another, the requirement of celibacy as Christ intended it and as the Latin Church has jealously preserved it. Similarly, one wonders how, in light of this doctrine, the people of God could even consider married priests. Even though they do not directly concern the priesthood, these words of the evangelist cannot be contradicted: "If any one comes to me and does not hate his own father and mother and wife and children and brothers and sisters, yes, and even his own life, he cannot be my disciple" (Lk 14:26).

No authority, no synod for any reason, or for any regional need, can claim the authority to separate purely and simply the priesthood from priestly celibacy, for as Vatican Council II recalls, the celibacy of clerics is not "only ... commanded by ecclesiastical law, but ... a precious gift of God."[8]

How far back in the history of the Church does this practice go?

From the first centuries of the Church, the law of continence and then of celibacy was considered to be of apostolic origin. All the ancient documents acknowledge an ontological connection between priesthood and continence. It would be false to say that the primitive tradition is not unanimous on this point. Indeed, the call of married men to the priesthood was always accompanied by a prescription of continence, even when the spouses continued to live under the same roof. Among the ancient documents, which are witnesses to the tradition, we find no trace of a contrary discipline before a certain confusion sets in at the end of the seventh century in the East.

The Council of Elvira in 305, the decretals of Pope Siricius in 385 and 386, and the Council of Carthage in 390 are the first written testimonies to a tradition that appears at that time as indisputable, firmly established, and furthermore not contested. If another discipline had been practiced at that time, we would inevitably have some trace of a controversy. Now, for the oldest documents, the discipline is

---

[8] Vatican Council II, Decree on Priestly Training *Optatam totius* (October 28, 1965), no. 10.

established and peacefully accepted by the whole undivided Church. These magisterial acts set forth the necessity of perfect continence for deacons, priests, and bishops. They assert that this discipline comes from the apostles. They appear as the first instances of an undisputed and indisputable oral tradition being set down in writing.

As early as the Second Council of Carthage, on June 16, 390, the Council Fathers voted for the following canon:

> Epigonius, Bishop of the Royal Region of Bulla, says: The rule of continence and chastity had been discussed in a previous council. Let it [now] be taught with more emphasis what are the three ranks that, by virtue of their consecration, are under the same obligation of chastity, i.e., the bishop, the priest, and the deacon, and let them be instructed to keep their purity.
>
> Bishop Genethlius says: As was previously said, it is fitting that the holy bishops and priests of God as well as the Levites, i.e., those who are in the service of the divine sacraments, observe perfect continence, so that they may obtain in all simplicity what they are asking from God; what the apostles taught and what antiquity itself observed, let us also endeavor to keep.
>
> The bishops declared unanimously: It pleases us all that bishop, priest, and deacon, guardians of purity, abstain from [conjugal intercourse] with their wives, so that those who serve at the altar may keep a perfect chastity.[9]

This canon indirectly confirms the existence of many married men in the ranks of the clergy, but all of them are called to continence. The subjects of the law are the deacons, the priests, and the bishops, in other words, the members of the three higher degrees of the clergy, which a man attains by *consecrationes*. These consecrations set men apart to perform functions that concern the divine mysteries. Here the service of the Eucharist is the specific foundation of the continence demanded of the ministers who exercise the priesthood. To celebrate Christ's sacrifice sacramentally demands that they live it out, even in their flesh. Bishop Lobinger is on the wrong track, far from the apostolic tradition, when he proposes the priestly ordination of

---

[9] *Corpus Christianorum* 149, p. 13, quoted in Christian Cochini, S.J., *The Apostolic Origins of Priestly Celibacy*, trans. Nelly Marans (San Francisco: Ignatius Press, 1990), 5.

married men for the purpose of celebrating the Eucharist. The service of the Eucharist is precisely what requires the perfect continence of the sacred ministers. The celebration of the Eucharist implies a close configuration of the priest to the poor, chaste, and obedient Christ.

In addition, there is a second motive that underscores the purpose of the obligation: the possibility of clerics obtaining in all "simplicity" what they ask of God. Without chastity, the minister would lack an essential quality when he presented to God the requests or the offerings of his human brethren and in a way would deprive himself of the freedom of speech that is gained for him by the renunciation of all the earthly ties of family. With chastity, in contrast, he enters into "simple" relations with the Lord because he is entirely free and dedicated. He no longer has anything to lose because he has already given everything.

The African canon of the Second Council of Carthage in 390 has decisive weight in the history of priestly celibacy because it vouches for a tradition that goes back to the apostles: "What the apostles taught and what antiquity itself observed, let us also endeavor to keep."

Many people would like to see women priests some day. They reject this unjust "discrimination" against women who are excluded from sacred orders. What do you think about this?

From the Old Testament on, God chose men and entrusted the priestly ministry to them: "[As for you, Moses], bring near to you Aaron your brother, and his sons with him, from among the sons of Israel, to serve me as priests" (Ex 28:1).

Jesus appointed only his twelve apostles as priests of the New Covenant. Nevertheless, in the midst of the apostles there were some very generous women, "who had followed Jesus from Galilee, ministering to him; among whom were Mary Magdalene, and Mary the mother of James and Joseph, and the mother of the sons of Zebedee" (Mt 27:55–56). God wanted men exclusively to be able to exercise the priesthood, even though Mary his mother was holier than the apostles.

In the Letter to the Hebrews it is written that the high priest is always chosen from among men and commissioned to intervene on behalf of mankind in their relations with God. This is not an honor that one takes upon oneself; one receives it through a call from God, as Aaron did. So it is indeed with Christ. On the day when he became high priest, he himself was not the one who gave himself this glory; he received it from God, who told him: "You are my son, today I have begotten you" (Ps 2:7). In one psalm he speaks as follows: "You are a priest for ever, according to the order of Melchizedek" (Heb 5:1–6).

The priesthood is from God. It is not a human creation. One does not become a priest in accordance with a desire or a simple human wish. It is necessary to be called by God. Now, for this mission, God decided to choose men only. The Judeo-Christian tradition and the teaching of the Latin Church confirm it.

Some people clamor for priestly ordination for women. Some Reformation communities have yielded to the world's pressure and have fabricated what they call female priests and bishops. This so-called priesthood is not Christ's but, rather, a human fabrication without any sacramental value.

Some high-ranking Catholic prelates apparently seem to wish for the ordination of women. In doing so, they oppose the definitive and infallible teaching of John Paul II. In his Apostolic Letter *Ordinatio sacerdotalis* dated May 22, 1994, the pope solemnly declared:

> Although the teaching that priestly ordination is to be reserved to men alone has been preserved by the constant and universal Tradition of the Church and firmly taught by the Magisterium in its more recent documents, at the present time in some places it is nonetheless considered still open to debate, or the Church's judgment that women are not to be admitted to ordination is considered to have a merely disciplinary force.
>
> Wherefore, in order that all doubt may be removed regarding a matter of great importance, a matter which pertains to the Church's divine constitution itself, in virtue of my ministry of confirming the brethren (cf. Lk 22:32) I declare that the Church has no authority whatsoever to confer priestly ordination on women and that this judgment is to be definitively held by all the Church's faithful.[10]

Any contrary statement amounts to a direct denial of the authority of the pope and a radical challenge to the authority of the Magisterium.

---

[10] Pope Saint John Paul II, Apostolic Letter *Ordinatio sacerdotalis* on Reserving Priestly Ordination to Men Alone (May 22, 1994), no. 4.

I wish to underscore the fact that this is not a matter of discussing the pertinence of the historical, theological, or scriptural arguments used. Saint John Paul II affirmed, by his irrevocable magisterial authority, the inability of the Church to proceed to the ordination of women. According to the Congregation for the Doctrine of the Faith, this topic is one of the positions that all priests have sworn to God to hold firmly, by their *Professio fidei*: "I also firmly accept and hold each and everything definitively proposed by the Church regarding teaching on faith and morals." Furthermore, the Congregation's Commentary dated June 29, 1998, explains, with regard to this teaching of John Paul II about the priesthood being reserved to men, that "The Supreme Pontiff ... intended to reaffirm that this doctrine is to be held definitively, since, founded on the written word of God, constantly preserved and applied in the Tradition of the Church, it has been set forth infallibly by the ordinary and universal Magisterium."[11] From the biblical, theological, and canonical perspective, therefore, the question is settled.

The proposals coming from the most important personages in the Church who attack head-on such an eminent act by Pope Saint John Paul II therefore deny his ability to issue decrees on his own initiative. By insinuating that an ecumenical council is the only authority that is qualified to decide certain ecclesiological matters, they are participating in the erosion of faith and order in the Church. I would like to be perfectly clear here. Such proposals renew the serious errors of those who assert that the council can act without the pope or against him. The college of bishops can make decisions only with its head, the Roman Pontiff. As canon law recalls, "There is neither appeal nor recourse against a decision or decree of the Roman Pontiff" (canon 333, §3). An appeal to the college of bishops against an act of the pope would amount to denying the primacy of the Supreme Pontiff and his constitutive function with regard to the episcopal college itself.

Even more profoundly, some people show that they have not understood why the eminent dignity of women does not consist merely in doing what men do. We get the impression that they

---

[11] Congregation for the Doctrine of the Faith, Commentary on the Concluding Formula of the *Professio Fidei* (June 29, 1998), no. 11.

want to reduce women to be "men just like the rest"! The Church needs women insofar as they have what is specifically feminine. They have, among other things, custody of the mystery of physical and spiritual motherhood. Pope Francis, in his homily on January 1, 2018, declared:

> The gift of the Mother, the gift of every mother and every woman, is most precious for the Church, for she too is mother and woman. While a man often abstracts, affirms and imposes ideas, a woman, a mother, knows how to "keep", to put things together in her heart, to give life. If our faith is not to be reduced merely to an idea or a doctrine, all of us need a mother's heart, one which knows how to keep the tender love of God and to feel the heartbeat of all around us.

The Church knows that she cannot live without this mystery that woman bears. But the priesthood is essentially connected with masculinity, to the mystery of the Bridegroom and of the Father.

Joseph Ratzinger saw the priesthood as an affirmation of the truth of the Cross. Is this an idea that you defend also?

Satan has a fierce hatred of priests. He wants to defile them, to make them fall, to pervert them. Why? Because by their whole life they proclaim the truth of the Cross. Priests and consecrated persons cannot leave the world indifferent. They proclaim down to the flesh this truth of the Cross. They will always be a subject of scandal for the world. They take Christ's place. Now, as Joseph Ratzinger said in a speech given in Rome in 1977, "the place of the true *vicarius Christi* is the Cross: to be a vicar of Christ is to be standing in the obedience of the Cross and thus to be a *representatio Christi* in time and in the world, to keep his power present as a counter-force to the power of the world.... Christ does not defend the Truth with legions of soldiers, but makes it visible through his Passion." Priests and consecrated persons, by their humble, dedicated lives, are a formidable challenge to the power of the world.

I would like to recall this. All you hidden and forgotten priests and religious, you whom society sometimes despises, you who are faithful to the promises of your ordination, you make the powers of this world tremble! You remind them that nothing can resist the strength of the gift of your life for the sake of truth. Your presence is unbearable to the prince of lies. You are not the defenders of an abstract truth or a party. You have decided to suffer for love of the truth, for Jesus Christ. Without you, dear brother priests and consecrated religious, humanity would be less great and less beautiful. You are the living rampart of the truth because you agreed to love it even to the Cross:

> The true measure of humanity is essentially determined in relationship to suffering and to the sufferer.... The capacity to accept suffering for the sake of goodness, truth and justice is an essential criterion of humanity, because if my own well-being and safety are ultimately more important than truth and justice, then the power of the stronger prevails, then violence and untruth reign supreme. Truth and justice must stand above my comfort and physical well-being, or else my life itself becomes a lie. In the end, even the "yes" to love is a source of suffering, because love always requires expropriations of my "I", in which I allow myself to be pruned and wounded. Love simply cannot exist without this painful renunciation of myself, for otherwise it becomes pure selfishness and thereby ceases to be love.
>
> To suffer with the other and for others; to suffer for the sake of truth and justice; to suffer out of love and in order to become a person who truly loves—these are fundamental elements of humanity, and to abandon them would destroy man himself.[12]

Priests and consecrated persons, because of their extraordinary gift of their whole body, their whole heart, and their whole strength to the Lord, are crucified with Christ and in profound communion with his sufferings. They want to become conformed to him in his death. Each one of them can say with Saint Paul: "I have been crucified with Christ; it is no longer I who live, but Christ who lives in me; and the life I now live in the flesh I live by faith in the Son of God, who loved me and gave himself for me" (Gal 2:20).

The experience of the Cross is the experience of the truth of our life. The truth and the Cross are our places of true human and

---

[12] Pope Benedict XVI, Encyclical Letter *Spe salvi* on Christian Hope (November 30, 2007), nos. 38–39.

Christian growth, for these are the places where we find Jesus, true God and true man.

The question of truth is first of all bound up with the Cross. The man or the cleric who proclaims God's truth inevitably mounts the Cross. All Christians, and priests in particular, are constantly on the Cross so that, through their witness, the truth may shine. In an eminent way, we carry in our body the sufferings of the death of Jesus, so that the life of Jesus, too, many be manifested in our body.

The bond between the truth and the Cross is a fundamental idea of Benedict XVI. He returns to it often in *Spe salvi*:

> In the history of humanity, it was the Christian faith that had the particular merit of bringing forth within man a new and deeper capacity for these kinds of suffering that are decisive for his humanity. The Christian faith has shown us that truth, justice and love are not simply ideals, but enormously weighty realities. It has shown us that God— Truth and Love in person—desired to suffer for us and with us. Bernard of Clairvaux coined the marvellous expression: *Impassibilis est Deus, sed non incompassibilis*—God cannot suffer, but he can *suffer with*. Man is worth so much to God that he himself became man in order to *suffer with* man in an utterly real way—in flesh and blood—as is revealed to us in the account of Jesus's Passion. (no. 39)

The pope adds: "Let us say it once again: the capacity to suffer for the sake of the truth is the measure of humanity" (no. 39). The Christian priesthood is the rampart of this saved humanity. By his life and his being, each priest is a light that brings hope. But this flame reveals also the ugliness of sin; it denounces the emptiness of this world. Dear priests, one could say about each of you what is said about the Cross of Christ itself: a scandal for some, folly for others! And yet, as Benedict XVI said in a homily that he gave in Nicosia in 2010:

> The Cross, then, is something far greater and more mysterious than it at first appears. It is indeed an instrument of torture, suffering and defeat, but at the same time it expresses the complete transformation, the definitive reversal of these evils: that is what makes it the most eloquent symbol of hope that the world has ever seen. It speaks to all who suffer—the oppressed, the sick, the poor, the outcast, the victims

of violence—and it offers them hope that God can transform their suffering into joy, their isolation into communion, their death into life. It offers unlimited hope to our fallen world.

That is why the world needs the Cross. The Cross is not just a private symbol of devotion, it is not just a badge of membership of a certain group within society, and in its deepest meaning it has nothing to do with the imposition of a creed or a philosophy by force. It speaks of hope, it speaks of love, it speaks of the victory of non-violence over oppression, it speaks of God raising up the lowly, empowering the weak, conquering division, and overcoming hatred with love. A world without the Cross would be a world without hope, a world in which torture and brutality would go unchecked, the weak would be exploited and greed would have the final word. Man's inhumanity to man would be manifested in ever more horrific ways, and there would be no end to the vicious cycle of violence. Only the Cross puts an end to it. While no earthly power can save us from the consequences of our sins, and no earthly power can defeat injustice at its source, nevertheless the saving intervention of our loving God has transformed the reality of sin and death into its opposite.[13]

Dear brother priests, your mission is to carry the Cross into the heart of the world. Your life is centered on the daily celebration of the Sacrifice of the Mass, which renews the sacrifice of the Cross. Your daily life is a continuation of the Cross. You are the men of the Cross! Be not afraid! With all my heart as a bishop, I wish to encourage you. Do not let yourselves be troubled by the rumors of the world. They mock your celibacy but they are afraid of you. Do not depart from the Cross. It is the source of all life and of all true love. In anchoring your lives to the Cross, you settle at the source of all good:

That is what we celebrate when we glory in the Cross of our Redeemer.... When we proclaim Christ crucified we are proclaiming not ourselves, but him. We are not offering our own wisdom to the world, nor are we claiming any merit of our own, but we are acting as channels for his wisdom, his love, his saving merits. We know that we are merely earthenware vessels, and yet, astonishingly, we have been chosen to be heralds of the saving truth that the world needs to

[13] Pope Benedict XVI, Homily at Holy Mass, June 5, 2010, Nicosia.

hear. Let us never cease to marvel at the extraordinary grace that has been given to us, let us never cease to acknowledge our unworthiness, but at the same time let us always strive to become less unworthy of our noble calling, lest through our faults and failings we weaken the credibility of our witness.... As we proclaim the Cross of Christ, let us always strive to imitate the selfless love of the one who offered himself for us on the altar of the Cross, the one who is both priest and victim, the one in whose person we speak and act when we exercise the ministry that we have received.[14]

Are priestly celibacy, the priesthood, the Cross, and truth irreducibly connected?

Celibacy, the priesthood, the Cross, and the truth are closely connected realities in Jesus, who is the stumbling block. I believe profoundly that the connection among these four points is the victory of love over fear. Accepting the truth presupposes going beyond the poison of suspicion. Accepting the Cross requires believing in love. Priestly life in celibacy is a proclamation of absolute trust in God. But our world is dominated by fear. It is paralyzed by this feeling exuded by the devil that isolates persons. Each one prefers to live in sadness and solitude rather than to agree to depend on someone else's love. During the vigil with priests on Saint Peter's Square for the conclusion of the Year for Priests, Benedict XVI insisted on this fundamental dimension:

> Celibacy ... is a definitive "yes". It is to let oneself be taken in the hand of God, to give oneself into the hands of the Lord, into his "I". And therefore, it is an act of loyalty and trust.... It is the opposite of this "no", of this autonomy that accepts no obligations, which will not enter into a bond.... So, we want to go ahead and make present this scandal of a faith that bases all existence on God. We know that besides this great scandal that the world does not want to recognize, there are also the secondary scandals of our shortcomings, our sins, which obscure the true and great scandal and make people think: "They are not really living on the foundation of God." But there is also so much loyalty! Celibacy—as its adverse criticism shows—is a great sign of faith, of the presence of God in the world. We pray to

[14] Ibid.

the Lord to help us, to set us free from the secondary scandals in order to make relevant the great scandal of our faith: the confidence, the strength of our life, which is founded in God and in Jesus Christ![15]

Priests, by their celibacy, pierce the cloak of distrust and suspicion that weighs on the world and cuts it off from God. Their example is necessary and makes them credible. How could we encourage young people to embark on the adventure of indissoluble marriage if we ourselves are not capable of giving our lives forever? Maybe the habit of too much wealth is what little by little makes us incapable of risking our lives for love. We become avaricious, settled in our ways of comfort and security. This reminds me of what Cardinal Ratzinger prophetically calls "bourgeois Christianity", that way of reducing Christianity to a philosophy of life from which any love that seemed radical or excessive would be banished.

For Jesus, one thing only counts: the truth (Jn 18:37–38). All his life, he served the truth, he gave witness to the truth. The truth about the Father, the truth about eternal life, the truth about the battle that man must wage in this world, the truth about life and about death are Christ's great battles. So many essential areas where lies and error are lethal. In the presence of Pilate, before being loaded down with his Cross and led off to Golgotha, he said: "For this I have come into the world, to bear witness to the truth. Every one who is of the truth hears my voice" (Jn 18:37). There is a profound bond between the truth and chastity. This bond is the gratuitousness of love. The truth is loved for its own sake and not for what it brings us. Joseph Ratzinger [Benedict XVI] expressed this in an enlightening passage of his homily on October 6, 2006:

> A beautiful phrase from the First Letter of Saint Peter springs to my mind. It is from verse 22 of the first chapter. The Latin goes like this: "Castificantes animas nostras in oboedentia veritatis." Obedience to the truth must "purify" our souls and thus guide us to upright speech and upright action. In other words, speaking in the hope of being applauded, governed by what people want to hear out of obedience

---

[15] Dialogue of the Holy Father Benedict XVI with Priests, Vigil on the Occasion of the International Meeting of Priests, June 10, 2010.

to the dictatorship of current opinion, is considered to be a sort of prostitution: of words and of the soul.

The "purity" to which the Apostle Peter is referring means not submitting to these standards, not seeking applause, but rather, seeking obedience to the truth. And I think that this is the fundamental virtue for the theologian, this discipline of obedience to the truth, which makes us, although it may be hard, collaborators of the truth, mouthpieces of truth, for it is not we who speak in today's river of words, but it is the truth which speaks in us, who are really purified and made chaste by obedience to the truth. So it is that we can truly be harbingers of the truth.

Thus the priest's chastity is the sign of his bond to the truth that is the crucified and risen Christ. This vital bond to the truth enables the priest to avoid the duplicity of leading a double life in which he lies to himself while seeking to seduce rather than to give himself.

What will be your stance during the synod for the Amazon region that will be held in October 2019, where it is obvious that the question of celibacy will be raised?

As we saw in the context of the place of women in the Church, I note with alarm that some persons would like to fabricate a new priest hood with human dimensions. If the Amazon region lacks priests, I am certain that we will not resolve the situation by ordaining married men, *viri probati*, who are called by God, not to the priesthood, but to married life so that they might prefigure the union of Christ and the Church (Eph 5:32). If, in a missionary impulse, each diocese of Latin America generously offered one priest for the Amazon region, then this region would not be treated with so much disdain and humiliation through the fabrication of married priests, as though God were incapable of raising up in that part of the world generous young men willing to make the total gift of their bodies and their hearts, their whole capacity to love and all their being in consecrated celibacy.

I have heard people say that, throughout the five hundred years of her existence, the Church of Latin America has always considered the "indigenous people" incapable of living out celibacy. The result of this prejudice is plain: there are very few indigenous priests and bishops, even though things are starting to change.

If because of a lack of faith in God and because of pastoral short-sightedness the synod for the Amazon region met to decide on the ordination of the *viri probati*, on the fabrication of ministries for women, and other incongruities of this sort, the situation would be extremely serious. Would these decisions be ratified on the pretext that they emanate from the will of the Synod Fathers? The Spirit blows where he wills, certainly, but he does not contradict himself and does not create confusion and disorder. He is the Spirit of Wisdom. On the question of celibacy, he has already spoken through the councils and the Roman pontiffs.

If the synod for the Amazon region made decisions along the above-mentioned lines, it would definitively break with the tradition of the Latin Church. Who can honestly say that such experimentation, with the risk of involving the distortion of Christ's priesthood, would remain restricted to the Amazon region? Certainly, we want to address emergencies and pressing needs. But the pressing need is not God! The current crisis is comparable in its seriousness to the great hemorrhage in the 1970s, during which priests left the priesthood by the thousands. Many of those men no longer believed. What about us? Do we still believe in the grace of the priesthood?

I want to make an appeal to my brother bishops: Do we believe in the omnipotence of God's grace? Do we believe that God calls workers to his vineyard, or do we want to replace him because we are convinced that he has abandoned us? Worse, are we ready to abandon the treasure of priestly celibacy under the pretext that we no longer believe that he would grant us the grace of living it in its fullness today? Dear brother bishops, every moment of our priestly life is a gratuitous gift of Almighty God's mercy; do we not experience this every day? How can we doubt? How can we believe that the Lord is not here with us in the midst of the storm? For pity's sake, let us not act as though he had left us to our own judgment. Benedict XVI was quite fair in the words that he spoke on this subject at the vigil on June 10, 2010, on the occasion of the International Meeting of Priests:

> [What's to be done about] the lack of vocations, because of which local Churches are in danger of perishing, for lack of the Word of life, missing the presence of the Eucharist and other Sacraments? ... The

temptation to take things into our own hands is great, the temptation to transform the priesthood—the Sacrament of Christ, to be chosen by him—into a normal profession, a "job" with specific working hours, and for the rest one belongs only to oneself. If we do so, we make it just like any other vocation; we make it accessible and easy. But this is a temptation that does not solve the problem.... If we too only perform a profession like any other, giving up the sacred, the novelty, the diversity of the sacrament which only God can give, that can only come from his calling and not from our "doing", we would not solve anything.... One great problem of Christianity in today's world is that it does not think anymore of the future of God. The present of this world alone seems sufficient. We want to have only this world, to live only in this world. So we close the doors to the true greatness of our existence. The meaning of celibacy as an anticipation of the future is to open these doors, to make the world greater, to show the reality of the future that should be lived by us already as present. Living, then, as a testimony of faith: we truly believe that God exists, that God enters into my life, and that I can found my life on Christ, on the future life.[16]

What a sign of faith and of trust in God a clear reaffirmation of the greatness and necessity of priestly celibacy would be! I know a bishop who, given the shortage of seminarians in his diocese, announced that he himself would make on foot, once a month, a pilgrimage to a Marian shrine. He has done this for several years to show how much he believes in the spiritual efficacy of his gesture. Today, his seminary has to be enlarged!

I want to emphasize also that the ordination of married men is by no means a solution to the lack of vocations. The Protestants who accept married pastors are likewise suffering from a shortage of men dedicated to God. Moreover, I am convinced that although in some Eastern Churches the presence of ordained married men is tolerated by the faithful, this is because it is complemented by the massive presence of monks. The people of God know intuitively that it needs radically dedicated men.

It would show disdain for the inhabitants of the Amazon region to propose "second-class" priests for them. I know that some theologians,

[16] Ibid.

like Father Lobinger, are seriously considering the idea of creating two classes of priests, one made up of married men who would only administer the sacraments, while the other would be made up of full-fledged priests who carry out the three priestly responsibilities: sanctifying, preaching, and governing. This proposal is theologically absurd. It implies a functionalist concept of the priesthood, while planning to separate the performance of the three priestly responsibilities, the *tria munera*, thus doing the opposite of what the Second Vatican Council teaches about their radical unity. I do not understand how anyone can indulge in such theologically regressive speculations. I think that, under the cloak of pastoral concern for mission countries that are short of priests, some theologians want to test their weird, dangerous theories. Basically, they disdain the peoples in question. A recently evangelized people needs to see the entire truth of the priesthood, and not a pale imitation of what a priest of Jesus Christ is. Let us not despise the poor!

The inhabitants of the Amazon region have a profound need of priests who do not limit themselves to doing their work on fixed schedules and then going back to their families to take care of their children. They need men who are passionate about Christ, burning with his fire, consumed by the zeal for souls. What would I be today if missionaries had not come to live and die in my village in Guinea? Would I have had the desire to be a priest if they had been content to ordain one of the men of the village? Has the Church grown cold to the point where among her children there are not enough magnanimous souls to get up and go off to proclaim Christ in the Amazon region? I think, on the contrary, that the prospect of a total gift to God can wake up the drowsy souls of many young Christian men. It is necessary also that we bishops have the courage to call them!

Saint Matthew spoke about eunuchs for the Kingdom of God....

The evangelist's words are luminous:

> The Pharisees came up to [Jesus] and tested him by asking: "Is it lawful to divorce one's wife for any cause?" He answered, "Have you not read that he who made them from the beginning made them male and female, and said, 'For this reason a man shall leave his father and

mother and be joined to his wife, and the two shall become one'? So they are no longer two but one. What therefore God has joined together, let no man put asunder." ... The disciples said to him: "If such is the case of a man with his wife, it is not expedient to marry." But he said to them, "Not all men can receive this precept, but only those to whom it is given. For there are eunuchs who have been so from birth, and there are eunuchs who have been made eunuchs by men, and there are eunuchs who have made themselves eunuchs for the sake of the kingdom of heaven. He who is able to receive this, let him receive it." (Mt 19:3–6, 10–12)

The Gospel is radical. Some people today reject these words. In the name of a personal pseudo-fulfillment, understood in a secular way, they reject the idea that a man could renounce the realization of his sexuality in marriage. Nevertheless, when someone gives to God, God returns the gift a hundredfold. Priestly celibacy is not a psychological mutilation. It is the free, joyous offering of one of our natural potentials. If it is lived out in intimacy with Christ, then far from creating any frustration in the priest, the gift of self develops our ability to love and expands it to the dimensions of Christ's heart. Because he is entirely dedicated to God, the priest becomes free to love all his brethren with a chaste love. Benedict XVI said to the clergy of Bolzano in August 2008:

There will always be a need for the priest who is totally dedicated to the Lord and therefore totally dedicated to humanity. In the Old Testament there is the call to "sanctification" which more or less corresponds to what we mean today by "consecration", or even "priestly Ordination": something is delivered over to God and is therefore removed from the common sphere, it is given to him. Yet this means that it is now available for all. Since it has been taken and given to God, for this very reason it is now not isolated by being raised from the "for", to the "for all". I think that this can also be said of the Church's priesthood. It means on the one hand that we are consigned to the Lord, separated from ordinary life, but on the other, we are consigned to him because in this way we can belong to him totally and totally belong to others. I believe we must continuously seek to show this to young people—to those who are idealists, who want to do something for the whole [community]—show them that precisely this "extraction from the common" means "consignment to the whole" and that this is an important way, the most important way, to serve our brethren. Part of this, moreover, is truly making oneself available to the Lord in the fullness of one's being and, consequently, finding oneself totally available to men and women. I think celibacy is a fundamental expression of this totality and already, for this reason, an important reference in this world because it only has meaning if we truly believe in eternal life and if we believe that God involves us and that we can be for him.[17]

Since antiquity, priestly celibacy has been guarded carefully as one of the purest glories of the Catholic priesthood. Saint John XXIII declared during the second session of the Roman Synod, on January 26, 1960:

We are upset that certain persons could imagine that the Catholic Church would go so far as to renounce deliberately or as a matter of convenience what was for long centuries and still remains one of the noblest and purest glories of its priesthood. The law of ecclesiastical celibacy and the concern to make it prevail always recall the battles of the heroic times when the Church of Christ had to engage in the struggle and won the triumph of her glorious trilogy, the constant emblem of her victory: the Church of Christ, free, chaste, and catholic.

Similarly, Saint Paul VI, in his encyclical *Sacerdotalis caelibatus* dated June 24, 1967, wrote:

Hence We consider that the present law of celibacy should today continue to be linked to the ecclesiastical ministry. This law should support the minister in his exclusive, definitive and total choice of the unique and supreme love of Christ; it should uphold him in the entire dedication of himself to the public worship of God and to the service of the Church; it should distinguish his state of life both among the faithful and in the world at large.

As for the Ecumenical Council Vatican II, in its decree *Presbytero-rum ordinis*, on the Ministry and Life of Priests, it taught that

---

[17] Meeting of the Holy Father Benedict XVI with the Clergy of the Diocese of Bolzano-Bressanone, August 6, 2008.

Perfect and perpetual continence for the sake of the Kingdom of Heaven, commended by Christ the Lord and through the course of time as well as in our own days freely accepted and observed in a praiseworthy manner by many of the faithful, is held by the Church to be of great value in a special manner for the priestly life. It is at the same time a sign and a stimulus for pastoral charity and a special source of spiritual fecundity in the world. Indeed, it is not demanded by the very nature of the priesthood, as is apparent from the practice of the early Church and from the traditions of the Eastern Churches, where, besides those who with all the bishops, by a gift of grace, choose to observe celibacy, there are also married priests of highest merit. This holy synod, while it commends ecclesiastical celibacy, in no way intends to alter that different discipline which legitimately flourishes in the Eastern Churches. It permanently exhorts all those who have received the priesthood and marriage to persevere in their holy vocation so that they may fully and generously continue to expend themselves for the sake of the flock commended to them.…

For these reasons, based on the mystery of Christ and his mission, celibacy, which first was recommended to priests, later in the Latin Church was imposed upon all who were to be promoted to sacred orders. This legislation, pertaining to those who are destined for the priesthood, this holy synod again approves and confirms, fully trusting this gift of the Spirit so fitting for the priesthood of the New Testament, freely given by the Father, provided that those who participate in the priesthood of Christ through the sacrament of Orders—and also the whole Church—humbly and fervently pray for it. This sacred synod also exhorts all priests who, in following the example of Christ, freely receive sacred celibacy as a grace of God, that they magnanimously and wholeheartedly adhere to it, and that persevering faithfully in it, they may acknowledge this outstanding gift of the Father which is so openly praised and extolled by the Lord. Let them keep before their eyes the great mysteries signified by it and fulfilled in it.[18]

Through the Gospel and the voice of the popes and of the councils, the voice of Jesus himself resounds in our ears. It comes to strengthen the hearts of priests who doubt or who are struggling to be faithful. It comes to enlighten the minds of the lay people who

[18] Vatican Council II, Decree on the Ministry and Life of Priests *Presbyterorum ordinis* (December 7, 1965), no. 16.

sense the importance of this question and want to count on priests who have dedicated their lives. Anyone who would dare to break and ruin this ancient treasure, this safe deposit box of the priestly soul, by seeking to separate the priesthood from celibacy, would hurt the Church and the priesthood of the poor, chaste, and obedient Jesus.

Is renouncing celibacy ultimately agreeing to reduce God to the level of an idol for the world?

Celibacy is a precious treasure, a splendid jewel that the Church has preserved for centuries. Throughout history it was difficult to understand it correctly and to preserve it intact. The renunciation of celibacy would be a defeat for all humanity. Many of our contemporaries think that it is impossible to love in perfect continence. There are many who think that celibacy puts the priest in an unnatural physical and psychological condition that is harmful to the equilibrium and maturity of the human person. Priestly celibacy, in this view, would therefore be a kind of violence done to nature. But in the Church's faith, it is instead a very sure manifestation of the great mystery of the divine love. Indeed, the priest is *Ipse Christus*. He is Christ himself. He carries within himself sacramentally Christ, the incarnation of God's love for man. This Christ, God made man, was sent into the world and appointed Mediator between heaven and earth, between God the Father and the human race.

In complete harmony with this mission, Christ remained throughout his earthly life in the state of virginity, which signifies his gift and his total dedication to the service of God and of mankind. The perfect chastity of the priest means to signify not only this imitation, this configuration to Christ, but also the intense presence of Christ in each priest. Priestly celibacy anticipates what we will be in God in the fullness of life in the heavenly Kingdom. Celibacy is an anticipation of eternal life with God.

Practical needs cannot drive the men of the Church to act according to the logic of profitability. We are laborers of the eternal Kingdom of God and not agents of an international business. There is a great risk of committing a tragic mistake, and history would blame us for it. The twelve apostles turned the world upside down. Why are we so preoccupied about the number of priests?

Did Jesus not tell us that the Kingdom of heaven possesses within itself a force, its own secret energy that enables it to grow, to develop, and to arrive at the harvest without man knowing it? "And he said, 'The kingdom of God is as if a man should scatter seed upon the ground, and should sleep and rise night and day, and the seed should sprout and grow, he knows not how. The earth produces of itself, first the blade, then the ear, then the full grain in the ear. But when the grain is ripe, at once he puts in the sickle, because the harvest has come.'" (Mk 4:26–29)

The harvest of the Kingdom of God is immense, and the laborers are very few today, as in the first days. They never were so numerous as to be sufficient according to human standards. But the Lord of the Kingdom asks us to pray that the Master himself might send laborers into his field. Little human plans cannot usurp the role of the mysterious wisdom of the One who over the course of history has challenged man's wisdom and power by his folly and weakness.

How would you define as precisely as possible the relation between ordination and belonging to Christ?

There is a specific ontological bond that unites the priest to Christ by virtue of the consecration that he received through the Sacrament of Holy Orders. He is therefore configured in a special way to Christ, who is "the way, and the truth, and the life" (Jn 14:6). He is possessed, immersed in Christ, so intimately that he must live and act in the truth, like Christ, and in the power of the Holy Spirit through humble service to God, to the Church, and for the salvation of souls. Thanks to this consecration, the spiritual life of the priest is imprinted, modeled, and marked by Christ's own behaviors.

The homily given by Benedict XVI during the Chrism Mass on Holy Thursday, April 9, 2009, is unambiguous:

> On the eve of my priestly ordination, fifty-eight years ago, I opened the Sacred Scripture, because I wanted to receive once more a word from the Lord for that day and for my future journey as a priest. My gaze fell on this passage: "Sanctify them in the truth; your word is truth." Then I realized: the Lord is speaking about me, and he is speaking to me. This very same thing will be accomplished tomorrow

in me. When all is said and done, we are not consecrated by rites, even though rites are necessary. The bath in which the Lord immerses us is himself—the Truth in person. Priestly ordination means: being immersed in him, immersed in the Truth. I belong in a new way to him and thus to others, "that his Kingdom may come". Dear friends, in this hour of the renewal of promises, we want to pray to the Lord to make us men of truth, men of love, men of God. Let us implore him to draw us ever anew into himself, so that we may become truly priests of the New Covenant.

He also said:

To be immersed in God's truth and thus in his holiness—for us this also means to acknowledge that the truth makes demands, to stand up, in matters great and small, to the lie which in so many different ways is present in the world; accepting the struggles associated with the truth, because its inmost joy is present within us. Nor, when we talk about being sanctified in the truth, should we forget that in Jesus Christ truth and love are one. Being immersed in him means being immersed in his goodness, in true love. True love does not come cheap, it can also prove quite costly. It resists evil in order to bring men true good. If we become one with Christ, we learn to recognize him precisely in the suffering, in the poor, in the little ones of this world; then we become people who serve, who recognize our brothers and sisters in him, and in them, we encounter him.

I wonder whether the crisis through which we are going in the world and in the Church has one of its deep roots here. We have forgotten that the source of all truth and of all good does not belong to us. We have forgotten to let ourselves be immersed in Christ. We have tried to accomplish by ourselves and according to our human plans what he alone can do. Priests have thought of themselves as carrying out a generous but all-too-human plan. Nevertheless, in our midst they are the incessant reminder that God breaks in at the heart of the world. Christians urgently need to tell priests who they are. They urgently need to stop asking them to be sympathetic friends or efficient managers. Today, I would like each Christian to go and find a priest and to thank him for what he is! Not for what he has accomplished, but for what he is: a man radically dedicated to God!

How I would love it if all the Christians in the world would pray that priests might devote themselves irrevocably to this consecration. I think that women have a special role to play in this prayer. In a mysterious spiritual maternity, they must carry the priests of the whole world: "Mothers are the strongest antidote to our individualistic and egotistic tendencies, to our lack of openness and our indifference. A society without mothers would not only be a cold society, but a society that has lost its heart, lost the 'feel of home'", Pope Francis said in his homily on January 1, 2017. "Recalling God's goodness in the maternal face of Mary, in the maternal face of the Church, in the faces of our own mothers, protects us from the corrosive disease of being 'spiritual orphans'. It is the sense of being orphaned that the soul experiences when it feels motherless and lacking the tenderness of God, when the sense of belonging to a family, a people, a land, to our God, grows dim."

Dear brother priests, we are not orphans! We have a Mother, who is Mary, who is the Church. Dear priests, the Church loves you as only a mother can love. Together we form a family, the holy people of God. Let us love the Church passionately. In her, we will find the grace to live our priesthood joyfully and ardently, the grace to give away everything once again so as to follow Christ and to offer him our lives to save souls.

3

THE CRISIS OF THE CHURCH

Nicolas Diat: Can we talk about a crisis of the Church?

Robert Cardinal Sarah: A superficial onlooker might be surprised that we talk about a crisis of the Church. From a human perspective, Christianity is expanding rapidly in some parts of the world. But I do not want to talk about the Church as a business to be evaluated by numerical results. The crisis that the Church is experiencing is much deeper; it is like a cancer eating away at the body from within. Many theologians, like Henri de Lubac, Louis Bouyer, Hans Urs von Balthasar, and Joseph Ratzinger, have analyzed this crisis at length. I will be only the humble echo and extension of their analysis.

Surely the most alarming symptom is the way in which men and women who call themselves Catholics pick and choose among the truths of the Creed. Joseph Ratzinger mentioned it in these terms during a conference that he gave in Munich in 1970: "What was hitherto unthinkable becomes normal: that men who long ago abandoned the Church's Creed should in good conscience regard themselves as the truly progressive Christians. For them, however, the only standard by which to measure the Church is the expediency with which she functions."[1]

In large sectors of the Church, we have lost the sense of God's objectivity. Each individual starts from his subjective experience and creates for himself a religion that suits him. What a shame! Each one tries to construct his Church to fit himself according to his own plan.

---

[1] Joseph Ratzinger/Pope Benedict XVI, "Why I Am Still in the Church", in *Fundamental Speeches from Five Decades*, trans. Michael J. Miller et al. (San Francisco: Ignatius Press, 2012), 138–39.

But this sort of business interests nobody. People will have nothing to do with a Church that is a party, a club, or a freethinkers' society. We already have more than enough human institutions of that sort. The Church is of interest only because she is the Church of Jesus Christ. In her, he gives himself, he surprises me.

Cardinal Ratzinger said in his book-length interview, *The Ratzinger Report*:

> "It is necessary to recreate an authentically *Catholic* climate, to find again the meaning of the Church as Church of the Lord, as the locus of the real presence of God in the world. That mystery of which Vatican II speaks when it writes those awesomely challenging words which correspond nonetheless to the whole Catholic tradition: 'the Church, or, in other words, *the Kingdom of Christ now present in mystery*'" (*Lumen Gentium*, 3).[2]

The loss of this way of looking at the Church in faith causes all the symptoms of her secularization. Prayer is eaten away by activism, true charity turns into humanistic solidarity, the liturgy is handed over to desacralization, theology is transformed into politics, and the very idea of the priesthood comes into crisis. This secularization is a terrible phenomenon. How can it be defined? One could say that it consists in a voluntary blindness. Some Christians decide to stop being enlightened by the light of faith. They decide to remove one part of reality from this light, then another. They decide to live in darkness. That is the sickness that is eating away at the Church. We decide to do without the light of faith in practice and even in theory. We study theology while making God a mere rational hypothesis. We read Scripture as a profane book and not as God's inspired Word. We organize the liturgy as a spectacle and not as the mystical renewal of the sacrifice of the Cross. We have come to the point where priests and consecrated religious live in a way that is sheer worldliness. Soon Christians themselves will live "as though God did not exist".

---

[2] Joseph Cardinal Ratzinger with Vittorio Messori, *The Ratzinger Report: An Exclusive Interview on the State of the Church*, trans. Salvator Attanasio with Graham Harrison (San Francisco: Ignatius Press, 1985), 47–48.

"God's face is noticeably disappearing. 'The death of God' is a very real process, which today extends deep into the interior of the Church. God is dying in Christendom, so it seems", Joseph Ratzinger said sorrowfully in his speech at the Catholic Academy of Bavaria on June 4, 1970.[3] At the heart of the crisis of the Church, faith becomes like a cumbersome reality even in the eyes of Christians. Pope Francis says:

> In the process, faith came to be associated with darkness. There were those who tried to save faith by making room for it alongside the light of reason. Such room would open up wherever the light of reason could not penetrate, wherever certainty was no longer possible. Faith was thus understood either as a leap in the dark, to be taken in the absence of light, driven by blind emotion, or as a subjective light, capable perhaps of warming the heart and bringing personal consolation, but not something which could be proposed to others as an objective and shared light which points the way. Slowly but surely, however, it would become evident that the light of autonomous reason is not enough to illumine the future; ultimately the future remains shadowy and fraught with fear of the unknown. As a result, humanity renounced the search for a great light, Truth itself, in order to be content with smaller lights which illumine the fleeting moment yet prove incapable of showing the way. Yet in the absence of light everything becomes confused; it is impossible to tell good from evil, or the road to our destination from other roads which take us in endless circles, going nowhere.
>
> There is an urgent need, then, to see once again that faith is a light, for once the flame of faith dies out, all other lights begin to dim. The light of faith is unique, since it is capable of illuminating *every aspect* of human existence. A light this powerful cannot come from ourselves but from a more primordial source: in a word, it must come from God. (*LF* 3–4)

When we speak about a crisis of the Church, it is important to specify that the Church, as the Mystical Body of Christ, continues to be "one, holy, catholic and apostolic". Theology, doctrinal, and moral teachings remain unchanged, unchangeable, and inviolable. The Church, as the continuation and extension of Christ in the world, is not in a crisis. She has the promises of eternal life. The gates of hell will never prevail against her. We know, we firmly believe,

---

[3] Ratzinger, "Why I Am Still in the Church", 138.

that, in her bosom, there will always be enough light for those who sincerely wish to seek God.

Saint Paul's appeal to Timothy, his son in faith, applies to us all: "In the presence of God who gives life to all things, and of Christ Jesus who in his testimony before Pontius Pilate made the good confession, I charge you. . . . Guard what has been entrusted to you [i.e., the deposit of faith]. Avoid the godless chatter and contradictions of what is falsely called knowledge, for by professing it some have missed the mark as regards the faith" (1 Tim 6:13, 20–21).

Faith continues to be a supernatural divine gift. But we, who have been baptized into Christ's death, are the ones who are reluctant to let our thoughts, our actions, our freedom, and our whole life be enlightened and guided at every moment by the light of the faith we profess. There is a tragic dichotomy and a spectacular incoherence between the faith we profess and our concrete way of life. In a letter taken from his correspondence included in the volume *Combat pour la vérité*, Georges Bernanos wrote: "You claim to be stones of the Temple called God, the fellow citizens of the Saints, the children of the Heavenly Father. Admit that that is not always visible at first glance!"

Today the crisis of the Church has entered into a new phase: the crisis of the Magisterium. Of course the true Magisterium, as a supernatural function of the Mystical Body of Christ, ensured and led invisibly by the Holy Spirit, cannot be in crisis: the voice and the action of the Holy Spirit are constant, and the truth toward which he guides us is firm and unchangeable. The Evangelist John tells us: "When the Spirit of truth comes, he will guide you into all the truth; for he will not speak on his own authority, but whatever he hears he will speak, and he will declare to you the things that are to come. He will glorify me, for he will take what is mine and declare it to you. All that the Father has is mine; therefore I said that he will take what is mine and declare it to you" (Jn 16:13–15).

Today, however, a veritable cacophony reigns in the teachings of pastors, bishops, and priests. They seem to contradict each other. Each one imposes his personal opinion as something certain. The result is a situation of confusion, ambiguity, and apostasy. The minds of many Christian faithful have been inculcated with major disorientation, profound disarray, and destructive uncertainties. The philosopher Robert Spaemann clearly described this disarray with a quotation taken from the First Letter of Saint Paul to the Corinthians:

"And if the bugle gives an indistinct sound, who will get ready for battle?" (1 Cor 14:8).

Nevertheless, as we know, the Magisterium remains the proof of unity of the faith. Our ability to receive the Church's teaching in the spirit of discipleship, with docility and humility, is the true mark of having the mind of sons and daughters of the Church. Unfortunately some, who ought to transmit divine truth with infinite caution, do not hesitate to mix it with fashionable opinions, or even with the ideologies of the day. How can we discern? How can we find a sure path in this confusion?

In his classic work the *Commonitorium*, Saint Vincent of Lérins sheds invaluable light on the subject of progress or change in the faith:

> Shall there, then, be no progress in Christ's Church? Certainly; all possible progress. For what being is there, so envious of men, so full of hatred to God, who would seek to forbid it? Yet on condition that it be real progress, not alteration of the faith. For progress requires that the subject be enlarged in itself, alteration, that it be transformed into something else. The intelligence, then, the knowledge, the wisdom, as well of individuals as of all, as well of one man as of the whole Church, ought, in the course of ages and centuries, to increase and make much and vigorous progress; but yet only in its own kind; that is to say, in the same doctrine, in the same sense, and in the same meaning....
>
> Our forefathers in the old time sowed wheat in the Church's field. It would be most unmeet and iniquitous if we, their descendants, instead of the genuine truth of wheat, should reap the counterfeit error of tares. This rather should be the result—there should be no discrepancy between the first and the last. From doctrine which was sown as wheat, we should reap, in the increase, doctrine of the same kind—wheat also; so that when in process of time any of the original seed is developed, and now flourishes under cultivation, no change may ensue in the character of the plant.[4]

I wish to beg bishops and priests to watch over the faith of the faithful! Let us not rely on commentaries posted hastily on the Internet by so-called experts. It takes time to receive magisterial teaching

---

[4] Vincent of Lérins, *Commonitory* 54, 67, in *Nicene and Post-Nicene Fathers*, Second Series, ed. Philip Schaff and Henry Wace (Peabody, Mass.: Hendrickson, 1994), 11:147–48.

and to interpret it according to a hermeneutic of continuity. Let us not yield to the pace of the media, which are so quick to talk about changes, turning points, or revolutions. The Church's time is a long time. It is the time of contemplated truth that bears all its fruit if we allow it to sprout peacefully in the ground of faith. John Henry Cardinal Newman wrote in 1878 in his *An Essay on the Development of Christian Doctrine*:

> From the nature of the human mind, time is necessary for the full comprehension and perfection of great ideas; and that the highest and most wonderful truths, though communicated to the world once for all by inspired teachers, could not be comprehended all at once by the recipients, but, as being received and transmitted by minds not inspired and through media which were human, have required only the longer time and deeper thought for their full elucidation.[5]

When the storm is raging over a ship, it is important to be secured to something stable and solid. It is not the time to run after fashionable novelties that are in great danger of fading even before anyone has had a chance to grasp them. It is necessary to stay on course, without swerving, while waiting for the horizon to be revealed. I wish to say to Christians: Do not let yourselves be troubled! You have in your hands the treasure of the Church's faith. It was passed on to you by centuries of contemplation, by the constant teaching of the popes. You can nourish your faith life on it without fear.

Does this crisis date back to Vatican Council II?

The seeds of it were present a long time before that, but there is no disputing the fact that Vatican Council II was followed by a profound and universal crisis of the Church. The postconciliar period was not the hoped-for ideal. Thus Jacques Maritain, in his memoir, *The Peasant of Garonne*, mentions

> the neo-modernist fever..., very contagious, at least in circles described as "intellectual," compared to which the modernism of Pius

---

[5] John Henry Cardinal Newman, *An Essay on the Development of Christian Doctrine* (Westminster, Md.: Christian Classics, 1968), 29–30.

X's time was only a modest hayfever, . . . this second description gives us the picture of a kind of "immanent" apostasy. . . . In preparation for many years, hastened by certain veiled hopes of the repressed regions of the soul which were stirred up here and there on the occasion of the Council, the manifold manifestation of this apostasy is sometimes falsely ascribed to the "spirit of the Council".[6]

At that time, many Christians, and in particular clergymen, experienced an adolescent identity crisis. Sons of the Church, we are simple heirs of the treasure of the faith, without any merit on our part. The truth of the faith was transmitted to us so that we might guard it and might live by it. In this regard, we are insolvent debtors with respect to all our ancestors. To receive the treasure of tradition presupposes a filial spirit. We are, in a way, dwarves perched on the shoulders of giants. But above all we are debtors of God. Aware of our unworthiness and weakness, we gratefully contemplate him placing into our hands the treasures of divine life: the sacraments and the Creed. What must our reaction be to such divine generosity with regard to our poverty? There is nothing else for us to do but to share the inheritance that we have received and to hand it on. The awareness of our fundamental unworthiness ought to drive us to tell the world the Good News, to proclaim it, not as our property, but in the manner of a precious deposit that has been presented to us by mercy. Incidentally, this was the reaction of the apostles after Pentecost. In the postconciliar years, it seems that some people had an incorrect awareness of this status as unworthy heirs. As Joseph Ratzinger says in *Principles of Catholic Theology*, they wanted to make "a great examination of conscience" of the Catholic Church. They reveled "in the confessions of guilt, in the intensity of the self-accusations", in a "concept of a Church that was sinful in a general and fundamental way". He observes that they went so far as "to take seriously the whole arsenal of complaints against the Church".[7] An examination of

---

[6] Jacques Maritain, *The Peasant of Garonne: An Old Layman Questions Himself about the Present Time*, trans. Michael Cuddihy and Elizabeth Hughes (Eugene, Ore.: Wipf & Stock, 2011), 5–6.

[7] Joseph Cardinal Ratzinger, *Principles of Catholic Theology: Building Stones for a Fundamental Theology*, trans. Sister Mary Frances McCarthy, S.N.D. (San Francisco: Ignatius Press, 1987), 371.

conscience ought to have led us to hand on our heritage all the more joyfully and attentively, since we would have realized how unworthy of this gift we are. On the contrary, Cardinal Ratzinger notes that this period "led ... to uncertainty about the Church's own identity, ... to a deep rift in her relationship to her own history, ... a radically new beginning."[8] But in this attitude there was a great danger of a subtle pride. Some clerics claimed to be heirs no more but, rather, creators. Sometimes they set about proclaiming an altogether human faith in place of the divine deposit. Instead of transmitting what we had received, they noisily proclaimed what they had invented. I am convinced that there was a spiritual fault at the root of this crisis. Much humility is necessary in order to agree to receive a gift. But, all at once, we refused to be undeserving heirs. Nevertheless, this reality is at the heart of every family. A child receives the love of his parents freely. He has not merited it. He will give it in turn. The fundamental humility that consists of agreeing to receive without deserving it and to hand on freely is the mold in which familial love is formed. The Church has been losing her familial spirit since it started to become diluted. She is prey to divisions and to harshness. She is undermined by a partisan spirit, suspicion, ideology. I must express my profound suffering given the degrading maneuvers and the manipulations that are making their way into ecclesial life. We ought to be the family of God. Almost constantly we present the lamentable spectacle of a court in which everyone is seeking power and influence. The morals of politicians are invading our ranks. Where is charity? Where is benevolence? We will find our peaceful unity again only by forming a body around the deposit of the faith. It is time to reject the hermeneutics of rupture, which break the transmission of the heritage but also the unity of the ecclesial body, as Joseph Ratzinger puts it clearly in *The Ratzinger Report*:

> To defend the true tradition of the Church today means to defend the Council. It is also our fault if we have at times provided a pretext (to the "right" and "left" alike) to view Vatican II as a "break" and an abandonment of the tradition. There is, instead, a continuity that allows neither a return to the past nor a flight forward, neither

[8] Ibid., 372.

anachronistic longings nor unjustified impatience. We must remain faithful to the *today* of the Church, not the *yesterday* or *tomorrow*. And this today of the Church is the documents of Vatican II, without *reservations* that amputate them and without *arbitrariness* that distorts them.[9]

It is time for us to rediscover a peaceful and joyful spirit, a spirit of sons of the Church who accept all her history as grateful heirs. The council must not be retracted. Instead, it is necessary to rediscover it by carefully reading the official documents that were issued by it. It is necessary to read the council without a guilty conscience but with a spirit of filial gratitude toward our mother the Church.

One of the problems posed by the conclusions of the council is the meaning that has been given to *Gaudium et spes*. Joseph Ratzinger recalls already in the *Principles of Catholic Theology* that "what was most effective was not its content ...; rather, it was the general intention ... of introducing a fundamental change."[10] The concept of "world" is not clearly defined in the document: "The Church cooperates with the world for the building up of society.... The text serves as ... an attempt at an official reconciliation with the new era inaugurated in 1789.... Neither embrace nor ghetto can solve for Christians the problem of the modern world."[11]

Basically, if the popes and the Council Fathers thought that they could confidently be open to everything positive in the modern world, it is precisely because they were certain about their identity and about their faith. They were proud of being sons of the Church. On the other hand, among many Catholics, there was an unfiltered, unrestrained opening to the world, in other words, to the prevailing modern mentality, at the very moment when scholars were questioning the foundations of the *depositum fidei*, which for a great number of people were no longer clear.

Some identified with "the spirit of the Council" in order to chase after perpetual renewal. Many stopped thinking of themselves as sons of the Church. They adopted the world's ways and criteria because they had a guilty conscience. If the Church is no longer perceived

---

[9] Ratzinger, *Ratzinger Report*, 31.
[10] Ratzinger, *Principles of Catholic Theology*, 379.
[11] Ibid., 381, 382, 391.

as the loving mother who feeds her children, then Christians will no longer understand why they are sons. If they are no longer sons of one and the same mother, they will no longer be brothers to each other. I would like to repeat here the words of Pope Francis in his homily on January 1, 2018: "To set out anew, let us look to our Mother. In her heart beats the heart of the Church. Today's feast tells us that if we want to go forward, we need to turn back: to begin anew from the crib, from the Mother who holds God in her arms." What he says about Mary must be understood about the Church, too. "Where there is a mother, there is unity, there is belonging, belonging as children", he declared on the same occasion the previous year.

What do you mean by a crisis of the Creed?

It is first of all a crisis of fundamental theology, a crisis of the foundations of the faith. This is connected with a wrong interpretation of Vatican II in the form of a hermeneutic of rupture, which ought to be countered with a hermeneutic of reform in the continuity of the Church as a single subject. It is manifested chiefly in "ecclesiology", or the theology of the Church.

I must note also a crisis of the place of theology in the life of the Church. We observe among specialists in sacred doctrine a claim of autonomy with regard to the Magisterium, which causes them to lean toward heterodox teachings that are presented as unchangeable truths. Theologians lose sight of their authentic mission, which is not the creation but the interpretation of what has been revealed: a more in-depth study of it, and not the development of their own academic skills.

Theologians must not think of themselves merely as intellectuals in a universe consisting solely of universities and academic journals. Theology is an ecclesial service. A priest-theologian is above all a pastor. It must not be forgotten that dogmatic definitions are a service rendered to the "little ones" of the Church, and not a way of lording it over others. In formulating the faith by means of words, the Magisterium allows everyone to share in the light that Christ left to us. The practice of theology starts with catechism and preaching. It consists of scrutinizing the mysteries of the faith so as to express them in human words that allow them to be transmitted to the greatest number possible. I am sometimes amazed by the profound theology that some believers develop intuitively based on the truths of the catechism. In *L'Humilité de Dieu* (The humility of God), François Varillon writes: "When she does theology, the Church does not honor her God under the title of Supreme Professor who discourses about his being in logically articulated statements for the satisfaction of the intellect." The Church simply makes sure that, at all times and in all places, people receive the light of Christ, of whom she is the sacrament. This concern leads her to formulate about a mystery, at a particular moment in history, what she has contemplated, so that the relation of her sons to the living God might not be perverted. These formulations, which are made at the conclusion of a long study, also inaugurate a new reflection. They are points of departure as much as, and even more than, they are points of arrival. If one wording becomes outmoded, nothing prevents the Church from renewing it, in fidelity to the meaning that it encloses. Yes, it is necessary to say better what has already been said, to formulate it in an ever more accurate way, without breaking with tradition. We must remain firm, unshakable in upholding the tradition, the doctrine, and the dogmas of the Church. Without polemics, impatience, or fuss.

The work of deconstruction carried on by a certain theology that has lost the ecclesial spirit has repercussions sooner or later on catechetical teaching. In that way, the catechism loses the certitude and harmony that ought to characterize it. It was an initial and serious error to attack the catechism by declaring it "outmoded". Nowadays, it is too often presented as a series of exegetical hypotheses, without logical or chronological connections. This approach adds no clarity at all for the children. We have to teach the faith, not the latest fashionable theories of historical-critical exegesis that will soon be outdated.

The crisis is evident also at the level of the relations between the two channels that transmit to us the one divine revelation, namely, Sacred Scripture and tradition, thus between the Bible and the Church who hands on what she has received from the Lord. Under the influence of Protestantism and its main idea, *sola scriptura*—Scripture alone, without the Magisterium—Catholic exegetes have touted a so-called "scholarly" interpretation of the Bible, encumbered by a set of working hypotheses and philosophical, scientific, or Hegelian prejudices, to the detriment of the patristic and traditional reading by the saints, the only ones who fully understood Scripture.

Finally, Scripture is considered nothing more than a set of ancient documents, fascinating of course, but devoid of supernatural importance, the understanding of which is no longer possible except for specialists. Now tradition is the chief criterion in matters of faith. Every Catholic must have the audacity to believe that his faith, in communion with the faith of the Church, is above any new magisterium of experts and intellectuals. One may legitimately wonder what the purpose and the spiritual interest are in trying to separate tradition and the Word of God.

The Dogmatic Constitution *Dei Verbum* had solemnly proclaimed the essential connection between the Magisterium and the Word of God: "It is clear, therefore, that sacred tradition, Sacred Scripture and the teaching authority of the Church, in accord with God's most wise design, are so linked and joined together that one cannot stand without the others, and that all together and each in its own way under the action of the one Holy Spirit, contribute effectively to the salvation of souls."[12] *Dei Verbum* also declares more explicitly that sacred tradition and Sacred Scripture "form one sacred deposit of the word of God, committed to the Church" (*DV* 10). The council thus emphasizes that the Word of God cannot subsist without the Magisterium of the Church, since the Church is the one who receives "the sacred deposit of the word of God" and, within the Church, the "living teaching office" alone has the office and the responsibility of interpreting with a specific authority received from Christ (*authentice, in nomine Christi*) the Word of God that is found in the Sacred Scriptures and in tradition (*DV* 10). Of course, "this teaching office is not above the word of God, but serves it, teaching only what has been handed on" (*DV* 10), that is, the same Word of God contained in the sacred deposit of the faith entrusted to the Church.

Today there is a great danger of thinking that sacred tradition could be made obsolete by a change of the Magisterium. Some say that the truths handed down by the Church must be reinterpreted in their context, and they take advantage of this to request changes from the Magisterium. Given this peril, the council firmly reminds us that tradition is the Word of God itself and that, although the Magisterium

[12] Vatican Council II, Dogmatic Constitution on Divine Revelation *Dei Verbum* (November 18, 1965; hereafter cited as *DV*), 10.

tries to abstract from it, it cannot take the place of it. The authentic Magisterium can never break with tradition and the Word of God. Our faith in the Church gives us the assurance of that.

Do you go so far, then, as to speak about a crisis of ecclesiology?

The great temptation for ecclesiology would be to reduce the Church to a sociological level. The spouse of Christ becomes the object of a purely human and profane examination. Some would like to see her as a society that promotes a project of essentially earthly social liberation. But they forget that she is nothing less than "Jesus Christ widespread and communicated", as Bishop Bossuet put it. They forget that she is really the Mystical Body of Christ: "The authentically Catholic meaning of the reality 'Church' is tacitly disappearing, without being explicitly rejected. Many no longer believe that what is at issue is a reality willed by the Lord himself. Even with some theologians, the Church appears to be a human construction, an instrument created by us and one which we ourselves can freely reorganize according to the requirements of the moment", Joseph Ratzinger explained in *The Ratzinger Report*.[13]

The Mystical Body of Christ, the Church, must make that same light shine everywhere and in every age, exactly like the sun that rises each morning and illumines the world. The first purpose on which God's mind and infinitely loving will are set eternally is the infinite perfection of Christ the Redeemer. All was created through him and without him nothing came into being (Jn 1:3), and God leads all things and all the events in history toward him. The Church is Jesus Christ extending his life, which is the very life of God, to all Creation that has been redeemed, sanctified, and divinized by him.

In October 2018, the Synod on "Young People, the Faith and Vocational Discernment" caused some perplexity because of its controversial interpretation of the episode of the "disciples on the road to Emmaus" taken from the Gospel of Luke (Lk 24:13–35).

You remember those two men trudging along, turning their backs on Jerusalem and heading toward a town called Emmaus. Along the way, they were joined by a stranger who caught up with them,

---

[13] Ratzinger, *Ratzinger Report*, 45.

slowed down, and questioned them. "What is this conversation which you are holding with each other as you walk?" he asks them. The two men's answer is simple: "Are you the only visitor to Jerusalem who does not know the things that have happened there in these days?" "What things?" he asks. "Concerning Jesus of Nazareth!" The stranger replies with a sort of vehement reproach: "O foolish men, and slow of heart to believe all that the prophets have spoken!" It is necessary to remember also the episode of the apostles in the boat when they are shaken by a violent wind: it is cause for panic, the storm is terrible, and their lives are in danger. Christ wakes up and scolds them: "Where is your faith?" (Lk 8:25). Why? To lack hope and faith is to distrust God, to doubt that he is present, that he is faithful, that he is active, at the heart of our life and in the midst of our anguish. When dealing with Christ, it is always wrong to despair. Then he reproaches them by saying: "Was it not necessary that the Christ should suffer these things and enter into his glory?" (Lk 24:26), and he explicitly condemns their lack of hope. During this trip to Emmaus, Jesus speaks and the disciples listen. Starting with Moses and mentioning all the prophets, he interprets the Scriptures concerning him.

This passage from the Gospels is certainly the most beautiful *lectio divina*. A commentary on Christ is given by Christ, Christ is explained by Christ, Christ is considered by Christ.

But it will be necessary to part ways. Nevertheless, something in the hearts of these men refuses to separate. "Stay with us, for it is toward evening and the day is now far spent" (v. 29). Jesus agrees. All three go into an inn. Then something quite strange happens. Saint Luke uses here the vocabulary of the Eucharist: "[Jesus] took the bread and blessed and broke it, and gave it to them" (v. 30). It is in fact the Eucharist, the Sacrament of Christ's Paschal Mystery. All this takes place on the evening of Passover. Only at that moment do they recognize him. But then they no longer see him. For one can meet Christ only in his Eucharistic Presence. They could have stayed a moment with him and listened to him again, feasting their eyes on his glorious face: "That which ... we have seen with our eyes, which we have looked upon and touched with our hands", Saint John writes in his First Letter (1:1). Faith opens their eyes to see the Risen Lord. That is what this marvelous passage reveals to us.

"And they rose that same hour and returned to Jerusalem" (Lk 24:33). They depart in the cold of night. That day they do not sleep. They return to the holy city and join the group of apostles; the pilgrims of Emmaus would be among the first witnesses of the Resurrection.

This passage helps us to understand that we are not the ones who construct the Church, but rather Christ, through his Word and the Eucharist: "the household of God [is] built upon the foundation of the apostles and prophets, Christ Jesus himself being the cornerstone" (Eph 2:20). As the Eternal Shepherd, he leads us. In his Church, he meets us by delivering his Word to us.

Christ spoke, and their hearts burned with love. At their departure, their pace had been sluggish and their faith—lukewarm. But while Christ explained the Scriptures to them, they started to walk at the pace of the Risen Lord. A change of pace, a change of life, a change of heart—maybe that is what the Lord expects of us when we listen to his Word. Then came the moment to break bread, the moment of the Eucharist. It is often said that this episode unfolded just like the Eucharistic celebration: at the beginning, the heaviness of sinful man who turns his back on Jerusalem, the place of the Cross and of Christ's suffering. He is then touched by the Word, the Liturgy of the Word, and the commentary on the Word—the homily. Then comes the breaking of the bread, and the disciples are sent on a mission. These men set out again for Jerusalem after having had the whole Christ: Christ the Word, Christ the Body, Christ the Blood, Christ the Eucharist. Thus surrounded again by this Presence, with their hearts filled with this silent glory of the Risen Lord, they meet the apostolic group: the Church founded on the apostles (Eph 2:20). They had broken their ecclesial and fraternal communion. Discouragement, despair, diminished faith: remaining aloof from the members of the Church, they had left for a distant place, Emmaus. And they rediscover ecclesial communion. They reconnect with the Eucharistic Christ, they rediscover the Church, they re-establish communion and will be fearless witnesses of the Risen Lord. Jesus Christ is the one who builds up the Church by his Word and by the Eucharist. We become members of the Church and missionaries of the Gospel, witnesses of the Risen Lord, after having been fed with the Word, with the Body and Blood of Jesus Christ. Saint Paul warns us: "According to the commission of God given to me, like a skilled master builder I laid a foundation, and another man is building upon it. Let each man take care how he builds upon it. For no other foundation can any one lay than that which is laid, which is Jesus Christ" (1 Cor 3:10–11). Let us follow the work of the apostles and of their successors down through the centuries. Let us build nothing according to the ways of the world. It is Christ who builds up his Church, and we are his useless collaborators.

Is the hierarchical form of the Church still acceptable to our contemporaries? Many people call for a more democratic government: What do you think?

We are witnessing today a misinterpretation of the human reality of the Church, conceived in certain laboratories where the utopia of a people of God is distilled into a dialectical opposition to the Magisterium. The role of the latter, and especially of the Congregation for the Doctrine of the Faith, has been misunderstood.

A horizontalist vision of the Church inevitably leads to the desire to align her structures with those of political societies. If it is only a human creation that was not directly instituted by Christ, then it has to be rethought ceaselessly, reorganized according to rational schemes answering the needs of the moment. Cardinal Ratzinger said in *The Ratzinger Report*:

> If the Church, in fact, is *our* Church, if *we alone* are the Church, if her structures are not willed by Christ, then it is no longer possible to conceive of the existence of a hierarchy as a service to the baptized established by the Lord himself. It is a rejection of the concept of an authority willed by God, an authority therefore that has its legitimation in God and not—as happens in political structures—in the consensus of the majority of the members of an organization. But the Church of Christ is not a party, not an association, not a club. Her deep and permanent structure is not *democratic* but *sacramental*, consequently *hierarchical*. For the hierarchy based on the apostolic succession is the indispensable condition to arrive at the strength, the reality of the sacrament. Here authority is not based on the majority of votes; it is based on the authority of Christ himself, which he willed to pass on to men who were to be his representatives until his definitive return. Only if this perspective is acquired anew will it be possible to

rediscover the necessity and fruitfulness of obedience to the legitimate ecclesiastical hierarchies.[14]

Nowadays Christians see their bishops as nothing more than men seeking power. They comment on the influence of this one or the career of another. How can they forget that governing in the Church is a service? To hold part of Christ's authority is precisely to enter into his status as servant, to be divested of one's whole being, of one's personal ideas, of one's preferences and tastes so as to become the humble servant of the salvation of all: "And Jesus ... said to them, 'You know that those who are supposed to rule over the Gentiles lord it over them, and their great men exercise authority over them. But it shall not be so among you; but whoever would be great among you must be your servant, and whoever would be first among you must be slave of all'" (Mk 10:42–44).

The service of governing is a way of the Cross at every moment. It ought to become a path of sanctification in imitation of him who emptied himself, taking the form of a servant. I want to insist: it is as servants of the faith and of the salvation of all that bishops must sometimes reprove and correct. Out of concern for protecting the faith of all, especially of the littlest ones, it happens that the Congregation for the Doctrine of the Faith condemns a book or forbids a priest to teach. This governing is a loving service to God and to souls. It is a holy and sanctifying task, although difficult and thankless.

Similarly, we do not obey in the Church as we do in a political society. The reason why we obey those who hold power is not that we are afraid of them. Truly Catholic obedience relates to God. Through the hierarchy, he is the one whom we love, he is the one whom we obey. We have lost the supernatural sense of this obedience, only to make it a power play. As early as 1976, the Archbishop of the Metropolitan See of Lyon, Alexandre Renard, noted in his book *Où va l'Église?* (Where is the Church going?): "The Church has come down with a case of horizontalism. We see the human beings, with their limitations and their tendencies, rather than their mission and their grace; our attitude toward bishops—including the pope—is like our attitude toward leaders and bosses; we criticize them rather

[14] Ibid., 49.

often, instead of working in communion with them, whose responsibility is so great and so heavy."

I would like to remind everyone about Jesus' words to Saint Peter.
"You are Peter, and on this rock I will build my Church" (Mt 16:18).
We have the assurance that this saying of Jesus is realized in what we
call the infallibility of the Church. The spouse of Christ, headed by
the successor of Peter, can live through crises and storms. Her members may sin and err. But if we remain united to Peter, we will never
be able to separate ourselves from Christ profoundly or lastingly. *Ubi
Petrus, ibi Ecclesia.* Where Peter is, there is the Church. In an important speech to the Sacred College [of Cardinals] and to the Curia on
June 28, 1980, John Paul II declared:

> The mandate of the episcopal college, which is closely united to the
> humble successor of Peter, is therefore to safeguard, to protect, to defend
> this truth and this unity. We know that, in carrying out this mandate,
> the teaching Church is assisted by the Holy Spirit with the specific
> charism of infallibility. This infallibility is a gift from on high. Our duty
> is to remain faithful to this gift, which does not come to us from our
> own meager strength or our own poor abilities, but solely from the
> Lord. It is to respect and not to disappoint the *sensus fidelium,* in other
> words, this particular "sensibility" by which the people of God perceive
> and respect the richness of the revelation that has been entrusted by God
> to the Church and which requires that she protect it absolutely.

Similarly, on November 18, 1980, in a speech to German theologians in Altötting, John Paul II said:

> The Magisterium exists only in order to determine the truth of God's
> Word, especially when it is threatened by distortions and misunder
> standings. The infallibility of the Church's Magisterium is to be seen
> in this context, too. The Church must ... be very humble and certain
> that she remains in the same truth, in the same teaching about faith and
> morals that she received from Christ, who in this domain equipped
> her with the gift of a special "infallibility". Admittedly, infallibility has
> a less central position in the hierarchy of truths, but it is in a certain
> way the key to the certainty with which the faith is professed and
> proclaimed, and also to the life and conduct of the faithful. For if
> this essential foundation is shaken or destroyed, the most elementary
> truths of our faith begin to dissolve at the same time.

We never advance in our search for the truth by challenging the Magisterium, present or past, or by casting doubt on it. It is true that in this area we get little help from those who appropriate the Magisterium and interpret it according to their own ideas, while breaking with the theological tradition. Alas, they are quick to hurl anathemas at all those who do not follow their line of thought. Given such theological hysteria, it is time to rediscover a bit of peace and benevolence. Only faith, confidence in the Magisterium and its continuity down through the centuries, can give us unity.

Do you think that we are confronted with an identity crisis of the Catholic religion in connection with ecumenism and interreligious dialogue?

The ecumenical effort is necessary, but sometimes it has proceeded with excessive haste, and we have forgotten that the reaffirmation of inviolable points of dogma is a service rendered to our interlocutor. An incorrect understanding of the true nature of ecumenism causes indifferentism about Christian confessions to set in.

The desire for a more fraternal, less hostile, and less strained relation between Christians is just and praiseworthy. But ecumenism cannot be reduced to that. True ecumenism lies in abandoning our sins and our lukewarmness, together freeing ourselves from our lack of faith, rediscovering the same faith in the Christian mysteries, in the sacraments, the same doctrine, the same Church that was entrusted to Peter and not one that we have built by our own ingenuity. True ecumenism consists of letting ourselves be guided solely by the one light of the Gospel, with its moral requirements. True ecumenism is to keep God's Word faithfully and to live according to his commandments. For "whoever keeps his word, in him truly the love for God is perfected. By this we may be sure that we are in him: he who says he abides in him ought to walk in the same way in which he walked" (1 Jn 2:5–6). Without a strong reaffirmation of Christ's teaching as it has always been handed down by the Magisterium of the Church, there is no ecumenism.

Who remembers the words of Saint Paul VI at his General Audience on August 28, 1974? He fearlessly declared: "What sort of ecumenism could we construct in that way? . . . Where would Christianity end up, and, moreover, where would Catholicism be if today, under pressure from a specious but inadmissible pluralism, we accepted as legitimate the doctrinal disintegration and therefore also the ecclesial disintegration that it can bring with it?"

I am surprised by the irenicism that we show toward non-Catholic Christian confessions. On some subjects, ecumenism toward our separated brethren in the East poses difficulties at the theoretical level, always with regard to questions of ecclesiology, particularly concerning papal primacy from the perspective of communion. Sometimes they avoid mentioning the real meaning of the primacy of Peter so as not to trouble the Orthodox. I am not sure that we will advance toward greater unity through that form of doctrinal diplomacy. I do not think that our separated brethren expect that of us. On the contrary, I think that they are grateful to us when we assume all of Catholic doctrine, explain it, and proclaim it without false prudence. It seems to me that the most productive steps have been the fruit of the ecumenism of the martyrs. When Catholics and Orthodox found themselves in the same gulags, they prayed together, witnessed to the faith together, and sometimes shared the same sacraments.

Moreover, we observe in some Catholic circles a fascination with the Protestant model. It must be possible for charity to get rid of our rough places so as to allow the Holy Spirit to work on our conversion. Nevertheless, it is pointless to deny the profound differences that separate us. Our faith in the Lord's Real Presence in the Eucharist, our fidelity to the Mass as the renewal of the sacrifice of the Cross, our faith in the sacramental character of the priesthood require us to be truly consistent: it is impossible for a Protestant to receive Communion during Holy Mass. That would have no other meaning but to express a kind of sympathy. But the Eucharist must not be manipulated just to signal good human relations. It is the locus of communion with the God of truth. Since the council, we have observed a greater openness on both sides, but the journey toward unity in truth is still a long one.

There is, furthermore—and this is more serious—an irenicism toward non-Christian religions. Some go seeking in these religions things that already exist in the Church. In the West, pagan and even animist religions are praised to the skies. Similarly, the philosophical-religious ideas of the Far East become models. Of course you have to be an African to dare to say (without a psychological complex) that these pagan "traditional religions" are zones of fear and lack of freedom. Unfortunately those extraordinary paths of salvation—and I am thinking in particular of the implicit baptism of desire that is present among some non-Christians—have been transformed into the ordinary path. Of course, the souls of some pagans are just, and they live according to an upright conscience. But it is urgent to bring the fullness of salvation to these souls. The Rahnerian theory of the "anonymous Christian" runs the risk of extinguishing our sense of the urgency of mission. Do we still have the anguish about salvation that gripped Saint Dominic, for example, and led him to spend entire nights in prayer, during which they heard him groan: "What will become of the souls of poor sinners?"

You often say that the crisis of the Church is not an institutional problem. Can you explain your point of view?

I have seen many institutional reforms. They often created all sorts of commissions and councils. Have we noticed many results? You do not correct a bad book by changing the binding or the paper. In his *Introduction to Christianity*, Cardinal Ratzinger wrote:

> Those who really believe do not attribute too much importance to the struggle for the reform of ecclesiastical structures. They live on what the Church always is; and if one wants to know what the Church really is one must go to them. For the Church is most present, not where organizing, reforming, and governing are going on, but in those who simply believe and receive from her the gift of faith that is life to them. Only someone who has experienced how, regardless of changes in her ministers and forms, the Church raises men up, gives them a home and a hope, a home that is hope—the path to eternal life—only someone who has experienced this knows what the Church is, both in days gone by and now.[15]

What we urgently need is to start looking again at everything with the eyes of faith. By reforming institutions non-stop, you maintain the illusion that the important thing is what we are doing, our human

---

[15] Joseph Cardinal Ratzinger, *Introduction to Christianity*, trans. J. R. Foster (San Francisco: Ignatius Press, 2004), 343–44.

action, which we regard as the only effective measure. This type of reform, therefore, only shifts the problem. I think that it is essential and urgent to discern the true nature of the crisis and to realize that the evil is not found solely in the ecclesial institutions. Minor modifications made to the organization of the Curia cannot rectify mind-sets, feelings, and morals. What is a "reform" in the profound meaning of the term? It is about a reformation. A return to the pure form, the one that comes from God's hands. The true reform of the Church consists of allowing ourselves to be shaped by God once again. In *The Ratzinger Report*, Cardinal Ratzinger declared:

> Hence, true "reform" does not mean to take great pains to erect new façades (contrary to what certain ecclesiologies think). Real "reform" is to strive to let what is ours disappear as much as possible so [that] what belongs to Christ may become more visible. It is a truth well known to the saints. Saints, in fact, reformed the Church in depth, not by working up plans for new structures, but by reforming themselves. What the Church needs in order to respond to the needs of man in every age is holiness, not management.[16]

It is necessary to find concrete ways to stop being an obstacle to the divine action. But as long as our souls are lukewarm, all measures will be in vain. Routine is a terrible threat. It hardens us. It makes us blind. It makes us deaf to any questioning. It closes the doors and the shutters against the divine light. It prevents us from understanding the mistakes that we make. It prevents us from reacting, correcting ourselves, converting, and advancing. It fosters carelessness, degradation, corruption. Above all, it prevents us from going against the current. Nothing great can be accomplished with men of routine who have settled for mediocrity once and for all. Nothing substantial can be accomplished with the lukewarm and the half-hearted. Lukewarmness leads to cowardice and treason. The Lord is merciless toward the lukewarm: "I know your works: you are neither cold nor hot. Would that you were cold or hot! So, because you are lukewarm, and neither cold nor hot, I will spew you out of my mouth" (Rev 3:15–16). In his book *Note*

---

[16] Ratzinger, *Ratzinger Report*, 53.

conjointe [Joint note], Charles Péguy expressed his severe views on this subject:

> There is something worse than having a wrong idea: having a ready-made idea. There is something worse than having a bad soul: having a soul that is quite set in its ways. There is something worse than having a perverse soul: having a soul governed by force of habit.... The worst sorts of distress, the most despicable acts, and sin itself are often chinks in man's armor,... through which grace can penetrate the breastplate of man's hardened heart. But everything slides over this inorganic breastplate of habit, and against it every sword is blunted!

As long as we are unaware of the seriousness of our failure, we will not react. Will the vile, filthy deeds of some clergymen that have recently come to light wake us up? Maybe this humiliation, this slap on the face was necessary to make us realize our profound need of reform, in other words, of conversion. How can anyone not react when confronted with so much cynicism on the part of men who are consecrated to God? How can we fail to look for the deep cause of these demeaning and organized acts of abuse committed against minors? This, surely, is the most extreme and revolting sign of a life that slipped little by little until it became a life without God, a life marked by practical atheism, a life that tipped from the sacred to the profane and even to profanation. It is necessary to take measures, and the Church is doing this, to protect the children, who are the sacred image of the divine innocence. But how can anyone fail to see that no measure will replace a profound look at our whole life with the eyes of faith? Above and beyond the abominable crimes committed against children, who will tell of the profound crisis that is eating away at the life of the clergy? Their chastity is being attacked in principle. Conduct contrary to consecrated celibacy is proliferating in some regions of the world. But the worst thing is not so much the sin of weakness, which always deserves mercy if it is regretted and confessed. The worst thing is that some clergymen claim that these acts are normal and benign. How can they fail to see that they do profound damage to their consecration to God? There is one problem that no structural reform will resolve: ignorance of God. Lukewarmness, the rejection of the evangelical requirements, the loss of the sense of sin, attachment to money have a common root in the loss of the sense of God. The degradation of the liturgy to a spectacle, negligence in liturgical celebrations and confessions, and spiritual worldliness are only symptoms. The structures or the institutions are not the things in crisis, but rather our faith and our fidelity to Jesus.

The changes to be made are not only in the institutions, not even in morals, but first of all in the interior life of souls, in the depths of minds and hearts, in the convictions and the orientation of consciences. What must change radically is our relation to God.

Of course, we must find concrete ways of putting this radical conversion into practice. Where is the true compass that can orient us? Do the popes have to write? Church teaching is no longer like an anchor to which the people of God want to hang on. Recent popes fought with all their might against the crisis they saw developing. Who still remembers the documents by Paul VI or by John Paul II? Who even reads them? More importantly, who takes them as a rule of life? We get the impression that words slide over people's souls without managing to break the shield of habit and indifference. What we need more than words is to re-experience God. This is perhaps the heart of all reform. Benedict XVI said in his address to the clergy of Rome on February 22, 2007: "Only if there is a certain experience can one also understand." We must therefore ask ourselves the question: How can we have the experience of God? We must therefore re-experience the Church as the place where God gives himself

From this perspective, I wish to note two priorities. First, there is a place where we can have this experience of God and of the Church: the liturgy. There it is not possible to hide from God. Benedict XVI wrote in his preface to the French edition of the volume of his Complete Writings on the liturgy that "the true renewal of the liturgy is the fundamental prerequisite for the renewal of the Church." Indeed, "the existence of the Church draws its life from the correct celebration of the liturgy. The Church is in danger when the primacy of God no longer appears in the liturgy or, consequently, in life. The deepest cause of the crisis that has upset the Church is found in the obscuring of God's priority in the liturgy." I humbly beg bishops, priests, and the people of God to care more for the sacred liturgy, to put God at the center of it, to ask Jesus Christ once again to teach us to pray. We have desacralized the Eucharistic celebration. We have transformed our Eucharistic celebrations into a folklore exhibition, a social event, an amusement, an insipid dialogue between the priest and the Christian assembly. Is there still a place for the Most High in our liturgies? Can we still experience God in them? Lay people sometimes claim a "ministry" at Mass so as to feel that they are taking part and actively involved. Let us reflect a bit on the nature of the active participation of Mary and of Saint John on Golgotha. They were there, silently allowing themselves to be penetrated, imbued, and shaped by the mystery of the Cross. Should I not, in turn, be concerned about knowing how I die with Jesus in each Eucharist and whether I agree to die to my sin? Is my Christian life built on prayer and on true intimacy with God? What place do prayer and the Word of God have in my life? In each of our Eucharistic celebrations, we ought to be able to say, like Saint Paul: "In Christ Jesus our Lord, I die every day!" (1 Cor 15:31).

There is another place where we can have the experience of God who gives himself in the Church: the monasteries. We find there a concrete actualization of what the whole Church ought to be. I have often said so, and I am not afraid to repeat it. The renewal will come from the monasteries. I invite all Christians to share for a few days the experience of life in a monastery. There they will experience "in miniature" what the Church is "at large". In the monasteries, they will experience the primacy given to the contemplation of God. Go back to the monasteries! In contrast with a world of ugliness and sadness, these sacred places really are oases of beauty, simplicity, humility, and joy. In the abbeys, the faithful can understand that it is possible to put God at the center of their whole lives. This primacy of contemplation was proclaimed by Christ himself when he declared that "one thing [only] is needful" and that "Mary has chosen the good portion, which shall not be taken away from her" (Lk 10:42), and even more when Jesus said to God his Father: "This is eternal life, that they know you the only true God, and Jesus Christ whom you have sent" (Jn 17:3). Contemplation is the heart of Christianity. In the monasteries, it is proclaimed for all eternity and will never be repealed. We must protect these precious places of contemplation. They are the present and the future of the Church. God dwells there: he fills the hearts of the monks and the nuns with his silent presence, and all of life there is liturgical. It is nourished by faith and the Divine Office and on fire with love and the burning bush of the Divine Presence.

In the monasteries, we have also the experience of the early Church, where the believers held everything in common. Each day they shared their bread. Today, the crisis of the Church is manifested particularly in her fragmentation; a partisan spirit has torn her apart. Christ did not found a Church where the voices would be so discordant. The life of the monasteries allows us to have the experience of rediscovered unity. Following their examples, our Christian communities ought to become places where one can understand the primacy of God, through the beauty of the liturgy, of silence, of charity, and of the common sharing of goods. People must be able there to "take this path which leads to discovery of the Gospel, not as a utopia but as the full form of life", as Benedict XVI said during the diocesan ecclesial congress in Rome on June 13, 2011. Our communities must become oases where one can experience the true nature of the Church. Now, "in ecclesiality", he said again during his General Audience on May 14, 2008, one has "an experience of God which is loftier than that attained by reflection. In it we really touch God's Heart."

Would you speak about the possibility of a false reform of the Church?

It is of capital importance to read and to understand the conference given in 1970 in Munich by Joseph Ratzinger, entitled, "Why I Am Still in the Church":

> The contemporary perspective has further modified our view of the Church: in practice, we see the Church now exclusively under the aspect of feasibility, what we can make out of her. The intensive effort for reform in the Church finally caused everything else to be forgotten; to us today she is only a structure that we can change, which confronts us with the question of what we ought to change so as to make her "more efficient" for whatever purposes the individual may have in mind. In the popular mind-set, the idea of reform has to a great extent degenerated into this way of framing the question and thus has been robbed of its essence. For reform, in the original sense, is a spiritual process, quite closely related to conversion and in this sense part of the core of Christianity: only through conversion does one become a Christian; this is true for the individual throughout

his lifetime, and this is true for the Church throughout all of history. She, too, as Church, lives on the fact that she is converted again and again to the Lord and turns away from her stubborn insistence on what is her own, on mere habit, which, although comforting, can so easily be contrary to the truth. But when reform is separated from this context, from the drudgery of conversion, and salvation is now expected solely from change in other people, from ever new forms and ever new adaptations to the age, then many useful things may still happen, but overall it becomes a caricature of itself. Strictly speaking, such reform can affect only the unimportant, secondary things in the Church; no wonder the Church herself in the end appears to be of secondary importance![17]

I think that we have arrived at a turning point in the history of the Church. Two perspectives are offered to us. Either we continue to pretend to save the Church by our restructuring efforts, which only add all-too-human excess weight to her divine essence, or we decide to let ourselves be saved by the Church, or rather by God acting in her, and then we will have to find the means of our conversion. We are perhaps at the eve of a great reform of the Church, like the Gregorian reform of the eleventh century or the reform of the Council of Trent in the sixteenth century. Historians analyze these moments in the life of the Church as structural changes. I think that in reality the saints are the ones who change things and who make history advance. The structures follow; they only perpetuate the action of the saints. In *Brother Martin*, Bernanos wrote:

> Whoever pretends to reform the Church with ... the same means used to reform temporal society: not only will he fail in his undertaking, but he will infallibly end by finding himself outside the Church.... The only way of reforming the vices of the Church is to lavish on her the example of one's own most heroic virtues. It's quite possible that Saint Francis of Assisi was not any less thrown into revolt than Luther by the debauchery and simony of prelates. We can even be sure that his suffering on this account was fiercer, because his nature was very different from that of the monk of Wittenberg. But Francis did not challenge iniquity; he was not tempted to confront it; instead, he threw himself into poverty, immersing himself in it as deeply as

---

[17] Ratzinger, "Why I Am Still in the Church", 136–37.

possible along with his followers. He found in poverty the very source and wellspring of all absolution and all purity. Instead of attempting to snatch from the Church all her ill-gotten goods, he overwhelmed her with invisible treasures, and under the hand of this beggar the heaps of gold and lust began blossoming like an April hedge.... [Thus the Church does not need reformers, but saints.][18]

We are awaiting the saints who will dare to get down to this interior reform. Who will they be? Popes like Saint Gregory VII or Saint Pius V? Poor unknown individuals like Saint Francis of Assisi? Fathers and mothers of families like the parents of Saint Thérèse of Lisieux? Each of us is called to begin with himself. We must rely on all the empirical initiatives that help put God back at the center. There is no lack of them. Let us not wait for a reform that comes from above, as in a governmental administration. Structures will not evolve unless they are led to do so by the saints. Again Joseph Ratzinger declared in the same conference given in Munich in 1970:

If we reflect on that, then we also understand the paradox that seems to have resulted from present-day efforts of renewal: the effort to loosen up rigid structures, to correct forms of ecclesiastical ministry that date back to the Middle Ages or, even more, to the era of absolutism, and to free the Church from such accretions for the sake of a simpler service in the spirit of the Gospel—this effort has in fact led to an overemphasis on the official element in the Church . Behind this another point, the crucial one, becomes visible: the crisis of faith, which is the actual nucleus of the process.... The Church still extends far beyond the circle of actual believers, and through this institutionalized untruth she has become profoundly alienated from her true nature.... The applause for the Council came partly from those who had no intention whatsoever of becoming believers themselves, as Christian tradition understands it, but rather greeted the "progress" that the Church was making toward their own stance as a corroboration of their way.... Through these developments, the reform program has tragically drifted into an odd ambiguity for which many people no longer see any solution.[19]

---

[18] As quoted in Hans Urs von Balthasar, *Bernanos: An Ecclesial Experience*, trans. Erasmo Leiva-Merikakis (Communio; San Francisco: Ignatius Press, 1996), 357.
[19] Ratzinger, "Why I Am Still in the Church", 137–39.

The road may be long, and the purification—painful. But we know that God does not abandon his Church. And "if God is for us, who is against us?" (Rom 8:31).

Do you think that it is possible to say that the Church is becoming more worldly?

Pope Francis often speaks about this terrible spiritual illness, worldliness, and its alignment with the criteria of the world. In an impulse of openness and trust, the doors and windows were opened, and the world rushed in, even into the most sacred spaces. Some Catholics seem to be contaminated by the anthropocentrism of the Western societies and man's attempt to make himself God. But a Church that has become worldly does not even have the world's charms. Henri de Lubac wrote in *Paradoxes*:

> When the world makes its way into the Church itself, it is worse than just being the world. Of the world it has neither the greatness in its illusory glamor nor that sort of loyalty it has in mendacity, ill-nature and envy, which are taken for granted as being its law. When the ecclesiastical world is worldly, it is only the caricature of the world. It is the world, not only in greater mediocrity, but even in greater ugliness. Yet never does that world, even in the worst moments, completely triumph. How many secret little islands there always are, refreshing oases, genuine and pleasing splendors![20]

How well I understand all the Christians who are suffering at the sight of the Church disfigured by so many betrayals and abuses. Because we are her sons, our hearts are sometimes full of shame. Let us take refuge in the heart of Mary. I would like to invite you to make with me a spiritual visit to the back of Saint Peter's Basilica in Rome. Let us contemplate this Mother who carries in her arms the body of her Son, who has been tortured, humiliated, covered with spittle and marks from the whip. His hands are pierced, and his forehead is lacerated by the crown of thorns. And, nevertheless, the Mother carries her Son's body with great gentleness and infinite

---

[20] Henri de Lubac, *Paradoxes of Faith*, trans. Paule Simon et al. (San Francisco: Ignatius Press), 225.

delicacy. Her face, the face of a the young mother, is at the same time recollected, pained, and peaceful. Without understanding him, she adores this Son who is so beautiful although scorned, this Son who is her God. Like Mary, let us be able to recognize the face of Christ beneath the soiled face of the Church. Neither our sins and betrayals nor our lukewarmness and infidelities can disfigure the Church. She remains quite beautiful, with the beauty of the saints. She remains quite young, with the youth of God. Let us be able to love the Church and to look at her in faith as Mary looked at Jesus dead in her arms. Let us be able to weep for the Church, let us be able to suffer because of the Church, if necessary, but let us always treat her with this loving and altogether Marian gentleness that the marble statue by Michelangelo reveals so well.

Is the Roman Curia in crisis because the institution has become too human?

The Curia must be the government of God's affairs. It must make the divine mystery known so as to gather people for the purpose of salvation. The Curia is a spiritual and divine government. It is entirely subjected to and guided and enlivened by God. Its methods, its means, and its strength can come from God alone. Its strength is in its humble, intense, persevering prayer that is totally attentive to God's holy will. If the Curia does not have an interior dimension, if the prelates, priests, and laymen who work in it do not have the mysticism of the apostles and prophets, if they are not nourished by the silent presence of God in their daily lives, it becomes a purely human structure. It has its competencies, but it is no longer at the service of God. Careerism, the ambition for political or diplomatic success, and worldliness then take hold of this government. Christ's kingship is not of this world (Jn 18:36). It is in heaven. It is about following the path of service and love, after the example of Christ, who "loved us and gave himself up for us, a fragrant offering and sacrifice to God" (Eph 5:2; cf. 2 Cor 2:14–15). Christians must be the fragrance of God. All who belong to God and work for his glory and for the salvation of souls must be like "a fragrant offering, a sacrifice acceptable and pleasing to God" (Phil 4:18).

If God created us in his image and we are made for God, how can we not work and stand before God, constantly offering him our bodies, our hearts, all our abilities to love, and the purity of our priestly chastity? In his First Letter to the Corinthians, Saint Paul writes:

> [Brethren,] do you not know that you are God's temple and that God's Spirit dwells in you? If anyone destroys God's temple, God will destroy him. For God's temple is holy, and that temple you are.
>
> Let no one deceive himself. If any one among you thinks that he is wise in this age, let him become a fool that he may become wise. For the wisdom of this world is folly with God. For it is written, "He catches the wise in their craftiness," and again, "The Lord knows that the thoughts of the wise are futile." So let no one boast of men. For all things are yours, whether Paul or Apollos or Cephas or the world or life or death or the present or the future, all are yours; and you are Christ's; and Christ is God's. (1 Cor 3:16–23)

In the Acts of the Apostles, Saint Paul preaches again: "For 'In him we live and move and have our being'; as even some of your poets have said, 'For we are indeed his offspring'" (Acts 17:28).

Is it possible to imagine curial life along the lines of monastic community life?

The Gospel would have to imbue our life completely, and sanctification would have to be our first impulse, our essential concern. It would be necessary for Jesus to have seized us entirely as Saint Augustine was seized. In early Christian times, bishops lived surrounded by their priests. They worked and prayed together. We are well acquainted with the community life of the bishop of Hippo. When he became a bishop, Augustine had been living in that city for six years and had already become familiar with the Christian district of the city, particularly the *insula* [island], where the buildings associated with worship are grouped together. At that time, there were two basilicas in Hippo: the old, or Leontine, basilica, in which Augustine had been appointed a cleric by the acclamation of the crowd; and the new one, or the basilica of Peace, where the council of bishops was held in 393. Augustine ordinarily preached in the latter. The *insula* also contained the residence of the bishop and of the clergy. In his Sermon 355, Augustine explains why he had two communities of laymen and clerics at his side: "I arrived at the episcopate. I saw that the bishop is under the necessity of showing hospitable kindness to all visitors and travelers; indeed, if a bishop didn't do that he would be said to be lacking in humanity. But if this custom were transferred to the monastery it would not be fitting. And that's why I wanted to have a monastery of clergy in this bishops' residence."[21] This model was at first founded on a common spiritual life. The bishop and his entourage attended the Divine Office and Holy Mass together. This is not about a life withdrawn from the world. Prayer and community life are means of strengthening our personal relationships with God and then of going out to proclaim Christ. Perseverance in prayer is often nourished by mutual assistance. The words of the Sacred Scriptures are luminous: "They held steadfastly to the apostles' teaching and fellowship, to the breaking of the bread and to the prayers" (Acts 2:42).

Common life could bolster our courage as it stimulated Saint Augustine to preach, denounce, reprimand, edify, and bear the demands of the Gospel together. This is a difficult responsibility, a harsh constraint, and an important effort. Saint Augustine loved that life, described as follows by Catherine Salles:

> Let your works be sometimes this, sometimes that, depending on the season, the hour, the day. Can one always speak? Always be silent? Always regain one's strength? Always fast? Always give bread to the poor? Always clothe the naked? Always visit the sick? Always stop quarrels? Always bury the dead? Sometimes do this, sometimes that, calmly, serenely, and lovingly. But the principle that commands these actions neither starts nor must it end. May fraternal charity remain, as it is written.

It is important for us to have moments without speech, moments for study, moments for activities, moments for leisure, and moments to stand in the presence of God so as to love him intensely.

If the Church can rediscover this life of communion, her witness will be more edifying and her influence more luminous. This model could apply to the Curia, but it would imply a radical conversion

---

[21] St. Augustine, Sermon 355, in Saint Augustine, *Essential Sermons*, trans. Edmund Hill, O.P., Works of Saint Augustine: A Translation for the 21st Century, pt. 3 (New York: New City Press, 2007), 408.

and a greater awareness that we are working for the Kingdom of God. The Lenten retreat planned by Pope Francis outside of Rome is along these lines. But this time is insufficient and very specific.

It is often said that we are seeking greater collegiality in the Church. But what is the model of this collegiality if not the apostles, who persevered together in prayer, having one heart and one soul? Often people create institutions, councils, or commissions to promote this collegiality. Why not model our efforts on those of the apostles? If we want to form an ecclesial college, let us begin by praying together; we must be diligent about reciting the Divine Office. Every bishop could implement this in his cathedral and thus give the example of a life of ecclesial unity with his priests. That is the true source of charity and unity.

The deleterious climate that prevails in some assemblies of the Church causes me consternation. Charity has been replaced by defamation, work by careerism, and joy by jealousy. Pope Francis had the right words with which to describe this atmosphere and this situation when he said that gossips, those "rumor mills", are "like terrorists" who kill by their vulgar, pretentious words.[22]

Priests must possess the charism of keeping secrets and keeping silent. If they squander this gift of God on facile, superficial words, the confidence of the people of God will melt like snow in the sunlight.

Is a prophetic government of the Church possible?

The prophet is God's interpreter. He gives the meaning of history, of events, and of politics according to the divine plans. The prophet is only a channel: he is the mouthpiece and the eyes of God, but he must be self-effacing and disappear while wrapping himself in the Word and the presence of God.

The men of the Church must be true prophets. A prophet does not speak his own word. He says God. The words of the false prophets are lies. They caress us, but they are like lethal poisons. They darken the path and lead us astray. A pope, a bishop, or a priest must not speak in his own name but must be solely the voice and the presence of God.

Today false prophets try to charm the people of God and put them to sleep by diluting the Gospel in ambiguous, confused language that

---

[22] Pope Francis, General Audience, November 14, 2018.

threatens to make our faith insipid, so as to get the world's benevolent attention. The great writer Paul Claudel wittily said: "The Gospel is salt, but you have made sugar out of it." By trying too much to reconcile everything, they become insipid, they lose the corrosive strength of the Gospel salt in our life. If we sacrifice the truth in order to avoid the difficulties that are inherent in the witness of our faith, then the Christian loses his salt; he is no longer good for anything. If the Christian, like a chameleon, takes on the color of his surroundings, then he is no longer the tangible sign of the Kingdom of God. On the contrary, we are called to give flavor to our era by clear, solid testimony to our Catholic faith. This is the responsibility incumbent in the first place on all Christians, and especially on bishops and priests.

There are false prophets today who, for ideological reasons, in order to please men or to make the Church more attractive, falsify God's Word. About them, too, Jeremiah says: "The prophets are prophesying lies" (Jer 14:14).

After the recent canonization of Pope Saint Paul VI, would it not be appropriate to meditate on the example of that prophetic pope? In publishing the encyclical *Humanae vitae*, on the one hand, and the *Credo of the People of God*, on the other, Paul VI gave us the example of prophetic government, contrary to currents and pressures.

Do you consider the model of Benedict XVI, who has retired to his monastery, to be a message for the whole Church?

In a world where God no longer counts, where spirituality is lowered to the level of self-help philosophy, Benedict XVI is an extraordinary beacon. He shows us that God deserves all our love, all our time, that prayer is the most important human activity. Silence is the door that gives us access to God by enabling us to encounter him.

Benedict XVI unceasingly reminds us of the superior value of the things of heaven. He says that God deserves the gift of our all. For this reason, he has chosen to spend the last days of his earthly life in silence, prayer, reading, and meditation on the Word of God. He is at the head of the great cohort of contemplatives who mysteriously carry the world. The pope emeritus contrasts contemplation and prayer with petty earthly ambitions. Humbly, he bears witness to the divine absolute: God alone suffices!

4

ACEDIA AND THE IDENTITY CRISIS

NICOLAS DIAT: How would you describe the spiritual situation of the West?

ROBERT CARDINAL SARAH: I think that the West is experiencing what the Desert Fathers called the temptation of the noonday devil, which occurs in the middle of the day, when the heat is most oppressive. It is called acedia. It is a form of depression, a relaxation, a spiritual lethargy. It is a sort of atrophy of interior vitality, a form of discouragement, an "atonia of the soul", as Evagrius of Pontus said in the fourth century.[1]

Jean-Charles Nault, the Abbot of the Benedictine Abbey of Saint-Wandrille [in Normandy, France] emphasizes in *La Saveur de Dieu: l'acédie et le dynamisme de l'agir* [Zest for God, acedia and the dynamism of action] that the spiritual and monastic tradition defines acedia even more profoundly as a sadness that takes hold of the soul in the presence of what ought to be its greatest happiness: its friendship with God. It attacks the joy that should characterize the soul in its relationship with God. The soul no longer rejoices in knowing and loving God. It bores it, disgusts it, weighs it down. It would prefer to love something else. What? It does not matter what! Anything rather than God. This sadness in the presence of God's gift generates in it disgust with anything that could draw it closer to God. Acedia is a general disgust with everything that makes up the spiritual life. "It is monotonous because you lack love",[2] Josemaría Escrivá said in his book *The Way*.

---

[1] Jean-Charles Nault, O.S.B., *The Noonday Devil: Acedia, the Unnamed Evil of Our Times*, trans. Michael J. Miller (San Francisco: Ignatius Press, 2015), 28.

[2] Josemaría Escrivá, *The Way* (New York: Image/Doubleday, 2006), no. 77, p. 13.

During the spiritual exercises that he preached in the presence of John Paul II in 1996, Christoph Cardinal Schönborn remarked: "It seems to me that the deepest crisis in the Church today is that we no longer dare to believe in what God can do for the good with those who love him. The spiritual masters traditionally call this torpor of mind and heart *acedia*."[3] For my part, I would go even farther. The ailment that characterizes Western society is a self-conscious sadness. The West refuses to love. I think that this is extremely serious. It is killing within itself the motivating force of all spirituality: the desire for God. Faced with the intoxicating grandeur of God's call to holiness, Western man withdraws into himself. He pouts. He refuses to let himself be attracted. He chooses to remain in sadness and rejects the joy that God offers him. This attitude produces an immediate result. A thick bitterness spreads in souls and in society. All social relations are marked by this profound disgust. When divine life is rejected, nothing else can make us happy. Depression has captured the heart of Western man. It has settled there and secretes its dangerous venom.

Allow me to cite the heartrendingly sad lines by Jean-Paul Sartre in his novel *Nausea*: "The word absurdity is coming to life under my pen.... Absurdity was not an idea in my head, or the sound of a voice, only this long serpent dead at my feet.... I understood that I had found the key to Existence, the key to my Nauseas, to my own life. In fact, all that I could grasp beyond that returns to this fundamental absurdity."[4] We have refused to let joy come to us from someone other than ourselves, from God. So we have preferred to extinguish any hope within us. Nothing is left but the terrible, monstrous sense of the absurd. We do not want to be bothered by the invitation to endless happiness that God offers us. We prefer to remain alone with ourselves, while hating our own greatness. In a way, I think that the West is experiencing the radical, deliberately willed solitude of the damned.

The story of the West is related for us in the Gospel through the episode of the rich young man (Mk 10:17–31). He is seeking eternal

---

[3] Christoph Cardinal Schönborn, *Loving the Church: Spiritual Exercises Preached in the Presence of Pope John Paul II*, trans. John Saward (San Francisco: Ignatius Press, 1998), 56.

[4] Jean-Paul Sartre, *Nausea*, trans. Lloyd Alexander and Robert Baldick (Tokyo: Ishi Press, 2017), 182.

life. His heart is filled with the desire for happiness. He keeps the Commandments. He is the face of the Christian West in the first half of the twentieth century, generous and full of great desires. This West sent missionaries into the whole world. And about it one can say what the Gospel says about the young man: "Jesus looking upon him loved him" (v. 21). The Lord adds, inviting him to share his supreme joy and to follow him more closely: "You lack one thing; go, sell what you have, and give to the poor, and ... follow me" (v. 21). Jesus offers the young man a close association with himself. The Gospel concludes: "At that saying his countenance fell, and he went away sorrowful; for he had great possessions" (v. 22). There you have the story of the West. It refused at the last moment to give everything. It balked at the supreme sacrifice. It was afraid, held back by its riches. So it sank into sadness.

What are the consequences of acedia?

Acedia has three consequences that are the hallmarks of contemporary Western society: torpor, bitterness, and agitated flight. First this despair leads to torpor, a form of slow paralysis. As though life refused to thrive and flourish. Then, given such a state, we observe resentment, a bitterness toward the good that one has refused to desire. Finally, there is flight into disorderly agitation, flitting about so as to forget the state in which one is voluntarily confined. Torpor, bitterness, and agitation form the tragic triptych of our time. It affects all walks of life, as Father Jean-Charles Nault emphasizes in his beautiful book *The Noonday Devil*.

Married couples are particularly affected. When someone refuses to enter into the joy of conjugal love, with all the giving and generosity that it requires, little by little a kind of routine between the spouses sets in. Avarice in giving oneself gives rise to timidity and torpor in love. Often our contemporaries no longer even believe that people can love each other for their whole lives. They are, so to speak, disillusioned. "It is too beautiful to be possible", they say, referring to fidelity. I am struck when I see the extent to which young people hesitate to marry. This is not a form of laziness, but a lack of hope and of confidence in their love. They consent to mediocrity in love; they renounce their great desires. This is the temptation of lukewarmness. It inevitably gives rise to a bitterness and a resentment toward more generous families. We see the development of a discourse that despises fidelity and fertility. Finally, couples are tempted to replace the joy that the gift of themselves ought to bring with a certain agitation, flitting around. For some, this will mean going from partner to partner. In others, we can observe a multiplication of activities that eventually try to mask the interior emptiness.

We observe the same phenomenon among priests and religious. As the future Pope Francis emphasized in spiritual exercises that he gave to priests (later published in book form as *Reflexiones Espirituales sobre la Vida Apostólica* [Spiritual reflections on the apostolic life]), "acedia can assume several forms in our lives as pastors.... Sometimes it is the paralysis when you no longer manage to keep up with the pace of life. Other times it affects the acrobatic pastor who, in his comings and goings, displays an inability to take God as his foundation." In all these cases, the rejection of the joy of giving oneself to God leads to disgust with Christian life, with its demands, with prayer, and a bitter critique of our brother priests or bishops. Finally, it is expressed by a frantic agitation, travels, an excessive presence on the Internet and in the social media, which attempts to fill up the void that has been created. This scattered attention serves to mask the fear of admitting one's sadness and of recognizing one's timidity, one's miserliness in giving oneself. I am not saying that all this is conscious. I am noting the steps of a process. I want to emphasize above all that acedia is always "a syndrome of a rich man", the reaction of a heart that is tired of giving itself. At some point these men refuse to rejoice in God's call to go farther! Pope Francis, in his homily on Sunday, October 14, 2018, for the canonization Mass of Paul VI, spoke these trenchant words:

Jesus is radical. He *gives all and he asks all*: he gives a love that is total and asks for an undivided heart. Even today he gives himself to us as the living bread; can we give him crumbs in exchange? We cannot respond to him, who made himself our servant even going to the cross for us, only by observing some of the commandments. We cannot give him, who offers us eternal life, some odd moment of time. Jesus is not content with a "percentage of love": we cannot love him twenty or fifty or sixty percent. It is either all or nothing.

In this sense, acedia is really a wound inflicted on our life of faith, hope, and charity. It is a rejection of the joy that charity ought to bring about in us. It is an indifference to the gift that is God himself. It is a refusal to respond to God's radical call.

I think that people do not realize the extent to which all of Western culture is marked by this blasé indifference to God that gives rise to sadness and hopelessness. "Admiration is happy self-surrender; envy is unhappy self-assertion", said Kierkegaard in his treatise on despair, *The Sickness unto Death*.[5] There is no better description of the situation of the West with respect to God. I think that contemporary man refuses to adore, to admire, so as not to find his deepest joy in someone other than himself. The result is an envious, sad solitude. The malady is so profound that it can affect a person's entire spiritual life, turn him away from prayer, and lead to disgust with God. One is paralyzed in the presence of this phenomenon that affects our way of reacting before one even notices the progress of the malady.

Are there any remedies?

Saint Thomas Aquinas says that the major remedy for acedia is not in us but in God. It is the Incarnation, the coming of God in our flesh. Indeed, since heaven seems so far away and we can grow tired in our search for God, he himself came to meet us so as to facilitate our desire to love him, so as to make tangible the good that he offers us. In this sense, I think that the feast of Christmas is the moment when it is easiest to fight against acedia. In contemplating the manger and the Infant Jesus, who makes himself so close, our hearts cannot remain indifferent, sad, and disgusted. Our hearts open and warm up. The Christmas carols and the customs that surround this feast are imbued with the simple joy of being saved. In this sense, contemplation of the Incarnation is the source of any remedy against acedia. This is where we can draw the strength to put into practice the recommendation of the Desert Fathers, those first monks in Church history. Their experience is summed up in a word: perseverance! This already implies accepting acedia as a trial. "Sadness is burdensome and acedia

---

[5] Søren Kierkegaard, *The Sickness unto Death*, trans. Howard V. Hong and Edna H. Hong (Princeton, N.J.: Princeton University Press, 1980), 86.

is [intolerable], but tears shed before God are stronger than both", Evagrius says.[6] The sole remedy is still returning to prayer, for it is an interior energy and strength whose source is God himself. Asceticism, mortification, acts of penance and self-denial are the humble, poor means of manifesting our perseverance in the spiritual combat.

I wish to emphasize that the perseverance that enables us to overcome acedia is joyful. This is not some Pelagian hardening of the will. Acedia is a sadness that seems to have no particular causes, because in fact I lack nothing. It affects the spiritual dynamism itself. Thus, in order to fight it, there is nothing else to do but to be faithful to one's commitment, to persevere in prayer, and to guard against calling everything into question. And what we have to keep above all is the altogether interior, supernatural joy of knowing that we are saved and loved by God. "Restore to me the joy of your salvation", the Psalmist says (Ps 51:12). I think, therefore, that it is of fundamental importance for the West to rediscover the meaning of thanksgiving! Wonder is the characteristic feature of children. A blasé old man is no longer astonished by anything, no longer enchanted by anything. The West sometimes resembles an embittered old man. It lacks the candor of a child. Spiritually, the continents that came to know the Good News more recently are still astonished and enchanted by the beauties of God, the marvels of his action in us. The West is perhaps too accustomed to it. It no longer shivers with joy before the manger scene; it no longer weeps with gratitude before the Cross; it no longer trembles in amazement before the Blessed Sacrament. I think that men need to be astonished in order to adore, to praise, to thank this God who is so good and so great. Wisdom begins with wonder, Socrates said. The inability to wonder is the sign of a civilization that is dying.

Would you speak about a fall of the sacred?

Everything connected with God is sacred. The more a reality is marked by the divine seal, the more it inspires in us the feelings that overcome our souls in the presence of God himself. These feelings make up what is called the sense of the sacred. How can it be

6 Nault, *Noonday Devil*, 39.

described? We find in it, on the one hand, the fear of the soul that adores, its respectful retreat in the presence of a reality that surpasses us, and, on the other hand, the desire to approach and to commune with this fascinating, desirable reality. These two feelings are not contradictory. They are ordered to each other.

In order to be able to commune with divine things, it is necessary to agree to acknowledge that one is radically unworthy of them. Unless we enter into fear and adoration, we never arrive at love and union. Look in the Gospel at the experience of Saint Peter on the occasion of the miraculous catch of fish (Lk 5:1–11). What a magnificent scene! Imagine the shores of the Lake of Tiberias in the early morning. The apostles are washing their nets on the bank after laboring the whole night without catching anything. They must be exhausted, numb with fatigue, and almost falling over for lack of sleep. Jesus walks by. He gets into a boat to teach the crowd and suddenly asks Simon to set out into the deep and to cast the nets. Just imagine the exchange of glances that must have followed, the several seconds of hesitation in Simon Peter's heart. He was a professional fisherman. He knew very well that, humanly speaking, it was impossible to have a productive catch after a night of toiling in vain. He could have protested and relied on his experience as a tradesman to contradict Jesus. We know that Peter did not have an easy-going character; he might have become angry and explained to the Lord that on the subject of fishing he was a specialist. But he decides to trust the Lord: "At your word I will let down the nets" (v. 5). He decides to renounce his human supports and takes Jesus' words as his sole foundation. And behold, the nets are filled to the breaking point. He agreed to enter into faith, and to him is given the concrete experience of God's omnipotence. How does he react? Does he leap for joy at this manifestation of divine glory? Does he immediately start to praise the glory of the Most High? No, he begins by prostrating himself before Christ and declares: "Depart from me, for I am a sinful man, O Lord" (v. 8). Imagine the bank of this particularly charming lake. The scenery is magnificent. Nature forms the marvelous setting for a gesture that constitutes the very first teaching of the first of our popes. The others are already disembarking, but Peter is on his knees, prostrate with his forehead on the ground before Jesus. The head of the apostles teaches us the sense of the sacred. He shows us by his example that holy fear is the doorway that leads us to divine intimacy. I cannot have access to God on an equal footing. I must make myself little so that he may admit me gratuitously to his infinite height.

The question about the sense of the sacred is not just a question of liturgical discipline. It affects the spiritual life, I dare say, the mystical life. To teach Christians to disdain the sense of the sacred as a secondary reality amounts to depriving them of the fullness of intimacy with God. Theologians of the liturgy who look down on the manifestations of this sense of sacred adoration bear a heavy spiritual responsibility. I am struck by this saying of Jesus to Saint Catherine of Siena: "I am He who is, you are she who is not!" And yet the intimacy between that Italian Dominican nun and the Lord Jesus was sublime. She could also say: "A person becomes one with his friend. A person does not become one with his master."

I think that the deepest mystical union presupposes the sense of sacred distance and of adoration. We cannot do without displays of our littleness or of our lowliness before the Divine Majesty. They are the mark of a sensitive soul. All gestures that amount to putting a hand on God destroy our true relation to him and prevent the creation of intimacy with him. I am thinking here of the casual attitude during the liturgy. I am thinking of the attitude that has sometimes set in at the moment of Eucharistic Communion when there is no apparent gesture of adoration. Should we not instead let ourselves be fed like little children? Priests bear a heavy responsibility. They must be exemplary in this area. In the Eastern churches, the only way to leave the house of God is to walk backward! In contrast, how many Western churches serve as concert halls? People talk there as they would in an ordinary place, a common meeting room. The true model is Moses before the burning bush! Let no one say that the interior attitude is the essential thing. It is neither real nor lasting unless it is manifested by external, concrete gestures.

In the West, the disappearance of God has brought in its wake the banishment of everything that is sacred in human life. The sacred has become a negligible quantity. The rift between man and God seems to be increasingly large, to the point where desacralization provokes no reaction at all. We walk past eminently sacred things without even being gripped by the respect and fear that they inspire. I wish to emphasize one unexpected consequence of this phenomenon. For the sense of the sacred is expressed by means of all the thresholds, all the separations that surround and protect the sacred realities: the church, the chancel or "choir", the altar, the tabernacle. Today, in many places, everything is accessible to everyone. They have done away with symbolic limits like the barrier that used to surround the sanctuary of the church, the steps that surrounded the altar. With the result that everything becomes common or profane.

In rejecting the presence of the sacred in our life, we create a uniform, featureless world, a flattened world. It makes no difference whether one is in a church or in an auditorium to celebrate Mass. It is all the same to celebrate on a consecrated altar or on a simple table. In these circumstances, how could we possibly have the experience described by the Psalmist: "I will go to the altar of God, to God my exceeding joy" (Ps 43:4).

In a world where everything is on the same level, everything becomes sadly equal. A profane, I would even say a profaned, world is a joyless world. Basically, the loss of the sense of the sacred is reason for sadness. How enchanting it is for a young altar server to approach the altar for the first time! His joy is that much greater because he is approaching God. To do so, he has put on the sacred garment of his ministers. The sacred is a precious good; it is the door by which joy enters into the world. It offers us a share in profound joys. Who has not trembled profoundly during the Easter Vigil while following the flame of the Paschal candle in the night? Who has never tasted the spiritual joy produced by singing the Gregorian chant *Salve Regina* in a monastery? The shiver of fear that it inspires is a thrill of joy. The voices of the monks join to proclaim the love of our Lady in a slow, grave, solemn chant that luminously expresses the true sense of the sacred: a joyous, confident fear. We literally experience in our flesh Goethe's words: "The sacred is what unites souls." I would add that it unites them in a profound joy.

We have lost these great sacred signs that ought to bring about the unity and the joy of the Christian people. Nowadays we see people turn to magical and pagan practices that are only the caricature of the sacred. Such behaviors show how severe a famine for sacred gestures the clergy have created among the most faithful believers. It is time for us to rediscover the simplicity of Saint Peter on the shores of the lake!

Has God become for modern man a negligible quantity in the midst of a multitude of occupations and pleasures?

I wish first to describe a fact that to me seems symptomatic of the modern world. In many libraries, books on spirituality are shelved in the section on "Personal Development". They have managed to make God a self-help method for attaining our own petty fulfillment. What an inversion! I think that that shows a total reversal of the logic of faith. God is not at my service. Of course, I can be happy only through him and with him. To believe in God is not contrary to our happiness. But it is necessary to put things back in order.

We were created to know, love, and serve God. In the past that was the first sentence in the catechism that was taught to little children. What wisdom! God is not just an element of my life alongside all my preoccupations. He is my all. "God alone suffices", Teresa of Avila used to say.

In a church, our contemporaries come to see a work of art. Rarely God. When they are present at a Eucharistic celebration, they spend most of their time taking photos or tapping on their cell phones. In family or professional life, God is absent. There are few families that turn their eyes toward heaven when they rise and go to bed. In the West, God has become like those elderly parents in the nursing home whom the children forget to visit. God must adapt to our use of time and to our weariness. We allow him a little room, thinking that we are doing much. What an illusion!

However, I do see also some Christian families that put God at the center of their lives. In them, prayer in common becomes self-evident. In some cities I have seen many Catholics participating daily not only in the Eucharist but also in the Liturgy of the Hours. These families restore God to his rightful place. They are building their lives on the only firm foundation. They are the hope of the Church.

Can we go so far as to mention a return to polytheism?

We live in a pagan system in which gods are born and die depending on our interests. We want nothing to do with the one true God. So we fabricate our own divinities.

We create gods, but also prophets and priests, depending on the moods of the moment. The postmodern world is the kingdom of the idols, sorcerers, and astrologers. These gods and their clergy are cruel. They do not care about life and joy. Behind the black curtains of a false humanism, they are at the service of financial capitalism. I think that the idol of money is enthroned at the summit of this new pantheon. I wish to recall the words spoken by Benedict XVI in Paris:

> Apart from the people of Israel, who had received the revelation of the one God, the ancient world was in thrall to the worship of idols. Strongly present in Corinth, the errors of paganism had to be denounced, for they constituted a powerful source of alienation and they diverted man from his true destiny. They prevented him from recognizing that Christ is the sole, true Savior, the only one who points out to man the path to God.
>
> This appeal to shun idols, dear brothers and sisters, is also pertinent today. Has not our modern world created its own idols? Has it not imitated, perhaps inadvertently, the pagans of antiquity, by diverting man from his true end, from the joy of living eternally with God? This is a question that all people, if they are honest with themselves, cannot help but ask. What is important in my life? What is my first priority? The word "idol" comes from the Greek and means "image", "figure", "representation", but also "ghost", "phantom", "vain appearance". An idol is a delusion, for it turns its worshipper away from reality and places him in the kingdom of mere appearances. Now, is this not a temptation in our own day—the only one we can act upon effectively? The temptation to idolize a past that no longer exists, forgetting its shortcomings; the temptation to idolize a future which does not yet exist, in the belief that, by his efforts alone, man can bring about the kingdom of eternal joy on earth! Saint Paul explains to the Colossians that insatiable greed is a form of idolatry (cf. 3:5), and he reminds his disciple Timothy that love of money is the root of all evil. By yielding to it, he explains, "some have wandered away from the faith and pierced their hearts with many pangs" (1 Tim 6:10). Have not money, the thirst for possessions, for power and even for knowledge, diverted man from his true Destiny, from the truth about himself?[7]

[7] Pope Benedict XVI, Homily at the Eucharistic Celebration in Notre Dame. Paris, September 13, 2008.

The hearts of many Christians are divided between love of the one true God and veneration of this idol, money. In this sense they become true polytheists. If there is only one God, then everything else becomes relative. The love of money is manifested in the excessive worry that it causes. I see people whose standard of living is secure and enviable worrying about the state of their bank accounts. I see some Christians becoming set in their ownership without taking care to detach themselves from their property. The words of Jesus are clear: "Woe to you that are rich, for you have received your consolation" (Lk 6:24). I think that attachment to material goods is like an anesthesia that prevents us from feeling our hunger for God. One can end up dying of spiritual hunger while thinking that one is full because of the abundance of material goods. The solution has to be radical. A Father of the Church, Clement of Alexandria, reminds us of it: "Any possession that you own for yourself, as though it belonged to you, and that you do not place at the service of those who need it, is unjust." Unless we detach ourselves from' riches by a sense of gratuitousness and service, they will suffocate us.

Do you think that it is possible to link the symbolic profanations of our era and this new reign of polytheism?

The profanations are multiplying. We have lost count of the churches that have been profaned, defiled. Sometimes they take it out on the images of the Blessed Virgin, sometimes the tabernacle itself is the target. Even cemeteries are no longer considered sacred spaces. The dead are not respected; their resting places are destroyed.

Each time, through sacred realities, Jesus is the one being attacked head-on; the whole Church is affected. When a place consecrated for divine worship is attacked, it is as though the heart of every Christian is broken. Those who desecrate take out their anger on the Blessed Sacrament, hating and despising Almighty God, who made himself little and weak in order to save us. Let us pray for them, that the diabolical hatred in their hearts will give way to a respectful fear of God and to grateful adoration. Actually their hearts, inhabited by Satan, are deeply profaned.

Let us not be surprised when we experience rejection and hatred. God's love for mankind, which was manifested at the time of the

Nativity, triggered the devil's anger. Recall that the horror of the massacre of the Holy Innocents followed shortly after the joy of Christmas. When God reveals his gentleness and his love, the devil responds with blind, gratuitous violence. The Church is in the world as a sign of contradiction. The more she preaches him who is "the way, and the truth, and the life" (Jn 14:6), the more she disturbs and the more she is rejected.

The Church unceasingly reminds the world about what it refuses to hear: that we are saved by the Cross. The Cross reveals at the same time God's infinite love and man's unfathomable misery. Is it any surprise that the sign of the Cross triggers so much hatred? "A servant is not greater than his master. If they persecuted me, they will persecute you", Jesus warned us (Jn 15:20). Many Christians are persecuted today throughout the world, although the silence in the media is deafening and the powerful are complicit by their indifference. Consecrated persons, priests, men and women religious, are abducted and assassinated in sordid conditions. The devil manifests himself only through hatred. He builds nothing; he destroys. His name is nothingness.

You often mention the marks of the devil . . .

The sign of Satan is division. Today there are serious conflicts within the clergy. And the devil is partying. The devil loves to divide the Church. The prince of darkness wants first to sow opposition among us. He sets a terrible trap for us through the media amplification of the least important episcopal statements. Everyone is ordered to take sides, to choose his camp. But in the Church, there are no sides! There are no camps! Synods are not political assemblies. Is each Christian supposed to judge everything? Have an opinion about everything? This sometimes hysterical politicization of what ought to remain a calm debate among theologians who love the same God is the mark of the demon. He lures us onto his own terrain. He leads us toward hatred, invective, manipulation, and Machiavellian calculation. Must we give up denouncing error? Certainly not! But we must do so in a spirit that is Catholic, in other words, profoundly supernatural and benevolent.

When the barque of the Church is beset by storms, the demon tries to terrify us. He sows anguish. He secretes doubt and suspicion.

People look for a scapegoat on which to take out these anxieties. While certain that they are defending the good, they perform a work of hatred. Then the devil bursts out into his cold laughter. He has won: the children of God are tearing each other apart. The spirit of faith and charity is covered by the glacial fog of mistrust and lying. Let us listen to the words of Jesus in the storm: "Why are you afraid, O men of little faith?" (Mt 8:26). If Jesus is in the boat with us, even though he seems to be asleep, we are not in danger at all. Peace and joy are the signs of God; fear and sadness are the attributes of hell.

He loves to utilize confusion. Dominican Father Marie-Dominique Molinié declared: "The devil's tactic is to propose to us what is 'reasonable'. Yes, he is the prince of lukewarmness, the king of compromise. His aim is not to make us fall into specific errors but, on the contrary, to leave us in vague uncertainty: because it is impossible to stake one's life on vague ideas and, consequently, to become a saint in those circumstances."[8]

He tries to make us believe that there is nothing serious about sin and that we can transgress God's Law without worrying too much. Satan loves to muddle our correct perception of God in his relations with mankind. He deceives us and tranquilizes us so that the reign of sin can extend its night. We, however, know the beautiful words of the psalm: "Blessed is the man who makes the LORD his trust" (Ps 40:4). Apart from him, there is, for the believer, only partial truth and partiality.

The devil tries to tear the Church apart, first by attacking the priesthood. Satan intends to destroy priests and the teaching of doctrine. He is horrified by the liturgy, the sacraments, and the apostolic succession. In trying to take out his hatred on consecrated persons, he means to ridicule the Church. Priests frighten him because they are the ministers of mercy. He knows that he will be vanquished by mercy. He seeks to instill lukewarmness and doubt in priests. He seeks to win the hearts of some and to draw them to renounce chastity. Worse yet, he has driven some priests to profane the bodies of children. How can we not see Satan's work in these lives of priests or bishops who have behaved like predators, spreading evil and spiritual

[8] Luc Adrian, "Du Désespoir à l'adoration: Une interview du Père Molinié", *Famille chrétienne*, no. 1161 (April 15, 2000).

death all around them? How can we not see that, in attacking both priests and children at the same time, the demon reveals his hatred of two reflections of God's goodness?

The speech given by Cardinal Karol Wojtyła to the American bishops in August 1976 was extraordinarily and prophetically powerful:

> We are now standing in the face of the greatest historical confrontation humanity has ever experienced. I do not think that the wide circle of the American Society, or the whole wide circle of the Christian community realize this fully. We are now facing the final confrontation between the Church and the anti-Church, between the Gospel and the anti-Gospel, between Christ and the antichrist. The confrontation lies within the plans of Divine Providence. It is, therefore, in God's Plan, and it must be a trial which the Church must take up, and face courageously.

He continued his reflection [as pope] in a question-and-answer session in Fulda in November 1980: "We must be prepared to undergo great trials in the not-too-distant future; trials that will require us to be ready to give up even our lives, and a total gift of self to Christ and for Christ. Through your prayers and mine, it is possible to alleviate this tribulation, but it is no longer possible to avert it.... How many times, indeed, has the renewal of the Church been effected in blood? This time, again, it will not be otherwise."[9]

Throughout recent decades, the activity of the popes has consisted essentially of driving back the assaults of the devil by offering to the world clear spiritual, doctrinal, and moral teaching that is faithful to Church tradition. In this way, they intended to offer to the people of God healthful foods that would give them strength with a view to the battle that is to be fought today. But I think that we must not be afraid of the devil. He makes noise, he agitates. Nevertheless, all his activity is in vain. As for the good, it makes no noise. It builds patiently and perseveringly. The demon was so afraid of the poor Curé of Ars that he tried to prevent him from sleeping. The demon trembles in the presence of saints, then tries to cover up their silent,

---

[9] Pope St. John Paul II, Interview with Catholics at Fulda, Germany, November 1980, as quoted by Regis Scanlon, "Flood and Fire", *The Homiletic and Pastoral Review*, April 1994.

discreet work with his cries and gesticulations. Let us not be taken in by that pathetic liar.

"We have no authority against the truth", said the apostle Paul in his Letters to the Corinthians . . .

In the Second Letter of Saint Paul to the Corinthians, we indeed find this extraordinary sentence: "We cannot do anything against the truth, but only for the truth" (2 Cor 13:8). This statement by Saint Paul expresses the absolute primacy of the truth. It refers us to the tragic dialogue between Pilate and Jesus. Pilate is the man of authority. He does not understand who Jesus is, this king who seems to have no human authority. Jesus seeks to make him understand that the power to dominate is nothing compared to the truth. Then Pilate takes refuge in calling it into question. The truth frightens him. Our world is like Pilate. It knows that the truth could cause its empire to collapse, and so it hides behind the question: What is truth? It asserts that this question has no possible answer. In political or legal debate, the question of truth is taboo. People want to ignore the fact that the truth can be recognizable. Benedict XVI wrote in *Jesus of Nazareth*:

> It becomes recognizable when God becomes recognizable. He becomes recognizable in Jesus Christ. In Christ, God entered the world and set up the criterion of truth in the midst of history. Truth is outwardly powerless in the world, just as Christ is powerless by the world's standards: he has no legions; he is crucified. Yet in his very powerlessness, he is powerful: only thus, again and again, does truth become power.... The kingship proclaimed by Jesus, at first in parables and then at the end quite openly before the earthly judge, is none other than the kingship of truth. The inauguration of this kingship is man's true liberation.[10]

Only the truth is powerful in and of itself. It does not need to rely on the strength of armies or on money. Our world veils its face in the presence of truth; it does not want to see it. Many people in our time

---

[10]Joseph Ratzinger/Pope Benedict XVI, *Jesus of Nazareth*, part 2: *Holy Week: From the Entrance into Jerusalem to the Resurrection*, trans. Philip J. Whitmore (San Francisco: Ignatius Press, 2011), 194.

get irritated and go away disdainfully as soon as someone talks about truth or refers to an objective truth that precedes us. That appears to them to be the synonym of dogmatism and intolerance, opposed to progress. But the truth is a light, an indisputable and liberating reality. The truth is indestructible because it comes from God; it is a face of God.

Can we say that at the origin of these crises there is first of all a crisis of moral theology?

Indeed, the field of moral theology has become an area of tensions between theologians. Many reject obedience to the Church's Magisterium in this field. Unfortunately, this has immediate consequences for the Christian people.

While dogmatic theology teaches us what God revealed and what we can deduce from it through reason enlightened by faith, moral theology proposes to show us what it is necessary to do. In *L'Église* [The Church], Cardinal Garrone lamented: "Theologians ... have a tendency to make themselves the arbiters of situations and to understand their vocation as a true teaching authority of which the bishop's magisterium would be no more than the faithful echo." Both the principles of fundamental moral theology and the supernatural virtues, particularly the virtue of religion, and the natural law or the Decalogue, in particular justice and chastity, are under attack.

The crisis of fundamental moral theology is due to the eclipse of the sense of the good. Morality does not aim to impose a constraining law on us externally. The good is fundamentally the truth about what we are. This is why it is false to say that the Church imposes too heavy a burden that would weigh upon the liberty of Christians. The Church only points out the path of full happiness and true liberty.

A false conception of good, replaced by duty, gives rise to erroneous theories like consequentialism. According to this system, nothing is good or bad in itself; the goodness of an act depends solely on its end or purpose and its foreseeable consequences. The end then justifies the means. There is an American form of moderate consequentialism, proportionalism, in which the morality of the act results from the calculation of the proportion of good and evil that the subject sees involved in it.

On the subject of these intellectual constructs, John Paul II was able to say that "Concrete situations are unfavorably contrasted with the precepts of the moral law, nor is it any longer maintained that, when all is said and done, the law of God is always the one true good of man."[11]

How can anyone claim that, in certain situations, an attitude that contradicts the profound truth of man would become good or necessary? It is impossible! "Circumstances or intentions can never transform an act intrinsically evil by virtue of its object into an act 'subjectively' good or defensible as a choice" (VS 81).

Consequently, there is no situation in which the moral norm would be impossible to put into practice. Indeed, that would imply that the Creator contradicts himself and asks us to go against the wise order that he himself inscribed in Creation. Pastorally, much is at stake here. It is false to set the truth of the law in opposition to contrary practical courses of action. One error that has become commonplace is to assert a "gradualness of the law" in cases concerning negative precepts forbidding acts as intrinsically evil. One must not pit pastoral practice against the universal truth of the moral law. Concrete pastoral care is always the search for the most appropriate means of putting into practice the universal teaching, never of departing from it.

I think that the real source of the crisis of moral theology is the fear that has overcome the hearts of clergymen. We are afraid of being thought of as cruel inquisitors. We do not want to be unpopular in the world's sight. Nevertheless, Saint Paul VI, who had this experience with regard to contraception, reminds us: "it is an outstanding manifestation of charity toward souls to omit nothing from the saving doctrine of Christ."[12]

Dear brother priests, it is our duty as fathers, guides, and pastors to proclaim the Good News of the Gospel! For our part, the consequence of our silences, uncertainties, or ambiguities is to veil human and Christian truth and to deprive the simplest believers of them. Out of paternal love for them, out of missionary zeal, out of generosity in

---

[11] Pope St. John Paul II, Encyclical Letter *Veritatis splendor* (August 6, 1993; hereafter cited as *VS*), no. 84.

[12] Pope St. Paul VI, Encyclical Letter *Humanae vitae* on the Regulation of Birth (July 25, 1968; hereafter cited as *HV*), no. 29.

evangelization, let us not be afraid to preach and to proclaim this Good News. Paul VI showed us a fine example of pastoral charity; let us not be afraid to imitate it! Our silence would be complicit and culpable.

Let us not abandon Christians to the deceitful sirens of ease and comfort! We should note, incidentally, that our celibacy is a pledge of credibility. If we truly and joyfully live a life dedicated to the Kingdom in total continence, we can preach the joy of a demanding Christian life. Of course, the more forcefully we preach the truth, the more patiently and kindly we will be able to accompany persons, as the Lord did, who was uncompromising with the wicked and merciful with sinners.

Faith is not a disorderly cry, a political act, or a strategy of media communications. It is participation in the divine truth itself.

So there is a crisis of the virtue of religion, of the liturgy, and of the sacraments?

I think that it is no exaggeration to say that the Church is going through the most serious crisis of the sacrament and Sacrifice of the Eucharist in her entire history. The *aggiornamento* of the liturgy did not produce the expected fruits. It is absolutely necessary to continue efforts to eliminate all the folklore elements that turn Eucharists into a spectacle. In the celebration of the Mass, the most incredible fantasies have come to tarnish the Paschal Mystery. Strange sorts of music have been broadcast during Masses. There have even been "theme" Masses. Respect for the liturgical rules has been insufficiently safeguarded. Fidelity also means respect for the liturgical norms promulgated by the ecclesiastical authority, and it excludes both arbitrary, untested innovations and the stubborn rejection of what has been legitimately foreseen and introduced into the sacred rites.

Joseph Ratzinger correctly remarked in the book-length interview *The Ratzinger Report*: "We must be far more resolute than heretofore in opposing rationalistic relativism, confusing claptrap and pastoral infantilism. These things degrade the liturgy to the level of a parish tea party.... With this in mind we shall also have to examine the reforms already carried out, particularly in the area of the *Rituale*."[13]

---

[13] Joseph Cardinal Ratzinger with Vittorio Messori, *The Ratzinger Report: An Exclusive Interview on the State of the Church*, trans. Salvator Attanasio with Graham Harrison (San Francisco: Ignatius Press, 1985), 121.

Furthermore, after the 1960s, some riches of the liturgy were abandoned, such as its hieratic invariance, but also its geographic and historical unity, which was assured by Latin as the language of the liturgy, by the rites that had been handed down, by the beauty of its art and of the solemnity that accompanied it. The disappearance of linguistic unity in the liturgy in favor of the vernacular languages is, to my mind, one possible factor of division. Were not some misunderstandings between Greeks and Latins at the origin of the schism between the Christian Churches of the East and the West?

The Second Vatican Council explicitly demands that the Latin language be preserved. Have we been faithful to it? The use of Latin in some parts of the Mass can help us to rediscover the profound essence of the liturgy. Being a fundamentally mystical and contemplative reality, the liturgy is beyond the reach of our human activity. Nevertheless, it presupposes on our part some openness to the mystery being celebrated. Thus the conciliar Constitution on the Liturgy recommends a full understanding of the rites, and it prescribes "that the faithful may also be able to say or to sing together in Latin those parts of the Ordinary of the Mass which pertain to them".[14] Indeed, understanding the rites is not the work of human reason left to itself, as though it were supposed to grasp everything, understand everything, master everything. But will people have the courage to follow the council to this conclusion? I encourage young priests to abandon courageously the ideologies of those who fabricate horizontal liturgies and to return to the directives of *Sacrosanctum concilium*. May your liturgical celebrations lead people to meet God face to face and to adore him, and may this encounter transform and divinize them. "The sacred liturgy is above all things the worship of the divine Majesty", the council teaches us (*SC* 33). It puts us in the presence of the mystery of divine transcendence. It has a pedagogical value only insofar as it is entirely ordered to the glorification of God and to divine worship. In his homily for the Feast of Corpus Christi, June 7, 2012, Benedict XVI said: "Christ ... did not abolish the sacred but brought it to fulfillment, inaugurating a new form of worship, which is indeed fully spiritual but which, however, as long as we are journeying in time, still makes use of signs and rites."

---

[14] Second Vatican Council, Constitution on the Sacred Liturgy *Sacrosanctum concilium* (December 4, 1963; hereafter cited as *SC*), no. 54.

I think that it is important to safeguard the riches of the liturgy that the Church's great tradition has handed down to us. In particular, the orientation of the altar, which we have in common with most of the Eastern Churches, whether united with or separated from Rome. I have had the opportunity to speak about how important this point is. It is a matter of knowing to whom we intend to look and to go. Is it toward the glorified Lord, who comes from the East? "When the focus on God is not decisive, everything else loses its orientation", Benedict XVI tells us in his preface to the German and English editions of his *Theology of the Liturgy.*[15] The converse is true: when we lose the orientation of our heart and body toward God, we cease to define ourselves in relation to him; literally, we lose the sense [meaning, direction] of the liturgy. To be oriented toward God is above all an interior fact, a conversion of our soul toward the one God. The liturgy must bring about in us this conversion toward the Lord who is the Way, the Truth, and the Life. For this purpose, it utilizes signs, simple means. Celebrating *ad orientem* is part of this. It is one of the treasures of the Christian people; it allows us to preserve the spirit of the liturgy. Oriented celebration must not become the expression of a partisan, polemical attitude. On the contrary, it must remain the expression of the most intimate and most essential movement of every liturgy: turning us toward the Lord.

The liturgy has sometimes become a battlefield, the place for confrontations between the supporters of the preconciliar Missal and those of the Missal resulting from the 1969 reform. The sacrament of love and unity, the sacrament that enables God to become our food and our life and to divinize us while living in us and we in him, had become an occasion for hatred and contempt. The Apostolic Letter given *motu proprio Summorum Pontificum* by Benedict XVI definitively put an end to that situation. Indeed, Pope Benedict declares with all his magisterial authority in his letter to the bishops dated July 7, 2007: "It is not appropriate to speak of these two versions of the Roman Missal as if they were 'two Rites'. Rather, it is a matter of a twofold use of one and the same rite."

---

[15] Joseph Ratzinger, "On the Inaugural Volume of My Collected Works", in *Theology of the Liturgy: The Sacramental Foundation of Christian Existence,* ed. Michael J. Miller, trans. John Saward et al., Joseph Ratzinger Collected Works, vol. 11 (San Francisco: Ignatius Press, 2014), xv.

Thus he dismisses all the combatants in the liturgical war. And just because the Extraordinary Form of the Roman Rite, the one that was in use before the reforms in 1969, was one of Archbishop Marcel Lefebvre's warhorses does not mean that we must disparage it. Archbishop Lefebvre's disciples were not the only ones to appreciate the possibility of rendering God worship according to the Extraordinary Form, or at least to be offended by the way in which Mass was often demeaned in numerous celebrations.

"The liturgy is precisely entering into the mystery of God, letting oneself be carried by the mystery and being in the mystery", Pope Francis said on February 10, 2014. The Extraordinary Form allows this to an excellent degree; let us not turn it into an occasion for division! The use of the Extraordinary Form is an integral part of the living patrimony of the Catholic Church; it is not a museum piece, a witness to a glorious but bygone past. It will be fruitful for Christians today! And so it would be fortunate if those who use the old Missal were to observe the essential criteria of the conciliar Constitution on the Divine Liturgy. It is indispensable for these celebrations to integrate a correct concept of the participation of the faithful who are present.

John Paul II and Benedict XVI were right to make a place for this ancient rite in the Church, provided that those who attend it observe the conditions of adherence to the Magisterium specified on several occasions and do not refuse on principle to celebrate with the new liturgical books.

It is necessary to encourage strongly the possibility of celebrating according to the old Roman Missal as a sign of the Church's permanent identity. For what was until 1969 the liturgy of the Church, the most sacred thing for us all, cannot become, after 1969, the most unacceptable thing. It is indispensable to acknowledge that what was of fundamental importance in 1969 remains so today as well: it is one and the same sacral character, one and the same liturgy. I appeal to priests with all my heart to put into practice the liturgical reconciliation taught by Pope Benedict, in the pastoral spirit of Pope Francis. The liturgy must never become the banner of a party. For some, the expression "reform of the reform" has become synonymous with the domination of one clan over another. I prefer to speak about liturgical reconciliation. In the Church, the Christian has no adversary! As

Cardinal Ratzinger wrote in his book *Kunder des Wortes und Diener eurer Freude* (Heralds of the Word and servants of your joy) [volume 12 of his collected works, on the priesthood], "We must rediscover the sense of the sacred, the courage to distinguish what is Christian from what is not; not so as to set up barriers, but so as to transform, so as to be truly dynamic."

Even more than a question of a "reform of the reform", this is a matter of a reform of hearts, a reconciliation of the two forms of the same rite, a mutual enrichment. The liturgy must always be reconciled with itself, with its profound being.

Enlightened by the teaching of the *motu proprio* by Benedict XVI, strengthened by the audacity of Pope Francis, it is time to take to its conclusion this process of reconciling the liturgy with itself. What a magnificent sign it would be if, in the next edition of the reformed Roman Missal, we could insert as an appendix the prayers at the foot of the altar from the Extraordinary Form, perhaps in a simplified, adapted version, and the prayers of the Offertory that contain such a beautiful epiclesis that complements the Roman Canon. Then it would finally be obvious that these two liturgical forms throw light on each another mutually, in continuity and without opposition. Then we could restore to the people of God a good to which they are so deeply attached!

In *The Ratzinger Report*, Cardinal Ratzinger says that the concept of active participation in the liturgy is

> no doubt correct. But the way it has been applied following the Council has exhibited a fatal narrowing of perspective. The impression arose that there was only "active participation" when there was discernible external activity—speaking, singing, preaching, reading, shaking hands. It was forgotten that the Council also included silence under *actuosa participatio*, for silence facilitates a really deep, personal participation, allowing us to listen inwardly to the Lord's word. Many liturgies now lack all trace of this silence.[16]

Sacred music, which nevertheless was praised highly by Vatican II, was set aside in favor of " 'utility music', songs, easy melodies, catchy tunes.... Experience has shown that the retreat to 'intelligibility for

---

[16] *Ratzinger Report*, 127.

all', taken as the sole criterion, does not really make liturgies more intelligible and more open but only poorer."[17]

We must always take more care of the sacred liturgy, because its genuine renewal is the fundamental condition for the future of the Church. In order to show the importance of the liturgy in the life of the Church, Benedict XVI acted very concretely. In his celebrations, he always put God at the center. Indeed, the liturgy must make us experience the centrality of the Cross. The theology of the Cross is the premise and the foundation of Eucharistic theology. While many churchmen insisted on the necessary structural or administrative reforms, Pope Benedict XVI reoriented us toward the essential thing: God! Boldly, he dared to denounce the danger of a self-satisfied Church that settles down in this world, is self-sufficient, and adapts to secular criteria. Sometimes she assigns more importance to organization and institutionalization than to her call to be open to God. In order to correspond to the grace of her authentic task, the Church must once again make an effort to detach herself from her "worldliness" so as to be open to God.

It is also important to understand better the Holy Sacrifice of the Mass, in other words, the sacrifice of the Cross, the unique sacrifice of the New Law, made present sacramentally on our altars. It is not an *agape* banquet in which Communion would be obligatory and necessary, but above all Christ's sacrifice.

This sacrifice must not be reduced to the sacramental Communion of the faithful. The latter presupposes, incidentally, that the communicant is in the state of grace, which the Holy See has had to recall on numerous occasions, in keeping with the Council of Trent. Unfortunately, even on this very important point, we seem to give up asking the Christian faithful to examine their consciences before approaching the Body of Christ. You will note, moreover, that at the Mass on Holy Thursday evening, in memory of the Last Supper, and on the feast of the Solemnity of the Most Blessed Sacrament of the Body and Blood of Christ, the reading from the First Letter to the Corinthians has unfortunately been truncated by the omission of verses 27 to 29 of chapter 11, which are in a way the conclusion of Saint Paul's teaching: "Whoever, therefore, eats the bread or drinks the cup of the Lord in an unworthy manner will be guilty of profaning the body and blood

---

[17] Ibid., 128.

of the Lord. Let a man examine himself, and so eat of the bread and drink of the cup. For any one who eats and drinks without discerning the body eats and drinks judgment upon himself" (1 Cor 11:27–29). In large Eucharistic gatherings, it is necessary to recall that only Christians in the state of grace can receive Communion. It is urgent to stop the profanation of distributing Communion to non-Christian tourists who are passing through; sometimes they take the consecrated Host home with them as a souvenir.

It is also urgent to train the faithful in the gestures of respect toward the Eucharist, even when custom has introduced Communion in the hand, and to avoid the abuse of having Communion distributed by extraordinary ministers while priests are present in sufficient number to provide that service.

The piety of the faithful must not be reduced either to the Eucharist alone or to the liturgy alone: popular piety also has its role, and especially adoration of the Eucharist (even outside of Mass), the Way of the Cross, and the Rosary. Purified, rid of certain aspects of folklore that disfigure it, popular piety can become a mystical experience and the occasion for a genuine encounter with the Lord.

We are returning, then, to the crisis that you consider the origin of all the others: the crisis of the Sacrament of Holy Orders and of consecrated life ...

Unquestionably the crisis manifested itself first at the level of the discernment of priestly vocations, and this was so even before Vatican Council II. Moreover, in discerning the qualifications of the candidates, some vocation directors inappropriately appealed to psychoanalytical methods. The Holy See, therefore, implemented criteria for discernment in the form of directives, indeed, imperatives, including in the area of the use of psychology.

The crisis however continued with the decrease of vocations. I want to recall here the very serious idea of Gabriel-Marie Cardinal Garrone in his book *L'Église*:

> Except for very rare exceptions, this crisis is universal. In whole sectors of the world today it assumes such serious dimensions that one can speak, according to appearances, of a short-term extinction of the priesthood.... Even today, some want to break with the nevertheless

quite moderate directives of the council; it does not take them long, though, to realize that they have gone astray and that the disappearance of the elements considered indispensable by the council has created a total vacuum.

Nevertheless, after the council, the Roman dicasteries, especially the Congregation for Catholic Education, Seminaries, and Pontifical Universities, published documents on each of the various aspects of the content of the formation of future priests with regard to philosophy, theology, Sacred Scripture, patrology, liturgy, Church history, spirituality, and preparation for celibacy.

The crisis became apparent above all at the level of priestly identity. The statistics speak for themselves. According to the international news agency *Fides* of the Congregation for the Evangelization of Peoples, in 2017 Europe lost 240,000 Catholics and 2,583 priests.

Some advocate a reform of the structures and a rejection of clericalism, which is supposedly the source of all the problems. It seems to me that the crisis is deeper. It affects the very identity of the priest. Priests no longer know what they are in this world. And so the black clouds of discontent, depression, suicide, and enormously serious moral failings point to a disastrous prospect. Yes, the priestly crisis is profound. It results directly from the crisis of faith, which shook the confidence of churchmen in their own identity: they end up doubting the importance and the specificity of their role. In *L'Église*, Cardinal Garrone writes: "One of the most serious dangers today is to consider the theological problem of the priesthood as a completely new problem and to begin all over again.... The profile of the priest is blurring. He is losing his awareness of himself, and the faithful who need him no longer find in him the indispensable support that they need, either for their faith or for their life." This has repercussions on vocations: "How could some priests have the idea and the courage to direct young men toward the seminary and toward the priesthood when they themselves are in an uncertain state of soul and, as they say, doubt 'their own identity'?"

Priests have increasingly had the tendency to consider their office as that of a delegate of the community, as though the Church were a democracy. They no longer have an accurate idea of the transcendental function of the priesthood.

During the Mass, the distinction between ministerial priesthood and the common baptismal priesthood has tended to become blurred, in particular by the absence of any distinction of liturgical spaces. Some theologians have claimed that, in cases of necessity, the community of the faithful could celebrate the Mass without a priest.

As for the bishops, their office of divine right is partly hobbled by the bureaucracy of the episcopal conferences; they run the risk of losing their inalienable and personal responsibility as "teachers of the faith". It is necessary to restore the balance between this responsibility and the genuine concept of collegiality, as it was taught by the Second Vatican Council. National bishops' conferences are useful in practice, but strictly speaking they have no magisterial mission; they must not forget that truth is not the result of votes, much less of the quantity of documents published.

Consecrated religious have been affected directly by the crisis. Cardinal Garrone writes these alarming words in *L'Église*:

> The protests have not spared the religious: they have been found at the forefront of the protesters. They have often been among the "angry militants". The phenomenon has affected even the large orders that, because of their tradition and their principles, seemed destined to remain more completely sheltered from the storm for a longer time. It has also affected the fundamental components of the structure of religious life. What seemed to be part of the essence of the religious state has been called into question. Prayer, with its demands. The vows, and, strange to say, all the vows, from obedience to chastity. In the painful spectacle of defections throughout the Church, the religious were hit the hardest, and the sickness among them seemed more difficult to treat than anywhere else.

Under the impact of the postconciliar period, the major religious orders, which are traditionally the pillars supporting the always necessary reform of the Church, wavered, emptied out by substantial defections and a crisis of vocations. To this day, they are shaken by an identity crisis. Many religious men tried to remedy it by throwing themselves into external works and by seeking "liberation" in society and politics. Many religious women, on the contrary, seem to be seeking this same liberation in depth psychology. Perhaps without noticing the reasons for it, a nun senses a profound uneasiness living in a Church in which Christianity finds itself reduced to the ideology of activism, according to that ecclesiology imbued with harsh masculinity, which is nevertheless presented—and perhaps believed as well—to be closer to women and to their "modern" demands.

Among consecrated religious, "renewal" was often confused with "convenience". Thus the abandonment of the religious habit is regrettable, and also the replacement of the nocturnal office with community vigils. Some have even called religious poverty into question and, more generally, the usefulness of the vows. Nevertheless, religious life is necessary for the Church: it unceasingly reminds her of the radical character of the Gospel.

PART II

Man Belittled

The modern world is demeaning. It demeans civilization; it demeans man. It demeans love; it demeans woman. It demeans the human race; it demeans the child. It demeans the nation; it demeans the family. It even demeans, it has managed to demean, what is perhaps the most difficult thing in the world to demean: it demeans death.

—Charles Péguy
Cahiers de la quinzaine

5

HATRED OF MAN

NICOLAS DIAT: One topic that has cropped up in many contemporary debates is a contempt for filiation. This is allegedly the cornerstone of the modern hatred of man. What is your perspective on this subject?

ROBERT CARDINAL SARAH: I would like to go back to the origin of this hatred that modern men seem to devote to themselves as well as to their own nature. At the root of this mysterious process there is fear. Our contemporaries have been convinced that in order to be free, it is necessary for them not to depend on anyone. This is a tragic error.

The modern mistrust of all dependence explains many ills. Alas, it has not finished displaying its deleterious effects. For, if depending on another person is perceived as a negation of freedom, then every true and lasting relationship appears dangerous. The other person always becomes a potential enemy. Now only a radically autonomous and independent man, a man who is alone, without any bond, can be a free man. He finds that he is shut off in himself. Hence filiation, depending on a father and a mother, becomes for our contemporaries a hindrance to full freedom. We do not choose our parents, we receive them! This first experience is unbearable for contemporary man, who wishes to be the sole cause of everything that happens to him and of all that he is. To him, receiving appears to be contrary to his dignity. The education that we have received from our parents seems like an offense against a freedom that is thought of as self-creating. With greater reason, the idea of receiving our nature as man and woman from a Creator-God becomes humiliating and alienating. In this way of thinking, it is necessary to deny the very notion of human nature or the reality of a sex that has not been chosen.

I think it is time to liberate man from this hatred of all that he has received. In order to do that, we urgently need to discover the true nature of our liberty, which flourishes and is strengthened by agreeing to be dependent through love. Indeed, all love creates a relation with the object of our love that is a bond, a gift, a free dependence.

The fundamental rejection of all bonds, of all filiation, is basically nothing but the renewal of what the Book of Genesis describes for us as original sin. In a homily given on December 8, 2005, Benedict XVI asked:

What picture does this passage show us? The human being does not trust God. Tempted by the serpent, he harbors the suspicion that in the end, God takes something away from his life, that God is a rival who curtails our freedom and that we will be fully human only when we have cast him aside; in brief, that only in this way can we fully achieve our freedom.

The human being lives in the suspicion that God's love creates a dependence and that he must rid himself of this dependency if he is to be fully himself. Man does not want to receive his existence and the fullness of his life from God.

He himself wants to obtain from the tree of knowledge the power to shape the world, to make himself a god, raising himself to God's level, and to overcome death and darkness with his own efforts. He does not want to rely on love that to him seems untrustworthy; he relies solely on his own knowledge since it confers power upon him. Rather than on love, he sets his sights on power, with which he desires to take his own life autonomously in hand. And in doing so, he trusts in deceit rather than in truth and thereby sinks with his life into emptiness, into death.

Love is not dependence but a gift that makes us live. The freedom of a human being is the freedom of a limited being, and therefore is itself limited. We can possess it only as a shared freedom, in the communion of freedom: only if we live in the right way, with one another and for one another, can freedom develop.

We live in the right way if we live in accordance with the truth of our being, and that is, in accordance with God's will. For God's will is not a law for the human being imposed from the outside and that constrains him, but the intrinsic measure of his nature, a measure that is engraved within him and makes him the image of God, hence, a free creature.

If we live in opposition to love and against the truth—in opposition to God—then we destroy one another and destroy the world. Then we do not find life but act in the interests of death.

I think that we can assign a truly theological meaning to the "death of the father" that a certain Western philosophy demands. In truth, this is about the ancient, destructive desire to receive nothing from anyone so as to owe nothing to anyone. Man's dignity consists of being fundamentally a debtor and an heir. How beautiful and freeing it is to know that I exist because I have been loved! I am the product of a free decision by God, who, from all eternity, willed my existence. How sweet it is to know that one is the heir of a human lineage in which children are born as the most beautiful fruit of their parents' love. How productive it is to know that one is indebted to a history, to a country, to a civilization. I do not think that it is necessary to be born an orphan in order to be truly free. Our freedom has meaning only if other persons give substance to it for us, gratuitously and through their love. What would we be if our parents did not teach us to walk and to talk? To inherit is the condition for any true freedom.

If a man were deprived of a received nature, what meaning would his freedom have? At the foundation of the hatred of man is this refusal to accept oneself as a creature. Nevertheless, our creaturely state is our finest claim to glory and the fundamental condition of our freedom. As a son of Africa, I am struck to see the extent to which Westerners are sometimes filled with hatred, but more often with anguish and rebellion, when they consider their condition as heirs and creatures. Nevertheless, as Benedict XVI put it on February 20, 2009,

> Man is not an absolute, as if the "I" can isolate itself and behave only according to its own will. It is contrary to the truth of our being. Our truth is that above all we are creatures, creatures of God, and we live in relationship with the Creator. We are relational beings. And only by accepting our relationality can we enter into the truth; otherwise we fall into deception and in it, in the end, we destroy ourselves.
>
> We are creatures, therefore dependent on the Creator. In the Age of Enlightenment, to atheism especially this appeared as a dependence from which it was necessary to free oneself. In reality, however, it

would be only a fatal dependence were this God Creator a tyrant and not a good Being—only if he were to be like human tyrants. If, instead, this Creator loves us and our dependence means being within the space of his love, in that case it is precisely dependence that is freedom. In this way we are in fact within the charity of the Creator; we are united to him, to the whole of his reality, to all of his power.... To be a creature means to be loved by the Creator, to be in this relationship of love that he gives us, through which he provides for us.[1]

At the root of the human condition there is the joyful experience that we are not at the origin of our being, that we are not our own creator, that even before we existed we were wanted and loved. This experience is foundational: "The LORD called me from the womb, / from the body of my mother he named my name" (Is 49:1). I am profoundly convinced that this certitude, founded on our experience, is at the root of all civilization. Without it, deprived of our origin, we are condemned to create everything by our own efforts. We are reduced to the state of nomads wandering through life and randomly thrown into the world by blind evolution.

In order to establish a solid life in this world, we must connect with others. Our freedom is made, not so much in order to say a frightened, suspicious No to others, as to say Yes to them, to commit ourselves to lasting bonds of trust and love. The archetype of this contract is marriage, through which one man and one woman, accepting their profound nature as sexed beings, realize that they need one another and choose to give themselves to each other forever. It is significant that modern man has become almost incapable of a total commitment. He is literally paralyzed by fear of this prospect, which involves confidence in himself and in the other. There is a common root to the crisis of marriage and to that of vocations. The two go hand in hand.

How can we make a lifelong commitment if we suspect the other *a priori* of not wanting our good? The suspicion cast on the benevolence and love of God the Creator has spread throughout human society like a slow, paralyzing poison. All relationships are now a

---

[1] Pope Benedict XVI, Address to the Community of the Roman Major Seminary for the Annual Feast of Our Lady of Trust, February 20, 2009.

source of fear. A commitment out of love appears to be a dangerous folly. Cold solitude gains ground with every passing day. It has become the characteristic of our society. Nevertheless, as Benedict XVI went on to say in February 2009,

> But creaturely relationality implies a second type of relationship as well. We are in relationship with God, but together, as a human family, we are also in relationship with each other. In other words, human freedom is, in part, being within the joy and ample space of God's love, but it also implies becoming one with the other and for the other. There is no freedom in opposing the other. If I make myself the absolute, I become the enemy of the other; we can no longer live together and the whole of life becomes cruelty, becomes a failure. Only a shared freedom is a human freedom; in being together we can enter into the harmony of freedom.
>
> And therefore this is another very important point: only in the acceptance of the other, accepting also the apparent limitations on my freedom that derive from respect for that of the other, only by entering into the net of dependence that finally makes us a single family am I on the path to communal freedom.[2]

And so another element of the hatred of all against all appears. If our freedoms must collaborate in order to flourish, it is necessary for them to share some standard, a just and objective common order that precedes them. Indeed, if the only standard of our action is a positive law imposed by the will of a majority, we will ceaselessly be obliged to bow before something extrinsic to us that is imposed from outside. Thus, all submission to a law, to an order, seems like a form of slavery to which one is compelled to consent in the name of the need to live together. Now such an interior disposition could not possibly make us happy. It could not possibly serve as the foundation of a peaceful, just society. Ultimately, in such circumstances, latent rebellion and profound resentment settle in man's heart. They are the secret driving forces of a desire to transgress limits continually. Since we are compelled to submit to the civil law by the political authorities, we push the reality of our freedom by trying all sorts of moral transgressions, while rejecting all the limits of our nature.

---

[2] Ibid.

This resentment against imposed law, against the nature we have received, has given rise to what we call "societal evolutions". The harsher and more repressive the globalized mercantile society becomes in imposing the laws of the marketplace, the more men try to prove to themselves that they are still free by transgressing the heritage of the natural law and by rejecting any notion of a received human nature. But such logic is a dead end that leads to self-hatred and the self-destruction of our nature—gender ideology and transhumanism are the latest avatars of this.

It is of capital importance here to rediscover the notion of human nature as the condition for the flourishing of our freedom. Indeed, what are we talking about when we mention the notion of natural law? Our contemporaries understand it as a slavery imposed by a God whom they imagine to be a competitor with our freedom. This is a tragic misunderstanding! The natural law is nothing other than the expression of what we profoundly are. It is, so to speak, the instruction manual of our being, the handbook for our happiness. When the Church condemns homosexual behavior or divorce, many think she is seeking to impose her dominion over consciences in a logic of power and repression. On the contrary, the Church humbly makes herself the guardian of man, of his profound being, of the conditions for his freedom and happiness.

God and man do not face off in a duel to gain dominion over the world! God the Creator wants to help man govern himself. For this purpose, he entrusted to the Church the mandate to remind everyone of what each person can discover in his conscience: the laws that rule our being profoundly. In a way, the natural law is the grammar of our nature. All we need to do to discover it there is to examine it with goodwill and gratitude.

Allow me to confide something to you. I am convinced that Western civilization is going through a lethal crisis. It has reached the limits of self-destructive hatred. Like at the time of the fall of the Roman Empire, when everything was on the road to destruction, the elites cared only about increasing the luxury of their daily life, and the common people were anesthetized by increasingly vulgar amusements. Today, too, the Church preserves what is most human in man. She is the guardian of civilization. In the first centuries of our era, the bishops and the saints were the ones who saved the cities that were threatened by the Barbarians. The monks were the ones who preserved and transmitted the treasures of ancient literature and philosophy.

More profoundly, the Church makes herself the guardian of human nature. The immense misunderstanding that prevails on this subject with the modern world is frightening. When the Church defends the lives of children by fighting against abortion, when she defends marriage by showing the profound harmfulness of divorce, when she preserves the conjugal relationship by warning against the dead end of homosexual relations, when she tries to protect the dignity of the dying against the temptation of euthanasia, when she warns against the dangers of gender ideology and transhumanism, in reality she makes herself the servant of humanity and the protectress of civilization. She seeks to protect the little ones and the weak against the unwitting extravagances of sorcerer's apprentices who, out of fear and out of hatred of their own humanity, risk leading so many men and women toward solitude, sadness, and death. The Church tries to set up the rampart of humanity against the neo-barbarism of the post-humans. The Barbarians are no longer at the city gates and beneath the ramparts; they are in positions of influence and in government. They shape the laws and public opinion, often animated by a genuine contempt for the weak and the poor. And so the Church stands up to defend them, convinced of the truth of Jesus' words: "As you did it to one of the least of these my brethren, you did it to me" (Mt 25:40).

Bishops do not seek to take control over consciences. They take seriously their mission as *defensor civitatis*, defenders of cities and of civilization! Believe me, I know from experience that the bishop is sometimes the last recourse against oppression. Precisely because we have no political interest, because, through our consecration, we have renounced the search for secular power and money, we are free. It is necessary to have given away everything in order to have nothing more to lose and to gain a true freedom of speech and of action. In Guinea, I had to take up the defense of my people against the dictatorship of Sékou Touré. I protested against the violent repression by the enemies of liberty. I do nothing different today in fighting against the enemies of man. No one will silence me! "If [we] were silent, the very stones would cry out!" (Lk 19:40). I will defend the true meaning of human freedom to the end. I will never abandon man to the ravings of the enemies of human nature. They threaten us; they tell us: Be quiet, you are losing popularity, you are not well regarded by the media world, you risk losing your faithful!

I am not here to be popular or to increase the numbers in the churches or on the social networks. The profound love for all my brethren in humanity that animates my soul forbids me to be silent. The Church has always stood up against ideologies. The bishops have paid the price of blood for having opposed Nazism, Communism, and all sorts of racism. Never will I be complicit by my silence in this new ideology of hatred for man and for human nature. The same is true of our love for God and our brethren!

What is your analysis of gender theory?

Gender theory is based on an observation: femininity and masculinity are expressed in various societies by codes inherited from the cultures that shape us. It morphs into an ideology by affirming that the very notions of femininity and masculinity are cultural creations that have to be deconstructed in order to be liberated from them. It is up to each person, therefore, to construct freely his gender, his sexual identity. It would be contrary to the dignity of our free will to be born with a sexual identity that is received and not chosen. Here we find the ambiguity that I mentioned previously. According to this ideology, only what I construct is worthy of me. Conversely, what I receive as a gift is not completely human. Nevertheless, we all have the experience of being born with a sexed body that we did not choose. This body tells us something about what we are. We have to cultivate our nature and not deny it! Our humanity attains the fullness of its flourishing by accepting the gift of its sexed nature, while cultivating and developing it. Our nature indicates the direction in which our freedom can express itself fruitfully and happily. But for the advocates of gender ideology, I can be free only in denying the natural given.

A man could therefore think of himself and construct himself as a woman. This claim can go so far as the alleged freedom to transform one's body by a surgical operation, thought of as the recreation of a sex chosen and fabricated by oneself. Here we have the illustration of what Pope Francis described with great subtlety in *Laudato si'*:

The basic problem goes even deeper: it is the way that humanity has taken up technology and its development *according to an undifferenti- ated and one-dimensional paradigm.* This paradigm exalts the concept of a subject who, using logical and rational procedures, progressively approaches and gains control over an external object. This subject makes every effort to establish the scientific and experimental method, which in itself is already a technique of possession, mastery and trans- formation. It is as if the subject were to find itself in the presence of something formless, completely open to manipulation. Men and women have constantly intervened in nature, but for a long time this meant being in tune with and respecting the possibilities offered by the things themselves. It was a matter of receiving what nature itself allowed, as if from its own hand. Now, by contrast, we are the ones to lay our hands on things, attempting to extract everything possible from them while frequently ignoring or forgetting the reality in front of us. Human beings and material objects no longer extend a friendly hand to one another; the relationship has become confrontational.[3]

We must rediscover the fact that our own nature is not an enemy or a prison. It extends a hand to us so that we might cultivate it.

Through our nature, ultimately the Creator himself is the one who extends his hand to us, who invites us to enter into his wise and loving plan for us. He respects our freedom and entrusts our nature to us as a talent that is to be made productive. In the gender ideol- ogy, there is a deep rejection of God the Creator. This ideology has real-life theological and spiritual consequences. In opposing it, the Church is not making herself the intransigent, inflexible guardian of a supposed moral order. She is fighting so that each human being may encounter God. The first place where he awaits us is precisely our nature, our profound being that he offers us as a gift. I tremble when I observe that some individuals among the clergy are attracted and tempted by the gender ideology. In reality, it bears within it the original temptation of the serpent: "You will be like gods." It seems that the West, inebriated by the power of its science and technology, can think of itself only as an all-powerful demiurge and that all that it has not authored ultimately appears to it as an affront to its dignity!

---

[3] Pope Francis, Encyclical Letter *Laudato si'* on Care for Our Common Home (May 24, 2015; hereafter cited as *LS*), no. 106.

In expressing season's greetings to the Roman Curia in December 2012, Benedict XVI said: "When the freedom to be creative becomes the freedom to create oneself, then necessarily the Maker himself is denied and ultimately man too is stripped of his dignity as a creature of God, as the image of God at the core of his being."[4]

Gender ideology aims to deconstruct the specificity of man and woman, to abolish their anthropological differences. It works relentlessly to fabricate a new unisex global culture, without masculinity, without femininity, which will make possible the coming of a new age of humanity. But in a world where everything is produced by man, there is nothing human left! Our planet runs the risk of resembling those industrial areas where no room is left for nature, which then become inhuman. The absurdity and the perversity of our own inventions ought to make us dizzy!

Some international organizations like the Bill and Melinda Gates Foundation, International Planned Parenthood Federation (IPPF), and its affiliates are spending extraordinary sums to introduce this ideology in Africa. They do not hesitate to put pressure on the governments and the populations. Relying on their financial power and their partisan certainties, they deploy a new form of ideological colonialism. With frenetic energy, some militants act with no respect whatsoever for the African peoples. They sometimes behave like dominating, contemptuous crusaders toward those whom they consider backward. I do not fear, nevertheless, to state that the poor people in Africa, Asia, or South America are profoundly more civilized than the Westerners who dream about fabricating a new man to their own specifications. Will the poor be the last defenders of human nature? I wish to pay homage to them here. All you who, in the eyes of men, are powerless and without influence, you who in the depths of your hearts know what it is to be human: have no fear of those who try to intimidate you! You have a great mission, "it consists in preventing the world from destroying itself ... reestablishing ... a little of that which constitutes the dignity of life and death", according to the words pronounced by the writer Albert Camus during the speech with which he accepted the Nobel Prize

---

[4] Pope Benedict XVI, Address on the Occasion of Christmas Greetings to the Roman Curia, December 21, 2012.

in 1957. Given the powers of money and of the media, given the pressures of the international lobbies, I want to emphasize what an immense value your simple, everyday, quite simply human life has. For, as Camus said at a conference four days later,

> Great ideas, it has been said, come into the world as gently as doves. Perhaps then, if we listen attentively, we shall hear, amid the uproar of empires and nations, a faint flutter of wings, the gentle stirring of life and hope. Some will say that this hope lies in a nation; others, in a man. I believe, rather, that it is awakened, revived, nourished by millions of solitary individuals whose deeds and works every day negate frontiers and the crudest implications of history. As a result, there shines forth fleetingly the ever-threatened truth that each and every man, on the foundation of his own sufferings and joys, builds for all.

Why do you say that gender theory endangers children and the most vulnerable?

Gender ideology puts societies into chaotic situations. It endangers the institutions of fatherhood and motherhood. In the view of some Western governments, the words "father" and "mother" have become improper. They speak about "parent 1" and "parent 2". The first victims of these behaviors are obviously the children. While greeting the Roman Curia in December 2012, Benedict XVI addressed this topic with keen insight:

> While up to now we regarded a false understanding of the nature of human freedom as one cause of the crisis of the family, it is now becoming clear that the very notion of being—of what being human really means—is being called into question. [Everyone knows] the famous saying of Simone de Beauvoir: "one is not born a woman, one becomes so" (*on ne naît pas femme, on le devient*). These words lay the foundation for what is put forward today under the term "gender" as a new philosophy of sexuality.... [People] deny their nature and decide that it is not something previously given to them, but that they make it for themselves. According to the biblical creation account, being created by God as male and female pertains to the essence of the human creature. This duality is an essential aspect of what being human is all about, as ordained by God. This very duality as something previously given is what is now disputed. The words of the creation account: "male and female he created them" (Gen 1:27)

no longer apply. No, ... [from now on] man and woman as created realities, as the nature of the human being, no longer exist. Man calls his nature into question. From now on he is merely spirit and will. The manipulation of nature, which we deplore today where our environment is concerned, now becomes man's fundamental choice where he himself is concerned.... But if there is no pre-ordained duality of man and woman in creation, then neither is the family any longer a reality established by creation. Likewise, the child has lost the place he had occupied hitherto and the dignity pertaining to him.... The defense of the family is about man himself. And it becomes clear that when God is denied, human dignity also disappears. Whoever defends God is defending man.[5]

Whoever defends God defends the child and his right to be born of a father and a mother. Without that, there is no longer any clear filiation. The latter disappears on the altar of politically correct thinking that claims to fight discrimination against homosexuals who want to have a child. Who, then, is leading the march toward the abyss in which children will never be able to know their origins? Born of the process of surrogate gestation, they will bear for their whole lives the burden of an anonymous birth. This system threatens to muddle the very notion of filiation and to turn children into perpetually displaced persons. How can anyone deny a child the right to know and to love his biological father and mother? Man must reflect before the consequences are irreversible. Laws that promote such practices are profoundly unjust. We will end up with incredible inequalities in which humanity will be divided in two: people who know their parents and those who are deprived of that joy, the perpetual orphans. I know that persons living as a same-sex couple are capable of love for children. I say, though, that they cannot meet all the needs of those children. I simply ask my readers: Beyond all ideology, in all honesty, do you not know, by experience, how necessary a father and a mother are?

In reducing fatherhood and motherhood to role-playing, gender ideology profoundly destroys the very notion of family. For mysterious reasons, over the course of the last decades of the twentieth century, we have seen a visceral hatred of the family develop. Very often

[5] Ibid.

the family appears in literary works or films as a place that oppresses and stifles personalities. Is that really our experience? Certainly, there are pathological cases. But I can say also that the family is the great rampart of love! It is the ultimate recourse of all who know that they are in danger. When everything is going badly, one naturally returns to his family. Nevertheless, from divorce to gender theory, by way of abortion and contraception, it seems that the institution of the family has become the focus of all the attacks and all the contempt. In his *Letter to Families*, Saint John Paul II wrote:

> It is evident that in this sort of a cultural situation the family cannot fail to feel threatened, since it is endangered at its very foundations. Everything *contrary to the civilization of love* is contrary to the whole truth about man and becomes a threat to him: it does not allow him to find himself and to feel secure, as spouse, parent, or child. So-called "safe sex", which is touted by the "civilization of technology", is actually, in view of the overall requirements of the person, radically *not safe*, indeed it is extremely dangerous. It endangers both the person and the family. And what is this danger? It is *the loss of the truth about one's own self and about the family*, together with the risk of a loss *of freedom* and consequently of a loss *of love* itself. "You will know the truth", Jesus says, "and the truth will make you free" (Jn 8:32): the truth, and only the truth, will prepare you for a love which can be called "fairest love" (cf. Sir 24:24, Vulgate).[6]

Indeed, I think that the family is an institution that is utterly unbearable to the devil. Because it is, par excellence, the place of love and gratuitous self-giving, it arouses his hatred and violence. Even more profoundly, the union of father, mother, and child is a trace of the fruitful unity of the Divine Trinity. Through families, the devil tries to profane the Trinitarian Unity. Above all, he wants to deprive innocent children of love and a happy childhood. In destroying families, the one who is "a murderer from the beginning" does nothing but reenact the massacre of the Holy Innocents. Because God made himself an infant, the innocence of every child has become unbearable to him because it reflects the very innocence of God. It

---

[6] Pope St. John Paul II, Letter to Families *Gratissimam sane* (February 2, 1994; hereafter cited as *GS*), no. 13.

is therefore urgent to defend and support families. This is not only
a moral duty; it is part of the spiritual combat. It is necessary to help
spouses love each other faithfully their whole life long. They bear the
image of God's very own fidelity to his people and particularly to
the most vulnerable and to the children. In his address to the Pontifical Council for the Family in 2010, Benedict XVI declared:

> Indeed, it is precisely the family founded on the marriage between
> a man and a woman that can give children the greatest help. They
> want to be loved by a mother and a father who love each other, and
> they need to live and grow together with both their parents, because
> the maternal and paternal figures are complementary in the raising
> of children and the development of their personality and identity.
> It is therefore important that everything possible be done to enable
> them to grow up in a united and stable family. To this end, it is
> necessary to urge spouses never to lose sight of the profound reasons
> and sacramentality of the conjugal covenant and to strengthen it by
> listening to the word of God and by prayer, constant dialogue, recip-
> rocal acceptance and mutual forgiveness. A family environment that
> is not serene, the separation of the parental couple, particularly with
> divorce, is not without consequences on the children. On the other
> hand, supporting the family and promoting its true good, its rights, its
> unity and its stability is the best way to protect the rights and authen-
> tic needs of minors.[7]

*Pope Francis seemed to note a development of Church teaching on the ques-
tion of homosexual marriage and LGBT rights.*

First I would like to emphasize that we cannot reduce a person to his
sexual orientation. Rather than speaking about "LGBT", I prefer to
speak about persons who engage in homosexual behavior or have a
homosexual orientation. These persons are fundamentally loved by
God, just as every man and every woman is. The Lord shed his blood
during his Passion for each of them. We must show them the greatest
compassion. As true pastors, we must also go to those who aggres-
sively claim the legitimacy of their behavior. They are the lost sheep

---

[7] Pope Benedict XVI, Address to Participants in the 19th Plenary Assembly of the Pontifical Council for the Family, February 8, 2010.

that we must go and seek in the distance, even if it means taking risks, so as to bring it back to the fold by carrying it on our shoulders. The first form of charity that we owe to them is the truth. No one expects an indulgent word from the Church. A partnership between two persons of the same sex will never be a marriage. There is no judgment of persons in this statement. They may show affection and generosity, but they will never be able to claim to experience the distinctive element of conjugal love, which is the mutual gift of the spouses' bodies in fruitful love. I think that the pope is inviting us not to allow any ambiguities in this regard. As a son of Saint Ignatius, to whom we owe the sublime *Spiritual Exercises*, he knows that Christ's standard is not that of confusion and insinuation. He invites us to charity through the truth and to truth in charity.

I think that the first victims of the LGBT ideology are the persons who experience a homosexual orientation. They are led by its militants to reduce their whole identity to their sexual behavior. Thus it is politically correct to speak about the "gay community" as though they were a separate class of people with a common culture, a particular way of dressing and speaking, neighborhoods set aside in the cities, and even their own stores and restaurants. They are described as if they were an ethnic community! I sometimes get the impression that the gay ideology unconsciously promotes a form of communitarianism. I beg Catholics who are tempted by homosexuality not to let themselves be shut away in this prison of LGBT ideology. You are a child of God by baptism! Your place is in the Church, like all Christians. And if sometimes the spiritual combat becomes too hard, fraternal charity will support you.

As for the churchmen who deliberately entertain ambiguities about the Christian view of homosexual behavior by saying that, morally speaking, all forms of sexuality are strictly equal, I tell them that they are doing the work of the prince of lies and that they lack charity toward the persons involved. Why such statements? Is it to justify their own behavior? Is it because they seek popularity? How can they offer ideological talk to those who ask us for the Word of God?

I would simply like to remind priests about the words of Saint Irenaeus of Lyon in *Against Heresies*: "Error, indeed, is never set forth in its naked deformity, lest, being thus exposed, it should at once be detected. But it is craftily decked out in an attractive dress, so as, by its outward form, to make it appear to the inexperienced (ridiculous as the expression may seem) more true than the truth itself."[8] Let us beware of becoming accomplices! Those whom we have deceived will demand an accounting in eternity.

What must we do? Ceaselessly recall the divine plan that is expressed in the nature of man and woman. This is an integral part of our mission of evangelization. We do not have the right to abandon those who expect us to show them the way to holiness, including in the area of sexuality. I want to emphasize the prophetic keenness of the words of John Paul II. In his apostolic exhortation *Ecclesia in Europa*, he wrote:

> The Church in Europe at every level must faithfully proclaim anew *the truth about marriage and the family*. She sees this as burning need, for she knows that this task is integral to the mission of evangelization entrusted to her by her Bridegroom and Lord, and imposes itself today with unusual force. Many cultural, social and political factors are in fact conspiring to create an increasingly evident crisis of the family. In varying ways they jeopardize the truth and dignity of the human person, and call into question, often misrepresenting it, the notion of the family itself. The value of marital indissolubility is increasingly denied; demands are made for the legal recognition of *de facto* relationships as if they were comparable to legitimate marriages; and attempts are made to accept a definition of the couple in which difference of sex is not considered essential.
>
> In this context the Church is called to *proclaim with renewed vigor what the Gospel teaches about marriage and the family*, in order to grasp their meaning and value in God's saving plan.[9]

On this fundamental issue of the family, people the world over expect clear, firm, and steady teaching from the Church.

---

[8] St. Irenaeus *Against Heresies*, book 1, preface, no. 2, in *Ante-Nicene Fathers*, vol. 1, *The Apostolic Fathers, Justin Martyr, Irenaeus*, ed. Alexander Roberts and James Donaldson (1885; Peabody, Mass.: Hendrickson, 1995), 315.

[9] Pope St. John Paul II, Post-Synodal Apostolic Exhortation *Ecclesia in Europa* on Jesus Christ Alive in His Church, the Source of Hope for Europe (June 28, 2003; hereafter cited as *EE*), no. 90.

In your first book, God or Nothing, *published in 2015, you judged that in the West a woman's body is often exploited, devalued, and trampled on. Has your opinion changed?*

On the contrary, the situation ceaselessly deteriorates. Advertising often reduces a woman's body to the level of merchandise used for commercial purposes. They expose it, they display it for everyone to look at. It seems that they find this contempt and humiliation normal. The female body is seen as an object meant to provoke sensual desire. They invite men to look at this sacred and maternal body in a way that is akin to rape, or at least violent domination. In Italy, on the church doors, this degradation is posted everywhere. When her relation to man is presented only under an erotic, sexual aspect, woman is always the loser. Advertising caricatures her as a mere trophy for her husband, at least in middle-class circles. Unwittingly, woman has become an object at the service of man.

Some feminist movements want to promote the dignity of women, but I think they do not address the problem at its root. In trying to "liberate" woman from the "slavery of reproduction", as Margaret Sanger, the founder of Planned Parenthood, put it, they cut her off from the greatness of motherhood, which is one of the foundations of her dignity. That sort of liberation is deceptive and illusory. It can even aggravate the problem. Without realizing it, one kind of feminism pushes women to look at themselves from the viewpoint of perverse, contemptuous men who reduce them to a sex object. It is necessary to be freed from that prison, from that false, humiliating leer! Women will be emancipated, not by rejecting their profound femininity, but, on the contrary, by welcoming it as a treasure. They will be happy, not by adopting a male-inspired psychology, but rather by discovering the profound dignity of their specific character as women.

I would like to go back to the source of the problem. I am borrowing the words of the Dominican theologian Jean-Miguel Garrigues, spoken during his conference on "Man and Woman in God's Plan": "From a theological perspective, the root of the crisis of the mystery of woman seems to be connected to the phenomenon of desacralization. Indeed, secularization erases the dimension of the sacred. Now woman is, so to speak, the pivot of the sacred in the history of humanity." Indeed, woman has a natural superiority over man, for it is from her that every man comes into the world. This link to the origin gives her a special subtlety and depth in everything concerned with the order of life. She is the one who gives life. Woman knows from experience the sacred mystery of the beginnings of a human being's life. Her ability to welcome life in her womb predisposes her to receive the mystery of grace, in other words, the divine coming to hide itself and to germinate in our soul. This is why in the Bible God is presented as the Bridegroom and asks us to learn from woman to receive him. Every soul must learn to enter into this mystery of the Bride. The Church herself is fundamentally Bride and mother. Women have in the Church the immense responsibility of teaching men this sacred mystery of being spousal. With regard to God, every creature is like a bride. This is why women have historically been the first to discover the mystery of consecrated life, of religious life. They are the ones who transmitted it to men. Woman causes the sacred to enter into the world. From the Virgin Mary on, they are the ones through whom God passes. They know how to welcome and guard his presence. Should we not render them homage here? In 1988, in *Mulieris dignitatem*, John Paul II wrote:

> The present reflections ... have sought to recognize, within the "gift of God", what he, as Creator and Redeemer, entrusts to women, to every woman. In the Spirit of Christ, in fact, women can discover the entire meaning of their femininity and thus be disposed to making a "sincere gift of self" to others, thereby finding themselves.
>
> During the Marian Year *the Church desires to give thanks to the Most Holy Trinity* for the "mystery of woman" and for every woman—for that which constitutes the eternal measure of her feminine dignity, for the "great works of God", which throughout human history have been accomplished in and through her. After all, was it not in and through her that the greatest event in human history—the incarnation of God himself—was accomplished?
>
> Therefore *the Church gives thanks for each and every woman:* for mothers, for sisters, for wives; for women consecrated to God in virginity; for women dedicated to the many human beings who await the gratuitous love of another person; for women who watch over the human persons in the family, which is the fundamental sign of the human community; for women who work professionally, and who at times are burdened by a great social responsibility; for *"perfect"* women and

for "weak" women—for all women as they have come forth from the heart of God in all the beauty and richness of their femininity; as they have been embraced by his eternal love; as, together with men, they are pilgrims on this earth, which is the temporal "homeland" of all people and is transformed sometimes into a "valley of tears"; as they assume, together with men, *a common responsibility for the destiny of humanity* according to daily necessities and according to that definitive destiny which the human family has in God himself, in the bosom of the ineffable Trinity.

The Church gives thanks *for all the manifestations of the feminine "genius"* which have appeared in the course of history, in the midst of all peoples and nations; she gives thanks for all the charisms which the Holy Spirit distributes to women in the history of the People of God, for all the victories which she owes to their faith, hope and charity: she gives thanks for all *the fruits of feminine holiness* [10]

This is why the Church is in the front lines in defending the dignity of women. In Africa, the Church regularly condemns the practice of female circumcision. This practice appeared even before animism, Islam, and Christianity. Some researchers find an origin for it in Nubia, in the Horn of Africa, in the regions corresponding to today's Egypt and Sudan. I think that the battle against this unacceptable mutilation will ultimately be successful. However, in Africa and Asia, despite the appearances, women are profoundly respected. No one would ever dare to reduce them to some of the degrading images found in the West. Someone might object that an African woman is conditioned to have children. This way of caricaturing the large African family is contemptuous. I wish to denounce this hypocrisy of making people believe that Western woman is respected and flourishing because she is liberated from the "burden" of maternity and because she is man's equal from every perspective.

Are you really certain that postmodernity is fundamentally characterized by the negation of the father figure?

I even think that the problem is deeper. We can talk about a crisis of the masculine figure.

---

[10] Pope St. John Paul II, Apostolic Letter *Mulieris dignitatem* on the Dignity and Vocation of Women on the Occasion of the Marian Year (August 15, 1988), no. 31.

There is a mortal danger in trying to set the two sexes in opposition. Man and woman are complementary. They have a vital need of one another. They must seek and cultivate this difference so that each one may be fully realized. Allow me to repeat what I told you already in *God or Nothing*: "African philosophy declares: 'Man is nothing without woman, woman is nothing without man.'"[11] And both are nothing without the child. God willed them to be inseparably complementary, and each is the blessing and the joy of the other. Each one is a precious gift that God gives to the other, and the two receive each other reciprocally in love, while giving thanks to God.

The war between the sexes that has stupidly been launched, as though to replace the last gasp of the class struggle, only leads to the caricature of masculinity and femininity. Virility is reduced today to a form of violence or vulgar rudeness. I think, on the contrary, that the masculine soul is characterized by his vocation to fatherhood in all its forms, carnal, spiritual, intellectual, or artistic. The masculine soul is sometimes tempted by violence because man experiences his virility as a certain power. He is called to develop moral fortitude, that virtue which allows him to expend his energy in the service of the good. Then he discovers that he is strong so as to be the servant of the good of others, and especially of the common good of the family and of society. Allow me to mention the fine figures of Christian politicians like the English philosopher Thomas More or the former mayor of Florence Giorgio La Pira (1904–1977). They are models of courage and manly fearlessness in confronting the political or financial powers of their time. Another possible temptation for the masculine soul is that he may come to dominate and disdain anything that seems to him weaker and less powerful. There is a resurgence of this temptation in the neo-pagan and eugenicist movements. Man must then discover that his virility unfolds in the service and protection of those who are weak and fragile, particularly women and children. Here I think of Saint Louis, King of France, kneeling before the lepers whom he treated, or of Cyprien Rugamba, the Rwandan husband who, after a life of sin and violence, became the very gentle protector of his home. Finally, moral laziness is another masculine

---

[11] Robert Cardinal Sarah with Nicolas Diat, *God or Nothing: A Conversation on Faith*, trans. Michael J. Miller (San Francisco: Ignatius Press, 2015), 163.

temptation, and the manly soul remedies it by a generosity that causes him to discover the true meaning of his authority as service to the flourishing of those who are entrusted to him. The summit of this generosity is practiced in the fatherhood that, by word and example, guides, strengthens, and confirms the child.

I wish to say to men that their souls are made for heroism and not for comfortable half-measures. Saint Paul says, does he not: "Husbands, love your wives, as Christ loved the Church" (Eph 5:25)? How did Christ love the Church? By giving himself even unto death on the Cross. This is what every husband is called to do: to love as Christ did! We should not think that heroism is always spectacular. There is an everyday, silent holiness for which Saint Joseph is the model. It presupposes the development of an interior manliness that our society ignores and disdains, so much so that fathers doubt themselves and are sometimes humiliated.

Now a fatherless society cannot be a balanced society. I know that the images of the father have often changed in social discourse and depictions. But the real question is elsewhere. When the symbolic figure of what a father signifies is changed, or even made to disappear, neither a mother nor a child can be happy. For several years, the symbolism of the sexes has been blurred. The father is the symbol of transmission, difference, and otherness: realities that have become difficult for the modern world to understand.

Finally, I wonder how children will be able to pray the Our Father if they no longer have the intimate experience of a benevolent, just father. The father of a family is the first image of the Eternal Father. This is not the least of his claims to glory.

Can we speak about the problem of the commercialization of the body?

Prostitution, pornography, and their derivatives have become huge markets. Politicians who do not take the appropriate measures to fight against prostitution make themselves guilty of a deliberate attack against women. In many respects, prostitution is only a contemporary form of slavery. We are witnessing the implementation of genuine trafficking in human beings from one continent to another. The West buys sex slaves from the poorest countries and hides behind the screen of a pseudo-liberty of morals. The exploitation of the human body within the context of prostitution is not the subject of serious legislation. The slave trade involving thousands of women from Eastern Europe who come to the West to rent their bodies is a disgrace. I must also denounce the hypocrisy of the rich countries that continue to tolerate sex tourism in Asia and elsewhere in order the exploit women's poverty, while shouting through the media megaphone that they want to liberate the women in poor countries from the slavery they suffer.

We observe, moreover, a form of eroticization of entire sectors of society. I am thinking in particular of pornography on the Internet. Defenseless young people are exposed to these violent visual aggressions, and the parents are disconcerted, since it is extremely difficult for them to protect their children. Now which governments are taking courageous measures to put an end to the scandal of pornography? Do the financial interests underlying these activities explain the total silence of many leaders? The ease with which children gain access to pornographic images on the Internet resembles a rape of the consciences of these minors. I think that the psychological and spiritual consequences of this invasion of pornography for a whole generation of children and young people have not yet been measured. Doctors are beginning to sound the alarm, since they so often encounter young people who are disturbed by increasingly violent images or are prisoners of addiction to pornography. Who will tell them that all these images do not depict the truth about sexuality? Who will tell them that sexuality is made up of self-gift and sensitivity and not of violence and humiliation? Once again, the Church is on the front lines in defending the truth and the dignity of sexuality. In this area as in many others, she becomes the guardian and protectress of what is most human in man.

Furthermore, trafficking in human organs, especially between poor countries and rich countries, is a disgrace that is too little known. Mafia bands assassinate children, remove their organs, and sell them to rich patients. Meanwhile, Western societies clamor everywhere for greater respect for human rights.

And how many people know that, in the West, cosmetics have been manufactured with the remains of aborted fetuses? Many scandals related to these practices have affected Planned Parenthood in the United States. I sometimes have the feeling that the most amoral, godless societies promote human rights at the top of their lungs in order to cover up their own shame.

In your [Nicolas Diat's] magnificent book, *Un temps pour mourir* [*A Time to Die*], I was quite struck by the testimony of Benedictine Father Abbot of En Calcat, Dom David d'Hamonville, who mentioned the trend toward profitability that may prevail in French hospitals. If a patient is profitable, he can be treated. Otherwise, they can just let him die.

The human body has become a mass of cells that the financial and political powers intend to control. Tremendous sums of money and liberal ideology are transforming this world into a genuine hell. Anything can be bought nowadays, from human organs to sperm, even the wombs of surrogate mothers.

Contrary to what it proclaims everywhere, the modern world has a profound contempt for the human body. It turns it into an object. Paradoxically, the Church, which is so often accused of making no room for fleshly realities, exists to defend vigorously the incomparable dignity of the body. I think that Christians, disciples of a God who took flesh, will never be able to disdain the human body or to abandon it to the voraciousness of merchants or of unscrupulous researchers. We priests, who hold in our hands every day the Lord's Eucharistic Body, know well the fragility and the price of the body. Perhaps we share this privilege with mothers who have experienced the care that is given to fragile, precious newborns. Following the example of John Paul II in his *Letter to Families*, we will never tire of recalling that

When the human body, considered apart from spirit and thought, comes to be used as *raw material* in the same way that the bodies of animals are used—and this actually occurs for example in experimentation on embryos and fetuses—we will inevitably arrive at a dreadful ethical defeat.

Within a similar anthropological perspective, the human family is facing the challenge of a *new Manichaeanism*, in which body and spirit are put in radical opposition; the body does not receive life from the spirit, and the spirit does not give life to the body. Man thus *ceases to live as a person and a subject*. Regardless of all intentions and declarations to the contrary, he becomes merely an *object*. This neo-Manichaean culture has led, for example, to human sexuality being regarded more as an area *for manipulation and exploitation* than as the basis of that *primordial wonder* which led Adam on the morning of creation to exclaim before Eve: "This at last is bone of my bones and flesh of my flesh" (Gen 2:23). This same wonder is echoed in the words of the Song of Solomon: "You have ravished my heart, my sister, my bride, you have ravished my heart with a glance of your eyes" (Song 4:9). How far removed are some modern ideas from the profound understanding of masculinity and femininity found in Divine Revelation! Revelation leads us to discover in *human sexuality* a *treasure proper to the person*, who finds true fulfilment in the family but who can likewise express his profound calling in virginity and in celibacy for the sake of the Kingdom of God. (*GS* 19)

Without God, human dignity is called into question. "If God does not exist, then everything is permissible", Dostoyevsky declared. Without God, the worst possible outcome happens. Man ends up showing contempt for man.

The twenty-first century will certainly be the time of new utopias, of transhumanism, of the search for a perfect, eternal man. Are you worried?

The current revolution has a name: augmented humanity, or transhumanism. Its methods range from nanotechnologies and biotechnologies to information sciences and brain sciences (French acronym: NBIC). The purpose is to surpass the limits of humanity and to create a superman. This theoretical project is on the way to becoming a reality. We are reaching here the end of the process of self-rejection and of hatred of human nature that characterizes modern man. Man hates himself to the point where he wants to reinvent himself. But he runs the serious risk of disfiguring himself irremediably. Faced with this prospect, any sensible person ought to tremble. In fact, there is a real sense that many people are profoundly helpless. Some declared that human freedom was an absolute. They rejected the Creator. They disdained the very notion of human nature. What is left? Here we are, alone, disarmed, and helpless, at the mercy of an ultimately nightmarish movement. We have transgressed all the limits. But we did not see that the limits were protecting us. Beyond the limit, there is nothing but the infinity of the void. Today some men of goodwill, some lawmakers, seek to put the brakes on this movement. But it is not a question of speed. The movement itself is what is dragging us toward nothingness. We speak about "post-human", but after the human there is nothing! We are locked into the idea that everything is possible as long as the law authorizes it. This legal positivism set up as a principle is reaching its endpoint today. It is no longer capable of protecting us. It is no longer playing its role, which is to say what is right and just. Men are abandoned to their own devices. How can this headlong flight forward be stopped? Where can we find the limit that will protect mankind? Where should we look for the principle that can guide us? Benedict XVI, in an address to the German parliament, spoke prophetic words that resound like a solemn and at the same time humble warning for all mankind:

> Where positivist reason considers itself the only sufficient culture and banishes all other cultural realities to the status of subcultures, it diminishes man, indeed it threatens his humanity.... In its self-proclaimed exclusivity, the positivist reason which recognizes nothing beyond mere functionality resembles a concrete bunker with no windows, in which we ourselves provide lighting and atmospheric conditions, being no longer willing to obtain either from God's wide world.... The windows must be flung open again, we must see the wide world, the sky and the earth once more and learn to make proper use of all this.
>
> But how are we to do this? How do we find our way out into the wide world, into the big picture? How can reason rediscover its true greatness, without being sidetracked into irrationality? How can nature reassert itself in its true depth, with all its demands, with all its directives?... If something is wrong in our relationship with reality, then we must all reflect seriously on the whole situation and we are all prompted to question the very foundations of our culture. Allow me to dwell a little longer on this point. The importance of ecology is no longer disputed. We must listen to the language of nature and we must answer accordingly. Yet I would like to underline a point that seems to me to be neglected, today as in the past: there is also an ecology of man. Man too has a nature that he must respect and that he cannot manipulate at will. Man is not merely self-creating freedom. Man does not create himself. He is intellect and will, but he is also nature, and his will is rightly ordered if he respects his nature, listens to it and accepts himself for who he is, as one who did not create himself. In this way, and in no other, is true human freedom fulfilled....

Nature therefore could only contain norms ... if a will had put them there. But this ... would presuppose a Creator God, whose will had entered into nature.... Is it really pointless to wonder whether the objective reason that manifests itself in nature does not presuppose a creative reason, a *Creator Spiritus*?[12]

We are arriving at the end of a cycle. The issue of transhumanism confronts us with a choice of civilization. We can continue in the same direction, but then we risk literally renouncing our humanity. If we want to remain human, we must accept our creaturely nature and once again turn to the Creator. The world has chosen to organize itself without God, to live without God, to think about itself without God. It is in the process of making a terrible experiment: wherever God is not, hell is there. What is hell if not the privation of God? The transhumanist ideology illustrates this perfectly. Without God, nothing remains but what is not human, the post-human. More than ever the alternative is simple: God or nothing!

A little while ago, the philosopher Guy Coq said in a conference entitled "Face of God, Faces of Men":

Savagery, in other words the possibility of destroying what is essential to civilization, proceeds by small steps. Savagery does not confront us, saying: Look, here I am. Be afraid. See the extent of the inhumanity that I am bringing.... Our civilization is like a drunk human being walking around near an abyss. Some steps bring him closer to it; others lead him away from it. But he does not know exactly where the edge of the abyss is. So it may happen that one simple little step more toward the edge will cause the definitive catastrophe. It was one little step too much. If the stroller wants to avoid the worst, he must carefully study his trajectory and try to understand that such a step ought to be avoided.[13]

The transhumanist temptation is this little step too far that hurls us into the void. By producing modified or augmented human beings,

---

[12] Pope Benedict XVI, Address to the Bundestag, *The Listening Heart, Reflections on the Foundations of Law* (September 22, 2011).

[13] *Visage de Dieu, visages de l'homme: La vie spirituelle dans le monde contemporain*, July 22, 2003 (Paris: Parole et Silence; Paris: Carmel, 2003).

it would lead us to abolish the boundary between subject and object. Today when I see a person, I am aware that he is not a thing that can be bought and disposed of but, rather, another self. Tomorrow, who will say where the boundary is between what is human and what is non-human? If human beings become manufactured products, who will be able to measure their fundamental dignity?

Are we really aware of what they are saying when they talk about augmented men? Will there soon be several classes of humans: the diminished humans and the augmented humans? What will be the value, the price, the rights of these and of those? I tremble to think that maybe soon some men will be able to feel and believe that they are superior to others because of their technological prostheses.

It must be emphasized that this project departs from the rationale for medicine. This is no longer a matter of treating or repairing an organism damaged by an accident. It is about creating, inventing a new, patented race. John Paul II wrote in *Fides et ratio*:

> It follows that certain scientists, lacking any ethical point of reference, are in danger of putting at the center of their concerns something other than the human person and the entirety of the person's life. Further still, some of these, sensing the opportunities of technological progress, seem to succumb not only to a market-based logic, but also to the temptation of a quasi-divine power over nature and even over the human being.[14]

Thus the mad advocates of augmented man speak about establishing a vast program of improving the population. They envisage increasing people's IQ. By implanting in the brain devices linked with computer technologies, they hope to give new faculties to some of them. They want to make men high-performing and efficient. Already techniques of artificial procreation, pre-implantation embryonic triage, and universalized prenatal diagnosis of genetic illness have little by little inoculated the popular mind with eugenic ideas. It is considered normal to eliminate embryos, in other words, very tiny human beings, who do not correspond to our norm. Who will set the norm tomorrow?

---

[14] Pope St. John Paul II, Encyclical Letter *Fides et ratio* on the Relationship between Faith and Reason (September 14, 1998), no. 46.

Who will say whether this individual or that one is high-performing enough or should be augmented? Does transhumanism seek to create a master race? These questions are terrifying and blood-chilling. The terrible experience of the murderous follies of the twentieth century ought to serve as an object lesson for us.

Confronted with this temptation to omnipotence, I wish to proclaim my love and my infinite respect for weakness. You sick persons, you who are weak in body or mind, you who suffer from a handicap or a malformation, you are great! You have a special dignity because you have a singular resemblance to Christ crucified. Allow me to tell you, the whole Church kneels down before you because you bear his image, his presence. We want to serve you, to love you, to console you, to soothe you. We also want to learn from you. You preach to us the gospel of suffering. You are a treasure. You show us the way, as Cardinal Ratzinger recalled in a conference given during an international meeting organized by the Pontifical Council for Pastoral Assistance to Health Care Workers:

> In this way the light of divine love lies specifically upon suffering people, in whom the splendor of the creation has been externally dimmed. Because these people are in a special way similar to the crucified Christ, to the icon of love, they have drawn near to a special shared nature with him who, alone, is *the* image of God.
>
> We can say of them, as Tertullian said of Christ, "However wretched his body may be ..., it will always be my Christ" (*Adv. Marc.* III, 17, 2). However great their suffering may be, however disfigured or dimmed their human existence may be, they will always be the favorite children of our Lord and they will always be his image in a special way.

The Cross is the final response to this ideology that, in order to escape weakness, dreams of doing away with all finitude: fatigue, pain, sickness, and even death. I think, on the contrary, that the heart of our civilization is accepting and loving finitude. The Promethean dream of an unbounded life, of an infinite power, is a lure, a diabolical temptation. Transhumanism promises that we will become gods "concretely". This utopia is one of the most dangerous in all of human history: the creature has never before tried to distance himself definitively from the Father to this extent. The words of Nietzsche in *The Gay Science* are becoming a reality: "God is dead!... And we have killed him!... The holiest and the mightiest that the world has hitherto possessed has bled to death under our knife.... Is not the magnitude of this deed too great for us? Shall we not ourselves have to become Gods, merely to seem worthy of it?"[15]

Scientists will certainly ridicule me and my ignorance. But as a man of faith, I would like to proclaim without shame or fear that the "superman" is a myth and that the Promethean project is fundamentally wrong.

This folly paradoxically expresses the tragic nostalgia for a lost paradise. Before original sin, man was not supposed to experience death but to remain eternally with God. Man seems to want to regain by his own efforts the good that he lost through his own fault. We know deep down that death and suffering cannot have the last word. We sense within us the call of eternity and of the infinite. Nevertheless, man cannot cease to be because of his human nature a creature at an infinite distance from his Creator. By his human effort, man will never manage to meet God, to raise himself to his level, and to live with his life. Man cannot live by God's life, which is called sanctifying grace, unless God gives it to him as an altogether gratuitous gift. Man has no right to it, for on God's part it is sheer gratuitous love, and it infinitely transcends all the potentials of human nature. Man is fundamentally dependent. He knows that he is called by God to a purpose that surpasses him. God willed it so; we do not find the full realization of our happiness on this earth alone. God did not create us for a merely natural perfection. In creating us in his image and likeness, God had a purpose infinitely superior to the perfection of nature. We exist only for this supernatural life. God created man for eternity.

Sanctity is the maximum fullness that lifts us to God's height. Our perfection, our sanctity is the work of God and of his grace. An infinite abyss exists between the natural order and the supernatural order, between the life of human nature and the life of grace, which is the very life of God given to man, and this abyss will never disappear. Sanctity assumes nature and does not contradict it, but surpasses it infinitely.

---

[15] Friedrich Nietzsche, *The Gay Science*, trans. Thomas Common (Digireads/Neeland Media, 2018), 104–5.

The Church prolongs the mission of Christ, who wants to lead man to perfection, to his divinization: "Remember your leaders, those who spoke to you the word of God; consider the outcome of their life, and imitate their faith. Jesus Christ is the same yesterday and today and for ever. Do not be led away by diverse and strange teachings" (Heb 13:7–9).

6

HATRED OF LIFE

Nicolas Diat: The issues of abortion and of sexual and reproductive rights are always the arena of a difficult confrontation between the Church and the media. For his part, Pope Francis does not hesitate to compare abortion to "genocide in white gloves".

Robert Cardinal Sarah: In many countries, there is what Saint John Paul II called an "anti-life coalition". If a government, on its own authority, can authorize citizens to take the life of a child legally, all sorts of excesses are possible. The legalization of abortion is the matrix for all sorts of transgressions. Who has the right to live? Who is condemned to death? Does a child with trisomy 21 inevitably belong to the second category of human beings? God's commandment is clear: "Thou shalt not kill."

Mother Teresa thought that a society in which a woman has the right to kill her baby is intrinsically barbaric. To mitigate the seriousness of this crime, its defenders attempt to describe it in attractive terms. "Termination of pregnancy" sounds nicer to the ear and to the conscience. Whole populations have been anesthetized with regard to this issue and do not seem to understand the seriousness of what is at stake. And the assassination goes on. A murder becomes good, justified, legitimate. A crime becomes a right. The Catholic Church is radically opposed to this mass murder, this crime against humanity. They try to drive us away from the debate and to stifle our words. Our arguments are considered obscurantist. Lobbyists exalt the freedom to choose death instead of celebrating the joy of life and of childbirth. Some even make maternity out to be a form of alienation and slavery.

The cynical laws that legalize abortion attack the foundations of law and ultimately lead to social disintegration and the self-destruction of the State. The problem is all the more severe because Europe is going through an unprecedented demographic crisis. The replacement of generations is no longer certain. In some countries, like Italy, an aging population poses serious problems.

Today we must admit that the status quo is far from what Paul VI recommended to governments in his encyclical *Humanae vitae*:

> And now We wish to speak to rulers of nations. To you most of all is committed the responsibility of safeguarding the common good. You can contribute so much to the preservation of morals. We beg of you, never allow the morals of your peoples to be undermined. The family is the primary unit in the state; do not tolerate any legislation which would introduce into the family those practices which are opposed to the natural law of God. For there are other ways by which a government can and should solve the population problem—that is to say by enacting laws which will assist families and by educating the people wisely so that the moral law and the freedom of the citizens are both safeguarded. (*HV* 23)

The absence of a true policy of supporting the family and demographic growth on the part of Western countries is a profound mystery to me. From the merely human perspective, it is obvious that there is an emergency. I think that there is a deep lack of hope in this race to death. It is as though these countries no longer believed in their own future.

And meanwhile the tragedy of abortion continues to ravage society. Pre-born children are its victims, but so, too, are their mothers, who are subjected to many pressures urging them to abort. There are many women who carry within them for years this terrible wound and know that they have put an end to their child's life. I would like to recall the prophetic words of Mother Teresa when she received the Nobel Peace Prize. In the presence of the King of Norway and the entire Nobel Academy, this woman, so tiny in stature but so great in God's sight, imitated the cadences of the Old Testament prophets to put the truth in front of our eyes. She dared to assert that abortion threatened world peace. She said:

> And I feel one thing I want to share with you all, the greatest destroyer of peace today is the cry of the innocent unborn child. For if a mother

can murder her own child in her womb, what is left for you and for me [but] to kill each other? Even in the Scripture it is written: Even if mother could forget her child—I will not forget you—I have carved you in the palm of my hand. Even if mother could forget, but today millions of unborn children are being killed. And we say nothing. In the newspapers you read numbers of this one and that one being killed, this being destroyed, but nobody speaks of the millions of little ones who have been conceived to the same life as you and I, to the life of God, and we say nothing, we allow it. To me the nations who have legalized abortion, they are the poorest nations. They are afraid of the little one, they are afraid of the unborn child, and the child must die because they don't want to feed one more child, to educate one more child, the child must die....

And so today, let us here make a strong resolution, we are going to save every little child, every unborn child, give them a chance to be born. And what we are doing, we are fighting abortion by adoption, and the good God has blessed the work so beautifully that we have saved thousands of children, and thousands of children have found a home where they are loved, they are wanted, they are cared. We have brought so much joy in the homes that there was not a child, and so today, I ask His Majesties here before you all who come from different countries, let us all pray that we have the courage to stand by the unborn child, and give the child an opportunity to love and to be loved, and I think with God's grace we will be able to bring peace in the world. We have an opportunity here in Norway, you are with God's blessing, you are well to do. But I am sure in the families and many of our homes, maybe we are not hungry for a piece of bread, but maybe there is somebody there in the family who is unwanted, unloved, uncared, forgotten, there isn't love. Love begins at home. And love to be true has to hurt....

For the child is the greatest gift of God to a family, to a nation and to the whole world. God bless you![1]

I think that only a woman could speak with so much audacity; only a saint could speak with so much clarity. Mother Teresa reminds me of those women who were at the foot of the Cross when the apostles had fled, overwhelmed with fear! Even though we priests

---

[1] Mother Teresa, Acceptance Speech. NobelPrize.org. Nobel Media AB 2019. https://www.nobelprize.org/prizes/peace/1979/teresa/26200-mother-teresa-acceptance-speech-1979/.

and bishops are often so cowardly in teaching the truth, the Holy Spirit spoke to us that day through a woman.

In the encyclical Evangelium vitae,[2] *John Paul II denounced the expansion of a disturbing "culture of death" that is expressed not only in fratricidal wars, massacres, or genocides, but above all by attacks against life in its earliest stages and against aged and sick persons. How are we to understand the former pope's perspective?*

Our contemporary societies have become morbid. All the popes of the last century fought against this culture of death. Basically it is a rather strange situation. For no one can love death. We are naturally repulsed by the prospect of the end of our lives on this earth. Nevertheless, beneath the deceptive finery of progressive ideologies, the postmodern civilizations do not hesitate to deal death.

In *Evangelium vitae*, which appeared in 1995, John Paul II wrote:

> How did such a situation come about? Many different factors have to be taken into account. In the background there is the profound crisis of culture, which generates scepticism in relation to the very foundations of knowledge and ethics, and which makes it increasingly difficult to grasp clearly the meaning of what man is, the meaning of his rights and his duties. Then there are all kinds of existential and interpersonal difficulties, made worse by the complexity of a society in which individuals, couples and families are often left alone with their problems. There are situations of acute poverty, anxiety or frustration in which the struggle to make ends meet, the presence of unbearable pain, or instances of violence, especially against women, make the choice to defend and promote life so demanding as sometimes to reach the point of heroism.
>
> All this explains, at least in part, how the value of life can today undergo a kind of "eclipse", even though conscience does not cease to point to it as a sacred and inviolable value, as is evident in the tendency to disguise certain crimes against life in its early or final stages by using innocuous medical terms which distract attention from the fact that what is involved is the right to life of an actual human person.

[2] Pope St. John Paul II, Encyclical *Evangelium vitae* on the Value and Inviolability of Human Life (March 25, 1995; hereafter cited as *EV*).

In fact, while the climate of widespread moral uncertainty can in some way be explained by the multiplicity and gravity of today's social problems, and these can sometimes mitigate the subjective responsibility of individuals, it is no less true that we are confronted by an even larger reality, which can be described as a veritable structure of sin. This reality is characterized by the emergence of a culture which denies solidarity and in many cases takes the form of a veritable "culture of death". (*EV* 11–12)

The great Polish pope had witnessed the atrocities of war—several of his Jewish friends did not return from the extermination camps—and many other horrors. He was long since acquainted with the activities of those morbid passions.

International institutions work to spread this culture of death. Poor countries, where the family is still a fundamental anchor point of social life, are the prime targets of their eugenicist and Malthusian policies. Large foundations in the hands of Western billionaires develop programs for exterminating pre-born children. This struggle to spread death at all costs is a monstrosity and an unbridled use of economic power to destroy the weak and the defenseless.

This is a great paradox. Western man, who takes the greatest possible advantage of the charms of human existence, ferociously fights against life. The hatred of life is the hatred of love. Love always produces life. Someone who loves in truth possesses life. I would like to recall the beautiful words of the apostle Saint John:

We know that we have passed out of death into life, because we love the brethren. He who does not love remains in death. Any one who hates his brother is a murderer, and you know that no murderer has eternal life abiding in him. By this we know love, that [Jesus] laid down his life for us; and we ought to lay down our lives for the brethren. But if any one has the world's goods and sees his brother in need, yet closes his heart against him, how does God's love abide in him? Little children, let us not love in word or speech but in deed and in truth.

By this we shall know that we are of the truth, and reassure our hearts before him whenever our hearts condemn us; for God is greater than our hearts, and he knows everything. Beloved, if our hearts do not condemn us, we have confidence before God. (1 Jn 3:14–21)

The culture of death is the work of a counterculture of living dead persons. We are confronted with an erroneous concept of human destiny. An authentic civilization is based on the joy of the gift of life.

I was born in Guinea at the time of the dictatorship of Sékou Touré. I understood then that the sole response to the violence of the revolutionary dictatorship was in the passion of love. We did not have to fear the dictatorship; instead, we had to sow love: "There is no fear in love, but perfect love casts our fear. For fear has to do with punishment, and he who fears is not perfected in love" (1 Jn 4:18). I had to work, with the help of divine grace, to graft onto the heart of each Guinean and of all the families a piece of the heart of God so that they could love and forgive as he does. We knew that all our arrested brothers were being tortured. The regime sought to extract hypothetical secrets from them. I was forbidden to visit in prison my predecessor in [the Archdiocese of] Conakry, Archbishop Tchidimbo, but there was no doubt whatsoever that he was subjected to the worst possible treatment. We no longer had any news about the many persons locked up in the jails of Sékou Touré. Through some guards who acted as go-betweens, we sometimes heard of the death of one of them in the midst of abominable sufferings. The henchmen of the regime showed the utmost perversity; they liked to see their prisoners die. Given these diabolical horrors, it was necessary to lead the people of Guinea to love and to forgive as God does. We can oppose violence and hatred only by clinging to God so as to love excessively.

The only hope is in God. The Father gathers life and love in himself.

Euthanasia is another form of contempt for human life . . .

Western man experiences a panicked fear at the idea of suffering and dying. When there is no longer any pleasure in the rendezvous, why remain on this earth? As with abortion, we observe a semantic shift that seeks to facilitate the evolution of people's mind-set. They propose that everyone should die with dignity. But who would ever like to pass away in pain? The advocates of euthanasia use the moral and psychological distress of terminally ill people and of their families to push their views. They show a false pity that is nothing other than a hypocritical death wish.

From the very beginning, the Church has known how to accompany the dying. How many priests and religious men and women have spent hours with persons who were at the end of life? At the end of their earthly journey, men do not need a cold, death-dealing syringe. They need a compassionate, loving hand. I think again of the distressing words of Mother Teresa:

> Our poor people are great people, are very lovable people, they don't need our pity and sympathy, they need our understanding love. They need our respect; they need that we treat them with dignity. And I think this is the greatest poverty that we experience, [the poverty that] we have in front of them who may be dying for a piece of bread, but they die [with] such dignity. I never forget when I brought a man from the street. He was covered with maggots; his face was the only place that was clean. And yet that man, when we brought him to our home for the dying, he said just one sentence: "I have lived like an animal in the street, but I am going to die like an angel, [with] love and care," and he died beautifully. He went home to God, for death is nothing but going home to God. And he having enjoyed that love, that being wanted, that being loved, that being somebody to somebody at the last moment, brought that joy in his life.[3]

To die with dignity is to die being loved! All the rest is a lie! The persons who devote themselves with tireless generosity in services that provide palliative care, so as to diminish pain and to accompany and love patients in their solitude—they know well that it is extremely rare for a patient to ask for euthanasia. If he does, his request masks some kind of distress. Basically, I think that the reason why there is a debate today about euthanasia is because we who are well cannot bear the presence of the sick and suffering. They are begging for our love and compassion. We do not have the courage to look them in the eye. We no longer have enough love to give to them. Our society is experiencing a drought of love, and so it wants to get rid of those who need it most. Go visit the hospitals, go simply, each day, to hold the hand of a patient or of an elderly person who has been abandoned to solitude! I beg you, try it; you will be able to tell even

---

[3] Mother Teresa, Acceptance Speech.

in your flesh what it is to love! Mother Teresa also said: "And this is
what I bring before you [propose to you], to love one another until
it hurts, but don't forget that there are many children, many children, many men and women who haven't got what you have. And
remember to love them until it hurts."[4]

The response to euthanasia is love until death! Euthanasia is based
essentially on an economic rationale. It is necessary to get rid of persons who have become useless to society and costly. Profitability is
more important than life.

The media are fully engaged in this fight for euthanasia, claiming
that it helps to alleviate pain and to prepare for an easy, happy death.
They like to present forcefully the details of particularly moving cases
so as to play on the feelings of the public.

Euthanasia is a form of assisted suicide and a legal way of putting someone to death. A mere weakening in respect for human life
can have incalculable consequences. In Belgium or in Great Britain,
they want to authorize the euthanasia of minors without their parents' consent. Are medical professionals not exclusively at the service
of life? Can they administer death, too? Euthanasia is becoming for
some a form of treatment. Do we have to fear the physician as we
would an executioner?

A remark by the French geneticist who discovered the cause of
trisomy 21, Professor Jérôme Lejeune, comes to mind: "The quality
of a civilization is measured by the respect that it has for its weakest members."

The Church must not be afraid to fight in season and out of season.
Were the Belgian bishops sufficiently courageous at the time when
euthanasia was legalized? Did those men of God sufficiently help
King Philippe, a good, kind man, the worthy heir of King Baudoin,
at the time when euthanasia of minors was legalized? I know that the
American, Polish, French, and Spanish bishops show great courage in
addressing all these issues.

What will our world look like in a century? Abortion, the commercialization of the body, sexual excesses, gender theory, the disintegration of marriage, and euthanasia are the many fronts of one
and the same battle with the Western elite that knows only three

---

[4] Ibid.

principles: money, power, and pleasure. These people dance on the cadavers of hundreds of thousands of fragile human beings whom they have deliberately sacrificed in order to keep their dominance.

The Church is the last rampart against this macabre, suicidal new world ethic. She must enlighten the consciences of everyone. When the sun of the Church is hidden, men grow cold. It is necessary to rediscover the courage of Saint Athanasius and of Saint Irenaeus in order to topple these new heresies. John Paul II paved the way. As early as 1980, at the beginning of his pontificate, he wrote in the encyclical *Dives in misericordia*:

> The Church, having before her eyes the picture of the generation to which we belong, shares the uneasiness of so many of the people of our time. Moreover, one cannot fail to be worried by the decline of many fundamental values, which constitute an unquestionable good not only for Christian morality but simply for human morality, for moral culture: these values include respect for human life from the moment of conception, respect for marriage in its indissoluble unity, and respect for the stability of the family. Moral permissiveness strikes especially at this most sensitive sphere of life and society. Hand in hand with this go the crisis of truth in human relationships, lack of responsibility for what one says, the purely utilitarian relationship between individual and individual, the loss of a sense of the authentic common good and the ease with which this good is alienated. Finally, there is the "desacralization" that often turns into "dehumanization": the individual and the society for whom nothing is "sacred" suffer moral decay, in spite of appearances.[5]

Similarly, the encyclical letter *Evangelium vitae* by John Paul II remains a prophetic document, a hymn to life thrown in the face of a world at a time when, as he put is, "the attacks against life" were multiplying, particularly through abortion and euthanasia. Thus a pre-born child can be condemned to death in his mother's womb while the terrible logical sequel of infanticide is extended from the beginning of life to euthanasia with the proposal to finish off severely handicapped patients and persons at the end of life. What an astonishing paradox: at a time when most societies want to abolish the

[5] Pope St. John Paul II, Encyclical *Dives in misericordia* (November 30, 1980), no. 12.

death penalty for murderers, they reinstate it for innocent, vulnerable people, from the child in the womb to the sick or elderly person or even those who are tired of living. In each case, we lose the sense of solidarity with men and women who are in a difficult situation.

Western society is thus harking back to the most archaic reflexes of the primitive societies that claimed the power of life and death over children and certain categories of the population. Both abortion and euthanasia are new, sanitized forms of a silent barbarity. Medicine cannot be the secular arm of a death-dealing power. Physicians have the vocation to protect life, not to prevent it. Four centuries ago, in his *Pensées*, Pascal wrote: "The property of power is to protect."[6] Not to assassinate.

I think that it is urgent for the Church to respond by creating "oases of life": places where pregnant women can be welcomed and accompanied toward childbirth, without disapproval and joyfully; places where handicapped children can be welcomed at their birth with wonder and not be treated as failures of medicine; places where patients can die in the dignity of love. Some religious congregations are already doing admirable work. I am thinking of *Les Petites Soeurs des Maternités Catholiques* [The Little Sisters of the Catholic Maternity Hospitals] in Africa and in Europe, or of all who are involved in palliative care. How can we not admire the exceptional work of the Jeanne Garnier House in Paris, which accommodates the terminally ill? In the French capital, Cardinal Lustiger, his successor Cardinal Vingt-Trois, and now Archbishop Aupetit never feared to proclaim the Gospel of Life. This ought to be an urgent imperative for all bishops. In every diocese, they should fight against the culture of death not only in words, but even more by putting a culture of life into practice concretely. The Gospel is not a utopia; it has to become incarnate. Now Jesus tells us: "I came that they may have life, and have it abundantly" (Jn 10:10). The Church is the matrix of a civilization of life.

In your view what is the place of the Holocaust in human history?

I think that the Shoah was the greatest scandal of humanity, the worst crime in modern history. Hatred of the Jewish people and

---

[6] Blaise Pascal, *Pensées*, trans. W. F. Trotter (Mineola, N.Y.: Dover, 2018), 88.

the intention to do away with them are an abomination. Was it not basically a plan to kill God by eliminating the people who bore the memory of his covenant down through the centuries? I would like to quote on this subject an exceptional speech by Benedict XVI. During his visit to the concentration camp in Auschwitz on May 28, 2006, he declared:

> To speak in this place of horror, in this place where unprecedented mass crimes were committed against God and man, is almost impossible— and it is particularly difficult and troubling for a Christian, for a Pope from Germany. In a place like this, words fail; in the end, there can only be a dread silence—a silence which is itself a heartfelt cry to God: Why, Lord, did you remain silent? How could you tolerate all this? In silence, then, we bow our heads before the endless line of those who suffered and were put to death here; yet our silence becomes in turn a plea for forgiveness and reconciliation, a plea to the living God never to let this happen again ...
>
> Pope John Paul II came here as a son of the Polish people. I come here today as a son of the German people. For this very reason, I can and must echo his words: I could not fail to come here. I had to come. It is a duty before the truth and the just due of all who suffered here, a duty before God, for me to come here as the successor of Pope John Paul II and as a son of the German people—a son of that people over which a ring of criminals rose to power by false promises of future greatness and the recovery of the nation's honor, prominence and prosperity, but also through terror and intimidation, with the result that our people was used and abused as an instrument of their thirst for destruction and power. Yes, I could not fail to come here.... This is the same reason why I have come here today: to implore the grace of reconciliation—first of all from God, who alone can open and purify our hearts, from the men and women who suffered here, and finally the grace of reconciliation for all those who, at this hour of our history, are suffering in new ways from the power of hatred and the violence which hatred spawns.
>
> How many questions arise in this place! Constantly the question comes up: Where was God in those days? Why was he silent? How could he permit this endless slaughter, this triumph of evil? The words of Psalm 44 come to mind, Israel's lament for its woes: "You have broken us in the haunt of jackals, and covered us with deep darkness ... because of you we are being killed all day long, and accounted as sheep for the slaughter. Rouse yourself! Why do you sleep, O Lord? Awake, do not cast us off forever! Why do you hide

your face? Why do you forget our affliction and oppression? For we sink down to the dust; our bodies cling to the ground. Rise up, come to our help! Redeem us for the sake of your steadfast love!" (Ps 44:19, 22–26). This cry of anguish, which Israel raised to God in its suffering, at moments of deep distress, is also the cry for help raised by all those who in every age—yesterday, today and tomorrow—suffer for the love of God, for the love of truth and goodness. How many they are, even in our own day!

We cannot peer into God's mysterious plan—we see only piecemeal, and we would be wrong to set ourselves up as judges of God and history. Then we would not be defending man, but only contributing to his downfall. No—when all is said and done, we must continue to cry out humbly yet insistently to God: Rouse yourself! Do not forget mankind, your creature! And our cry to God must also be a cry that pierces our very heart, a cry that awakens within us God's hidden presence—so that his power, the power he has planted in our hearts, will not be buried or choked within us by the mire of selfishness, pusillanimity, indifference or opportunism. Let us cry out to God, with all our hearts, at the present hour, when new misfortunes befall us, when all the forces of darkness seem to issue anew from human hearts: whether it is the abuse of God's name as a means of justifying senseless violence against innocent persons, or the cynicism which refuses to acknowledge God and ridicules faith in him. Let us cry out to God, that he may draw men and women to conversion and help them to see that violence does not bring peace, but only generates more violence—a morass of devastation in which everyone is ultimately the loser. The God in whom we believe is a God of reason—a reason, to be sure, which is not a kind of cold mathematics of the universe, but is one with love and with goodness. We make our prayer to God and we appeal to humanity, that this reason, the logic of love and the recognition of the power of reconciliation and peace, may prevail over the threats arising from irrationalism or from a spurious and godless reason.

The place where we are standing is a place of memory, it is the place of the *Shoah*. The past is never simply the past. It always has something to say to us; it tells us the paths to take and the paths not to take. Like John Paul II, I have walked alongside the inscriptions in various languages erected in memory of those who died here: ... All these inscriptions speak of human grief, they give us a glimpse of the cynicism of that regime which treated men and women as material objects, and failed to see them as persons embodying the image of God. Some inscriptions are pointed reminders. There is one in Hebrew. The rulers of the Third Reich wanted to crush the entire Jewish people, to cancel it from the register of the peoples of the earth. Thus the words of the Psalm: "We are being killed, accounted as sheep for the slaughter" were fulfilled in a terrifying way. Deep down, those vicious criminals, by wiping out this people, wanted to kill the God who called Abraham, who spoke on Sinai and laid down principles to serve as a guide for mankind, principles that are eternally valid. If this people, by its very existence, was a witness to the God who spoke to humanity and took us to himself, then that God finally had to die and power had to belong to man alone—to those men, who thought that by force they had made themselves masters of the world. By destroying Israel, by the *Shoah*, they ultimately wanted to tear up the taproot of the Christian faith and to replace it with a faith of their own invention: faith in the rule of man, the rule of the powerful.

Then there is the inscription in Polish. First and foremost they wanted to eliminate the cultural elite, thus erasing the Polish people as an autonomous historical subject and reducing it, to the extent that it continued to exist, to slavery. Another inscription offering a pointed reminder is the one written in the language of the Sinti and Roma people. Here too, the plan was to wipe out a whole people which lives by migrating among other peoples. They were seen as part of the refuse of world history, in an ideology which valued only the empirically useful; everything else, according to this view, was to be written off as *lebensunwertes Leben*—life unworthy of being lived. There is also the inscription in Russian, which commemorates the tremendous loss of life endured by the Russian soldiers who combated the Nazi reign of terror; but this inscription also reminds us that their mission had a tragic twofold effect: they set the peoples free from one dictatorship, but the same peoples were thereby subjected to a new one, that of Stalin and the Communist system.

The other inscriptions, written in Europe's many languages, also speak to us of the sufferings of men and women from the whole continent. They would stir our hearts profoundly if we remembered the victims not merely in general, but rather saw the faces of the individual persons who ended up here in this abyss of terror. I felt a deep urge to pause in a particular way before the inscription in German. It evokes the face of Edith Stein, Theresia Benedicta a Cruce: a woman, Jewish and German, who disappeared along with her sister into the black night of the Nazi-German concentration camp; as a Christian and a Jew, she accepted death with her people and for them. The Germans who had been brought to Auschwitz-Birkenau and met their death here were considered as *Abschaum der Nation*—the refuse of the nation. Today we gratefully hail them as witnesses to the truth and goodness which even among our people were not eclipsed. We are grateful to them, because they did not submit to the power of evil, and now they stand before us like lights shining in a dark night. With profound respect and gratitude, then, let us bow our heads before all those who, like the three young men in Babylon facing death in the fiery furnace, could respond: "Only our God can deliver us. But even if he does not, be it known to you, O King, that we will not serve your gods and we will not worship the golden statue that you have set up" (cf. Dan 3:17ff.).

Yes, behind these inscriptions is hidden the fate of countless human beings. They jar our memory, they touch our hearts. They have no desire to instill hatred in us: instead, they show us the terrifying effect of hatred. Their desire is to help our reason to see evil as evil and to reject it; their desire is to enkindle in us the courage to do good and to resist evil. They want to make us feel the sentiments expressed in the words that Sophocles placed on the lips of Antigone, as she contemplated the horror all around her: My nature is not to join in hate but to join in love.

By God's grace, together with the purification of memory demanded by this place of horror, a number of initiatives have sprung up with the aim of imposing a limit upon evil and confirming goodness. Just now I was able to bless the Centre for Dialogue and Prayer. In the immediate neighborhood the Carmelite nuns carry on their life of hiddenness, knowing that they are united in a special way to the mystery of Christ's Cross and reminding us of the faith of Christians, which declares that God himself descended into the hell of suffering and suffers with us....

At Auschwitz-Birkenau humanity walked through a "valley of darkness". And so, here in this place, I would like to end with a prayer of trust—with one of the Psalms of Israel which is also a prayer of Christians: "The Lord is my shepherd, I shall not want. He makes me lie down in green pastures; he leads me beside still waters; he restores my soul. He leads me in right paths for his name's sake. Even though I walk through the valley of the shadow of death, I fear no evil; for you are with me; your rod and your staff—they comfort me.... I shall dwell in the house of the Lord my whole life long" (Ps 23:1–4, 6).

When major forms of violence prevail—all kinds of imperialism, whether bloody or camouflaged; brutal actions, blatant and entrenched disorder—people are often amazed at God's patience and silence and are scandalized by it. This divine silence in the presence of barbarity and crimes is for many a sufficient motive for unbelief. If we only knew how intense God's impatience is! It takes him nothing less to overcome it than the infinitude of his love. God does not will evil. I am sad when I hear people say, "God allows evil!" No! God does not allow evil. He suffers from it. He is mortally wounded by it. He is the first one struck by it! The more monstrous the evil, the more evident it is that God in us is the first victim. God is like a mother: through love a mother can suffer with her child more than her child and for her child. A completely healthy mother can experience her child's agony more painfully than the child himself, precisely because of this identification of love with the beloved. This is what love is capable of.

How can we imagine that God's love is less maternal than a mother's love, when all the love of all mothers, including that of the Blessed Virgin, is only a drop in the ocean of God's maternal affection? No one is struck without God being struck, in him, before him, more than he, and for him.

Silence is the most powerful and most fraught word spoken by love, and this absence is the most immediate presence at the heart of human suffering. The God-who-is-Love was silently present in Auschwitz-Birkenau, mysteriously flooding that martyred ground with his affection. No one can know how God welcomed into his arms all who passed from life to their demise in the death chambers.

In order to doubt it, we would have to have lost sight entirely of the dignity of our freedom. God gave us complete freedom. If God creates this freedom, it is not in order to petrify it and to replace it with himself. The task is ours. It is necessary to accomplish it in impatience and patience, "speaking (and living) the truth in love" (see Eph 4:15).

After the Holocaust, we might have thought that the horror of genocides would no longer be repeated. Alas, that is not the case at all . . .

If we believe that a man is made in the likeness of God, it is impossible to commit the slightest abuse against him. In killing a man, we kill God. In detesting a man, we detest God. In making a man suffer, we make God suffer. A genocide, the systematic, programmed elimination of a nation, ethnic, or religious group, is a perfect sign of the devil: a battle, an offensive, a radical opposition against God himself.

In Africa, many men and women have been reduced to slavery. As a child, I heard the old people talking about deported villagers. On the coast, along the ocean, we knew where there used to be buildings in which slaves were crammed before their departure by boat. They were nothing but worthless merchandise. I knew at a very early age the shameful lot reserved for many of my brethren. I was not unaware of the fact that some of my ancestors had been sold like animals. They never returned. This commerce lasted for centuries. The defenseless populations that were its victims had nothing with which to respond to the blows. Black slaves had less value than a piece of furniture or a field of grain. All the regions of Africa experienced this humiliation, this abasement, this total negation, this commerce in slaves that was designed, promoted, and vilely carried out by Christian or Muslim countries. I, too, am the son of that tragic history.

Since his accession to the throne of Peter, Pope Francis has quite bluntly denounced two genocidal policies of our era. On April 12, 2015, the Second Sunday of Easter, he concelebrated a Mass for the faithful of the Armenian Rite with Patriarch Nerses Bedros XIX Tamouni. This Mass set off a major diplomatic storm—Turkey immediately recalled its ambassador for consultations in Ankara. This reaction was caused by the preliminary greeting addressed by the Supreme Pontiff to the faithful who were present. In that speech, he mentioned "the first genocide of the twentieth century",[7] which struck the Armenian people in 1915; Turkey has not yet acknowledged that it was a deliberate extermination.

In 2018, he made extremely firm remarks on the subject of abortion, saying: "to have a nice life, they do away with an innocent." On that day in June, while receiving at the Vatican representatives of family associations, Pope Francis compared abortion performed in the case of a handicapped child to eugenics "with white gloves". "I have heard that it is in fashion—or at least customary—in the first months of pregnancy to have certain exams, to see whether the baby is not well, or has some problems.... The first proposal in that case is: 'Shall we do away with it?'... In the last century the entire world was scandalized over what the Nazis were doing to maintain the purity of the race. Today

---

[7] Quoting the Common Declaration of His Holiness John Paul II and His Holiness Karekin II at Holy Etchmiadzin, Republic of Armenia (September 27, 2001).

we do the same thing, but with white gloves." The pope also asked: "Have you ever wondered why you do not see many dwarfs on the streets? Because the protocol of many doctors—many, not all—is to ask the question: 'Will it have problems?' "[8] As the successor of Peter views it, with the tragedy of abortion, the West is experiencing a form of hidden, sanitized, and destructive genocide.

In his Cahiers de la quinzaine, *Charles Péguy wrote: "The modern world is demeaning. It demeans civilization; it demeans man. It demeans love; it demeans woman. It demeans the human race; it demeans the child. It demeans the nation; it demeans the family. It even demeans, it has managed to demean, what is perhaps the most difficult thing in the world to demean: it demeans death."[9] What reflections do these words of this great French author inspire in you?*

In our human relations, we have invented a justice without love, which quickly becomes an enraged beast. We become equally indifferent to truth and to lying. We want to become richer and richer, and we do not see that we are becoming poorer and poorer. We resemble beings that have lost their center of gravity. We do not know how to love because we do not know the true love of God. Our era loves to look at itself in a mirror. Men love themselves excessively. We are experiencing the triumph of egotism.

When people turn their backs on God, they darken love. For a Christian, God is the Almighty. But that does not mean dominating or having the power to crush others. God is eternally divesting himself. God exists, he is present, in order to give himself. He can only give himself. The presence of God in my life makes me incapable of demeaning love, incapable of demeaning a man or a woman. Because there is no greater proof of love than to give one's life.

Heroes and martyrs still exist. Saint Maximilian Kolbe and Arnaud Beltrame[10] are living examples of the greatness and nobility of love.

---

[8] Pope Francis, Address to the Delegation of the Forum of Family Associations (Saturday, June 16, 2018).

[9] Charles Péguy, *Cahiers de la quinzaine*, IX, 1 (October 1, 1907).

[10] Arnaud Beltrame was a French gendarme who gave his life in 2018 so that a hostage held by a terrorist might be set free.—TRANS.

I would like to quote also a passage by John Paul II. In the apostolic exhortation *Ecclesia in Europa*, he wrote:

> At the root of this loss of hope is an *attempt to promote a vision of man apart from God and apart from Christ*. This sort of thinking has led to man being considered as "the absolute center of reality, a view which makes him occupy—falsely—the place of God and which forgets that it is not man who creates God, but rather God who creates man. Forgetfulness of God led to the abandonment of man". It is therefore "no wonder that in this context a vast field has opened for the unrestrained development of nihilism in philosophy, of relativism in values and morality, and of pragmatism—and even a cynical hedonism—in daily life". European culture gives the impression of "silent apostasy" on the part of people who have all that they need and who live as if God does not exist.
>
> This is the context for those attempts, including the most recent ones, to present European culture with no reference to the contribution of the Christian religion which marked its historical development and its universal diffusion. We are witnessing the emergence of a *new culture*, largely influenced by the mass media, whose content and character are often in conflict with the Gospel and the dignity of the human person. This culture is also marked by a widespread and growing religious agnosticism, connected to a more profound moral and legal relativism rooted in confusion regarding the truth about man as the basis of the inalienable rights of all human beings. At times the signs of a weakening of hope are evident in disturbing forms of what might be called a "culture of death". (*EE* 9)

I am struck by modern man's talent for making everything he touches ugly. Look at outer space: the images of the planets and the stars are captivatingly beautiful. Everything is in its place. The order of the universe breathes peace. Look at the world, the mountains, the rivers, the landscapes: everything breathes a tranquil beauty. Look at the face of a child who bursts out laughing, the face of an old person wrinkled by the years. God made his Creation with so much love that it always inspires an impression of nobility and beauty. But look at what the modern world makes!

I think that man, even if he is poor, even if he is tired or sick, is beautiful when he remains simple and true, in other words, aware of and happy about his status as a creature. Modernity disfigures the beauty of the Creator that is reflected on the faces both of children and of the dying. This reflection is so unbearable to it that it wants to deform it. This reflection is an unceasing reproach that it cannot tolerate. It wants to demean it. I remember a very beautiful book written by a Polish author who was deported, when he was a child, to the gulag in Siberia during the Soviet era. At the moment when he boards the train that would take him to the camps, he asks himself why his mother, who was so beautiful, was being deported with him. What is more beautiful in a child's heart than his mother's face? He answers: "Because a beauty like the one that radiated from my mother was necessary there, too. Beauty is necessary wherever man makes himself an animal, wherever they try to make him a demon." I would like to adopt as my own this reflection by Piotr Bednarski. The modern world demeans the most sacred realities and makes them ugly: the child, the mother, death. And nevertheless, it will never be able to snatch completely from our souls the interior beauty that God has placed there. This beauty is inaccessible to it. Wherever holiness flourishes, a little of God's own beauty unfolds. In this same book that I just quoted, entitled *Les Neiges bleues* [The blue snows], the child, upon discovering the ugliness of the Soviet concentration system and of violent death, exclaims:

> "Christ they crucified. For us. He was young, wise, and handsome. He loved, and he was loved, he proclaimed love—and despite that, or perhaps because of that, they killed him.... Is love then an offense?" That was when something in me snapped. I pressed myself to the ground so as to release all my bitterness in tears. And when tears failed me, when my eyes became dry as the desert sand, my heart opened up. And I started to weep again, but interiorly, within myself, with tears that only He who had created us could see.

These interior tears that God alone sees wash the world of all ugliness and all meanness. They restore its beauty. Children, mothers, old people, and saints know this, but it is a secret that they share with God and that remains concealed from the world's eyes.

PART III

THE FALL OF TRUTH, MORAL DECADENCE, AND BAD POLITICAL HABITS

This invites a comparison with the decline of the Roman Empire: it was still functioning as a great historical context, but in practice it was already living off of those who would eventually break it up, because it no longer had any vital energy of its own.

—Joseph Cardinal Ratzinger
Europe Today and Tomorrow:
Addressing the Fundamental Issues

7

WHERE IS THE WORLD HEADED?

NICOLAS DIAT: *How do you view the skepticism of modernity toward the past and traditions?*

ROBERT CARDINAL SARAH: Modern man in the West disdains the past. He is proud of his civilization, which he thinks is superior to all that preceded it. Advances in the fields of science and technology give him this illusion; the latest revolutions of communications technology, and the Internet in particular, anchor this claim.

Modern man has amnesia. We aspire to break with the past, while what is new becomes an idol. There is, to my way of thinking, an aggressive form of hostility toward tradition and, more generally, toward all heritage.

Now, by living in a perpetual change, modern man deprives himself of a compass. Young people can condemn the errors of previous generations. I can understand that there are some pages they would like to turn: How can anyone blame the young Germans of the postwar era for not wanting to think anymore about the ghosts of the Nazi past? However, even the darkest pages of history must not be forgotten. It is of capital importance to maintain the memory of the Holocaust.

Fundamentally, tradition is an agreement with the future that we find in the past. Alas, I look with consternation at the Westerners' amnesia. We are far from the little primary school of my Guinean village where I learned that my ancestors were Gauls.... That lesson might seem strange, but it was not traumatizing. It resulted from a real intention to open up the French identity to the Guineans, at a time when the country was a French colony.

The crisis of memory cannot help but give rise to a cultural crisis. The precondition for progress lies in the transmission of the acquisitions of the past. Man is physically and ontologically bound to the history of those who preceded him. A society that rejects the past cuts itself off from its future. It is a dead society, a society with no memory, a society carried off by Alzheimer's disease.

This contemporary trend applies to Christianity. If the Church were to cut herself off permanently from her long history, it would not be long before she perished. In *L'Affrontement chrétien* (The Christian confrontation), Emmanuel Mounier explains that this desire to break with the past has caused a joint decline of Western civilization and of Christianity. Christianity was supported from its very beginnings by the "vigor of civilization"; it would suffer today from its collapse. But the crisis is, first of all, in his view, an internal matter in Christianity. There is a sort of porous membrane between Christian civilization and Christian religion. If Christianity makes a pact with the world instead of enlightening it, Christians are not being faithful to the essence of their faith. The lukewarmness of Christianity and of the Church causes the decline of civilization. Christianity is the light of the world. If Christianity no longer shines, it helps plunge humanity into darkness.

What do you think about the complex relation of modern thinkers to the idea of roots?

A root is the start and the food of life. It plants life in a fertile soil and waters it with a nourishing sap. It sinks into the groundwater so that life may remain green in every season. It enables leaves to form and flowers and fruits to appear. A life without roots leads to death. The complex relation of modern thinkers to the idea of roots is caused by the anthropological crisis that we mentioned earlier. Modern man fears that his roots might become a yoke. He prefers to deny them. He thinks he is free, although in fact he is more vulnerable. He is like a dead leaf detached from the tree, at the mercy of every gust of wind.

This difficulty is a Western phenomenon. In Africa and in Asia, we remain attached to our roots; they plunge our lives and our history into the depths of our ancestral origins. Ethnic groups, religions, and cultures have ancient histories by which they continue to be nourished. In them the past and the future overlap and are inseparable. Being anchored in this way is not a kind of determinism but rather the precondition of our freedom.

The rejection of Christian roots in the European Constitution is the most obvious symptom of this attitude. Today European institutions are reduced to an economic and administrative structure. Apart from the financial interests, which are promoted by a small oligarchy, Europe fabricates ideologies, feeds them on utopia, and loses its soul. Europe has cut itself off from what it is deep down. It has denied itself.

The West sometimes gives the impression of having progress as its only prospect . . .

Progress is a powerful idol of Western societies. It is the alpha and the omega that are supposed to facilitate the coming of a new man. Progress leads to the birth of a purely technological civilization concerned about opulence and a superabundance of the material goods that modern man avidly seeks.

Every day we are overwhelmed by the news and by fresh information. Each one of us is summoned to adapt, to change. Postmodern man is a perpetual nomad, a puppet tossed to and fro, at the mercy of all the winds of fashion.

The compulsive search for progress has led to the emergence of a virtual man. How could he possibly encounter God? Movement and instability are the most implacable enemies of contemplation.

In his *Confessions*, Saint Augustine writes: "You have made us for Yourself, Lord, and our hearts are restless until they rest in You." God is the very direction of all genuine progress. Speed and artificiality cannot lead us to God. The man of the moment is not the man of God. He ends up no longer understanding his reason for being.

In this state of being lost, it is not surprising that we show no uneasiness about the coming of humanoid robots endowed with artificial intelligence. We are vaguely astounded, certain that these hybrids equipped with brains composed of a network of artificial neurons are an opportunity for humanity. But in reality they herald its slow death.

Nevertheless, the Church has always contributed decisively to technological progress. How many scientific discoveries were made in a Christian milieu or even in the monasteries? The Church today must continue to encourage all scientific advances that are really at the service of man. In order to do that, she must remain herself and continue to preach what Christ handed on to her.

Does the coming of a society of robots herald the definitive death of God?

We must speak first about the death of man. I often think about Paul Tibbets, the pilot of the bomber *Enola Gay* that bombed Hiroshima. He is par excellence the obedient, irresponsible man of the civilization of machines.

In the 1947 essay *La France contre les robots* [France against the robots], Georges Bernanos referred lucidly to this phenomenon: "In the more or less insidious struggle against the interior life, the civilization of machines is not inspired, at least not directly, by any ideological plan; it defends its essential principle, which is the principle of the primacy of action. Freedom of action does not frighten it at all; freedom of thought is what it fears."[1]

In our world, man finds his place only insofar as he is useful in the vast spider web of robots. Man reduced to the role of technological underling is no longer a man, strictly speaking, but a cold operator who long since has renounced the use of his free will; he has lost contact with his soul. Bernanos continued: "Souls! One almost blushes to write that sacred word today.... Man has contact with his soul only through the interior life, and in the civilization of machines the interior life little by little assumes an abnormal character."[2]

Contemplative man is the one who does not subject himself to the technological imperative of production. He knows that the death of man heralds the death of God, and the death of God— the end of humanity.

Without God, the only things for the world to follow are utopias and idols. Without God, the world lives in the void, in nothingness, in permanent anxiety and suffering. If man no longer seeks God, if he creates for himself his own gods in the service of his flourishing, then the true God disappears from the world's horizon.

[1] Georges Bernanos, *La France contre les robots* (FV Éditions, 2019), 133.
[2] Ibid., 132.

The Life of life is vanishing from our societies. Nevertheless, God remains alive in us. He is in our souls, since man is the dwelling place, the most sacred temple of God.

Paradoxically, progress could make us discover God. Progress ought to be the most propitious setting for a constant discovery of what God has willed. All scientific or technological discoveries tell about God's Creation. A superficial science turns people away from God, but a deep, wise science draws us close to him.

Has the Church made the correct diagnosis with respect to the consequences of post-humanity?

The truth does not change. It is eternal. Its name is Jesus Christ, and "Jesus Christ is the same yesterday and today and for ever" (Heb 13:8). Humanity will never perish. It will be saved by Christ. Post-humanity is a lie. It wants to assert its autonomy with respect to its Creator, but it will never be able to kill its Creator.

Fundamentalist liberalism now seems to be the only rule in the world. It recommends the abolition of all rules, of boundaries, and of morality. It recommends the abolition of religion. Since God is dead, religion no longer links us with any divinity, and it becomes superfluous.

In the *Préface pour un traité du vide* (Preface for a treatise on the void), Blaise Pascal wrote: "The whole series of men, over the course of many centuries, must be considered as one and the same man who always exists and learns continually." The seventeenth-century philosopher is right. The idea that one man should be surpassed by another is arrogant and stupid. There is no difference between Adam and the man of today, ontologically speaking and in their ability to sin, to rebel against God; the only insignificant difference is that the man of today wears expensive clothing and has a mobile phone, while Adam and Eve discover they are naked.

What will be left of us, such as we are, "human, all too human", when the prospects opened up by cloning and the artificial womb have done away with birth, when sickness will be kept at bay by the advances of nanomedicine and biotechnologies, and when the Grim Reaper will no longer frighten us because we will be able to download our consciousness? Will we at last be delivered from our fleshly wrapping? Fascinated by the incredible possibilities of the machine, man wishes he could scrap his body of flesh and blood so as to put on a skin of silicon and steel. What a false liberation!

How can we fail to question political leaders and the powerful, given the enormous risks of biotechnology? It is obvious that it confronts us with a very serious moral dilemma. The specter of eugenics—the plan to bring into the world individuals selected according to certain criteria—still hovers over the entire field of genetics. Will States be able to authorize the sterilization of individuals deemed "imbeciles" while encouraging persons endowed with desirable characteristics to have as many children as possible? The eugenicist policy of the Nazis involved the extermination of entire categories of the population and authorized medical experiments on individuals who were considered genetically inferior and were described as *Untermenschen*, "subhumans"; will the legal arrangements of that policy become the new norm?

I would like to recall the wording of the decree of the European Council on human cloning: "The instrumentalisation of human beings through the deliberate creation of genetically identical human beings is contrary to human dignity and thus constitutes a misuse of biology and medicine."[3] These words are full of clarity and courage. They are the sign that Europe has not completely lost the heritage of wisdom.

The exhilarating fumes of a deep sleep have made us lethargic. We have forgotten the saying in the Book of Revelation: " 'I am the Alpha and the Omega,' says the Lord God, who is and who was and who is to come, the Almighty" (Rev 1:8).

"After me, the deluge", twenty-first century man seems to exclaim. This leap into the void is accompanied by an almost suicidal unwillingness to hand on tradition, is it not?

The notion of heritage is dead. Emptiness is the norm. For the high priests of the new world, culture, values, religion, and tradition

---

[3] Council of Europe, 1998 Convention on Human Rights and Biomedicine: Additional Protocol on the Prohibition of Cloning Human Beings. Cited by Dónal P. O'Mathúna, "Cloning and Stem Cell Research: Wrong Motives on Both Sides of the Atlantic", *Dignity* 6, no. 2 (2000): 3.

cannot be transmitted. They must remain buried in oblivion, and in order to make sure that no one hears any more about them, the tomb will be sealed by abolishing the school curricula.

This unwillingness to hand on tradition results from a death wish. How can we decide not to hand on what the past has given to us? This self-sufficient pride is terrible, oppressive, suffocating. Ever since they made rupture the driving force of modernity, Western societies have been incapable of ensuring and undertaking the transmission of their cultural heritage and of their past experience. To reject all heritage, to make a *tabula rasa* of the past and of the culture that preceded us, to disdain role models and all forms of filiation, to break systematically with the father figure: these modern acts, which bog societies down in the dictatorship of the present, lead to the worst human, political, and even economic catastrophes.

I have the feeling that the history of the Western countries has become a field of ruins. How can anyone transmit something that no longer exists? Will everything disappear? Will Christianity, history, civilization, human beings themselves disappear so as to be replaced by robots?

The younger generations are deprived of a centuries-long heritage that would have helped them to build their lives. A young person who sees a nativity scene scarcely understands the meaning of that display. A young person who sees a painting in a great museum is unable to recognize the major biblical figures. A young person who reads a nineteenth-century novel no longer understands anything about the life and the culture of that time. Without history, without roots, without landmarks, he becomes lost in the marshes of virtual reality. In these circumstances, the past is a *terra incognita* [unknown land] and the present—a tyranny.

Is rupture therefore the driving force of modernity?

Today, in order to appear modern, Westerners think that they are obliged to assume a permanent posture of rupture.

The globalized elites want to create a new world, a new culture, new men, a new ethics. The only things they cannot make are a new sun, a new moon, new mountains, new air, a new world. Rupture is the driving force of their political project. They no longer want to refer to the past. People who continue to identify with the values of the old world have to disappear, whether they like it or not. For the proponents of the new world, those subhumans belong to an inferior race. It is necessary to exclude them and to eliminate them. This desire to break with the past is tragically adolescent. A wise man is aware and proud of being an heir.

With dread I note attitudes that are sometimes similar within the Church. What would a Church be in which those who are attached to the treasures of the Christian tradition and are faithful to the unchangeable teaching of him who "is the same yesterday and today and for ever" (Heb 13:8) were eliminated?

Is our era living in an eternal present?

Living in a present moment that we wish could be endless manifests a rejection of the things of eternity. The present becomes superabundant, and God—invisible. Man seeks more and more to escape into alternate realities. I am struck by all the persons who spend endless time with their mobile telephone, absorbed by images, lights, ghosts. The eternal present is an eternal illusion, a little prison cell. A mobile phone constantly transports us outside of ourselves; it cuts us off from any interior life. It gives us the sense of always traveling across continents, allowing us to be in contact with everybody. In reality, it empties us of our interior life and puts us down in the world of ephemeral things. A mobile phone makes us lose real contact; it projects us toward what is far-off and inaccessible. It gives us the impression of generating space and time, of being gods capable of communicating without being stopped by any obstacle. These insane communication devices steal silence, destroy the richness of solitude, and trample on intimacy. It often happens that they snatch us away from our loving life with God to expose us to the periphery, to what is external to us in the midst of the world.

Nevertheless, the present, too, belongs to God. The Father dwells in all the dimensions of time. God is. If man knows his identity and lives reasonably in the present, he can once again become planted in God.

We pass through time in order to find God more intimately. Time is a long march toward God.

Does the cult of hic et nunc *[here and now] go hand in hand with the rejection of eternity?*

In the modern world, the present has become an idol. Now, in fact, man is born for the hereafter. Eternal life is inscribed within him. The culture of the present instant, therefore, creates a permanent nervous tension. It is necessary somehow or other to get contemporary man out of this dangerous idolatry of immediacy. Man can rediscover peace and true quiet only by placing himself back in God.

The cult of *hic et nunc* is the product of the philosophical crisis and of the cultural crisis of modern times. How can we make others understand that the greatest treasures are not those that we can touch with our hands? Being open to God is an act of faith that no one can quantify.

I think it is necessary to make the Western world understand that excessive attachment to material things is a trap. Our postindustrial materialist civilization is doomed to an imminent death. And the transhumanist civilization would be an ever bigger catastrophe. Humanity has to realize what a material and spiritual dead end it has reached. It does no good to inebriate oneself with little selfish, artificial, fleeting joys. In a conference held in Rio de Janeiro on December 22, 1944, Georges Bernanos rightly declared: "We reach hope only through the truth, at the cost of great efforts. In order to encounter hope, it is necessary to have gone beyond despair. When we go to the very end of the night, we meet another dawn."

Our world will not be able to do without the truth and hope in God. This path of truth will lead us to enormous sufferings. Let us learn to detach ourselves from material goods and from power. Let us be scrupulously attached to God and to his word of life. We will then arrive all together at unity in the faith and at the knowledge of the truth that has a name: Jesus Christ.

8

HATRED, RIDICULE, AND CYNICISM

NICOLAS DIAT: How do you view the various twentieth-century forms of totalitarianism and their posthumous children?

ROBERT CARDINAL SARAH: The past century had the misfortune of experiencing the most horrible political regimes and ideological systems. We know how Communism and Nazism shattered the lives of millions of persons.

In my country, Guinea, we lived for a long time under the Marxist dictatorship of Sékou Touré. Our people experienced the loss of freedom, the extortions of the political police, hunger, and poverty. Arbitrary arrests, deportation to torture camps, and summary trials were part of everyday life. What rivers of tears and blood inundated Guinean families! Not one was spared by the dictatorship and the political and ideological violence.

Totalitarianism spread like wildfire over all the continents. The totalitarian regimes destroyed man, crushed the faith and cultural values, trampled on human freedoms and dignity, whereas their ambition was to change man.

The Nazi regime, in particular, imagined that it would give rise to a flawless race, a master race. Its intention to exterminate the Jewish people, God's chosen people, left a brand mark on the entire history of humanity.

In the twenty-first century, totalitarianism has a more pernicious face. Its name is the idolatry of complete and absolute freedom, which is manifested in its most aggressive forms in gender ideology and transhumanism. Nazism, Fascism, and Communism have terrible successors. We are talking about new ideologies that deny human dignity and promote abortion and euthanasia, but also about Islamist fanaticism, which kills to establish a reign of terror. Some clues allow us to discern the same demonic origins of these movements. We see in them one and the same hatred of man, one and the same destructive pride.

Considering the current historical context, it is urgent for the Church, through the voice of her leaders, to make known to everyone, definitively, the Creator's will concerning man, the family, marriage, the sacredness of and respect for the human person. How many persons of goodwill would join in with such a splendid act of courage by the Church!

The atheistic ideology of the twentieth century intended to detach man from God. The new ideologies now hope to mutilate and control his nature. Man dreamed up his own earthly paradise. It was a bitter failure. Now he wants to change his own human nature.

John Paul II fought with all his might in favor of the fall of Communism. The Church must now protect the weakest persons from the madness of transhumanism and from gender ideology, with which the capitalist and liberal forces seem to be perfectly satisfied.

How would you describe the new attempts to transfigure the world?

In her book *La Haine du monde* [The hatred of the world], Chantal Delsol writes that "we are still living in the demiurgic era, and our demiurges are part of the same sphere of influence as the recent forms of totalitarianism. They inhabit the same process." Their hatred of God has remained the same.

Man, willingly deprived of God, seeks to transform his body. Science and the new technologies are the instruments of this contemporary demiurgic enterprise. Man and nature must bow under the relentless yoke of research. The promise is simple: augmented man will become immortal, his intellectual ability will be unequaled, and his physical forces will be increased tenfold. Genetics is a new god. No one knows in what disaster it will end, and nevertheless we continue on this foolhardy course. Is the catastrophe imminent? The answer of the mad ideologues is invariably simple: it is necessary to carry on with the forced march! We will pay dearly for this senseless process of self-destruction. Augmented man will ultimately be diminished man. This monstrous path will lead to the commercialization of man as a commodity.

The total emancipation of man conceals a programmatic rebellion that aims to show God that we are capable of accomplishing everything without him, by filling in his gaps and correcting his inability to achieve the perfect man. A river that is separated from its source continues to flow for a time. But it will ultimately dry up. A tree deprived of its roots will suffer the same fate. How can the excesses of boundless human pride be checked? How can temperance be regained? The Church knows the bonds between man and his Creator. She knows that a vessel needs its potter, bread—its baker, a house—its builder. A child needs his parents. And man needs God. The Church's word is a light. It reminds us that man has divine roots. The search for independence is an illusion. Without God, his creature is a stone that rolls aimlessly toward the abyss.

Our era seems divided between ridicule and cynicism.

The opposite of ridicule is always found in the sacred. Indeed, ridicule aims to defile, to crush, and to humiliate; it frees itself from all respect. On the contrary, the sacred implies deference and silence. The deification of ridicule inevitably leads to barbarity. On this subject I agree with the analysis that Chantal Delsol provides in her book *La Haine du monde*:

> Using sarcasm and destroying someone's reputation, self-esteem, and soul, so to speak, can prove to be more serious and cruel than using outright violence. For the scars of the soul often leave a deeper mark than the scars of the body. Similarly, trivializing a behavior that was formerly considered seriously wrong makes it possible to rearrange the hierarchy of values more surely than any physical threat.

I am convinced that the battle for civilization involves not using the weapons of evil. We must beware of ridicule. The good advances in silence. Christians and people of goodwill must not enter into a logic of struggle to own the media space. The true battle takes place in our hearts. A conscience that silently respects the Mystery of God and of man effectively thwarts the shouts of the ideologues in the media.

The Church is the only voice defending an authentic humanism. The Church is the last rampart, the only sure defense of man and of his dignity. Some U.N. agencies as well as European institutions, which have considerable financial and technological resources, have launched an aggressive campaign against her teaching. The populations no longer have the wherewithal to reflect. They have been anesthetized, hypnotized, and are now incapable of reacting reasonably. Profit is the only god of the globalized elites, who care nothing about man's future.

Transhumanism aims to create an eternal man. Is this not a utopia that has the great advantage of not showing its true face?

Transhumanism feeds into the mad plan to accelerate evolution by pushing back the limits of the human being and by creating new forms of life. It encourages genetic research that, in the near future, is supposed to make possible the birth of a hybrid man–machine. Scientists who promote transhumanism attempt to achieve what is, with no doubt whatsoever, the oldest dream of humanity, maliciously instilled in Adam and Eve by Satan. In the Bible, the serpent in fact reassures the woman in these terms: "You will not die. For God knows that when you eat of it your eyes will be opened, and you will be like God, knowing good and evil" (Gen 3:4–5).

The project to augment the human being is therefore not a new one. Because it confronts him with the unknown, because it destroys his very being, the Grim Reaper has always frightened man. Transhumanism intends to remedy death by postponing the age of the great journey toward eternity and by abolishing it. Now the heralds of transhumanism are proclaiming the death of death. Man will no longer die of death. He will be eternal.

In *La Haine du monde*, Chantal Delsol describes this somber future:

Because of individual freedom, they tell us, there are bound to be different human statuses—in the mid-twenty-first century, a people of immortal cyborgs will be mixed in with traditional human beings who are rather like the Amish. In other words: the task of incessant renewal, the vocation to create something new constantly, linked with the acceptance of death, will devolve upon a group of volunteers who remain mortal. The latter will save the heart of the world. For the immortal human beings will not have children: zero birthrate, zero mortality is the program for the society of the immortals, as in the novel *Globalia* by Christophe Ruffin. Silicon Valley's program for immortality forgets that nature is a perpetual renewal, which expresses the perpetual youth of the world, fresh beginnings, the indefinite succession of dawns—nothing else. And it is at the same time—these two things are connected—the diversity that constantly starts over from individual beings, who are ever new. There is no diversity, no singularity, no hope, unless death is accepted.

And she correctly concludes: "What Hannah Arendt calls *superfluous man*, with neither futility nor meaning because he is uprooted, in the sense of deprived of bonds and relations—that is the heart and the center of the revolutionary utopias, which is at the same time the heart and the center of the contemporary period."

This movement takes for granted a philosophy of constant evolution, According to this philosophy, the intellect is not a spiritual faculty at all, but the result of the development of matter over the course of history. Hence, there is no need whatsoever to question the pertinence—much less the morality—of modifying the genome, inserting electronic fleas into the body, or joining intelligent prostheses to it. Since he possesses the power and the technology, man must become the master of evolution and contribute to the coming of a post-humanity into the world.

There is a major paradox here, because this outlines a sort of new nostalgia for paradise lost. Fatigue, sickness, and death did not exist before original sin. But our hope is neither in man nor in science. It is in God. For Christians, the soul survives the earthly passing away of the body. According to God's plan, we will one day regain this bodily wrapping. The resurrection or eternal life is the work of the Father, and not of man. I observe, however, that the Church no longer devotes homilies to the soul, eternity, and the last things. Priests are afraid of provoking mockery. During funeral ceremonies, the suppression of the *Dies irae* is symbolic of this false modesty.

We should be joyous and full of hope. Man seeks eternity by the paths of science. But God alone will give it to us. A time will come when we will live with him eternally.

In the postmodern world, eternity becomes a commercial affair. In the best of worlds, charity will disappear inasmuch as the whole world will be strong and eternal. A hell on earth.

The Church does not have the right to be mediocre. If she refuses to denounce the Promethean dreams of this era, she will fail seriously in her divine mission. If she proposes nothing to remedy the transhumanist excesses, she will betray Christ. If she adapts to the spirit of the age, she will turn away from God. This is a considerable danger. What the utopias of the twentieth century did not accomplish, the postmodern, godless West will attempt to do.

In this context, how can we return to wisdom? It is necessary to listen to God. To accept our finitude. Through the Incarnation, Christ teaches us that the way of happiness is not the negation of our creaturely state. On the contrary, he came to take on our flesh. He shows us the way. He is the perfect man. Now, he did not decide to free himself from any limit of our human condition. No component of our humanity is foreign to him. Even suffering can be experienced in love after his example. To alleviate suffering is a work of charity; to deny it is an illusion. Christ shows us that death itself can open onto eternal life if we accept it. The transhumanist ideology is inspired by the unfortunate temptation to ape the resurrection. Only God-made-man can conquer death. And by passing through it by love, he conquered it definitively. By his death, he conquered death. He offers us his life, which is the only eternal life.

9

EUROPE'S CRISIS

NICOLAS DIAT: In this chapter, the great book by Joseph Ratzinger, Europe Today and Tomorrow: Addressing the Fundamental Issues, *which was published in 2005, will be the thread of our reflection. One year before his election to the throne of Peter, the cardinal wrote:*

> We notice a self-hatred in the Western world that is strange and that can be considered pathological; yes, the West is making a praiseworthy attempt to be completely open to understanding foreign values, but it no longer loves itself; from now on it sees in its own history only what is blameworthy and destructive, whereas it is no longer capable of perceiving what is great and pure. In order to survive, Europe needs a new ... acceptance of itself, that is, if it wants to survive.[1]

How could anyone not be struck by the prophetic aspect of Ratzinger's words?

ROBERT CARDINAL SARAH: With the passing years, and despite its economic development, the problem of Europe is becoming increasingly serious. The scientific and technological advances, the abundance of material goods, and the dissolving of all proper identity have blinded Europe, unbalanced it, made it proud, a-religious, and atheistic. Any man who denies his roots and no longer recognizes his own being is either denying himself or is afflicted with amnesia; the same goes for organizations. Europe seems to be programmed to self-destruct. The only vision that it has of the future is on the economic and military levels. Its Judeo-Christian roots have been forgotten. The West seems to hate itself and to be ready to commit suicide.

---

[1] Joseph Ratzinger/Pope Benedict XVI, *Europe: Today and Tomorrow: Addressing the Fundamental Issues*, trans. Michael J. Miller (San Francisco: Ignatius Press, 2007), 33.

Europe wants to be open to all the cultures—which may be praise-worthy and a source of richness—and to all the religions of the world, but it no longer loves itself. Just look at the younger generations and their poor knowledge of their own mother tongue.

Europe has lost its nobility. Ugliness is invading all sectors of society. Pretentiousness and pride are serious evils. The search for truth no longer exists. Evil and good are confused. A liar is no longer ashamed of himself; in a way he proudly shows off. Words are transformed into instruments of economic and financial war. People live in confusion. New words are created, but above all one must not give them a precise definition. People no longer know what a man or a woman is. Sex is no longer an objective reality. The family, marriage, and the human person have been redefined ceaselessly.

The picture that you paint is terrible. Could Europe be dead already?

I think it is on its last legs. A process of self-destruction is always reversible. But time is short. For several years, the decline has been accelerating. All civilizations that ignore the eminent dignity of the human person have vanished. Today, as at the time of the Roman Empire, Europe manipulates, commercializes, and toys with human life, thus creating the conditions for its own extinction.

The rejection of life, the murder of pre-born children, the murder of the handicapped and the elderly, the demolition of the family and of moral and spiritual values: all this is the first act in the tragedy of the suicide of an entire people. We are helpless spectators at the decline of a civilization. Europe's nosedive is unique in the history of humanity.

However, I must add that in Europe, alongside the institutions that seem suicidal and decadent, there are true seeds of renewal. I have met many generous families that are deeply rooted in their Christian faith. I have also seen fine religious communities that are faithful and fervent. They remind me of the Christians who, in the twilight years of the Roman Empire, kept watch over the flickering flame of civilization. I want to encourage them. I want to tell them: Your mission is not to save a dying world. No civilization has the promises of eternal life. Your mission is to live out with fidelity and without compromise the faith you received from Christ. In that way, even without realizing it, you will save the heritage of many centuries of faith. Do not be afraid because of your small numbers! It is not a matter of winning elections or influencing opinions. It is a matter of living the Gospel. Not thinking of it as a utopia, but experiencing it concretely. Faith is like a fire. A person himself must be on fire in order to be able to transmit it. Watch over this sacred fire! May it be your heat in the depths of the winter of the West. When a fire illumines the night, people gradually gather around it. That must be your hope.

In the same book, Europe Today and Tomorrow, *Joseph Ratzinger wrote: "Europe, precisely in this hour of its greatest success, seems to have become hollowed out, paralyzed in a certain sense by a crisis of its circulatory system, a crisis that endangers its life, which depends, so to speak, on transplants, which then, however, cannot help undermining its identity. This interior dwindling of the spiritual strength that once supported it is accompanied by the fact that Europe appears to be on the way out ethnically as well."[2] This severe observation seems to agree with your own analyses.*

In speaking about transplants, Cardinal Ratzinger is already mentioning migratory trends. Very soon, we know, there will be in Europe a singularly dangerous imbalance on the demographic, cultural, and religious levels. Europe is sterile; it is not replacing itself, for lack of a sufficiently high birthrate. Its house is filling up with foreigners because it is "empty, swept, and put in order" (Mt 12:44). It got rid of its historical and Christian treasures.

It seems that the European technostructures[3] are delighted about the migratory flows or encourage them. They reason only in economic terms. They need workers who can be paid little. They ignore the identity and the culture of every people. Just look at their overt contempt for the Polish government. Liberal ideology takes precedence over any other approach. As at Bethlehem, God is the only poor person for whom there is no room at the inn.

Europe claims to fight against all forms of discrimination based on race and religious affiliation. In this area, real progress has been

---

[2] Ibid., 23–24.
[3] Groups of technology experts who exert control over industry or government.—TRANS.

made. But some have taken advantage of it in order to impose a utopian spirit. The disappearance of fatherlands and the colonization of cultures could not be a form of progress. The European multiculturalist enterprise exploits an ideal of universal charity that is misunderstood. Charity is not a denial of self. It consists of offering to the other the best that one has and what one is. Now the best thing that Europe has to offer to the world is its identity, its civilization, which is profoundly imbued with Christianity. But what has it offered to the Muslim newcomers except irreligion and barbaric consumerism? How can anyone be surprised when the latter take refuge in Islamist fundamentalism? Europeans ought to be proud of their morals and customs that are inspired by the Gospel. The most precious gift that Europe could give to the immigrants living on its soil is not primarily financial aid, much less an individualist, secularized way of life, but rather a share in its Christian roots. The essential condition for wel coming the other person is: coming to terms with what one is. Given the danger of radical Islamism, Europe ought to be able to articulate firmly on what conditions one can share its life and its civilization. But it doubts itself and is ashamed of its Christian identity. So it ends up reaping contempt.

Joseph Ratzinger added: "Multiculturalism, which is continually and passionately encouraged and promoted, is sometimes little more than the abandonment and denial of what is one's own, flight from one's own heritage. But multiculturalism cannot exist without shared constants, without points of reference based on one's own values. It surely cannot exist without respect for what is sacred."[4]

Many flowers make up a garden, and each variety adds to its wealth. All the species are beautiful and different. The colors, the shades, and the perfumes combine to form a paradise. If the flowers were all alike, the beauty would be gone. True beauty is sacred. Cardinal Ratzinger was right to reflect that "for the cultures of the world, the absolute secularity that has been taking shape in the West is something profoundly foreign. They are convinced that a world without God has no future. And so multiculturalism itself calls us to come to

[4] Ratzinger, *Europe*, 33.

our senses and to look deep within ourselves again."[5] I believe that if migrants who arrive in Europe end up having contempt for it, this is basically because they find nothing sacred in it.

In Africa and in Asia, nothing is profane. Everything is sacred. Everything is connected to God and depends on him. Everything reaches its fullness in God. The smallest reality is connected to God. It is inseparable from its origin. A profane culture is an unexplored, contemptible country, "a waterless spring" (cf. 2 Pet 2:17). African man cannot understand a world without God. The river would no longer have sources, and the houses would be without foundations. A world without God and without morality is like a stillborn infant. The Sea of Galilee cannot exist without its source in the Jordan River. A world without God and without moral and religious values is a deadly illusion. Technological advances try to anesthetize man in an ever deeper sleep. The Egyptian and Roman civilizations disappeared in spite of their prowess and impressive accomplishments. Man without God rocks himself to sleep with the illusion of being immortal.

Cardinal Ratzinger knew that there are pathologies of religion, but he was still convinced that the pathology of reason totally detached from God is much more dangerous.

Indifference toward God is a serious pathology, because it leads to man's celebration of himself. There is a terrible arrogance in this crisis of faith. As we read the Sacred Scriptures, it is striking to note among our contemporaries the fundamental error of judgment whereby people seem to attach a lot of importance to things that have none. They give priority, for example, to the phantoms of money, material wealth, or political power. On the other hand, God, who ought to be the treasure and the source of all human flourishing, finds in the heart of man nothing but indifference and contempt. Man thinks he does not need God in order to take his own destiny in hand, to achieve fulfillment by himself, and to build today's world and tomorrow's.

In all things, God takes the initiative, accompanies us, supports us, and achieves our authentic humanity and our happiness.

---

[5] Ibid., 34.

Unfortunately, man does not want to acknowledge his errors. He is content with what he achieves without God. He is content with his decadence. He is content with chaos. He will soon be content with being replaced by robots or by transhumans. I say this trembling with fright.

Isn't the best guarantee of our freedom the fact that there are values that no one can distort?

Fundamental values govern the life of societies; this is a decisive fact. Relativism feeds on the negation of values in order to establish its deleterious influence. In a relativist regime, everything can be manipulated, including human life. Thus freedom is extinguished. But the authentic values will never die.

The Western project consists of detaching man from God so as to make him autonomous. This enterprise may seem triumphant, but it will be a failure. We cannot live out our humanity fully while being detached from our origins. What is good and beautiful, truth, love, and happiness, come from God. Without him, man is afraid of happiness. The call of happiness becomes more difficult than death. For many of our contemporaries, happiness comes from mere consumption and from an absolute freedom that nothing hampers in its expression, with each person following his own desires, inclinations, and appetites. This materialist enjoyment is an agony. Instinct, pleasure, and desire are the only masters of these disillusioned lives. What an almost bestial vulgarity! But man will always remain a divine creature. True freedom lies in the battle to agree with the Father's will and to correspond to it. Alexander Solzhenitsyn and all the prisoners in the Soviet gulags knew the cost of this path. They knew that God would always have the last word. However much one may deny it, God will always be God; he dwells in the midst of us, because he is the one who fully realizes us. All the believers in my country who suffered under the Marxist dictatorship of Sékou Touré can talk about freedom. And, always, they will affirm that freedom is absolutely connected to truth. In Africa they say that freedom and truth are like oil: you may try your best to drown them or to destroy them, but like oil they will always stay at the surface.

The freedom of the Western world is at the lowest possible point. But one day it could be restored. Unless men and their leaders stubbornly persist in their error. The coalition of the forces of evil who disguise themselves in the finery of purity seems to be prevailing. For nothing is impossible for God.[6]

Another remark by Cardinal Ratzinger is strikingly relevant to our age: "If the nations of the Western world were to commit themselves entirely to this path [of laicism], they would be unable in the long run to resist the pressure of ideologies and political theocracies."[7]

This statement is a prophecy. Cardinal Ratzinger speaks about pressures and theocracies; it is not a complicated problem to understand where they are today. Relativist liberalism and radical Islamism threaten many Western States. The theocracies have convictions rooted in a history that gives them an unfailingly combative power. Materialism and hedonism are infinitely fragile in comparison to those systems. The West no longer has any interior energy whatsoever; how will it defend itself against the attacks made by such terrible resolves to dominate and conquer? The West's only strength lies in a ferocious desire to self-destruct. Its exaltation of an imaginary strength is sometimes reminiscent of the last moments of the Soviet Union. We are helplessly witnessing the passage from a human age to a bestial age. Two kinds of barbarism are confronting each other: a materialist barbarism and another Islamist one. I fear that the second one will have the last word. This reminds me of the very strong words spoken by Cardinal Ratzinger during a conference that he gave in July 1987:

> In the name of an ambiguity between pluralism and religious liberty, they have completely separated the Christian fact from the requirement to shape the public order. The idea of a State that is completely neutral with regard to values, a State that keeps its distance from any religious and moral order is absurd. Bultmann himself said that although a non-Christian State is conceivable, an atheist State is not. I think that it is very important to remind consciences of the political

---

[6] Cited in *Ser cristiano en la era neopagana* (Madrid: Edicion Encuentro, 2008), 98.
[7] Ibid., 99.

and social dimension of Christianity, its unalterable character as a public fact.

The European crisis is essentially a spiritual crisis rooted in the rejection of God's presence in public life.

Cardinal Ratzinger's conclusion seems to describe a candle that is about to flicker out: "The State itself renounced any religious basis and claimed to be founded solely on reason and on its own intuitions. When confronted with the frailty of reason, these systems have proved to be fragile and have easily fallen victim to dictatorships; they survive, actually, only because parts of the old moral consciousness continue to exist, even without the previous social foundations, making possible a basic moral consensus."[8]

In the West, does an invisible, fragile Christian regime that has run out of steam still hold in its ancient hands the nations that it created? Possibly. But a State that would reject all moral norms is doomed sooner or later to destruction. Saint Paul tells us clearly that true authority comes from God. The powerful media use every means to try to break up the remnants of Christianity. The media system, the one genuine thought police, runs from one battle to the next in its campaign to transform man.

Unless Europe pays special attention to this warning, it will disappear. Its break with God will lead to an anthropological revolution without precedent in the history of humanity. In order to conclude this reflection, I would like to quote some brilliant remarks taken from the speech given by Cardinal Ratzinger at the Academy of Moral and Political Sciences on November 6, 1992, made beneath the dome of the Institut de France:

> Let us return to the question of how we can restore wholesome respect for high moral standards and rights to our societies and defend the right and the good against naïveté and cynicism, without a similar force of right being imposed or even arbitrarily defined by external coercion. In this regard, Alexis de Tocqueville's analysis of *Democracy in America* has always made a strong impression on me. For this structure, which

[8] Ibid., 26.

in itself is fragile, to retain its cohesion and make possible an order of liberties in freedom lived in community, the great political thinker saw as an essential condition the fact that a basic moral conviction was alive in America, one which, nourished by Protestant Christianity, supplied the foundations for institutions and democratic mechanisms.

In fact, institutions cannot maintain themselves and be effective without common ethical convictions. These in turn cannot come from a purely empirical reason. The decisions of the majority will themselves remain truly human and logical only if they presuppose the existence of a basic humanitarian sense and respect this as the true common good, the condition of all other goods. Such convictions require corresponding human attitudes, and these in turn cannot be developed unless the historical foundation of a culture and the ethical, religious judgments it contains are taken into consideration. For a culture and a nation to cut themselves off from the great ethical and religious forces of their history amounts to committing suicide. Cultivating the essential moral judgments, and maintaining and protecting them without imposing them by force, seems to me to be a condition for the survival of freedom in the face of all the forms of nihilism and their totalitarian consequences.

Finally, I am worried about the consequences of the annihilation of Christian Europe for all the other parts of the world. The missionaries from the Old Continent for a long time brought the Gospel message and the teaching of Christian values to Africa or to Asia. They enabled entire populations to leave their old pagan religions so as to find Christ. I am a product of that history. God gave a particular responsibility to Europe. For long centuries, it responded generously to that calling. Its new, fanatical egotism will inevitably have consequences. Yet I want to continue to believe in Europe even though I am aware that the illness seems incurable. The tragic thing about the Old Continent is not that it does not know the meaning of its mission but that it is less and less disturbed by not having one. Human civilization is at stake, and European man does not care. He is dancing on the edge of a volcano. And yet, some countries are waking up, little by little. Their voices carry. I am thinking of Poland, Slovakia, Austria, Italy, and Hungary. So let us hope!

10

THE ERRORS OF THE WEST

NICOLAS DIAT: *In our first book,* God or Nothing, *you established a connection between Enlightenment ideology and irreligious humanism. Could you return to that reflection?*

ROBERT CARDINAL SARAH: In his famous speech given at Harvard in 1978, Aleksandr Solzhenitsyn spoke with an honesty and candor that did not fail to surprise some Westerners who were already accustomed to "politically correct" language:

> But should someone ask me whether I would indicate the West such as it is today as a model to my country, frankly I would have to answer negatively. No, I could not recommend your society in its present state as an ideal for the transformation of ours. Through intense suffering our country has now achieved a spiritual development of such intensity that the Western system in its present state of spiritual exhaustion does not look attractive.[1]

When man assigns importance to his own reason alone, to material goods, and God disappears in the great roar of ideologies, is it any surprise that the West is going through an unprecedented crisis? The underlying characteristic of the Enlightenment ideology is to affirm that reason, in order to be reason, must cut itself off from all divine light. The Enlightenment ideology tried to exile God as far as possible from our earth. During the French Revolution, the cult of the Supreme Being perfectly expressed this momentous childishness. Man's pretentiousness and rebellion always end up turning against

---

[1] Aleksandr Solzhenitsyn, "A World Split Apart", Commencement Address, Harvard University, June 8, 1978, available at https://www.solzhenitsyncenter.org/a-world-split-apart/.

him. No civilization has ever professed atheism and irreligion to this extent. No civilization ever believed to this extent that reason alone was sufficient in order to get ahead in life.

Why should humanism inevitably be irreligious? On the contrary, the desire to care for man ought to lead the West to draw closer to God. I profoundly believe that reason finds its fulfillment only by being open to the light of faith.

Do you think there is a sort of artificial supremacy of law over morality?

Atheist civilizations inevitably lose the metaphysical sense. Transcendent realities are foreign to them. Man now thinks that he is sufficiently powerful to take his destiny in hand by himself.

Modern man wants nothing more to do with his Creator. And so he tramples the moral laws little by little, only to replace them with so-called democratic rules of law. The most rudimentary desires become the measure of everything. The majority, often represented by the parliamentary power of the States and manipulated by the powerful media, little by little rewrites the moral norm.

In this wayward development, individual freedom is the only criterion, and personal satisfaction—the only objective. Everyone can do what he wants. The moral law is detested. The media high priests burn incense to impulses. If a man wants to put an end to his life, he can. If a man wants to become a woman, he can. If a girl wants to prostitute herself on the Internet, she can. If an adolescent wants to look at pornography on the Internet, he can. If a woman wants to abort her child, she can. It is their right. Everything is possible.

This picture may appear to be a caricature. And yet this is the reality. We have entered into a civilization of the chaos of desires. And the deeper we sink into the chaos, the more obvious it becomes that when the primitive pleasures dry up, man prefers to have done with life. He prefers nothingness. There is no hope outside of this world. Man no longer looks to heaven. He struggles in his frustrations. Westerners have become the largest consumers of antidepressants. The offices of psychologists and other practitioners are always packed. Suicide among adolescents has become an ongoing phenomenon.

In Africa, suicide is almost nonexistent. In traditional societies, it does not exist. A human being is fully integrated in a small community.

He respects the laws of nature and of his people's customs. God remains the foundation of his life. He aspires to the hereafter following his brief stay on earth. If death comes, he accepts it as a path that leads us from this earth to the fatherland where our ancestors await us.

On my continent, all the men and women of the same tribe support one another. No one is marginalized. In the evening, each one speaks. Money has no vital meaning. Only human relations and the relation with God have genuine importance. The poor are happy; they are so happy and alive that they dance.

In the West, the new "rights" are actively supported by the powerful media and financial interests. The latter influence the populations and make them feel guilty. In order to popularize euthanasia, they incessantly cook up messages to overturn so-called "public opinion". When the communications media have done their work, the polling institutes come to explain in learned terms that the majority has changed ... The time is therefore ripe. A world of lies, conditioning, and manipulation is shamelessly set up. A world of slaves. The techniques of mental manipulation are of a rare subtlety. Evil becomes good through a grand magic trick.

If the Church does not denounce the illusion that these new "rights" bring, chaos will ensue. And it will lead the world into darkness. Paul VI showed this prophetic courage with his encyclical letter *Humanae vitae* on marriage and the regulation of births. John Paul II constantly spoke about the ravages of the culture of death. Benedict XVI called Europe to rediscover its Christian roots. And, today, Francis rejects the economic exploitation of man by man. The recent popes have not been followed by the governments of the West. The evil has worsened. But we must not throw up our hands.

John Paul II regularly denounced the ideal of freedom that degenerates into license and unbridled passions. What is your point of view on this subject?

There is a dictatorship of unbridled freedom. Aleksandr Solzhenitsyn understood very quickly that the West no longer knew the true meaning of freedom. In his speech at Harvard, he declared: "Such a tilt of freedom in the direction of evil has come about gradually, but it was evidently born primarily out of a humanistic and benevolent concept according to which there is no evil inherent to human nature;

the world belongs to mankind and all the defects of life are caused by wrong social systems which must be corrected."[2] Solzhenitsyn offers an objective critique of the Western idolatry of liberty. His reflection on liberty as it is experienced in the West deserves our attention.

The former prisoner of the gulag had made a very poignant appeal to the free peoples in the name of the oppressed peoples. He meant to point out the root of the evil. In *The Error of the West*, he wrote:

> The Western World has arrived at a decisive moment. Over the next few years, it will gamble the existence of the civilization that created it. I think that it is not aware of it. Time has eroded your notion of liberty. You have kept the word and devised a different notion. You have forgotten the meaning of liberty. When Europe acquired it, around the eighteenth century, it was a sacred notion. Liberty led to virtue and heroism. You have forgotten that. This liberty, which for us is still a flame that lights up our night, has become for you a stunted, sometimes disappointing reality, because it is full of imitation jewelry, wealth, and emptiness. For this ghost of the former liberty, you are no longer capable of making sacrifices but only compromises.... You have the impression that democracies can last. But you know nothing about it. Interior will is more important than policy. If the leaders of the East felt that there was the slightest flame in you, the slightest drive to make freedom survive on your side and spread, if they understood that you were ready to sacrifice your life, then at that very second they would give up. The battle now unfolding is not between them and you but between you and yourselves. Deep down, you think that liberty is won once and for all, and this is why you can afford the luxury of disdaining it. You are engaged in a formidable battle, and you behave as though it were a ping pong match. Now you are probably still holding the trump cards. But only if your will to play them breaks through your attitudes and no one doubts your resolve.[3]

That man suffered for years and years in the Soviet gulags. He weighs the price of true liberty, sound liberty. In these times of moral degradation and general resignation, he invites us to spiritual resistance and to an effort to discern what is at stake in liberty. How can we silence this forceful, severe challenge to the declining West?

---

[2] Ibid.
[3] Aleksandr Solzhenitsyn, *L'Erreur de l'Occident* (Paris, Grasset, 1980), a text quoted by Léon Arthur Elchinger in *Je plaide pour l'homme* (Paris: Fayard, 1976), 171–72.

The word *liberty* remains, but its profound meaning no longer exists. It has become an empty shell. Men confuse liberty and libertinage. Is liberty not the daughter of truth, which leads her to do good and to seek beauty? Or is she only a means of finding what is agreeable? Western liberty is a shadow play.

Genuine liberty is a conquest, a concrete struggle that demands overcoming oneself by discipline and effort. It requires, first of all, self-mastery and the discernment of one's own weaknesses and qualities. Liberty is a flame that lights up. It is the opposite of a blind feeling that draws us toward our abysmal passions.

Only those who have experienced the loss of liberty can understand its genuine meaning. They know its profundity.

Today liberty is an advertising slogan. It is bought and sold at the mercy of stock market fluctuations. I fear that Western parliamentary majorities are manufactured simply with money, rhetorical toppings, media theatrics, rigged electoral systems, gerrymandered districts, and a thousand different pressures or subterfuges. Western culture, which ought to bring liberty to the world, no longer knows the meaning of it.

The Church must speak about Christ the liberator. He comes to break the chains of evil and sin. God gives liberty. If the Church stops teaching about the liberty intended by God, she seriously fails at her mission. Man is not naturally good. Original sin exists. Liberty is achieved through detachment from that sin. God alone can help us. The Church must repeat this truth incessantly.

We sometimes get the impression that the rights of the individual are trampling on those of society.

We have forgotten that the common good is the most profound and intimate good of human persons. In an orchestra, the greatest good of each instrumentalist is basically the symphony that is played by them all. In a family, the common happiness is the primary good of each member. Today we prefer to pit society and the individual against each other. Now society must not victimize the individual. Economic policies too often leave men at the side of the road, deprived of everything, badly beaten, and half dead. I am horribly shocked to see the distress in which poor farming families are abandoned. This silent scandal is unspeakable.

But it is also true that personal flourishing must not harm the collective lot. In hedonistic Western societies, the primacy of the individual's pleasure tends to harm the proper running of societies. Individual choices and tendencies can pollute society and destabilize its foundations. A form of dictatorship of personal fulfillment prevails.

Individualism is a ruin. It worries me to note that European leaders themselves show signs of blatant individualism. For example, many have not been willing to start a family and have no children. In these circumstances, how can an ambitious family policy be promoted? How can the desire for children and love for them be cultivated at the heart of families?

The power of the media is regularly called into question. Nevertheless, they play a major role within our societies.

The media have a formidable power to seduce, to condition, to recruit, and to exert psychological pressure. Young people are easy prey. Given the chaotic diversity of the images that march past, they are often at a loss. They think that they are easily acquiring a sort of new liberty. In reality, they are enslaved, fettered, and disoriented, incapable of asking themselves the essential questions about life. They lack the wisdom, discernment, experience, and education to confront maturely everything that the media propose to them. They are exposed to an incessant flow of information that breaks into their virginal innocence.

I note with sorrow that some priests have fallen into the crude snares of the powerful media. They have become dependent on these forms of communication. Some seminarians, too, fall into these traps. Instead of building for themselves little by little an interior cloister that will allow them to be ever more intimately in the presence of God, they waste precious time that ought to be devoted to silence, prayer, and meditative reading of the Word of God. Television, the Internet, and many other communication technologies monopolize the time that is meant for God.

At the Vatican, in Saint Peter's Basilica, the media and televisions have invaded the pope's solemn Eucharistic celebrations. The ceremonies are treated like spectacles. We are witnessing a process of incredible desacralization. I am not unaware of the fact that, in front of their screens, some sick and elderly persons can nourish their faith in this way. But one cannot find God by watching a television program. God is a Real Presence hidden in the tabernacle. An image will never replace an intimate encounter. The Father accepts no imaginary intermediary in order to make a soul grow. We deceive ourselves when we pretend to believe that we have encountered God and taken part in the Eucharistic Sacrifice by watching a televised broadcast. No one can claim to have been at his mother's funeral by watching the film of the ceremony of her funeral Mass. It would distort our relations with God if we subjugated them to technological mediations. No truly intimate and personal human relationship can be formed through a mechanical intermediary. No machine, no technology, no robot can replace a man in his relation to God.

The media are no strangers to our loss of the sense of prayer and contemplation. They are the thieves of the sacred fire. The life of our soul has no importance to them. I would like to repeat here a message that I have already addressed to priests: Do not pray the Divine Office with your mobile phone. You cannot manipulate a machine on which there are all sorts of apps and pray at the same time. In the Eucharistic liturgy, there is a missal for Mass; in the same way, love the sacred book that is your breviary, because the Divine Office is an authentic liturgy.

The media are the main opponents of silence. Without silence, reason itself cannot flourish. I think we ought to inaugurate a great media fast during Lent. Christians should set the example of complete abstinence from the screen for forty days. Such a practice would have real consequences for our relations not only with God but also with each other. It is truly a matter of civilization. But are we capable of it? I pose the question to all my Christian readers: Will you dare to break your digital chains for at least forty days per year? That would be a prophetic stance!

Pius XI and his successor, Pius XII, expected much from the media as ways of increasing the possibilities for evangelization. The Vatican was a pioneer with Vatican Radio. There were high hopes then. Nevertheless, despite the implementation of these new communication technologies, evangelization has never been so weak. This is because evangelization is not a form of communication. It is primarily a witness. It is done with a body, with weariness and suffering. Christ's sacrifices are our model. Evangelization is a new incarnation of the Word of God.

Would I have left my little Guinean village if I had not had the chance to meet a missionary who was enthralled by Christ, consumed by the desire to die for him, filled with zeal to proclaim the Gospel? I was touched by the example of the prayer of the missionaries in our little church. I did not hear them on the radio. I saw Father Marcel Bracquemond and his confreres, Fathers André Mettan, André Besnir, and Daniel Denoual, in the half-light of the choir. Prayer is the foundation of evangelization.

We urgently need to rediscover the meaning of authentic Christian asceticism. Moreover, it takes great humility to make good use of the media. This quality is necessary for journalists.

Recently I was glad to read an interview with Bishop Batut of Blois, in which he explained that "the liturgy is not a show." The journalist asked him where to begin when initiating young people to the mystery of the Christian liturgy. I agree completely with the answer he gave him:

> It is necessary to get them out of their tablets and smart phones, get them out of their inability to experience silence.... Silence is the hardest thing for them, but also the most fruitful. Young people are capable of understanding that the important thing is not whether or not they are bored at Mass but going to Mass. We have to get them beyond the emotional side that often is 99 percent of their motivation. The most important thing is not to give them explanations about the liturgy, but to have them experience it! How many times have I seen young people in tears during beautiful liturgies? They were weeping because they were discovering a transformative newness. They were experiencing God.[4]

Certainly it is necessary to get young people out of their tablets and smart phones so as to experience God. I recommend extending this example to all priests.

---

[4] Samuel Pruvot, "Mgr Batut: 'La liturgie n'est pas un show'", *Famille chrétienne*, no. 2109 (June 16, 2018).

The accumulation of goods is certainly not an insignificant factor in the long siesta of the West.

God wants man to be happy on this earth. Earthly life is a prelude to eternal happiness. Therefore, it is not a matter of being opposed to the improvement of living conditions.

But nowadays, there is a reversal of priorities. Consumption has become an end in itself. Capitalist materialism has triumphed over Marxist materialism. The two are twin brothers. They cause the spiritual dimension of men to atrophy, so that they become enslaved consumers. Now it is necessary to replace the primacy of matter with the primacy of the spirit.

The more a man settles down and revels in material things, the more he tends to move away from God. Christ himself says: "Truly, I say to you, it will be hard for a rich man to enter the kingdom of heaven. Again I tell you, it is easier for a camel to go through the eye of a needle than for a rich man to enter the kingdom of God" (Mt 19:23–24).

Going against the grain of this soft life, monks voluntarily choose poverty so as to draw closer to God. Their ascetical practices allow them to develop an extraordinary cultural life. They adopt as their own the words of Deuteronomy:

> And you shall remember all the way which the LORD your God has led you these forty years in the wilderness, that he might humble you, testing you to know what was in your heart, whether you would keep his commandments, or not. And he humbled you and let you hunger and fed you with manna, which you did not know, nor did your fathers know; that he might make you know that man does not live by bread alone, but that man lives by everything that proceeds out of the mouth of the LORD. Your clothing did not wear out upon you, and your foot did not swell, these forty years. Know then in your heart that, as a man disciplines his son, the LORD your God disciplines you. So you shall keep the commandments of the LORD your God, by walking in his ways and by fearing him. (Deut 8:2–6)

The great saints Benedict of Nursia, Bruno of Cologne, and Francis of Assisi chose poverty so as to nourish their spiritual life better. They founded centers of extraordinary spiritual and cultural life.

Often the Virgin Mary has appeared to poor children. In Lourdes or in Fatima, the little shepherds who saw her possessed nothing. They were singled out by the Mother of Christ. God loves hearts that are poor, simple, meek, and burning with love. The pure heart is the most beautiful temple of God.

Faith and poverty are half-sisters. Comfort often leads to arrogance and selfishness.

Are the search for comfort and the obsession with material things contrary to the life of the soul?

Modern man takes care of his body and completely neglects his soul. He talks all day about the growth of the economy, about money, production, well-being, working conditions, and summer vacations. But he no longer knows God.

It is not a matter of being against comfort. There are immensely rich persons who have not lost their spiritual dimension—who, like Job, keep the faith while putting God at the center of their lives and their activities.

However, there is a modern obsession with money and luxury. Acquisition seems to be synonymous with happiness. This snare becomes a form of slavery, bringing jealousy and hatred along with it. Advertising perpetually keeps this illusory quest alive. It profoundly pollutes relations between men. How can people accept the fact that it is posted everywhere, on the smallest free wall of our cities and rural areas? Abolishing or at least reducing it is a public health issue. I know that some cities in Brazil have already had the courage to forbid it in the public space. This is a prophetic, courageous stance. Christians should unite with people of goodwill to drive out of our cities this invasion of ugliness and vulgarity. Maybe then we will rediscover a taste for works of art, which offer the comfort of beauty to everyone at no cost!

When this obsession with consumption and comfort makes its way into the Church, it leads to the betrayal of promises that have been made to Christ. The God whom we follow is poor and humble. Priests and bishops are influenced too much by secular mentalities. They should beware of falling into muddy ditches. The best remedy for it is to go off to the monasteries regularly. These enclaves are often the only way to find the path of the Gospel again. The voluntary poverty of the monks, their silence, their immersion in God, and their discretion are the models that can rebuild our lives and reorient them more toward God and his Church.

Are you acquainted with many contemporary priests who are willing to go off to proclaim Christ in the most remote regions, at the risk of their lives, like the missionaries of the past? Material comfort leads to a worldly, bourgeois bureaucratization of the clergy.

What do you think about the relations between the West, Russia, and Orthodoxy?

John Paul II was convinced that the two lungs of Europe had to work together. Today, Western Europe is employing extraordinary means to isolate Russia. Why persist in ridiculing that great country? The West is displaying unheard-of arrogance. The spiritual and cultural heritage of the Russian Orthodox Church is unequaled. The reawakening of faith that followed the fall of Communism is an immense hope. It is the fruit of the blood of martyrs. The testimony given by Aleksandr Solzhenitsyn in an article published by *Le Figaro* in 1985 is impressive:

> The world had never before known a godlessness as organized, militarized, and tenaciously malevolent as that practiced by Marxism. Within the philosophical system of Marx and Lenin, and at the heart of their psychology, hatred of God is the principal driving force, more fundamental than all their political and economic pretensions. Militant atheism is not merely incidental or marginal to Communist policy; it is not a side effect, but the central pivot. The 1920's in the USSR witnessed an uninterrupted procession of victims and martyrs amongst the Orthodox clergy. Two metropolitans were shot, one of whom, Veniamin of Petrograd, had been elected by the popular vote of his diocese. Patriarch Tikhon himself passed through the hands of the Cheka-GPU and then died under suspicious circumstances. Scores of archbishops and bishops perished. Tens of thousands of priests, monks, and nuns, pressured by the Chekists to renounce the Word of God, were tortured, shot in cellars, sent to camps, exiled to the desolate tundra of the far North, or turned out into the streets in their old age without food or shelter. All these Christian martyrs

went unswervingly to their deaths for the faith; instances of apostasy were few and far between. For tens of millions of laymen access to the Church was blocked, and they were forbidden to bring up their children in the Faith: religious parents were wrenched from their children and thrown into prison, while the children were turned from the faith by threats and lies.[5]

In Russia, the Orthodox Church has to a great extent resumed its pre-1917 role as the moral foundation of society. This arouses political opposition, but also a deep hatred on the part of the post-Christian elites of the West, not only vis-à-vis Russia, but also against the Russian Orthodox Church and, by extension, against Orthodox Christianity itself. The overtly political attack that aims to pit Ukraine against the Russian Orthodox Church under the authority of Patriarch Cyril of Moscow is a dangerous, stupid provocation. I think, on that contrary, that European Christians ought to unite to emphasize their heritage, which is in the first place that of the saints and martyrs.

[5] Quoted in "Russia and Islam, part two: Russian Orthodoxy", *The Saker*, February 18, 2013, at http://thesaker.is/russia-and-islam-part-two-russian-orthodoxy/.

11

RUTHLESS ENEMIES

NICOLAS DIAT: *Why do you relentlessly denounce what you call the psychological, moral, and spiritual weakness of Westerners?*

ROBERT CARDINAL SARAH: The West has become increasingly detached from the source of life. How could anyone forget the teaching of the prophet Jeremiah, who put these words in God's mouth: "For my people have committed two evils: they have forsaken me, the fountain of living waters, and hewed out cisterns for themselves, broken cisterns, that can hold no water" (Jer 2:13)? This break with God can only be fatal. How can Westerners suppose that the spiritual, moral, and psychological consequences are not serious? Despite worrisome symptoms, they refuse to call themselves into question. Let us take the example of the arts, architecture, poetry, painting, or music. Can anyone fail to note the terrible regression? Beauty disappears from the horizon. Ugliness is set up as an unsurpassable norm.

The West's denial of reality is the product of a terrible pride, a voluntary blindness, a death impulse. False values are cherished and propagated. Ugliness has become beauty, immorality is progress. Is the West really aware of the abyss that it is digging under its own feet? It is hard to imagine that such a brilliant civilization could decide to abandon so many riches without understanding anything of this loss. We must denounce this movement that leads to inventing riches that are not riches at all and transforming gold into mud.

The West seems happy to see its churches turned into gymnasiums, its Romanesque chapels fall into ruin, its religious patrimony threatened by a total desacralization. Russia, on the contrary, is spending considerable sums to restore the treasures of Orthodoxy. The West does not for an instant imagine the unlimited consequences of its spineless cowardice with regard to its Christian artistic history.

Would you go so far as to talk about the postmodern colonization of Africa?

In my own life in Africa, I was able to appreciate the finest fruits of Western colonization. The cultural, moral, and religious values that the French gave to my country were a great treasure. The colonists came with rich, living ancestral traditions ennobled by Christianity. Their concepts of the dignity and rights of man and of human values were emancipating. France gave me an extraordinary language. The missionaries from that country brought me the true God. I am not afraid to say that I am the child of a constructive colonization. Today, however, Westerners come to Africa with false, criminal values. I cannot accept this propagation of venom that threatens to destroy traditional African man. Why does the West want to annihilate what it built in the first place? The real enemy of the West is the West itself, its imperviousness to God and to spiritual values, which resembles a process of lethal self-destruction.

What do you think about globalization?

The earth was created by God. He wanted a pluralistic world. Men do not resemble one another. Nature, too, is multifariously rich, because God ordained it so. Our Father thought that his children could be enriched by their differences.

Today, globalization is contrary to the divine plan. It tends to make humanity uniform. Globalization means cutting man off from his roots, from his religion, from his culture, history, customs, and ancestors. He becomes stateless, without a country, without a land. He is at home everywhere and nowhere. Nevertheless, man's wealth is the land that saw his birth and growth. He draws incalculable resources from that particular geographical space. The earth cannot be an ocean without boundaries. This planet could become a nightmare.

God wanted to place his creature in a garden, in a country, on a continent. Nations are large families. God wanted man to be rooted. He knows how important attachments are for good health. Man was not created to be an economic agent or a consumer. Humanity enters into a divine plan that the Bible unceasingly describes. God seeks to protect us, but if men stray from the paths marked out by him, they will perish.

Countries like those in the Visegrad Group that refuse to get lost in this mad rush are stigmatized, sometimes even insulted. Globalization becomes an obligatory medical prescription. The world-fatherland is a fluid continuum, a space with no identity, a land without history.

How can Africa exist in this unbridled globalization?

The African continent has been structured for a long time by kingdoms. The Mandinka people occupied territories without marked or defined boundaries, whose only landmarks were the laws of the ancestors. The genuine relations within the kingdoms were not of an economic kind. Customary inspiration was the strongest bond between men. In this order, initiation was a decisive rite of passage for full membership in the ancestral family.

Colonization invented the nations that we know today. The colonists never completely abolished the ancestral traditions, values, and feasts. Now, though, globalization insidiously seeks to cut young people off from these roots. It is difficult for me to believe that this attempt will succeed: How could anyone build a life solely on an idolatrous belief in economic, financial, and commercial laws?

What is your position on the decisive issue of migration?

There is a grand illusion that consists of making Third World peoples believe that all boundaries will be abolished. Certainly, migratory flows have always existed. The search for a better life and the flight from poverty and armed conflicts are nothing new. On the other hand, the current movements are distinguished by their magnitude. Some people take incredible risks. There is a heavy price to pay. The West is presented to some Africans as the earthly paradise. Hunger, violence, and war can drive these people to risk their lives in order to reach Europe. But how is it acceptable for some countries to be deprived of so many of their sons and daughters? How will these nations develop if so many workers make the choice to go into exile? What are these foreign humanitarian organizations that crisscross Africa urging young men to flee while promising them better lives in Europe? Why are death, slavery, and exploitation so often the real result of the travels of my African brothers toward the El Dorado of their dreams? I am revolted by these stories. The Mafia-like networks of smugglers must be eradicated with the utmost firmness. Oddly, they remain completely unpunished. From this perspective, the situation in Libya is catastrophic. That country was cynically destroyed in order to pillage its oil. Why do the Western governments have so few projects to propose with a view to its reconstruction? On all sides, I am not sure that respect for and the protection of human life are observed.

Not long ago, General Gomart, the former director of French military intelligence who retired from the army in May 2017, explained: "This invasion of Europe by migrants is programmed, controlled and accepted.... None of the migratory traffic in the Mediterranean is unknown to the French military and civil authorities." The general in fact was in charge of collecting all the information that might help France to make its decisions. He analyzed how the migratory traffic in the Middle East and in the Mediterranean region was picked up by French intelligence agents. The latter knew the place where the smugglers exchanged their human cargos and where they were lodged. The French intelligence services see them preparing the departures for Europe from the beaches of Tripolitania and Cyrenaica, imposing an inflexible itinerary on the migrants.

Each time, before setting out to sea, the smugglers call the Italian Maritime Rescue and Coordination Centre, and so it is that the European ships will pick up the migratory streams right there at sea so as to lead them to a safe port, for fear that they might get lost along the African coasts ... The invasion is not unforeseeable. Thus there is no mystery, everything is known. They know where the smugglers are going to get supplies for their boats. They know that Turkey provides false passports and that the customs authorities prefer to shut their eyes. French intelligence services are well informed about the smallest details of migratory traffic in Africa.

Everything must be done so that people can remain in the countries that saw their birth. Every day hundreds of Africans die in the waters of the Mediterranean. I am still haunted by the story of those two young Guineans who sought to flee from Conakry clandestinely. They had climbed into the luggage bay of the airplane and died of cold during the flight. Close friends told me about young men coming from Africa who died in the refrigerators of ships that were transporting bananas. This barbarity cannot continue.

In Europe, the migrants are deprived of their dignity. Human beings are parked in camps and condemned to wait without anything to do with their days. In France, the Calais Jungle[1] was a disgrace. How is a man without a job supposed to be able to find genuine fulfillment? The cultural and religious uprooting of Africans thrown into Western countries that are themselves going through an unprecedented crisis is a lethal compost.

The only lasting solution is via the economic development of Africa. The heads of State of my continent have a great responsibility. Europe must not become the tomb of Africa.

I am not certain that the Marrakech pact, which was signed by several countries including France in 2018, whose purpose is to strengthen cooperation between countries with regard to migratory problems, is really contributing to any progress. This document promises us safe, orderly, and regular migrations. I fear that it is producing exactly the opposite. Why were the peoples of the nations that signed the document not consulted? Do the governments of these States, like France, think that the people are not fit to judge correctly concerning issues that are so important for the future of the world? Are the globalized elites afraid of the response of democracy to the migratory flows? Countries as diverse as Italy, Australia, Croatia, Estonia, Austria, Hungary, Slovakia, Poland, Switzerland, the Czech Republic, and even the United Stated refused to sign that pact. *A contrario*, I am astonished that the Holy See did not intervene to nuance and supplement this document, which to me seems seriously inadequate.

What should governments do for the migrants who are already present on European soil?

If governments have already welcomed these men and women, this implies that they have a precise plan for giving them all the guarantees of a dignified life, with housing, jobs, and stable familial and religious life. The contrary would be irresponsible and disturbing. Alas, I observe that they are far from fulfilling all these conditions. Without a precise plan for their integration, it is criminal to offer hospitality to migrants.

[1] The Calais Jungle was a refugee and migrant encampment in 2015–2016.—TRANS.

Does Islamist totalitarianism worry you?

Attacks perpetrated by radical Islamists have become daily events. In the Middle East, in Africa, and in Europe, it is constant violence with no truce. The list of cities affected grows ever longer: Paris, Nice, Brussels, Cologne, Berlin, Stockholm, London, Ouagadougou (Burkina Faso), Grand-Bassam (Ivory Coast), Nairobi (Kenya). I am struck, in particular, by the terrible crimes committed against the Egyptian Copts.

I wonder sometimes whether the Western governments are implementing adequate policies to fight against terrorism. How could the Islamic State come into existence and grow with such impunity? I do not want to criticize the work that is under way. But to a great extent it is insufficient. The religious causes are not addressed. Many of the Islamist terrorists have been in Europe for several generations. They are the children of the consumer society. Driven to despair by European nihilism, they throw themselves into the embrace of radical Islamism. I think that the causes of terrorism are in great part religious. This phenomenon can be combated only by proposing a true spiritual perspective to the young people who have come from immigration. They reject atheist society. They refuse be integrated into the secularized world. Who will have the courage to propose to them a Europe that is proud of its Christian heritage? Who will have the courage to invite them to embrace an identity that is founded on morality and Christian values? The evangelization of young Europeans of Muslim origin ought to be a pastoral priority. I am convinced that they expect a clear, firm witness from us. But in the name of a misunderstood interreligious dialogue, we are cowardly and timid in proclaiming Christ.

Fanatical fundamentalist Islamism that intends to attack and wound Christians and Muslims must be fought vigorously. In my country, I had the opportunity to become acquainted with a spiritual Islam that is inspired by Sufism. There the Muslims spur the Christians on in their own religious practices.

The deterioration of Christian morality has gone far in the West. Many Muslims are sincerely shocked by it. The majority of the migrants who depart for the West are young men. Can anyone imagine that they would not be offended upon arriving in European countries where senseless paganism reigns?

We observe also that Western governments are really fainthearted about welcoming persecuted Christian refugees. This fact was particularly notable during the administration of President Obama. In Canada, the Trudeau government is emblematic of this strange practice.

The West is suffering from a loss of its fundamental landmarks; the renunciation of its Christian roots is one aspect of it. In this context, utopian philanthropy exposes it to the attacks of radical Islamism. If Europe rediscovers its identity, it can lift up its head and fight terrorism. Identity is the melting pot of genuine mutual respect. In a so-called open society with no proper identity, men who possess a system of values are inevitably the victors.

What is your perspective on the military interventions of Western countries in the world?

Western governments claim to impose their type of political regime throughout the world. Why should American democracy be exported to the four corners of the world? It is absurd to impose the same rules on all countries. Perfect democracy does not exist. Do we have to recall the many problems caused by legislation about the death penalty in the United States? I respect the family policy of Russia more than that of Great Britain, Canada, or France.

The Obama administration tried to bring freedom to the Syrians. Today the country resembles an expanse of ruins. It is obvious that President Assad's regime is not the best possible one. The extortions of the Ba'athist regime [Iraq] are intolerable. The protection enjoyed by the Christian minority must not make us forget the worse crimes that are committed there en masse. Without Russia's intervention, an Islamist regime would have ended up winning the day. The Christians of that country owe their survival to Moscow. Russia played its role as protector of the Christian minorities, most of them Orthodox. The Russian government intended to defend a religion, but also a culture.

In Iraq, the Western coalition brought about the fall of Saddam Hussein, and chaos set in. John Paul II did everything he could to avoid military intervention against Saddam Hussein. We know today that the presence of chemical weapons—the pretext of the invasion—was a shameless lie. Which financial interests were hidden in that initiative? Western interventionism in the name of democracy can lead to a derailing of liberty.

In Libya, the fall of the leader's regime resulted in the streams of migration with which we are familiar and the destruction of all political structures in the country. Why did Nicolas Sarkozy suddenly decide to do away with a regime without considering the aftermath? France has a heavy responsibility in the Libyan tragedy. What a complete lack of moral sense! Do they talk about "respect for human rights" with regard to Syria? Do they talk about progress of civilization? When you think about the way in which Saddam Hussein and Muammar Gaddafi were tortured and killed ... Some rightly consider that these two men had a lot of blood on their hands. Still, did the West have to stage the atrocity of their agony and death? The worst bandits have a right to a dignified death. God alone is judge. The tragedy of the West is always the same. God is dead. The States have taken God's place.

The West must make an examination of conscience. How many countries have seen their most elementary rights trampled on by the Western powers? How can anyone say that some peoples are less worthy or less civilized than others? No State is entitled to impose its political, economic, or cultural views. The West brought great ideals into the world, but its propensity to impose its political system is reprehensible. Why is it unwilling to receive from other peoples?

The West has fatally lost its way. It is necessary to call into question the whole framework of its geopolitical policy.

12

THE DECEPTIVE SEDUCTIONS
OF SUPPOSEDLY EMANCIPATED LIFE

NICOLAS DIAT: Modern life is looking more and more like a permanent party.

ROBERT CARDINAL SARAH: People seem to be obsessed with monotony and sadness. In order to ward off fear, they continually lose their way and then dust themselves off. Now their joys are artificial, since they follow from the sad reign of enjoyment and ease.

In so-called developed societies, the moral and spiritual poverty is immense. Partying becomes the only means of forgetting the nothingness into which individuals have fallen.

The more man destroys himself, the more he feels the need to find treatments for his interior crisis: at the end of that passionate quest, Asian philosophies look like miracle drugs.

Man rushes from festivities to vacations, from trips to banquets. Life is one big game. Anything exotic is promising. Even funerals are not supposed to be sad now. You have to sing and laugh until the last moments. How can men applaud the dead as they enter or leave the church? How can they demean a moment that is so full of emotions and sacredness? Our thoughtlessness and superficiality in the presence of this mystery is stupid. In the presence of death, we should keep silence, recollect ourselves, pray, and turn to God so as to try to enter into the great divine mystery in which the departed person now finds himself. Death is not easy. Your book *Un temps pour mourir: Derniers jours de la vie des moines*[1] shows this very well. Man wants to drive death away, eliminate mourning. He no longer tolerates sadness and tears.

---

[1] English edition: *A Time to Die: Monks on the Threshold of Eternal Life* (San Francisco: Ignatius Press, 2019).

Suffering, whether interior or physical, no longer has a legitimate place. It is necessary to hide the handicapped, forget the sick, and warehouse the elderly. Old age is no fun. Therefore it must be hidden behind the gloomy walls of retirement homes.

Finally, indifference is the unspoken rule with regard to matters concerning God and religion.

Religious feasts are transformed into pitiful commercial days on which generosity is corrupted. This falsely luminous life is the high point of a decadent civilization. The search for enjoyment, success, and fulfillment leads people ever farther away from God. Life has become a feast without God.

In his *Pensées*, Pascal wrote: "All the unhappiness of men arises from one single fact, that they cannot stay quietly in their own chamber."[2] The philosopher neatly shows that man, in his pride and concupiscence, can find interior peace and genuine happiness only in God. According to him, the broken relationship between man and his Creator is what produces in a human being constant dissatisfaction with the life he is leading and the desire to forget, through "diversions", that he is mortal. He concludes as follows: "As men are not able to fight against death, misery, ignorance, they have taken it into their heads, in order to be happy, not to think of them at all."[3]

In order to avoid hearing God's music, we have chosen to use all the devices of this world. But heaven's instruments will not stop playing just because some people are deaf.

In our second book, The Power of Silence, *we dedicated a long reflection to the modern struggle of noise against silence.*

It is necessary to help the modern world by making it understand that noise has become a powerful dictatorship that unceasingly demeans it. Far away from noise, man can rediscover God. If the lights go out, if the sounds fall silent, he is capable of listening to God's voice in his heart.

The partying civilization seeks to stifle silence by every possible means. It promotes the scattering of feelings, superficiality, and hedonism. Noise is the twin brother of the lie. Silence is the seat of truth, the dwelling place of God.

[2] Blaise Pascal, *Pensées*, trans. W. F. Trotter (Mineola, N.Y.: Dover, 2018), 39.
[3] Ibid., 47.

How can we make our contemporaries understand that life is not a party and that silence liberates? We must help them grasp that silence is the fine flour of all genuine encounters. Interior silence is always difficult to achieve. In this search, the monasteries offer oases.

Would you say that there is a relentless battle between the search for pleasure and interiority?

Modern man neglects his interior life so much that he no longer knows what it means. He is submerged in the mud of passions, pre-occupied with amusing himself and enjoying all the pleasures of the world. It does not matter to him that he lives in a world dominated by evil, violence, corruption, loose morals, perversion, irreligion, and even contempt for God.

Exaggeration is the norm. There have always been periods in history in which sordidness, brutality, obscenity, foulness, and frenzy held the high ground. Our era is all the more disturbing in this regard because God is socially dead. This great absence is the worst possible threat for humanity. The danger is that the successor of Christian man will be amoral man.

The Church absolutely must play her role. What makes her work that much more complex is the fact that the moral consensus resulting from Judeo-Christian civilization, which for centuries left its mark on the world, has disappeared. The philosophical relativism denounced by Benedict XVI has swept it all away in its deadly waves. At the opening of the 2005 conclave, he courageously declared: "We are building a dictatorship of relativism that does not recognize anything as definitive and whose ultimate goal consists solely of one's own ego and desires."[4] In his book *Light of the World,* published in 2010, he continued this reflection:

> It is obvious that the concept of truth has become suspect. Of course it is correct that it has been much abused. Intolerance and cruelty have occurred in the name of truth. To that extent people are afraid when someone says, "This is the truth", or even "I have the truth." We

[4] Joseph Cardinal Ratzinger, Homily at the Mass "Pro Eligendo Romano Pontifice", April 18, 2005.

never have it; at best it has us. No one will dispute that one must be careful and cautious in claiming the truth. But simply to dismiss it as unattainable is really destructive. A large proportion of contemporary philosophies, in fact, consist of saying that man is not capable of truth. But viewed in that way, man would not be capable of ethical values, either. Then he would have no standards.[5]

Far from the truth, man scatters himself in vain pleasures. Confusion paves the way for the most immoral diversions.

The death of interiority is almost considered to be a good. Pleasure and error walk the same path, snickering proudly. We are witnessing the revenge of instinct. Self-control, a certain mental and emotional health, are attained through a genuine continence.

Alas, the individual is king and the sole judge of his conduct. He is left to his own discernment. How can a man who does not have adequate formation and education judge himself?

In order to rediscover an interior life worthy of this name, it is necessary to cultivate silence first. Silence is difficult, but it makes a human being capable of letting himself be led by God. Silence is born from silence. Through God, the silent one, we can reach silence. Man is unceasingly surprised by the light that then shines forth. Silence is more important than any other human work. Because it expresses God. The genuine revolution comes from silence; it leads us toward God and others so as to place us humbly and generously at their service.

Silence and reflection alone, enlightened by the divine realities, can bring about a rebirth of the interior life. It is necessary to give modern man the means to rediscover the path of his heart so as to flee the winter of his base instincts.

Could we speak about a pantheon of modernist idols?

In it, the idol of money dominates the others. A proverb says: "When money talks, even the devil listens!" Money runs the world. The worship of the golden calf is an obsession of the modern world.

---

[5] Pope Benedict XVI, *Light of the World: The Pope, the Church, and the Signs of the Times*, a Conversation with Peter Seewald, trans. Michael J. Miller and Adrian J. Walker (San Francisco: Ignatius Press, 2010), 50.

Liberty is another idol. Western man no longer tolerates any constraint. He claims an absolute independence from all moral norms. God cannot come to contradict any of his rights. From now on, life is entirely made up of rights. But idols are always liars.

Democracy is the third goddess. Alas, she is a bloody one. Nations, peoples, cultures, particularly in the Near East and in Africa, are massacred in the name of democracy. Its high priests, the Westerners, shed rivers of blood in order to impose the worship of her throughout the world.

In my view, men are controlled first by the powers of money.

In his book *Les Droits de l'homme dénaturé* [The rights of denatured man],[6] the legal scholar Grégor Puppinck writes:

> Human rights? After World War II, they appeared as a universal promise of peace and justice. Today they have become an ideological battlefield, the terrain on which clashing civilizations confront each other. For the rights of man are the reflection of our concept of man in the first place. Now, the latter has changed a lot since the composition of the Universal Declaration in 1948. Whereas that postwar declaration was still inspired by *natural rights*, the affirmation of individualism has generated new *anti-natural rights*, such as the right to euthanasia or abortion, or to homosexuality, leading in turn to the emergence of transhuman *transnatural rights* that today guarantee the authority to transform and to redefine nature, such as the right to eugenics, the right to have a child or to change one's sex. At work at the heart of this transformation we note an evolution that testifies to a profound transformation of the concept of human dignity, which tends to be reduced to the individual will alone, regardless of the body, or to the mind, as opposed to the body, and which regards any negation of nature and conditioning as a form of liberation and progress. Furthermore, human rights discreetly accompany transhumanism, working to make representative democracy outmoded.

Modern man is unaware. He does not gauge all the consequences of his acts. He lives in artifice so as to disguise his crimes. He prefers illusion to reality. False idols have led the West to its collapse. In his *Sermon on Honor*, Bossuet thundered: "Almost no men nowadays are

---

[6] Grégor Puppinck, *Les Droits de l'homme dénaturé* (Paris: Cerf, 2018).

concerned about avoiding vices; the sole concern is to find specious names and reasonable pretexts.... The name and dignity of a 'great man' is supported more by wit and industriousness than by honesty and virtue; and in fact the world considers someone virtuous and regular enough when he has the skill to look after himself and the inventiveness to cover himself."

Only the courage to resist will be able to overcome all the deceptive seductions of a supposedly emancipated life! Love for God and for others and the patient, stubborn search for the good are more than ever the kinds of dissidence the world needs.

13

THE DECLINE OF COURAGE
AND THE FATAL UTOPIAS OF THE
"BEST OF ALL WORLDS"

NICOLAS DIAT: How would you describe the modern civilization of well-being?

ROBERT CARDINAL SARAH: The exaggerated cult of well-being that is a sad sign of our era saps courage and resolve little by little. Courage is defined as strength of character and the firm determination of men when faced with difficult situations. It is the enemy of fear. Now our era lives in perpetual fear, anguish, and the most senseless obsessions, agonizing irrationality.

Courage does not work without a genuine interior strength. There can be combat only if it is supported by moral and spiritual values. Courageous men distinguish themselves by their determination to overcome obstacles. Often we notice that our courage comes from our relation to God. Heaven makes heroes. Alas, we unceasingly focus our interest exclusively on well-being and the enjoyment of material goods. Most of the life of Western man is directed toward this search for the pleasures of a life without suffering or obstacle. Therefore, it is necessary to work to bring this mania for acquisition and consumption under control. We must replace the primacy of matter with the primacy of spirit.

Why were immense crowds of young people, during the World Youth Days, so enthusiastic and so happy around John Paul II, Benedict XVI, and today around Pope Francis, undertaking long, expensive journeys just to meet them and to listen to them? Why are young people attracted by these men of God who speak fiery words? It is because, just as every athlete needs a trainer, so too young people need models, heroes who can train them to devote themselves to noble commitments and tasks. Young people want strong, provocative words, words that challenge their energy. They aspire to heroism and to noble conduct and to an intensely spiritual life. Young people are full of physical energy, filled with enormous spiritual reserves that are, so to speak, walled up, enclosed within the dam of their heart. Here is what one of them said in a column that appeared in the *Figaro littéraire* the day after the terrorist attacks in Paris that shook not only France but the entire world on November 13, 2015:

> Our civilization is suffering from a terrible, perhaps fatal disease that is called spiritual emptiness. We have bread, machines, exterior freedom, but we are petrified in matter. Not only that: the best part of ourselves is hungry. In my opinion, the collapse of the essential spiritual values—religion, art, love—is the reason why young people went out into the streets [to protest the attacks]. They were fighting because of a lack of soul. Unconsciously, but profoundly and vigorously, the young people of the whole world arose in defense of the spirit.

I am aware that unbelievers have well-founded complaints about the Church. The writer and dramatist Eugene Ionesco wrote: "So as not to lose her believers, the Church made sure that people no longer know what the supernatural and the sacred is. The religious sense is in each of us. It will not be able to develop as long as the Church is corrupted by her many, many compromises. Let her be above the world. That is the only way that people will strive to climb up to her level."[1]

We cannot fail to have the humility and the courage to accept words like these; they recall the genuine mission of the Church. Her mission is neither political nor social; it cannot resemble the mission statement of an NGO. It consists essentially of bringing men to God and enabling man's heart to become a sacred temple again, the temple and dwelling place of God.

I know that some people think that the spiritual life is possible only in a form of material flourishing. This is a serious error. The major periods of spiritual richness are often the fruit of poverty. Even today, the great spiritual centers are found at the heart of poor countries. I am thinking especially about the India of Mother Teresa.

The expansion of Christianity has occurred through the most deprived populations. They were the first to understand the revolutionary

---

[1] Eugène Ionesco (in conversation with Yves de Gibon), in *L'Église sous leur regard* (Paris: Beauchesne, 1975), 114–15, quoted by Léon Arthur Elchinger in *Je plaide pour l'homme* (Paris: Fayard, 1976), 118.

vigor of the Gospel—whether in Palestine, in Corinth, in Rome, or elsewhere. In the Book of Deuteronomy, one canticle refers to the reproaches leveled against Israel. It echoes, so to speak, various periods in which the Chosen People abandoned God, preferring money and material wealth to him: "But Jeshurun waxed fat, and kicked; you waxed fat, you grew thick, you became sleek; then he forsook God who made him, and scoffed at the Rock of his salvation" (Deut 32:15). The attitude of the great spiritual masters toward comfort has never changed. The words of Ecclesiastes have always been a source of inspiration: "A person who has no one, either son or brother, yet there is no end to all his toil, and his eyes are never satisfied with riches, so that he never asks, 'For whom am I toiling and depriving myself of pleasure?'" (Eccles 4:8). The persistence with which man torments himself in order to obtain riches, this "striving after wind", to borrow the metaphor from Ecclesiastes, is it not the vain, frantic pursuit of a satisfaction that always eludes us?

This is indeed Solomon's observation: he had done great things; he had houses, trees, flocks, servants, maidservants, and treasures. Nevertheless he has to say: "And behold, all was vanity,... and there was nothing to be gained under the sun" (Eccles 2:11).

Qoheleth looks all around him, and what does he see? He is alone, without having an assistant to help him; he has no son or brother, either; and there is no end to all his labor. He does not say to himself: "For whom, then, do I torment myself and deprive my soul of happiness?" All the wealth that this man acquired could not satisfy him.

Another man who loves money is not satisfied at all with money. His possessions increase, and those who consume them increase, also; what benefit does the master have from them? The rich man's worry about his possessions "will not let him sleep" [Eccles 5:12].

Hezekiah had paraded his possessions in front of the envoys from the King of Babylon. The prophet told him: "Hear the word of the LORD of hosts: Behold, the days are coming, when all that is in your house, and that which your fathers have stored up till this day, shall be carried to Babylon; nothing shall be left, says the LORD" (Is 39:5–6).

With regard to all this emptiness, it seems to me important to recall the Psalmist's warning: "If riches increase, set not your heart on them" (Ps 62:10).

The financial powers have no interest in seeing a genuine humanism grow. They have put man into a deep, sticky sleep. The civilization of well-being mutilates man. He is cut off from eternity. Man must arm himself with courage for the benefit of the interior man. The struggle against the dictatorship of matter is not easy. Our contemporaries are prisoners of a sort of glue. But the young people, who are fed up with this orgy of material goods and disgusted by the emptiness that they carve out in man, will reawaken this increasingly inhuman world so as to lift us by the strength of their energy toward our origins, toward God, and toward spiritual values.

It is necessary to make Pascal's bet. It is necessary to choose transcendence by agreeing to what is invisible.

In your opinion, what is the foremost utopia of our era?

The consumerist utopia is the strongest and most dangerous. Is man made for God or to spend his life consuming? In the capitalist system, one can even wonder whether someone who no longer has a "market value" still has a place in a world dominated exclusively by financial trends.

In these societies, the acquisition of material comfort and the massive production of consumer goods are the summit of earthly life.

The remark by Saint Ignatius of Loyola seems to have become the sad reply of a bygone world: "Oh, how vile does earth appear to me when I look up to heaven!"[2]

Certainly, material progress exists and can give man true benefits, a real human and earthly happiness. But in the postmodern world, the use of these advances is perverted.

Genuine consumption ought to help us attain greater interior, moral, and spiritual qualities. We should tend to be more human by ceaselessly drawing closer to God. If earthly things come to interrupt this course, we can be sure that it is the wrong road.

Christ always tried to remind people who were seeking the Kingdom of God that it is already in their own hearts. The life of faith, diligence in prayer, the constant thought of God, and charity are essential practices if we are to avoid sinking into an asphyxiating materialism. The benefits that we can derive from material goods depend on the richness of our moral life.

---

[2] Quoted by Stewart Rose, *St. Ignatius and the Early Jesuits* (London: Burns and Oates; New York: Catholic Publication Society, 1891), 333.

A man's interior qualities will cause authentic growth. We must detach ourselves from the tumult of exterior objects so as to burrow into the folds of our soul and to search there for the clarity of divine illumination and the silence that is so difficult to preserve. There is always a struggle within us between the exterior man, who turns away from God and lives in sin while falling prey to his carnal, worldly desires, and the interior man, who is open to grace and is sanctified by following the law of the Spirit and the will of God.

Saint Paul mentions this reality when he writes to the Corinthians: "So we do not lose heart. Though our outer man is wasting away, our inner man is being renewed every day. For this slight momentary affliction is preparing for us an eternal weight of glory beyond all comparison, because we look not to the things that are seen but to the things that are unseen; for the things that are seen are transient, but the things that are unseen are eternal" (2 Cor 4:16–18).

True material value is dependence on moral and spiritual wealth. The most important crisis is not of an economic sort. It is fundamentally spiritual. The utilitarian philosophy demonstrated an unsuspected power of corruption. A policy of unlimited productivity inevitably leads to human, cultural, or ecological catastrophes. Consumerism is a utopia that corrupts and debases man to the purely earthly level. This religion of immediacy looks only to the profit motive. Man no longer counts. He is bothersome. In some cases, why not replace him with robots? I think it is urgent for us to become reacquainted with the experience of gratuitousness. The most profoundly human acts are characterized by gratuitousness. It is the prerequisite for friendship, beauty, study, contemplation, and prayer. A world without gratuitousness is an inhuman world. I call on Christians to open oases of gratuitousness in the desert of triumphant profitability. We ought to ask ourselves the question: Does gratuitousness characterize each one of our days? It is not an optional supplement; it is the condition for the survival of our humanity.

Could the cult of consumerism that you ceaselessly denounce be the golden calf of the postmodern era?

In the Old Testament, despite God's solicitude at the time of the liberation of the slaves from Egypt, their extraordinary crossing of the Red Sea dry shod, and the gift of manna, Israel abandons its God to make for itself an idol that it can carry about. It wants a divinity that can be subjected to its whims. Instead of allowing itself to be shaped, educated, and led by the Lord, the God of Israel's armies, it molds for itself an idol, a golden calf, made out of women's earrings, melted down by Aaron, and it declares before this statue: "These are your gods, O Israel, who brought you up out of the land of Egypt" (Ex 32:4). Man then shows all his inconsistency, his ingratitude and meanness.

Today we have returned to the era of the golden calf. Money is at the heart of the preoccupations of the Western world, but also of many peoples throughout the world. Christ's teaching is simple: "No servant can serve two masters; for either he will hate the one and love the other, or he will be devoted to the one and despise the other. You cannot serve God and mammon" (Lk 16:13).

Money is thought to liberate us from slavery and poverty. Nevertheless, although we are unwilling to admit it, we are prisoners of the chains of materialism. The golden calf is incapable of leading us toward the Promised Land. From then on it sells us to other vulgar, vain gods: hedonism, egotism, and consumerism.

The furious tides of our passions prevail over our reason. Postmodern man is dragged through the unhealthiest sorts of mud. God is horrified by these diabolical movements. He would like to come to our aid, but we reject his love. The golden calf is destroying humanity. The finest part of man's being is amputated.

You have often denounced the utopia of a global religion. Can you explain to us what you mean by that?

The dream of the Western globalized elite is precisely to establish a new world religion. For this little group, the ancient religions, and in particular the Catholic Church, must be transformed or die. They must abandon their doctrine and their moral teaching. It is supposedly necessary to arrive at a worldwide, global religion, a religion without God, without doctrine, and without moral teaching, a religion of consensus. In reality, this religion would end up being at the service of financial interests alone.

Religion is a personal relationship between a man and God. How can anyone imagine the life of this love caught in the shapeless muddle of a worldwide ideology? The search for a global religious consensus is fallacious and stupid.

We are facing a political, ideological, atheistic approach, an aberrant, unacceptable dictatorship.

It would seem, from what you say, that this is the dawning of the utopia of a world without borders.

Alas, the European Union is a good example of this utopia. The abolition of ancestral boundaries hushes up the identity of the old nations. The roots, the millennial culture, and history of a country no longer matter. Commerce and free trade are the only valid norms. It is not surprising that the populaces rebel against this attempt to erase their own identity, their history, their language, and their specificity. The project that consists of trying to annihilate the history of States on the altar of financial interests is a dangerous utopia.

I can understand the idea of some cooperation of peoples. I can understand a certain opening of boundaries so as to improve economic exchanges. But the libertarian liberal ideology is nonsense. Europe is dying of this selfish delirium.

The U.N. elites dream of a world government that would rule peoples, cultures, and traditions that were formerly so different. It is a dream that borders on madness and is a sign of the contempt of the peoples for their riches. What will become of Africa, which has experienced so many humiliations over the course of history? Will we still have the right to live? It is enough to observe the work in our countries of the large Western philanthropic foundations to understand what African man means in the view of the billionaires who finance them. They are convinced that they know better than we do the best policies for our continent. In reality, this elite has two obsessions: the drastic decrease of the African birthrate and economic development in the service of the objectives of the Western multinational corporations.

This utopia absolutely intends to win this match. Indeed, the world in which we are living seems to have destroyed its boundaries. Why have wars never been as numerous as now? In Syria, in Libya, in Afghanistan, in Central Africa, the chaos is indescribable. They are trying to weaken, destroy, and dominate so as to pillage and control as absolute masters.

Does globalization have to benefit a few privileged individuals? Are Western armies not spending their time fighting poor people? The armaments contracts that produce large profits for the major powers and make it possible to wage the war in Yemen are a disgrace. They organize humanitarian conferences by day and sell weapons by night. The thousands of Yemenite children who are dying of hunger in atrocious sanitary conditions do not seem to keep the attention of the decision makers and the diplomats. They are nothing in comparison to the fabulous arms contracts.

In Africa, the West provides arms to the populations, which tear each other apart. While the poor are killing each other, major international groups exploit the natural resources of the countries at war.

The globalist ideology is based solely on financial interests. No one pities the poor and the weak. But the powerful have all the rights.

Many thinkers denounce the utopia of transparency. What are your reflections on this subject?

We live in so-called open societies in which the new means of communication are thought to be informing us about the least event. In reality, disinformation has never been so rampant. The father of lies and prince of this world has taken possession of the hearts of those who have power.

A transparent society is equipped with dangerous instruments of control over its population. The political and financial powers seek to seize them in order to influence opinions.

On the social networks, especially, people agree to give a lot of information about their private lives, which contributes to strengthening the instruments of control that I mentioned.

In these days of artificial intelligence, the regime of transparency is a falsification of genuine liberty. The control mechanism of the traditional dictatorship over consciences was relatively simple to understand. The tyranny of the postmodern regimes is subtler.

Genuine transparency is founded on the greatness of the relation between God and men. In his Letter to the Philippians, Saint Paul shows us the way: "Finally, brethren, whatever is true, whatever is honorable, whatever is just, whatever is pure, whatever is lovely, whatever is gracious, if there is any excellence, if there is anything worthy of praise, think about these things" (Phil 4:8). Nobility and virtue cannot be hidden.

Man must be vigilant and know how to analyze and test things with a critical, discerning mind. He must not take at face value the information that is ceaselessly brought to him on a silver platter. There are often false truths circulating. Above all, one must not repeat these fake news stores, because one ends up accepting them.

The man who truly loves God wants to be discreet. A godless man is ceaselessly exposed in the secular light. He is naked, buffeted by the winds of rumors, a prisoner to storms of lies and calumny.

For liberals, the utopia of egalitarianism is particularly dangerous.

Since the Enlightenment era, it has been taken for granted that justice cannot be achieved without equality among men. Nevertheless, we know that this state is impossible. During the last century, the search for equality led to the tragedy of Communism and Marxism, which tried to construct paradise on this earth. On the other hand, it is necessary to consider carefully the policies that fight against social inequalities. The promise of equality is often a banner waved by the most selfish financial powers. They need to keep up this illusion so that the peoples do not rebel.

We can be indignant, but, alas, inequality is part of human existence. All stages of life are marked with this seal. Death does not escape from this difficult rule. How can anyone deny that a European and an African are not equal before sickness and death? Some die at an advanced age, others die young. Some die suddenly, without suffering; others undergo a long agony. Is that fair? We are born with very different chances in life.

The utopia of egalitarianism ruins the meaning of human existence. Wisdom commands us to steer clear of its essentially proud, revolutionary whims.

We have to put our lives into God's hands. He is our best guide, our rampart. He created us, and he is the only one who knows the meaning of our destinies.

What do you say about the utopia of the digital revolution and about the tyranny of formatting minds?

Today we have to show courage in order to resist the primacy of technology and of technicians. We have to choose between what lifts us higher, toward what is true, and what drags us down. We know that the media can form and deform moral judgment. In the crisis through which we are going, they can save our civilization, just as they can corrupt it fatally. More and more they seem to enable our contemporaries to devise a certain idea of the world for themselves. In the past, it was necessary to work, to search, to make an effort in order to discover the truth. Today, it is enough to go on the Internet to have access to an impressive quantity of data. We are spared the trouble of reflecting and passing a critical judgment. Modern man has lost the notion of the long term. Man behaves only as a consumer. There is an urgent need to acquire interior maturity and a greater awareness of our responsibility.

Protecting nature has primordial importance, but this does not prevent some philosophers, like Alain Finkielkraut, from mistrusting an ecological utopia.

Alas, Africans know all too well the problems associated with the destruction of nature. Their minerals and other natural resources are often shamelessly pillaged and placed on the altar of financial interests. The rich countries do not care about the human and social consequences that they cause for defenseless populations.

In his encyclical *Laudato si'*, Pope Francis addressed these issues radically. Here are the prophetic lines near the beginning of this document:

> The urgent challenge to protect our common home includes a concern to bring the whole human family together to seek a sustainable and integral development, for we know that things can change. The Creator does not abandon us; he never forsakes his loving plan or repents of having created us. Humanity still has the ability to work together in building our common home. Here I want to recognize, encourage and thank all those striving in countless ways to guarantee the protection of the home which we share. Particular appreciation is owed to those who tirelessly seek to resolve the tragic effects of environmental degradation on the lives of the world's poorest. Young people demand change. They wonder how anyone can claim to be building a better future without thinking of the environmental crisis and the sufferings of the excluded.
>
> I urgently appeal, then, for a new dialogue about how we are shaping the future of our planet. We need a conversation which includes everyone, since the environmental challenge we are undergoing,

and its human roots, concern and affect us all. The worldwide ecological movement has already made considerable progress and led
to the establishment of numerous organizations committed to raising awareness of these challenges. Regrettably, many efforts to seek
concrete solutions to the environmental crisis have proved ineffective, not only because of powerful opposition but also because of a
more general lack of interest. Obstructionist attitudes, even on the
part of believers, can range from denial of the problem to indifference, nonchalant resignation or blind confidence in technical solutions. We require a new and universal solidarity. As the bishops of
Southern Africa have stated: "Everyone's talents and involvement
are needed to redress the damage caused by human abuse of God's
creation." All of us can cooperate as instruments of God for the care
of creation, each according to his or her own culture, experience,
involvements and talents. (*LS* 13–14)

In his encyclical *Caritas in Veritate*, Benedict XVI had blazed the
trail:

Today the subject of development is also closely related to the duties
arising from *our relationship to the natural environment*. The environment
is God's gift to everyone, and in our use of it we have a responsibility
towards the poor, towards future generations and towards humanity
as a whole. When nature, including the human being, is viewed as
the result of mere chance or evolutionary determinism, our sense of
responsibility wanes. In nature, the believer recognizes the wonderful
result of God's creative activity, which we may use responsibly to
satisfy our legitimate needs, material or otherwise, while respecting
the intrinsic balance of creation. If this vision is lost, we end up either
considering nature an untouchable taboo or, on the contrary, abusing
it. Neither attitude is consonant with the Christian vision of nature as
the fruit of God's creation. . . .

*The way humanity treats the environment influences the way it treats itself,
and vice versa.* This invites contemporary society to a serious review of
its life-style, which, in many parts of the world, is prone to hedonism
and consumerism, regardless of their harmful consequences. What is
needed is an effective shift in mentality which can lead to the adoption of *new life-styles* "in which the quest for truth, beauty, goodness and communion with others for the sake of common growth are
the factors which determine consumer choices, savings and invest-
ments". Every violation of solidarity and civic friendship harms the

environment, just as environmental deterioration in turn upsets relations in society. Nature, especially in our time, is so integrated into the dynamics of society and culture that by now it hardly constitutes an independent variable. Desertification and the decline in productivity in some agricultural areas are also the result of impoverishment and underdevelopment among their inhabitants. When incentives are offered for their economic and cultural development, nature itself is protected. Moreover, how many natural resources are squandered by wars! Peace in and among peoples would also provide greater protection for nature. The hoarding of resources, especially water, can generate serious conflicts among the peoples involved. Peaceful agreement about the use of resources can protect nature and, at the same time, the well-being of the societies concerned.

The Church has a responsibility towards creation and she must assert this responsibility in the public sphere. In so doing, she must defend not only earth, water and air as gifts of creation that belong to everyone. She must above all protect mankind from self-destruction. There is need for what might be called a human ecology, correctly understood. The deterioration of nature is in fact closely connected to the culture that shapes human coexistence: *when "human ecology" is respected within society, environmental ecology also benefits.* Just as human virtues are interrelated, such that the weakening of one places others at risk, so the ecological system is based on respect for a plan that affects both the health of society and its good relationship with nature.

In order to protect nature, it is not enough to intervene with economic incentives or deterrents; not even an apposite education is sufficient. These are important steps, but *the decisive issue is the overall moral tenor of society.* If there is a lack of respect for the right to life and to a natural death, if human conception, gestation and birth are made artificial, if human embryos are sacrificed to research, the conscience of society ends up losing the concept of human ecology and, along with it, that of environmental ecology. It is contradictory to insist that future generations respect the natural environment when our educational systems and laws do not help them to respect themselves. The book of nature is one and indivisible: it takes in not only the environment but also life, sexuality, marriage, the family, social relations: in a word, integral human development. Our duties towards the environment are linked to our duties towards the human person, considered in himself and in relation to others. It would be wrong to uphold one set of duties while trampling on the other. Herein lies a grave contradiction in our mentality and practice today: one which demeans the person, disrupts the environment and damages society.[3]

Genuine respect for nature is born of a contemplative attitude. It cannot be decreed; it requires a profound conversion of heart and a sense of loving adoration of the Creator.

[3] Pope Benedict XVI, Encyclical Letter *Caritas in Veritate* on Integral Human Development in Charity and Truth (June 29, 2009; hereafter cited as *CiV*), nos. 48 and 51.

14

THE FACE OF POSTMODERN
DEMOCRACIES AND CAPITALISM

NICOLAS DIAT: How would you define the cynicism that you speak about so often when talking about civil government?

ROBERT CARDINAL SARAH: In ancient Greek, this word is derived from *kuôn, kunos*, which means "dog". The theory of cynicism was developed by Antisthenes, a faithful disciple of Gorgias. When he reached manhood, he became attached to Socrates. From the latter's teaching, Antisthenes adopted above all else firmness of character, which he made into man's ultimate purpose, so to speak. Thus he arrived at a morality of individual self-sufficiency and a practical contempt for the institutions that Socrates, however, had respected at the cost of his life. This contempt for conventions was taken to its extreme by Diogenes of Sinope, whose radical individualism was expressed by the insolence that characterized all the philosophers called Cynics because of their attitude and their biting, obscene remarks—hence the comparison with a dog. They did not even consider the public good. Decorum, politeness, and respect for others did not enter into their reflection.

Today, moral principles and the welfare of peoples are insidiously trampled on by the cynicism of many governments and financial institutions. The media effectively play supporting roles to assist this disastrous movement.

Wars and economic crises are often the product of shameless policies whose true motivations are never stated.

It is enough for me to mention just one example. Who distributes the arms that the child soldiers use? The poor countries do not have the means to produce this military materiel. I condemn these lies. The countries of the Middle East, Libya, Syria, and, farther away, Afghanistan are broken, dismantled by the domineering spirit of the Westerners' economic interests. Thousands of children perish amid the most reprehensible indifference. Meanwhile, when an Italian or French soldier dies in combat, a period of national mourning is decreed immediately. The European lie, which practices the morality of "variable geometry",[1] is scandalous.

I remember the desperate appeals of John Paul II to prevent the First Iraq War. He had understood that this campaign that did not want to speak its name was only a commercial war started in the name of false humanitarian principles. The military/oil-industrial complex had no consideration for the rights of the Iraqi people. History has proved the Polish pope right. It is necessary to denounce these Machiavellian schemes in which the decadent West tries to impose its anthropological and moral vision on the whole world.

In Africa, we know this exploitation of the interests of the poor. Western ideology allows massacres to be perpetrated with complete impunity. The family is the great treasure of our continent. The governments of the Northern countries decided to break this incomparable advantage. I often think of the despicable statement of President Emmanuel Macron during the G20 summit in Hamburg, in July 2017: "When some countries still have seven or eight children per woman, you can decide to spend billions of Euros there and you will not stabilize anything." How can they refer to the independence of the African countries when they dare to talk that way?

It is necessary to denounce the major clearance sale of Africa's natural resources for the benefit of foreigners, carried out with the complicity of the national political leaders. Africa is literally being pillaged, exploited by the multinationals and the Western governments. They foment war; they track down its mineral resources with arms. Then, while the Africans are fighting each other, they exploit its subsoil. They pollute the environment and leave the continent in endemic poverty. The arms traffic in Africa is a horror that decimates the African populations, creates permanent instability and hatreds that

[1] A method of differentiated integration in the European Union as a means of coping with irreconcilable differences among countries.—TRANS.

ruin the peoples. The bishops of the Democratic Republic of Congo recently decided to protest, declaring on May 20, 2018:

> The economic policy of our country is increasingly extroverted, organized to the detriment of the Congolese but for the benefit of foreign economies: our mineral resources are pillaged, the surtaxes by public agents strangle and kill the Congolese economy with a disloyal competition organized by the very persons who have charge of protecting this nation! All this leads to the poverty of the Congolese populations and banditry on every side.[2]

It is necessary to fight against all forms of corruption, lying, and contempt for the peoples, their culture, and their faith. The common good is the only objective. The defense of life and of morality is a noble combat that is pleasing to God.

In her book Les Yeux ouverts [*With Open Eyes*], *Marguerite Yourcenar wrote:*

> *I condemn the ignorance that prevails at this time in the democracies as well as in the totalitarian regimes. This ignorance is so strong, often so thorough, that you would say that it is desired by the system, if not by the regime. I have often reflected on what the education of a child could be. I think that there would have to be basic, very simple studies in which the child would learn that he exists within the universe, on a planet whose resources he will have to use sparingly later on, that he depends on the air, on the water, on all living beings, and that the least error or the least violence runs the risk of destroying everything.*

How are we to react to the growing lack of education in our time?

At the root of the collapse of the West there is a cultural identity crisis. The West no longer knows who it is, because it no longer knows and does not want to know who made it, who established it as it was and as it is. Many countries today do not know their history. This self-suffocation naturally leads to a decadence that paves the way for new barbarian civilizations. I am certain of it: the paganization of the

---

[2] From "We Refuse to Die", a statement issued by the five bishops of the Bukavu province in the east of the Democratic Republic of Congo following their May 14–20 plenary meeting.

West will paganize the whole world, and the collapse of the West will cause a general cataclysm, a complete cultural, demographic, and religious upheaval.

In parallel with this phenomenon of an increasing lack of education, the elites, who have kept for themselves great literary, scientific, or political knowledge, have decided to eliminate all reference to a moral or Christian culture. Christian culture is the love of a wisdom embodied by a man, the Son of God, Jesus Christ. In him, all lives find a justification. In methodically detaching itself from God, modern culture can no longer offer a unified vision of the universe.

And nevertheless, the dark night of this world is still beautiful, because God exists.

Contemporary culture is the ruination of man. He has reverted almost to a bestial state. The dilution of culture engenders a form of perverse, empty sentimentalism. We must learn again to know Jesus Christ, to believe that he loves us and that he died out of love for us. It is necessary to relearn the catechism of the Catholic Church. It is necessary to have the courage and determination to acquire knowledge of the fundamental truths of the Creed of the Catholic faith. Why should many Catholics put up with illiterate, unreasoning piety, with a sentimental religion guided by emotional outbursts, with a blind morality deprived of the bedrock of solid doctrine?

Education leads us to clarity. But it is necessary to pass through demanding stages by means of intense work and shrewdly waged battles.

The Romans used to repeat this maxim: "Ars sine scientia nihil est" (Art without science is nothing). Failure to resort to the intellect is a shipwreck. It is not possible to arrive at faith without making an appeal to reason. A mystical identification with God without the aid of reflection is a dangerous sort of quietism.

The very etymology of the word "culture" involves a notion of growth: there is no cultivation without work and without effort. In order to rediscover an authentic meaning of culture, it is necessary to know what sort of humanity we wish to establish. Do we want a world in which man is in the image and likeness of God, or an earth cut off from all relation with transcendent realities, a totally secularized world, a world without God? In the first case, we will be able to promote the growth of a noble, beautiful culture; in the other, we will approach savagery little by little. Happiness consists of an ever richer perfecting of a culture inherited from our forefathers in God's sight. The barbarity of being uncultured is dominated by the search for endless enjoyment and by the satisfaction of our instincts and passions.

How would you define the lying that you ceaselessly bring to light?

Lying is a mask behind which man hides in order to fool and corrupt his fellow human beings. But he loses track and lies to himself, sometimes to the point of no longer being able to find solid ground.

Lying is the everyday practice of a world that no longer fears God.

Lying is an abyss where the devil rules as master. God is absent from that hole. It is necessary to accept the light of truth in order to return to the surface.

A liar is a man who infects himself with an incurable, mortal illness. Through its lies, our world today runs the risk of being a world condemned to die out. The poem by Charles Baudelaire, "L'amour du mensonge", which appears in the volume *Les Fleurs du mal*, admirably evokes the tragedy of a lying world cut off from God:

> Dear indolent, I love to watch you so,
> While on the ceiling break the tunes of dances,
> And hesitant, harmoniously slow,
> You turn the wandering boredom of your glances.
>
> I watch the gas-flares colouring your drawn,
> Pale forehead, which a morbid charm enhances,
> Where evening lamps illuminate a dawn
> In eyes as of a painting that entrances:
>
> And then I say, "She's fair and strangely fresh,
> Whom memory crowns with lofty towers above.
> Her heart is like a peach's murdered flesh,
> Or like her own, most ripe for learnèd love."
>
> Are you an autumn fruit of sovereign flavour?
> A funeral urn awaiting tearful showers?
> Of far oases the faint, wafted savour?
> A dreamy pillow? or a sheaf of flowers?

> I have known deep, sad eyes that yet concealed
> No secrets: caskets void of any gem:
> Medallions where no sacred charm lay sealed,
> Deep as the Skies, but vacuous like them!
>
> It is enough that your appearance flatters,
> Rejoicing one who flies from truth or duty.
> Your listless, cold stupidity—what matters?
> Hail, mask or curtain, I adore your beauty![3]

By its hatred for the truth, our age condemns itself to vanish. The Gospel tells us: "You will know the truth, and the truth will make you free" (Jn 8:32).

Satan is the first of liars. Saint John writes: "You are of your father the devil, and your will is to do your father's desires. He was a murderer from the beginning, and has nothing to do with the truth, because there is no truth in him. When he lies, he speaks according to his own nature, for he is a liar and the father of lies" (Jn 8:44). All lying is a form of slavery; it fetters us without our being aware of it. It causes us to enter into Satan's troubled waters.

Do you think that the Western democracies have been taken hostage by a financial oligarchy?

It is commonly admitted that democracy is the ideal political system. We are familiar with the quip by Winston Churchill: "Democracy is the worst form of government, except for all the others." This is one of the most durable aphorisms in the political debate.

Today, however, democracies are held hostage by powerful financial oligarchies. They have become the privileged system of powerful little groups that watch out primarily for their interests quoted on the stock market. Government of the people by the people has become the subjection of the people by high finance.

In Guinea, with Sékou Touré, I experienced Marxist democracy. The people were supposed to hold all the powers. In reality, they were oppressed, starving, crushed.

---

[3] "Love of Lies", in *Poems of Baudelaire*, trans. Roy Campbell (New York: Pantheon Books, 1952).

In the West, after the disasters of Nazism and Communism, they tried to assure the success of the so-called liberal democracies. These regimes claim to be open, tolerant, and progressive. Nevertheless, the power of the people has become an illusion that the media try to substantiate daily.

How can anyone continue to pretend that the people are sovereign? Look at the shameless way in which the power of the people is ceaselessly thwarted in order to strengthen the power of a small group of privileged persons.

Democracy is sick. The corruption of the Western governments is in no way inferior to that of the poor countries of the Southern Hemisphere. I am revolted by the violence that is perpetrated against the French demonstrators who are called the "gilets jaunes" (yellow jackets). Repression is becoming a more and more common *modus operandi* in the Western democracies. Furthermore, I cannot believe that the bureaucratic institutions of the European Union really want to defend the interest of the peoples. Democracy has been deified. Now, though, it is displaying totalitarian excesses. I am worried when I see the Western powers pretend to set up democracy in poor countries through armed intervention. Their populations know nothing about the characteristics of this form of government that others claim to establish by force.

How do you judge the truth of capitalism in practice?

A semantic shift has occurred. We no longer talk about capitalism but about economic liberalism or about a decentralized economy. The proponents of capitalism think that free competition is the only possible way to make progress. The profit earned by businesses is supposed to help all to improve their standard of living and to obtain more opportunities for development, convenience, and well-being.

In reality, capitalism is based on the idol of money. The lure of gain gradually destroys all social bonds. Capitalism devours itself. Little by little, the market destroys the value of work. Man becomes a piece of merchandise. He is no longer his own. The result is a new form of slavery, a system in which a large part of the population is dependent on a little caste.

In these conditions, do solidarity and development still have any meaning?

The truth of capitalism must be judged by the yardstick of the freedom that each person can keep and increase. It is clear that today the managers, like the hired workers, are caught in the gears of national and international decisions that limit their freedom. I often have the feeling that the material well-being of the West was acquired at the price of a sort of moral decline of the populations. Therefore, it is necessary to state clearly the distinction between an economy founded on freedom of enterprise and a capitalist system founded on the profit motive. Economic freedom implies our responsibility as men before God and our fellow citizens. It is not an absolute without rules or limits. It is at the service of everyone's good. Its objective is the friendship of all in the civilization. It must therefore be regulated by a certain sobriety and temperance, or else it becomes blind and violent. A freedom that aims only at profit ends up destroying itself.

What connection is there between the consumer society, mass culture, and the standardization of ways of life?

Capitalism tends to reduce humanity to one central figure: the consumer. All economic forces attempt to create a buyer who can be the same anywhere on the globe. The Australian consumer must resemble the Spanish or the Romanian consumer exactly. Cultural and national identities must not be a hindrance to the building of this interchangeable man.

The standardization of consumer products is the perfect reflection of the aridity of this soulless civilization. The consumer society encourages ever-increasing production, the ever-greater accumulation and consumption of material goods. It presents to man an unimaginable abundance of material goods to consume and attempts to stimulate human greed more and more. The abundance of material goods is almost frightening. A human being seems obliged to consume what happens to be within his reach.

Materialism seeks to provoke an unlimited need for enjoyment. It totally misunderstands the needs of the interior life. In order to flourish, each person must be recognized in his uniqueness. The essence of capitalism is contrary to this principle. Capitalism imprisons man within himself, isolates him, and makes him dependent.

Mass consumption leads to a dangerous, sterile form of gregariousness. The standardization of ways of life is the cancer of the postmodern world. Men become unwitting members of a great planetary herd that does not think, does not protest, and allows itself to be guided toward a future that does not belong to it.

Individual isolation and the degradation of persons, who are doomed to be no more than elements lost in the mass of consumers, are the two most horrible children of capitalism.

God's creature is deadened. He places his heart as a burnt offering on the altar of artificial happiness. He no longer knows the taste of true joys. He is an animal that eats, drinks, revels, and enjoys. The critical sense has become a ghost from the past.

Globalized humanity, without borders, is a hell.

Do you think that economic liberalism and societal libertarianism march to the same drummer?

Liberal capitalism needs to make men lose their beliefs and their morality. It mobilizes all its forces to arrive at an anarchic libertarianism. But a mind-set that is indifferent to evil, while tolerating everything, protects nothing.

May 1968 marked the turning point of this fatal alliance between economic liberalism and societal libertarianism.

The official thinkers of this trend, for example Jean-Paul Sartre or Michel Foucault, advocated the liberation of the instincts. They wanted to break all the taboos, the social frameworks, and the institutions, and to liberate spontaneity. Those who identified with this deconstructionist line of thought liked to proclaim the death of God.

This movement is based on an erroneous concept of freedom.

Father Henri de Lubac correctly summed up the atmosphere of the time: "If one [adversary] says that two and two make five, and the other that they make four, he [the broadminded man] prudently inclines towards the middle solution: two and two, he suggests, more or less make four and a half."[4] The revolution in May 1968 was a libertarian explosion. But if I say that two plus two makes five or four and a half, am I freer? Rather, I am more idiotic. Freedom is essentially connected to the truth.

---

[4] Henri de Lubac, *Paradoxes of Faith*, trans. Paule Simon et al. (San Francisco: Ignatius Press), 126.

In 1993, John Paul II tried to give a magisterial response to this crisis of truth in his encyclical *Veritatis splendor*: "The splendor of truth shines forth in the works of the Creator and, in a special way, in man, created in the image and likeness of God (cf. Gen 1:26). Truth enlightens man's intelligence and shapes his freedom, leading him to know and love the Lord. Hence the Psalmist prays: 'Let the light of your face shine on us, O Lord' (Ps 4:6)."

All the insurgents in 1968 shouted loudly, clamored for man's absolute freedom, even with regard to God. But this great and noble aspiration led to aberrations that destroyed the interior man.

What is the solution to inequalities caused by globalization and the remedy for situations of great poverty?

Since the Age of Enlightenment, Western man considers himself a model, a superman, a master who dictates to other peoples what man, freedom, democracy, culture, society, economy, and law are. During the era of the black slave trade, an African was worth less than his master's furniture. Some merchants even asked themselves the theological question as to the existence of the soul in Africans. But in the Church, the saints have always been the defenders of the slaves and of the little ones. I am thinking of Anne-Marie Javouhey, a woman who fought against governments to establish respect for the freedom of slaves in nineteenth-century Guiana. I am thinking also of Saint Peter Claver, the apostle to the slaves, of Saint Martin de Porres, a black Dominican of the seventeenth century, or also of Saint Josephine Bakhita, a slave who became a Canossian nun at the beginning of the twentieth century. The phenomenon to which we are referring is not that old. Racial segregation and discriminatory practices did not end legally in the United States until 1964, and the apartheid regime in South Africa lasted until 1994.

Within the Catholic Church, some voices have always been raised to condemn slavery. We find a very beautiful sign of this in Rome. On the façade of the church of San Tommaso in Formis there is a mosaic from the very early thirteenth century. On it Christ is depicted on his throne, holding in one hand a white slave and with the other a black slave whom he liberates together from their chains. At the heart of the Middle Ages, the white man and the black man are represented in the mosaic while observing strict equality. Once again, the Church was ahead of her times. It took centuries for Christians and the world to accept her message fully.

On another level, capitalism created in Europe a proletariat that was living in miserable, undignified conditions. From the very start, a dominant bourgeois class crushed a small, defenseless proletariat. In order to gauge the extent of this, it is helpful to reread certain pages by the French novelist Zola. Even though many Christian employers introduced laws to protect the workers, the spirit of capitalism spread its law of domination.

I am not surprised to observe that the capitalism of our time is able to extend this type of opposition on a worldwide scale. Capitalism is cynical. The rich are called to enrich themselves more and more while the poor must remain in the same state of deprivation. The humanist talk is so much deceptive tinsel. The elites want no change. Sentimentalism and cheap pity take the place of action.

Who caused the wars and the poverty that prompt Africans to flee their countries? Who destroyed Iraq, Libya, and the Democratic Republic of Congo because of their natural resources? Entire nations have been ravaged economically by the unscrupulous multinationals that pillage national economies. Neo-colonial policies that infantilize governments are a disgrace. Is it any surprise, then, when populations flee such situations in streams? They conceal the truth, and they dare to wonder whether it is necessary to welcome the populations that arrive on the European shores. And I am not talking about the Mafia-like practices of those who exploit the migrants' poverty.

The issue of Africa, the forgotten, exploited continent, has always been at the heart of your reflection.

In the 1995 Post-Synodal Apostolic Exhortation *Ecclesia in Africa*, John Paul II wrote some especially edifying words:

> Contemporary Africa can be compared to the man who went down from Jerusalem to Jericho; he fell among robbers who stripped him, beat him and departed, leaving him half dead (cf. Lk 10:30–37). Africa is a Continent where countless human beings—men and women, children and young people—are lying, as it were, on the edge of the road, sick, injured, disabled, marginalized and abandoned. They are in dire need of Good Samaritans who will come to their aid.

For my part, I express the hope that the Church will continue patiently and tirelessly its work as a Good Samaritan. Indeed, for a long period certain regimes, which have now come to an end, were a great trial for Africans and weakened their ability to respond to situations: an injured person has to rediscover all the resources of his own humanity. The sons and daughters of Africa need an understanding presence and pastoral concern. They need to be helped to recoup their energies so as to put them at the service of the common good.[5]

It is necessary to know that the richest countries of Africa are constantly at war. In Congo-Kinshasa, the international enterprises exploit the minerals without much oversight because the governments have been greatly weakened by the successive wars. Who distributes the arms to the various belligerents? Who profits from the crime? For many years, Angola experienced the same situation. On its soil were the largest diamond reserves in Africa. Similarly, the forest resources of Gabon and Central Africa go far to explain the bloody conflicts within those two countries.

Finally, I continue to wonder about the causes that helped hand Libya over to extremely dangerous Mafia-like powers, which play a leading role in the trafficking of migrants.

Is human enhancement the ultimate dream of capitalism?

Capitalism no longer needs men but, rather, consumers. Its sole objective is to improve the capacities for production and consumption. Enhanced man, the product of a technological revolution, is the latest avatar of the system to improve its profit. Just look at the developments taking place in the world of the powerful pharmaceutical industry. The blurring of the boundaries between classic therapeutic medicine and the medicine of enhancement is one of the chief characteristics of twenty-first-century biomedicine. In contemporary biomedicine, the new medications and medical technologies can be utilized not only to treat the sick patient, but also to enhance certain human abilities. Medicine is no longer exclusively therapeutic. The Promethean dream is at work. "I do not see how contemporary man

---

[5] Pope St. John Paul II, Post-Synodal Apostolic Exhortation *Ecclesia in Africa* on the Church in Africa and Its Evangelizing Mission towards the year 2000 (September 14, 1995), no. 41.

is so perfect that we should not seek to improve him": this terrible remark by the biologist Francis Crick, co-discoverer with James Watson of the structure of DNA in 1953, could be the motto of the transhumanist movement.

In the contemporary imagination, the robot appears as the model of future humanity. I have already said that man hopes to discard his body's flesh and blood so as to clothe himself in silicon and steel. Cells age, bodies wear out: metal, though, can be replaced. This is why the transhumanists are studying the ways to download the data in the brain and to transplant a personality into another body. Then immortality would be achieved! What an overwhelming desire to be a machine! What sort of human being would result from it?

This reminds me of the words of the prophet Daniel:

> "You saw, O king, and behold, a great image. This image, mighty and of exceeding brightness, stood before you, and its appearance was frightening. The head of this image was of fine gold, its breast and arms of silver, its belly and thighs of bronze, its legs of iron, its feet partly of iron and partly of clay. As you looked, a stone was cut out by no human hand, and it struck the image on its feet of iron and clay, and broke them in pieces; then the iron, the clay, the bronze, the silver, and the gold, all together were broken in pieces, and became like the chaff of the summer threshing floors; and the wind carried them away, so that not a trace of them could be found. But the stone that struck the image became a great mountain and filled the whole earth." (Dan 2:31–35)

For postmodern capitalism, man is a resource like any other. All that matters is the god Money.

Thus the primordial objective of a society, namely, the preservation of the human species and the protection of persons, comes into contradiction with the objective of capitalism, which prefers profits to human beings.

If men are merely consumers, they can only be the enemies of one another. Society then becomes the vast battlefield of an unbridled competition. We will not be able to recognize each other as brothers unless we discover that we have one and the same Father. Then we will take care of each other gratuitously. More than ever God is asking us: What have you done to your brother?

15

THE FUNERAL MARCH OF DECADENCE

NICOLAS DIAT: *How do you define decadence? How was it manifested within the Roman Empire?*

ROBERT CARDINAL SARAH: In his Sermon 81, Saint Augustine wrote, citing Psalm 102:

> Do you wonder that the world is failing? Wonder that the world is grown old. It is as a man who is born, and grows up, and waxes old. There are many complaints in old age; the cough, the rheum, the weakness of the eyes, fretfulness, and weariness. So then as when a man is old; he is full of complaints; so is the world old; and is full of troubles.... Choose not then to cleave to this aged world, and to be unwilling to grow young in Christ, who tells you, The world is perishing, the world is waxing old, the world is failing, is distressed by the heavy breathing of old age. But do not fear, "Your youth shall be renewed as the eagle's."[1]

These words of the aged bishop of Hippo seem to describe Rome, undermined by its immorality, its sin of luxury, and its cruel, bloody games in which slaves are sacrificed for the amusement of the Romans, who demand only *panem et cirenses*, bread and circuses. The Romans are overcome by their frantic search for enjoyment. They like to watch blood flow at the circus where famished wild beasts devour men. What horrible customs that age had!

---

[1] St. Augustine, Sermon 31, *Sermons on Selected Lessons of the New Testament*, trans. R. G. MacMullen, in *Nicene and Post-Nicene Fathers*, First Series, ed. Philip Schaff (1888; Peabody, Mass.: Hendrickson, 1995), 6:356, trans. rev. and ed. by Kevin Knight. http://www.new advent.org/fathers/160331.htm.

But Rome is besieged. And behold, it is captured, the city that had conquered the whole world. An ancient capital is falling down. For long years it was master of the world. The capture of the Eternal City symbolizes the decline and death of a thousand-year-old civilization.

If Rome can perish, Saint Jerome laments, what certainty is left? The whole world comes crashing down so quickly. "Who would believe that Rome, built up by the conquest of the whole world, had collapsed, that the mother of nations had become also their tomb?"[2]

In the early fifth century, at the time of the sack of Rome by the Visigoths under Alaric I, the bishop of Hippo was sad, but he tried to see Rome beyond its palaces and its triumphal arches: "It may be so; Rome will not perish, if the Romans do not perish.... For the question is not of her wood and stones, of her lofty insulated palaces, and all her spacious walls."[3] What Augustine feared occurred in a surprising and very painful way. Indeed, on August 24, 410, Alaric's troops invaded the capital of the empire. The fall of the *Urbs* gave rise to looting, fires, rapes, and massacres. The pagans then accused the Christians: "Look, everything is collapsing because of the Christian God!" they said, convinced that their gods were taking revenge for being abandoned in favor of this new religion. The Christians themselves were troubled. Despite the emperors who conspired with all their might against her, the Church succeeded in converting the empire, which became Christian in the fourth century. Then the Church saw it inundated by the barbarian invasions, but her life swelled with a new sap, and she converted the barbarian peoples so as to lead them to Christ. The youth of Rome, like our own, would be renewed only by converting to Christ. Then it would be able to gain vigor and strength.

The Church inspired and shaped the Middle Ages and created Europe. She saw the death of the medieval civilization that had sprung up and spread under her influence. She saw the birth of the modern world that increasingly escaped from her influence by radically opposing her doctrine.

---

[2] St. Jerome, preface to book 3 of his *Commentary on Ezekiel*, trans. W.H. Fremantle et al., in *Nicene and Post-Nicene Fathers*, Second Series, ed. Philip Schaff and Henry Wace (1893; Peabody, Mass.: Hendrickson, 1995), 6:500.

[3] St. Augustine, Sermon 31.

Centuries pass; the Church remains. Once again our time is marking the end of a civilization, with its share of anguish and fears.

In surveying world history, Montesquieu wrote in his work *Considerations on the Causes of the Greatness of the Romans and Their Decline* that "more states have perished by the violation of their moral customs than by the violation of their laws."[4] The fight against air and water pollution and the conservation of natural resources have become a respectable concern of society and the object of a new science: ecology. But there are other serious dangers for our future: the many forms of moral pollution. They, too, poison the air we breathe. They distort our conscience, pervert our judgment and our sensitivity, corrupt the reality of love, and lead to man's decline. The West is the chief point of departure of this moral pollution; this is why, like ancient Rome, it runs the risk of dying.

Why do you insist so much on the issue of moral exhaustion?

For the zealots of postmodernity, the traditional values issuing from the Judeo-Christian civilization are outmoded, useless, and dangerous. The family has never been heckled so much. Under the guise of humanism and fraternity, human dignity is trampled on. The corruption of morals and violence against women are reaching levels that have rarely been equaled. The West is poisoned by ideas that cause a deformation of consciences and a perversion of sensitivity.

Evil, violence, crimes, and sexual perversion have always existed. There have certainly been periods in history when squalor, brutality, obscenity, filth, erotic frenzy, and sexual inebriation ruled as much as they do today. But, in comparison to those eras, what rules now is an institutionalized hedonistic culture that threatens human life tomorrow. A little while ago, young people bathed in the great bath of the undisputed values that resulted from Judeo-Christian civilization. Today, those values are rejected as maladjusted and dilapidated, and they are combated.

---

[4] Charles-Louis de Secondat Montesquieu, *Considerations on the Causes of the Greatness of the Romans and Their Decline*, trans. David Lowenthal (1965; Indianapolis, Cambridge: Hackett, 1999), 86.

By relying on reason, the West attempts to have done with "the old world". The confusion between good and evil is the greatest tragedy of our time. The intellect no longer seems capable of making such a distinction. Reason no longer knows what is harmful to human nature, to human existence, and what is not. Too many young people and adults misunderstand or categorically deny the importance of the great principles of the world. We have lost the compass that must orient man's moral judgment.

Although reason remains capable of finding the truth, it seems to be lost in the marshes and the fogs that blind it and prevent it from being open to the truth.

Western man is his own worst polluter. We can observe a striking parallel between the pollution of nature and that of man himself. We know that certain chemical products must not be used to increase agricultural yields, but we continue to do so. The same goes for the moral life: man has lost the sense of the absolute. He is trapped in an anesthetizing relativism. Then he becomes scattered, depressed, and no longer finds his way.

One verse from the Second Letter of Peter poses a resoundingly relevant question: "Since all these things are thus to be dissolved, what sort of persons ought you to be . . . !" (2 Pet 3:11).

The impoverishment of educational institutions is frightening. They are nevertheless the origin of all major reforms. The teaching of history is symptomatic of this impoverishment. This noble subject, which once had a pivotal position in the humanities, is now debased to the role of an almost useless teaching.

In many Western countries, the desire to break with the past and all its traditions has caused situations of latent civil war. Man no longer loves himself. He no longer loves his neighbor or the land of his ancestors. He detests his culture and the values of the past. Many combat our religious, cultural, historical heritage and our very roots.

There is a new form of dictatorship and of cultural colonization that feeds the resentment of one part of the populace. This war of values is tragic. Because it denies its Christian roots, Europe no longer has a common cement. It is sinking little by little into violence and communitarianism. Civil wars are breaking on the horizon. Nations are falling apart; their specific traits are evaporating. Their citizens take refuge in artificial ideals. They confuse their feelings with the building of a collective project.

In the name of modernity and progress, they burn everything related to the past.

This is not a matter of nurturing nostalgia for a bygone past. But it is necessary for young people to have a clear identity, for them to know what history they are inheriting. More profoundly, I think that young Westerners aspire to a world in which each generation will not be overwhelmed by the burdensome duty of rebuilding everything from scratch. It is time to give them back the freedom to receive from their forefathers certitudes and rules based on experience. It is exhausting to have to reinvent everything ceaselessly. Receiving is a form of freedom.

Instead of that, what do they propose to us? The advocates of gender theory want to deconstruct the family. Gender theory itself is being taken to a decisively higher level by turning into the queer movement. The latter will not stop at the mere deconstruction of the human person; it is interested above all in the deconstruction of the social order. It is a matter of sowing confusion about sexual identities and behaviors, introducing suspicion about rules that are inherited and regarded as the expression of human nature, changing culture and social relations from within by transforming people's approach to sexuality.

John Paul II liked to talk about the nihilist passion of destruction.

Postmodern man likes to destroy. He is attracted by morbid things. From this perspective, contemporary art is significant. Ugliness is loved and exalted. The horrible virus spreads at full tilt; harmony is replaced by incomprehensibility.

The ancient institutions of our societies are under attack, which condemns these societies to enter into a process of decadence. I think we are now reaching a new level with the destruction of man himself. It is urgently necessary to help Western man—who is often very active, lucid, and restless, never satisfied with himself, always continually tending to improve himself and others—to find his rest in the humble, resolute acceptance of his weaknesses and limits. More than an active being, more than a manufacturer of objects, is the human being not a contemplative? Man does not create himself; he receives much as an inheritance.

We concluded our book *The Power of Silence* by emphasizing how the agitation, activism, and noise that characterize our time act as a force that destroys the interior life. Noise is the ultimate enemy of reflection, tranquility, and love. Now noise has become commonplace. It is part of our environment and of our way of life. And it keeps us from confronting our interior life.

And sadly, suicidal feelings are a commonplace part of everyday life.

Modern man consumes thoughtlessly, irresistibly caught up by the abundance and the advertising that encourages him to use things without any hindrance. Sooner or later he opens his eyes to the infinite sadness of his existence and realizes that he can no longer see heaven. He is caught in a vicious circle: produce, consume, produce even more, and consume still more.

Man is materially obese. On the spiritual level, he wanders like a poor tramp. For a long time he was not unhappy. The universe seemed to him full of material promises.

The decadence of our societies is gradually enveloping people in an anxiety-causing mist. Institutions, cultures, histories are dying out inexorably.

It is necessary to come and contemplate the ruins of the Roman forum to understand the finitude of civilizations.

The suicide of the West is tragic. Its rejections are leading all humanity to a dead end. It has no more strength, no more children, no more morality, no more hope. Its only hope of survival is to rediscover the One who said: "I am the way, and the truth, and the life" (Jn 14:6).

Christians have abandoned their mission, and the decadence of the West is the result. They no longer look to heaven. They are taken hostage by the new paradigms. They make themselves worldly. The life of prayer itself, which ought to feed and strengthen them and make them influential, runs the risk of being contaminated by the spirit of spectacle and the search for sensations. Nevertheless, for more than two thousand years, this prayer has nourished the life of saints and of all the disciples of Jesus. Prayer is the only great remedy.

16

RELIGIOUS LIBERTY

NICOLAS DIAT: *In 2008, in the majestic crypt of the Shrine of the Immaculate Conception in Washington, in the presence of more than four hundred American bishops, Benedict XVI declared: "Respect for freedom of religion is deeply ingrained in the American consciousness—a fact which has contributed to this country's attraction for generations of immigrants, seeking a home where they can worship freely in accordance with their beliefs."*[1] *In your opinion, is the United States a model of religious liberty that should be imitated by other nations?*

ROBERT CARDINAL SARAH: Some understood the words of Benedict XVI in that way. They thought that they could hold up the United States as the archetype of an open society, a model that should be exported to or else imposed on the whole world. They certainly forgot the sentence that preceded the one that you quote. Indeed, the pope recalled: "Your people ... have confidence in God, and they do not hesitate to bring moral arguments rooted in biblical faith into their public discourse." In fact, Benedict XVI intended in this way to recall the objective foundations of an authentic religious liberty.

The great temptation of political societies is to forget that they have neither their foundation nor their ultimate purpose in themselves. A State can never claim perfection; it will never be able to promise us complete happiness or absolute freedom. Earthly societies are always incomplete. I think that we need to remind Christians of

[1] Pope Benedict XVI, Address at the Celebration of Vespers and Meeting with the Bishops of the United States of America, National Shrine of the Immaculate Conception, Washington, D.C., April 16, 2008.

this: our hope is not in this world. The Kingdom of God will never be established on earth. The more a political society forgets this, the more it presents itself as the unsurpassable horizon, the more totalitarian it becomes.

In this sense, I want to recall forcefully what Benedict XVI said: there is a profound relationship between the Communist mirage, the Nazi madness, and democratic liberalism as we know it today.

These three ideologies resemble each other in several fundamental points. They claim to produce man's happiness at will or by force. Communism and Nazism invented the extermination camps. Democratic liberal ideology makes use of persecution by media and indoctrination from the earliest childhood. Those are the signs of a society that thinks it is humanity's only horizon, the sole political, economic, and social reference point. Christians will always be a thorn in the flesh for these soft or hard totalitarianisms. For Christians ceaselessly recall that we are not made for this world. Our fatherland is found in heaven!

This does not mean that our earthly fatherlands are nothing and that we do not have to apply ourselves to make them places of human flourishing, fraternity, decency, truth, and justice. On the contrary, we must look for ways to live there in unity, proud of our respective cultures. From this perspective, we must note the failure of the liberal democratic ideology. The peoples of the West have fallen prey to a profound identity crisis. They no longer know that they form a people.

On that same occasion, Benedict XVI emphasized the deep relationship between totalitarianisms and liberal ideology. If at the foundation of the democratic State there is nothing but a gathering of purely subjective individuals, how could the majority fail to become oppressive? Basically, it is nothing but the expression of a liberty void of meaning, left to the whims of opinions, at the mercy of the manipulations of the powerful and the rich. "Deprived of its content, individual freedom abolishes itself", Benedict XVI wrote in *Truth, Values, Power: Touchstones of Pluralistic Society*.[2] In *A Turning Point for Europe?* he also wrote, "What holds a society together and gives it

---

[2] Reprinted in Joseph Ratzinger/Benedict XVI, *Faith and Politics*, Selected Writings, trans. Michael J. Miller et al. (San Francisco: Ignatius Press, 2018), 97–105; here, 100.

peace is law".[3] A society that refuses to be founded on the objective good turns into a dictatorship of emptiness.

The Church owes it to herself to interrogate the democratic societies about the foundation of law. A society founded on itself collapses sooner or later. I was struck by the prophetic courage of Benedict XVI each time he addressed national parliaments, in Westminster in 2010 and also in Berlin in 2011. Each time he insisted on one point, which he repeats in the work *A Turning Point for Europe?*: "When God and the basic pattern of human existence laid down by him are ousted from public consciousness and relegated to the private sphere, ... the concept of law dissolves into thin air and, with it, the foundation of peace."[4] This remark sets forth a point of capital importance. Law needs a transcendent foundation, which is received by man. It cannot establish itself, unless the political authority gives in to the temptation of Prometheus and turns into a totalitarian power.

Do you mean that democratic societies may not be just societies?

I would like to quote a fine aphorism by Saint Augustine: "Remota itaque justitia quid sunt regna nisi magna latrocinia?" (When justice is banished from them, what are States but large bands of robbers?)[5] Cardinal Ratzinger pertinently echoes this reflection by Saint Augustine. Here is what he wrote in *A Turning Point for Europe?*:

> Merely pragmatic criteria, which are thereby necessarily the criteria of a party, determined by the group, are essentially the constitutive factor of structured robber societies. Something other than these— that is, something other than a large group that regulates itself only in accordance with its goals—exists only when a righteousness comes into play that is measured, not by the interest of the group, but by a universal criterion. Only this do we call the "justice" that constitutes the state. It includes the Creator and creation as its points of orientation. This means that a state that is in principle agnostic vis-à-vis God

---

[3] Joseph Cardinal Ratzinger, *Turning Point for Europe? The Church in the Modern World—Assessment and Forecast*, trans. Brian McNeil (San Francisco: Ignatius Press, 1994), 48.

[4] Ibid., 54.

[5] St. Augustine, *DCE*, IV, 4.

and constructs justice only on the basis of majority opinions inherently sinks down to the level of the robber band.[6]

A band of robbers does not even form a community but, rather, a momentary collection of interests that converge accidentally. A State that abandons the determination of the law to the fluctuations of majorities runs the severe risk of turning into a band of robbers. He continues: "Where God is excluded, the principle of the robber band exists, in variously harsher or milder forms. This begins to become visible where the organized killing of innocent human beings—unborn human beings—is clothed with the appearance of right because it is protected by the interest of a majority."[7]

I do appreciate the democratic form of government, because it gives each person the opportunity to realize his free responsibility in society, but it does not bear within itself the foundation of a genuine law. A society that is democratic in form needs some content: law, the good; otherwise, it is organized around nothingness. Justice is truly the goal but also the intrinsic standard of all politics. Politics is more than a mere technique for defining public ordinances: its origin and purpose are found precisely in justice, and that is of an ethical nature. Thus the State in fact finds itself inevitably confronted by the question: How can justice be done here and now?

But where can this content, this foundation, be found? Is it the Church's job to give it? Isn't there a risk of falling into a form of theocracy?

You put your finger on the problem of authentic religious liberty. Every human being must be able to seek the truth freely, above all in religious matters. The public debate must remain free in its expression. But it must be founded on an objective content that is fair and common to all men. Speaking to the British Parliament, Benedict XVI recalled that

> The Catholic tradition maintains that the objective norms governing right action are accessible to reason, prescinding from the content of

---

[6] Ratzinger, *Turning Point*, 132.
[7] Ibid., 132–33.

revelation. According to this understanding, the role of religion in political debate is not so much to supply these norms, as if they could not be known by nonbelievers—still less to propose concrete political solutions, which would lie altogether outside the competence of religion—but rather to help purify and shed light upon the application of reason to the discovery of objective moral principles.[8]

In his encyclical letter *Deus caritas est*, Benedict is much more explicit and precise. He writes:

> The Church's social teaching argues on the basis of reason and natural law, namely, on the basis of what is in accord with the nature of every human being. It recognizes that it is not the Church's responsibility to make this teaching prevail in political life. Rather, the Church wishes to help form consciences in political life and to stimulate greater insight into the authentic requirements of justice as well as greater readiness to act accordingly, even when this might involve conflict with situations of personal interest. Building a just social and civil order, wherein each person receives what is his or her due, is an essential task which every generation must take up anew. As a political task, this cannot be the Church's immediate responsibility. Yet, since it is also a most important human responsibility, the Church is duty-bound to offer, through the purification of reason and through ethical formation, her own specific contribution towards understanding the requirements of justice and achieving them politically.
>
> The Church cannot and must not take upon herself the political battle to bring about the most just society possible. She cannot and must not replace the State. Yet at the same time she cannot and must not remain on the sidelines in the fight for justice. She has to play her part through rational argument and she has to reawaken the spiritual energy without which justice, which always demands sacrifice, cannot prevail and prosper. (*DCE* 28a)

The principle of religious liberty is described nicely here. Man must freely discover and put into practice these objective norms that are, so to speak, the grammar of our human nature. The Church is here to enlighten free human reason, to correct it, to purify it of

[8] Pope Benedict XVI, Address to Representatives of British Society, including the Diplomatic Corps, Politicians, Academics and Business Leaders, Westminster Hall, September 17, 2010.

the temptation of omnipotence. Man must realize that reason that does not let itself be purified becomes totalitarianism, even though it may be dressed up in democratic procedures. Recall that Hitler was elected according to a democratic process.

What, then, is the role of Christians in politics?

Above all, they must set up a barrier against totalitarian arbitrariness that emancipates itself from the natural law. They must do this on behalf of their conscience. For the Creator inscribed this objective order on the conscience. It is inconsistent and harmful to separate the Christian on one side from the citizen on the other.

Christians must therefore attest to the fact that "man is capable of perceiving truth and that this ability ... sets a limit to all power", to repeat the words of Cardinal Ratzinger in *Values in a Time of Upheaval*.[9] Truth is the real rampart against the temptation of limitless power. We must at the same time maintain man's fundamental capacity to reach this truth and his right to search for it freely until he finds it. This objective natural order, which Christians must defend, is the good of every person. It is not necessary to profess the Christian faith in order to recognize it. This order is accessible to all men of good will. Christians should have no hang-ups about promoting it. They must speak fearlessly, because they are not acting on behalf of one party against another; rather, they are witnesses to the truth, defenders of human nature. But they must be ready to suffer and to die in order to bear witness to this truth.

Are Christians sometimes called to resist the political authority?

They are often called to spiritual resistance. Confronted with a State that requires some cooperation in evil or imposes evil, Christians are called in the name of their conscience to martyrdom, the summit of Christian political witness. "In the end injustice can be overcome only through suffering, through the voluntary suffering of those who remain true to their conscience and thereby authentically witness to

---

[9] Joseph Cardinal Ratzinger (Pope Benedict XVI), *Values in a Time of Upheaval*, trans. Brian McNeil (New York: Crossroad; San Francisco: Ignatius Press, 2006), 90.

the end of all power in their suffering and in their whole life", Cardinal Ratzinger wrote in his book *Church, Ecumenism, and Politics*.[10] It is necessary above all to refuse to allow oneself to be bought or corrupted by money. Christ and the apostles have absolutely nothing with which to carry out their mission. Many think that money fosters and promotes the Church's mission. Let them open their eyes and look at the opulent Churches of the West. They were more flourishing, more missionary, more fervent, more faithful and more dynamic in their evangelical testimony when they were supported by their faith in Jesus Christ and were poorer in financial means. As long as we emphasize and give priority to the material aspects and means, we asphyxiate the Church.

In the United States, some preferred to lose everything rather than to collaborate with the destruction of the natural order under the Obama administration. Spiritual resistance is the best service that Christians can render to political society. I think that in a human society, a Christian will always be more or less a dissident. Sometimes he will be put in prison to silence him. More often, his words will be disqualified by conformist irony or a media lynching.

Nevertheless, Christians are less persecuted in Western democracies than in countries ruled by Islamism, are they not?

The most destructive persecution of Christianity is unfolding today in the Western democracies. There, they have killed God. Increasingly, Christians are marginalized, terrorized, humiliated, ridiculed. Thus we must deplore the fact that a growing number of Christians apostatize. There is nothing Christian about them but the name. They still practice their religion but without conviction, as a purely cultural or social act. In saying this, I am not ignoring the millions of heroic Christians who are deeply faithful to Christ and to his teaching. Remember Christ's warning: "Do not fear those who kill the body, and after that have no more that they can do. But I will warn you whom to fear: fear him who, after he has killed, has power to cast into hell; yes, I tell you, fear him!" (Lk 12:4–5).

---

[10] Joseph Ratzinger/Pope Benedict XVI, *Church, Ecumenism, and Politics: New Endeavors in Ecclesiology*, trans. Michael J. Miller et al. (San Francisco: Ignatius Press, 2008), 165.

In pluralist democracies, the totalitarian temptation is the product of reason that refuses to let itself be purified by religion. This gives rise to the soft dictatorship of relativism and concealed persecution that little by little anesthetizes consciences, robbing men of their true liberty. Fanatical, fundamentalist Islamism experiences the opposite temptation: a religion that refuses to let itself be purified by reason. Christians know that God manifests himself through the conscience. There is no tension between the work of God the Creator and revelation. And so we can say that an essential part of human dignity is to seek and to find the truth freely. Christians trust reason; they call for religious liberty so that the truth might be embraced by all. Islamism, in contrast, imposes its belief against reason, by force and violence. It preaches a god who can command what is contrary to human dignity and violates conscience and freedom. Fanatical, fundamentalist Islamism promotes a religion founded on sheer obedience to an external law that is not revealed in the conscience but is imposed by political society. Here, too, Christians are figures in a spiritual resistance. In many countries of the Middle East, they are the only ones to resist, not on behalf of a party that would seek to take power and to impose itself on others, but on behalf of the rights of a conscience that is open to the truth.

Those who have been martyred by Islamism proclaim the "power of powerlessness" in confronting violence. I am thinking of all those brothers and sisters in Egypt, Pakistan, Syria, Iraq, Nigeria, and Sudan. They are models for us who do not experience bloody persecution. They are also a reproach for all our compromises with the power of lying. They question our middle-class Christianity, which proceeds from one compromise to the next so as to avoid any trouble. They tell us with blinding clarity: if Christianity makes its peace with the decadence of the West, the reason is because Christians are not faithful to the essence of their faith. Their faces are the true light for the Church of our time. Their example is truly the foundation of our hope. They are the face of Christ today.

"The Martyrs are the true glory of the Church", Pope Francis wrote last November [2018] to the Franciscans in Syria; nothing can demonstrate more clearly than martyrdom the Christian's characteristic manner of participating in the history of humanity's salvation. The martyrs have the Kingdom of God as their prospect. They are the true glory of the Church and our hope. Their testimonies are a warning not to lose our way in the midst of storms. Francis concluded: "Not a few times the sea of life has a storm awaiting us, but out of the existential waves we receive an unexpected sign of salvation: Mary, the Mother of the Lord, looking in astonishment and silence at the innocent, crucified Son who fills life and salvation with meaning."[11]

[11] Translation from the Vatican News website: https://www.vaticannews.va/en/pope /news/2018-11/pope-francis-franciscans-holy-land-custos.html.

PART IV

Rediscovering Hope:
The Practice of the Christian Virtues

In this life, virtue consists of loving what must be loved. Knowing how to choose it is prudence, not letting oneself be distracted by seductive powers is temperance, not letting oneself
be led astray by pride is justice.

Saint Augustine, Letter 155

17

GOD OPENS HIS HAND

NICOLAS DIAT: You paint a very somber picture of the state of the world and of the Church. How can we pave the way for a renewal? What program would you propose following?

ROBERT CARDINAL SARAH: I have no program. When you have a program, it is because you want to achieve a human project. The Church is not an institution that we have to achieve or fashion with our ideas. It is simply necessary to receive from God what he wants to give us.

John Paul II already warned us against this tendency to develop Church programs in his Apostolic Letter *Novo millennio ineunte*:

> It is not therefore a matter of inventing a "new programme". The programme already exists: it is the plan found in the Gospel and in the living Tradition, it is the same as ever. Ultimately, it has its centre in Christ himself, who is to be known, loved and imitated, so that in him we may live the life of the Trinity, and with him transform history until its fulfilment in the heavenly Jerusalem. This is a programme which does not change with shifts of times and cultures, even though it takes account of time and culture for the sake of true dialogue and effective communication. This programme for all times is our programme for the Third Millennium.[1]

This reminds me of a very beautiful text by Cardinal Ratzinger in which he asks himself what the reform of the Church should be like. He compares the Church to a statue. Michelangelo, when he received a block of marble, already saw the statue imprisoned within

---

[1] Pope St. John Paul II, Apostolic Letter *Novo millennio ineunte* at the Close of the Great Jubilee of the Year 2000 (January 6, 2001), no. 29.

the shapeless marble. For him, to sculpt was to remove the excess around the statue. Similarly, we do not have to sculpt the body of the Church according to our petty ideas. We do not have to invent a Church. The Church is Jesus' work. We have to remove all the surplus that our sins and compromises with the world have added on top of his work, to the point of masking its beauty. Yes, let us remove all the layers of worldliness, cowardice, and sins that hide from everyone's sight the holiness, the splendor, and the divine beauty of God's Church. What will we find then? First, the Christian virtues. They are given to us by God to divinize our human nature. They are received in baptism; they are the procession that accompanies the presence of the Trinity in our souls. They are our spiritual dynamism.

The word virtue in Greek means "excellence". The virtues bring each of our faculties to its most perfect fulfillment. In basing our lives on the Christian virtues, we are certain that we are not making a mistake.

What is the first virtue that you would like to mention?

I would like to begin by recalling the importance of prudence. This virtue makes us find the concrete means of putting into action the purposes that we have chosen. We are increasingly tempted by a disembodied Christianity. I often hear preaching about a religion of "good intentions". Now the best of intentions end up becoming a dream or a mirage unless they are turned into an actual reality.

It is not enough to have fertile ideas or grand desires. It is necessary to put them into practice, too. I have already underscored this pathology that is characteristic of the modern mind: under the pretext of being "spiritual", we disdain the concrete means, giving in to the temptation of a Christianity that is so "pure" that it ends up being intellectual. Basically, we refuse to let God be incarnate and to enter into the heart of our lives. I wonder whether there is not a subtle form of pride behind this attitude. Does it not quite simply reject our created nature, with its limits? Does it not refuse to receive this nature as a gift, of which we are not the author? Is this not a secret echo of Lucifer's rebellion against his creaturely condition?

Our relation to God must be based on attitudes and gestures. Of course, the essential thing takes place within the heart. It may happen, though, that one ends up despising the concrete means of preserving and developing this interior relation with God. Prudence consists of moving into action; otherwise, the best intentions remain pious wishes.

Let us take a few examples. I often hear supposedly enlightened Christians express disdain for forms of popular devotion such as pilgrimages, the Rosary, processions in honor of the Blessed Sacrament of the Body and Blood of Jesus Christ, or genuflection before Jesus in the Eucharist. Is it necessary to contrast faith and religion to this extent? What would a human love be if it were never expressed externally? Prudence teaches us that we need sacred gestures. We need to get down on our knees humbly, out of love, to be silent, to sing. We need these external signs. Saint Paul VI was not afraid to recall this in his General Audience on June 16, 1965:

> It is advisable to note that the external manifestation of religious sentiment is not only a right but also a duty, because of the very nature of the human being, who receives from external signs a stimulant for his interior activity and expresses it in the external signs, thus giving to it its full meaning and social value.... Consequently, external religious practices, when they are neither superstition nor an end in themselves, serve, so to speak, as clothing for the divine things that they make accessible to our cognitive faculty. In a way, they help us to present to the Heavenly Majesty the tribute of an earthly offering.

This is true in the sphere of repentance, too. Some are afraid of being too materialistic. Then, under the pretext of being more spiritual, they reduce fasting to a purely interior movement. The Christian fast, in order to become the fast of the heart, must first be the fast of the body. Thus, the Lenten fast ought to be a fine communal Christian ceremony. Christian asceticism is not an enemy of the body, but a discipline with a view to self-mastery and the intention to make the body participate in the surge of our soul toward holiness.

I am thinking also of the life of clerics. The teachings of the recent popes admirably lay the foundations for an authentic priestly spirituality. All that remains is to translate them into concrete methods. Benedict XVI and Francis envisaged a spiritual reform of clerical life, which ought to start with a spiritual reform of the life of the Curia. Christian prudence consists of seeking the concrete means of doing this in the light of the faith. Rather than copy the bureaucratic institutions of the secular world, let us return to the means that the apostles implemented from the very first Christian times. The Acts of the Apostles point the way: in order to put the Gospel into practice concretely, clerics must center their lives on the Word of God, common prayer, and the celebration of the Eucharist. It is necessary for them to listen to Saint Paul again as attentively and seriously as possible: "Be imitators of me, as I am of Christ" (1 Cor 11:1). In order to preserve their chastity, they must lead a common life of poverty, charity, and obedience. How can anyone be surprised by the rampant invasion of secularism in the mentality of pastors who live in opulence? In this sphere, Christian prudence consists of taking the concrete means of a life of poverty. A cleric cannot be content with an alleged spirit of poverty hovering over a life that is concretely oriented toward consumption and material goods. On September 30, 2001, in a homily, Saint John Paul II declared: "The *route of poverty* will allow us to transmit to our contemporaries the 'fruits of salvation'. As Bishops we are called upon, therefore, to be poor at the service of the Gospel."

Similarly, the life of clerics must follow concretely the precepts of holiness. As Benedict XVI reminded Irish Catholics on March 19, 2010, the most profound causes for the proliferation of the abuse of minors lie in the abandonment of that ideal: "All too often, the sacramental and devotional practices that sustain faith and enable it to grow, such as frequent confession, daily prayer and annual retreats, were neglected. Significant too was the tendency during this period, also on the part of priests and religious, to adopt ways of thinking and assessing secular realities without sufficient reference to the Gospel."[2] How can a priest remain faithful if his life is not structured by methods such as confession and spiritual direction?

However, it is necessary to go farther. Benedict XVI notes among the causes of the increase of infidelity to the commitment to celibacy "a well-intentioned but misguided tendency to avoid penal approaches to canonically irregular situations".[3] To my way of thinking, this point is particularly important. We need to rediscover the sense of punishment. A priest who commits a mistake must be

---

[2] Pope Benedict XVI, Pastoral Letter to the Catholics of Ireland (March 19, 2010), no. 4.
[3] Ibid.

punished. This is a manifestation of charity toward him, because it allows him to correct himself and to do penance. But it is also justice for the Christian people. A priest who fails to be chaste must receive a punishment. Canon law (canon 1340) foresees many ways of correcting. He should be sent, for a definite period of time, to do penance in a monastery. Under the guise of mercy, guilty priests have just been moved geographically, even in tragic cases of pedophile acts. This damages the credibility of the whole Church. It is urgently necessary to rediscover the meaning of the penal law. Who knows how many priestly souls could have been saved if there had been an attempt to correct them before something irreparable had been committed?

I want to remind bishops that their responsibility as fathers is at stake. Can the father of a family raise his children without ever punishing them? I think that exempting oneself from this method under the pretext of mercy or a supposedly adult faith is the most poignant manifestation of the clericalism so often denounced by Pope Francis.

We must use the means corresponding to our deep intentions. To be prudent is to provide oneself with the concrete means of attaining union with Christ and living as a Christian. This presupposes not living according to the world's standards. It is time to rediscover the courage of anti-conformism. Christians must have the strength to develop oases where the air is breathable, where, to put it quite simply, Christian life is possible. Our communities must be these oases in the middle of the desert. One must be able to devote time to prayer, the liturgy, and works of charity.

The world is organized against God. Our communities must organize themselves, not by being content to make some room for him, but by putting him at the center. I am struck when I see that many Christian families choose to settle near a monastery or a vibrant parish. They want to live by the rhythm of the Church and to make their existence a true liturgy. They want their children not only to have abstract Christian ideas but to experience concretely a milieu imbued with the Divine Presence and an intense life of prayer and charity: "We must open up avenues to experience faith for those who are seeking God",[4] Benedict XVI said.

---

[4] Pope Benedict XVI, Address at the Meeting with the Parish Priests and the Clergy of the Diocese of Rome (February 26, 2009).

Let us not think that we will be able to live as Christians if we adopt all the attitudes of a godless world. By not living as one believes, one ends up believing as one lives.

Being Christian is not only a disposition of the soul but a state of life. Monks take this disposition seriously. In a monastery, everything is organized to remind us of the presence of God and the need for fraternal charity. Christian lay people should organize themselves so that their concrete everyday life does not separate them from God and allows them to act in a way that is truly consistent with their faith. This implies rethinking all social and professional relations, the ways in which we relax, learn, stay informed, and educate our children. We cannot leave these things up to a world that is founded on atheism. Christian prudence commands us to discover the means of a personal, familial, and social life that is organized according to Christ.

The virtue of temperance has bad press today. Does it still have a place among the Christian virtues?

How can we claim to be disciples of Christ, who did not even have a stone on which to rest his head, if we live in opulence? How can a priest claim to imitate Christ if he lacks nothing? If he has a bourgeois, worldly life-style, if his priestly consecration does not distinguish him from the people in the world? Temperance is the virtue that makes us seek excellence in the enjoyment of pleasurable things. This enjoyment is good in itself, because it is created and willed by God.

The consumer society makes pleasure and possession an end in itself and an idol. Like all idolatry, consumption at all costs turns men away from God. Temperance is that moderation, that simple sobriety which protects our interior life and opens the way to contemplation. You know how close I am to the monks. How their lives, immersed in the praise of God and the search for him, lead us to grow in the will of God and to tend constantly toward perfection. With them you learn patiently to pass from the carnal to the spiritual. At the monastery you learn that asceticism is only a discipline of the soul's strength in mastering the body, with a view to making it participate in the splendor of the spiritual realities. Thus

Saint Bernard of Clairvaux could write to Guigues, the prior of the Grand Chartreuse:

> However, as we are in fleshly bodies, and are born of the desire of the flesh, it is of necessity that our desire, or affection, should begin from the flesh; but if it is rightly directed, advancing step by step under the guidance of grace, it will at length be perfected by the Spirit, because that is not first which is spiritual, but that which is natural, and afterwards that which is spiritual; and it is needful that we should first bear the image of the earthly and afterwards that of the heavenly (1 Cor 15:46, 49).[5]

Monks are mirrors and models to follow. Look at their example. They lead a simple, sober, and humble life. Do not think that they disdain the body. On the contrary, they know how to put it in its place. They know the necessity of contemplation. Moreover, monks live for a long time. They are in better health than most Westerners, who are gorged on the more or less corrupted consumer goods.

I think we must rediscover the meaning of moderation. I am struck by the fact that, in the rich countries, people no longer know how to rejoice and celebrate in a simple way. Joy does not necessarily come about through excess, immoderation, a profusion of means. Christian temperance is expressed in the simple, sober joys of the family. Unfortunately, modern communications technologies create desires and jealousies by spreading ever more excessive images. Immoderation has become the rule. I have heard reports that some families postpone baptisms or marriages for several years so as to plan a more luxurious party. What an inversion of priorities! Intemperance creates pride and immoderation.

Temperance should govern our relation to technology. The power represented by the technological means caresses temptation in us. We want to be more and more powerful, more and more connected, less and less dependent on our body. Intemperance could lead us to the Luciferian attitude of rejecting all limits. In the encyclical *Laudato si'*, Pope Francis thus says that "those who are surrounded with

---

[5] St. Bernard of Clairvaux, Letter 11, no. 8, to Guigues, the Prior, and to the Other Monks of the Grande Chartreuse, in *The Life and Works of Saint Bernard*, vol. 1, trans. Samuel J. Eales (Aeterna Press, 2014).

technology 'know full well that it moves forward in the final analysis neither for profit nor for the well-being of the human race', that 'in the most radical sense of the term power is its motive—a lordship over all.' "[6]

Instead of extending a hand toward nature to welcome it while bowing to the potentialities that it offers us, we try to possess it, manipulate it, and enslave it. We start worrying like someone who always wants to have more and is sad that he does not own enough things. This observation applies both to individuals and to nations. Sadness and anxiety are the poisoned fruits of intemperance.

I, in contrast, call for joyous self-limitation. In 1993, in his Liechtenstein Address, Alexandr Solzhenitsyn remarked:

> The time is urgently upon us to limit our wants. It is difficult to bring ourselves to sacrifice and self-denial, because in political, public, and private life we have long since dropped the golden key of self-restraint to the ocean floor. But self-limitation is the fundamental and wisest step of a man who has obtained his freedom.... We can only experience true spiritual satisfaction, not in seizing, but in refusing to seize. In other words, in self-limitation.... To limit ourselves is the only true path of preservation for us all. And it helps bring back the awareness of a Whole and Higher Authority above us—and the altogether forgotten sense of humility before this Entity.[7]

This reflection is extremely important. What is at stake ultimately in temperance is our capacity for adoration. Excess consumption anesthetizes the contemplative life and gives the illusion of power. The consumer society is inebriating; it sets man against God. Like a man who staggers because he has drunk too much, Western man defies God and refuses to adore him. He believes that he himself is all-powerful, whereas he has never been so frail.

Intemperance and consumption destroy friendship between men and dissolve the ties that unite nations. Alexandr Solzhenitsyn also said in the same speech: "If we do not learn to limit firmly our desires

---

[6] LS 108, quoting Romano Guardini, *The End of the Modern World* (Wilmington, 1998), 56.
[7] In *The Solzhenitsyn Reader: New and Essential Writings, 1947–2005*, ed. and trans. Edward Ericson, Jr., and Daniel J. Mahoney (Wilmington, Del.: Intercollegiate Studies Institute, 2006), 599–600.

and demands, to subordinate our interests to moral criteria—we, humankind, will simply be torn apart, as the worst aspects of human nature will bare their teeth.... If a personality is not directed at values higher than the self, corruption and decay inevitably take hold."[8]

It is difficult to escape this reasoning. The consumer society is a system by which all human beings seem to be fettered. I think we have to have the courage to perform prophetic acts. It is up to the Christians of our time to be inventive, even if that involves a certain marginalization. In *The Ratzinger Report*, the curial cardinal wrote:

> it is time that the Christian reacquire the consciousness of belonging to a minority and of often being in opposition to what is obvious, plausible and natural for that mentality which the New Testament calls—and certainly not in a positive sense—the "spirit of the world". It is time to find again the courage of non-conformism, the capacity to oppose many of the trends of the surrounding culture, renouncing a certain euphoric post-conciliar solidarity.[9]

Temperance is the source of joy and benevolence. Christians must invent new forms of work and consumption. In this sphere, too, in a consumerist world, they are the internal dissidents.

You speak about opposition to the world; is this not the very place where the virtue of fortitude appears?

You are right. Fortitude is the virtue that helps us to confront bodily and spiritual dangers. Often, while citing an intention to be kind and benevolent, some have extinguished genuine Christian fortitude. Jesus tells us that we are the salt of the earth, not the sugar of the earth!

Blessed are the meek! Woe to the soft and the lukewarm! Christians must reclaim this fine virtue of fortitude that is wedded so well with meekness. They must know that they will always be a sign of contradiction for the world. The Lord did not ask us to have no enemies but to love them.

---

[8] Ibid., 600.

[9] Joseph Cardinal Ratzinger with Vittorio Messori, *The Ratzinger Report: An Exclusive Interview on the State of the Church*, trans. Salvator Attanasio with Graham Harrison (San Francisco: Ignatius Press, 1985), 36–37.

Christian fortitude must give us the courage to confront fearlessly the contemptuous laughter of the conformists, the media, and the so-called elites. We must rediscover the audacity to brave the secularist inquisition that hands out good conduct certificates to some and stigmatizes others from the heights of its self-proclaimed authority. Our reference point is not in this world! We have nothing to do with society's applause; our city is in the heavens!

Our fortitude is not a kind of stiffening, violence, or rigidity. It is the confident, joyous certainty that made Saint Paul exclaim: "If God is for us, who is against us?" (Rom 8:31).

Our fortitude is founded on faith in God. We are not afraid to defy this world because we do not do so in the name of a temporal power. Our fortitude does not rely on money, powerful media pressure, influence, or military might. Our fortitude is Jesus' fortitude. In January 2013, a few weeks before his resignation, a weary Benedict XVI spoke in a frail voice: "God seems weak if we think of Jesus Christ who prays, who lets himself be killed. This apparently weak attitude consists of patience, meekness and love, it shows that this is the real way to be powerful! This is God's power! And this power will win!"[10] The only true power of God is the power of love that dies on the Cross for our salvation.

Christian fortitude is the fortitude of the martyrs who smile at their executioners. A little while ago someone told me the story of the fifteen-year-old Tuareg who was preparing to kill a young Christian Malian of the same age. He armed himself, and, when he walked up to the victim he had chosen, the young Malian smiled at him and said to him: "Before you kill me, I just want to tell you that I have a message for you: Jesus loves you." Then the Tuareg ran away, overwhelmed by the force of the truth. He converted, he was beaten, he was tortured. He had to flee his country and his family. The one who was violent became strong with Christ's fortitude. In October 2011, at a General Audience, Benedict XVI told us: "Those who want to be disciples of the Lord, his envoys, [must] be prepared for the passion and martyrdom, to lose their own life for him.... We must be willing to pay in person, to suffer misunderstanding, rejection, persecution in the first person. It is not the sword of the

---

[10] Pope Benedict XVI, General Audience, January 30, 2013.

conqueror that builds peace, but the sword of the suffering, of whoever gives up [his] own life."[11]

On this earth, martyrdom is no longer confined to Muslim countries. It takes a lot of fortitude to be the father or the mother of a family nowadays. It takes true magnanimity, that virtue which drives us to do great things, in order to embark on the adventure of a Christian family. I want to tell all Christian parents that they are the glory of the Church of the twenty-first century: your witness is sometimes a daily martyrdom. You must confront the contempt of the world when you choose to give life. You must confront the precariousness and the uncertainty of tomorrow. But your mission is great! You bear the hope of the world and of the Church! The smiles and the joy of your children are your most beautiful reward! Stand firm! Cling to the faith! By your fidelity to Christ's teaching about the married couple and the family, by your signs of everyday love, you are sowing seeds of hope. Soon the harvest will spring up.

I also know how much priests and consecrated religious need fortitude: dear priests, sometimes you work in obscurity, with a feeling of failure. Even if the boat seems to be swept along by the storm, hold fast! Do not give in to confused talk. Do not abandon the tradition of the Church: that would be to cut off your own roots. The boat is battered by the storm. It is taking on a great deal of water: hold fast to the boat; in other words, hold fast to doctrine, and pray intensely. Look at Christ and not at the violence of the wind. Fear not! Jesus is with us; he is the one at the helm. The Church is the only ship that will never be shipwrecked! Let us hang on to the Cross without letting go. It is the true sign of Christian fortitude. The fortitude that gives all but lets go of nothing.

To all Christians I would like to say that our strength against this world of violence and falsehood is the truth of Christ. In 1972, when the Nobel Prize was awarded to him, Aleksandr Solzhenitsyn declared:

Violence does not live alone and is not capable of living alone: it is necessarily interwoven with falsehood.... Any man who has once acclaimed violence as his *method* must inexorably choose falsehood as

[11] Pope Benedict XVI, General Audience, October 26, 2011.

his *principle*. At its birth violence acts openly and even with pride. But no sooner does it become strong, firmly established, than it senses the rarefaction of the air around it and it cannot continue to exist without descending into a fog of lies, clothing them in sweet talk. It does not always, not necessarily, openly throttle the throat, more often it demands from its subjects only an oath of allegiance to falsehood, only complicity in falsehood.

And the simple step of a simple courageous man is not to partake in falsehood, not to support false actions! Let *that* enter the world, let it even reign in the world—but not with my help....

And no sooner will falsehood be dispersed than the nakedness of violence will be revealed in all its ugliness—and violence, decrepit, will fall.

These words are prophetic! We have arrived at an era in which the world unceasingly solicits our complicity with falsehood. Christian fortitude is the strength of the truth and the strength of our faith, the strength of God's love, which has been poured out into our hearts by the Holy Spirit who has been given to us (Rom 5:5). Truth is the milieu in which faith and love are experienced authentically. This is why we must create little islands of truth. Each Christian family, each school, each parish must become a little island in which all falsehood is banished, a place where we refuse all compromise with the world's ideology, relativism, and seduction. Human relations must become true and simple again. It is our responsibility to bring the truth everywhere, to occupations, professional, political, and social relations. This is Christian fortitude: rejecting falsehood. The truth will make us free, the truth is our strength!

In listening to you, we get the feeling that all the human relations of Christians must be transformed. The virtue that governs these relations and must help to bring about the change is justice, is it not?

Yes, justice is the virtue that enables us to render to each person what is due to him. This begins, naturally, with our own parents. They gave us life! Once again, I want to pay my respects to all the parents of the world. We must honor them. Filial piety is a form of justice. Christians must have the sense of piety toward their elders. Africa is acquainted with this virtue. On my continent, an old man is not considered a problem because it is necessary to care for him and feed him when he no longer produces anything. The old people assure the transmission of culture. They are our archives, our libraries, and the guardians of our traditions. Without them, peoples become orphans, without affiliation, without origin, without memory, without history, without culture, without tradition. If we do not honor our old people, we cannot love our fatherlands. The latter confer our identity on us. They shape us by their languages, their customs, their history, and their culture. We owe them honor and affection. Pope Francis said in a video message on November 1, 2018:

> There are no laboratory identities, none. Every identity has a history. And as it has a history, it has ownership. My identity comes from a family, a village, a community. You can not talk about identity without talking about belonging. Identity is belonging....
>
> Do not be fooled. Take care of your own property. And so, when we see people among us who do not respect anything, ... each one of you, ask yourself: Do I sell my heritage? Do I sell the history of my people? Do I sell the culture of my people? Do I sell my culture and what I have received from my family? Do I sell the consistency of my life?... Do not sell our deepest aspect, that is, our belonging, our identity.[12]

Justice consists, first, of recognizing that we are heirs with regard to our history. We must be proud of our fatherlands, be aware that through our birth we belong to a community with a heritage and a destiny, without falling into national idolatry as a result. An identity that is accepted is the pledge of fraternal life among the peoples. Migrants themselves must enter into this feeling of belonging to a community with a heritage and a destiny when they settle definitively in a country that welcomes them. Their identity is then amplified and modified. They become heirs by adoption. They receive all the duties of children, which consist of honoring and loving the fatherland that adopted them.

When persons are cut off from their heritage and deprived of this sense of belonging, they are made cultural orphans: they are

---

[12] Pope Francis, video message for the Scholas Occurrentes in Buenos Aires, November 1, 2018.

weakened, uprooted, handed over to barbarism. To be a barbarian is to live without being attached to any heritage, be it historical, cultural, or national. I am struck when I see that, in the Gospel, Jesus loves his people and trembles with compassion at the sight of human sufferings. Jesus loves his fatherland to the point of weeping over Jerusalem. He has a profound relation with the city that embodies the destiny and the history of his people. Without this vital sense of belonging, we feel alone, lost, and abandoned. Filial piety is a form of Christian justice that is often forgotten and yet is fundamental. This sense of filial belonging, the foundation of all civilization, is all the more important because we live in an age when relations between peoples or between persons are reduced to relations of economic competition.

Indeed, we live under the influence of an ideology that asserts that the economy, left to itself, can replace the virtue of justice and regulate human relations. Market liberalism shares this postulate with Marxism. Both try to reduce man to a producer and a consumer. Both reject any idea of justice that is not strictly the result of an economic structure. We are talking here about two totalitarian ideologies. The idea of excluding any regulation of the market by the virtue of justice amounts to handing man over to a carnivorous mechanism of competition and globalized profit. In September 2001, John Paul II said in a homily: "As Bishops we are called upon ... to be servants of the revealed word, who when needed will *raise their voices in defense of the least....* To be prophets is to point out with courage the social sins that are the fruit of consumerism, hedonism, and an economy that produces an unacceptable gap between luxury and misery, between the few "rich men" and the many 'Lazarus's' condemned to misery."[13] In order for these words to be believable, our life must also in fact be sober, detached from material goods, and really poor!

We need a true freedom of enterprise in order to develop a just economy. But this freedom must be imbued with the virtue of justice. Our freedom has a purpose, a meaning; it must flourish in a form of friendship. It cannot give free rein to the appetites for ownership while leaving it up to hypothetical laws of the marketplace to regulate these unbridled desires.

[13] Pope St. John Paul II, Homily at the Inauguration of the 10th Ordinary General Assembly of the Synod of Bishops, September 30, 2001.

Benedict XVI stated this principle magisterially in the encyclical *Caritas in veritate*: "In *commercial relationships* the *principle of gratuitousness* and the logic of gift as an expression of fraternity can and must *find their place within normal economic activity*" (*CiV* 36). We must rethink the very essence of economic relations. They cannot be reduced to a mercantile relation. They must become in the proper sense just relations between just men. Economic relations must essentially be simultaneously mercantile and open to gratuitousness.

In his message for January 1, 2012, Benedict XVI declared:

> We cannot ignore the fact that some currents of modern culture, built upon rationalist and individualist economic principles, have cut off the concept of justice from its transcendent roots, detaching it from charity and solidarity: "The 'earthly city' is promoted not merely by relationships of rights and duties, but to an even greater and more fundamental extent by relationships of gratuitousness, mercy and communion. Charity always manifests God's love in human relationships as well, it gives theological and salvific value to all commitment for justice in the world."[14]

Here there is a depth in the concept of economy that I find striking. Freedom opens the economic relation up to the just relation, which flourishes in fraternal charity that gives glory to God. People do not realize the extent to which Benedict XVI profoundly renewed the social doctrine of the Church. He made a profound synthesis and gave the idea of justice all its fullness by connecting it with the idea of charity.

Charity surpasses justice, because to love is to give, to offer oneself to the other; but it cannot exist without justice that leads us to give to the other what is *his*, in other words, what falls to him because of his being and his action. I cannot "give" to the other from what is *mine* without having given him what is his according to justice. Someone who loves others with charity is first just toward them. Not only is justice not foreign to charity, not only is it not an alternative or parallel way to charity, but justice is also *inseparable* from charity. It is intrinsic to it. Justice becomes the first way of charity or, as Pope

Paul VI said, the "minimum" of it, an integral part of this love "in deed and in truth" (1 Jn 3:18). Moreover, Benedict XVI says again in his encyclical *Deus caritas est*:

> Love—*caritas*—will always prove necessary, even in the most just society. There is no ordering of the State so just that it can eliminate the need for a service of love. Whoever wants to eliminate love is preparing to eliminate man as such. There will always be suffering which cries out for consolation and help. There will always be loneliness.... The claim that just social structures would make works of charity superfluous masks a materialist conception of man: the mistaken notion that man can live "by bread alone" (Mt 4:4; cf. Dt 8:3)—a conviction that demeans man and ultimately disregards all that is specifically human. (*DCE* 28)

Nevertheless, relations in our globalized society develop in inverse proportion, approaching the limit beyond which the system will lose its equilibrium and collapse. Violence, less and less hampered by the restrictions imposed by centuries of lawfulness, is setting the West ablaze. Moreover, not only brute force triumphs in other regions, but also the enthusiastic justification of it.

The world is carried away by the cynical conviction that force can accomplish everything and that justice is powerless. The demons of Dostoyevsky creep through the world, in full sight, contaminating countries where, a short time ago, one could not even imagine them. Through terrorist acts of destruction, the explosions, and the nihilist fires of these recent years, they manifest their intention to shake and destroy civilization. And they might very well succeed.

The world, which has suddenly become civilized and timid, has found nothing else to set against the brutal renaissance of barbarism but smiles and concessions. The spirit of surrender is a sickness of the will among the wealthy peoples. There is a permanent state of soul in those who have abandoned themselves to the pursuit of prosperity at any price, those for whom material well-being has become the purpose of their life on earth. These men—and there are many of them in the world today—have chosen passivity and retreat so as to prolong their everyday pleasure a little, so as to elude tomorrow's difficulty. The price of cowardice is always evil. We will win the victory only if we have the courage to make sacrifices.

18

WHAT MUST WE DO?

NICOLAS DIAT: *Your diagnosis seems very somber. Are you not lacking in hope?*

ROBERT CARDINAL SARAH: Hope is not a smug optimism! Since a believer's hope has it source in God, one can truly hope only insofar as one has ties with God and is open to his influence. Hope is a constant combat. In this combat, the only weapons we wield are prayer, silence, the Word of God, and faith. We need an uprising of men and women who have the courage and spiritual energy to speak and to act, thus sowing around them the seed of good sense, truth, love, and peace. Yes! Hope is a difficult combat. The *Catechism of the Catholic Church* tells us that it is "the theological virtue by which we desire the kingdom of heaven and eternal life as our happiness, placing our trust in Christ's promises and relying not on our own strength, but on the help of the grace of the Holy Spirit" (*CCC* 1817). This virtue strengthens our trust. We have no doubt, Jesus told us: "I have conquered the world." He is the victor.

Christians are peaceful and confident because they know that Christ has already conquered. What reassures us is not our own effort or our power. The Church must remain peaceful and serene when facing the coalition of powers that forms to put her to scorn. Our hope is founded on the limitless goodness of God. Christian hope is calming and demanding. Benedict XVI declared in October 2011:

> St. John Chrysostom, in one of his homilies, comments: "For so long as we are sheep, we conquer: though ten thousand wolves prowl around, we overcome and prevail. But if we become wolves, we are worsted, for the help of our Shepherd departs from us" (*Homily* 33, 1:

PG 57, 389). Christians must never yield to the temptation to become wolves among wolves; it is not with might, with force, with violence that Christ's kingdom of peace grows, but with the gift of self, with love carried to the extreme, even towards enemies.[1]

Hope enables us to be perfectly lucid in our diagnosis.

I would like to emphasize how dynamic the virtue of hope is. It brings us to desire eternal life as our ultimate happiness. The anchor of our hope is cast there, in heaven, in paradise, in God, at the very heart of the Trinity. We do not desire an earthly kingdom. We know very well that this world will pass and that the Kingdom of heaven will never be established on earth. From this perspective, it seems to me that we priests and bishops do not preach enough about the object of our hope: heaven.

In the past, they used to talk about the four last things. There was rarely a retreat without a meditation on this subject. You sometimes get the impression that Christian hope has become secularized. Today, John Paul II says in his encyclical letter *Redemptoris missio*,

> the temptation ... is to reduce Christianity to merely human wisdom, a pseudo-science of well-being. In our heavily secularized world a "gradual secularization of salvation" has taken place, so that people strive for the good of man, but man who is truncated, reduced to his merely horizontal dimension. We know, however, that Jesus came to bring integral salvation, one which embraces the whole person and all mankind, and opens up the wondrous prospect of divine filiation [to their divinization].[2]

People hope only for a better world with more solidarity, one that is more ecological, more open, more just. That would not be enough to nourish a theological hope. The object of our desire is God himself! Our heart is too large for this limited world! We must adopt as our own the exclamation of Saint Augustine: "You have made us for yourself, Lord, and our hearts are restless until they rest in you" (*Confessions*, I, 1). Yes, we are cramped in the created world. Only

---

[1] Pope Benedict XVI, General Audience, October 26, 2011.

[2] Pope St. John Paul II, Encyclical Letter *Redemptoris Missio* on the Permanent Validity of the Church's Missionary Mandate (December 7, 1990), no. 11.

God is capable of slaking our thirst for happiness! If our contemporaries desert our churches, it is very often because they arrive with the desire for God and someone tries to satisfy them with good feelings that are human, all-too-human! Let us not live beneath our rank! We are children of God and, therefore, heirs, heirs of God, co-heirs with Christ, since we suffer with him so as to be glorified with him, too, and to share his eternal happiness (cf. Rom 8:17). We are, as the Eastern Fathers of the Church say, called to be divinized in fullness. That is what heaven is!

Maybe the fear of talking about hell makes us so timid about preaching our divine vocation to holiness. We can let ourselves be divinized by the Holy Spirit only by accepting him freely. A man who refuses this gift definitively cuts himself off from God. Hell is the reality of that separation. In trying to erase the tragic shadow that the greatness and the radical character of our freedom bring with it, we have cut man off from his call to a godly eternity, to divine beatitude, and to God himself. Christian hope, on the contrary, supports our desire for God. It expands the heart and protects us from the wear and tear of discouragement.

I firmly believe that it finds its deepest source in the Eucharist. Every time we receive Communion, something happens temporarily that will be definitive and complete in heaven. In my Communion, I taste God, and he divinizes me. This is why all liturgy is the source of joy and youth. A magnificent saying is attributed to Alcuin, the monk companion of Charlemagne: "Liturgy is the joy of God." Yes, the liturgy plunges us into the very life of God. It is the anticipation of heaven. How many times I have been struck by observing the faces of those old monks who are celebrating Mass, all lit up by a new youth, quite radiant with holiness, having haloes, as it were, of heavenly light. The child then shows through beneath the features of the old man. I would say the same about the face of Pope Emeritus Benedict XVI when he celebrated at the altar. What grace, what delicacy, and what interior joy! We had the impression of seeing the face and the white hair of an old man, but his features had the innocence, the candor, and the freshness of a child's face.

In *The Spirit of the Liturgy*, Romano Guardini wrote: "The liturgy preserves freedom of spiritual movement for the soul" and, as such,

offers "the best antidote to barbarism".[3] The liturgy is a hope treatment. It revives our desire for God and, at the same time, already sat-
isfies it! I understand why Benedict XVI affirmed that the authentic
renewal of the liturgy is the fundamental condition for the renewal of
the Church. The liturgy gauges the radical character, the vehemence
of our desire for God and for heaven. Without this desire, the driving
force of the Christian life grows languid and dies out.

Contact with the saints is another place where we renew our hope.
I have had the opportunity to meet some saints, old or young, sick
or well, known or unknown. I still see at the Casa dell'Allegria, the
house of the Missionaries of Charity of Mother Teresa of Calcutta,
the face radiant with purity, divine splendor, and joy of Sister Mary
Frederick, who had just celebrated her 102nd birthday. Or the face
of Brother Vincent of the Resurrection, a young canon at the Abbey
in Lagrasse, who died, carried off by sickness. I see again many faces
of fathers and mothers of families, of discreet priests who wore themselves out performing their duties. Their eyes always reflected that
light of hope, that youth of the desire for God, like an anticipated
presence of heaven. In *Jeanne relapse et sainte*, the novelist Georges
Bernanos wrote:

> Our Church is the Church of the saints. In order to be a saint, what
> bishop would not give his ring, his miter, his crozier; what cardinal—
> his purple vestments; what pope—his white robe? Who would be
> unwilling to have the strength to run that admirable race? For sanctity
> is an adventure, one can even say it is the only adventure. Once this
> has been understood, one has entered into the heart of the Catholic
> faith and has felt his mortal flesh thrill with a terror different from the
> terror of death: a superhuman hope.

Hope must be the virtue that makes us smile like a child when we are
alone against everyone.

All you who despair, I address you: you sick people abandoned
in the hospitals, you orphans whom war has torn from the arms of
a mother, you whom the modern world has forgotten, you who no

---

[3] Romano Guardini, *The Spirit of the Liturgy*, trans. Ada Lane, in Joseph Cardinal Ratzinger,
The Spirit of the Liturgy, with Romano Guardini, *The Spirit of the Liturgy*, commemorative ed.
(San Francisco: Ignatius Press, 2018), 287n7.

longer see the dawn at the end of the night. I dare to invite you to put your hope in God. *Spes non confundit*. Hope does not disappoint!

I appeal particularly to you, brother priests who despair because you are collapsing beneath the weight of your task without seeing any results of your efforts. I repeat to you the beautiful words of Georges Bernanos spoken in 1945 during a conference:

> Someone who has not seen the road at dawn between two rows of trees, quite fresh and quite alive, does not know what hope is. Hope is a heroic determination of the soul, and its highest form is despair that has been overcome. People think that it is easy to hope. But the only ones who hope are those who have had the courage to despair of the illusions and lies in which they found a security that they incorrectly take for hope. Hope is a risk to be run; indeed, it is the risk of all risks. Hope is the greatest and the most difficult victory that man can win over his soul.... One does not attain hope except through the truth, at the cost of great efforts. In order to encounter hope, it is necessary to go beyond despair. When one walks until the end of the night, one encounters another dawn. The demon of our heart is named "What's the use?" Hell is the cessation of love.

As I listen to you, I am reminded of the remark by G. K. Chesterton: "I could not abandon the faith, without falling back on something more shallow than the faith. I could not cease to be a Catholic, except by becoming something more narrow than a Catholic.... We have come out of the shallows and the dry places to the one deep well; and the Truth is at the bottom of it." [4]

Faith broadens our view; it allows us to look at everything as God himself does, with the eyes of God. Faith causes us to enter into the mystery. Unlike a very foolish idea, faith expands the intellect. Faith does not close off, it does not forbid us to reflect; on the contrary, it deepens our understanding of the world and of men. It helps us to delve into the depths of things, into their mysterious reality, into the secret of their intimate being. It allows us to see what is usually obscure to us. Without faith, a whole sector of reality is off-limits

[4] G. K. Chesterton, "The Well and the Shallows", in *Collected Works*, vol. 3 (San Francisco: Ignatius Press, 1990), 391.

to us. Faith opens for us a door to the depth of reality. Thanks to faith, the universe appears to us in all its breadth as "a cosmic Church whose 'nave' is sensible creation and whose 'choir' is the world of intelligible realities", to repeat the words of Hans Urs von Balthasar, quoting Saint Maximus the Confessor.[5]

The act of believing surpasses intellectual conviction. The act of faith is a real participation in the knowledge of God himself, in his view of everything. I remember a very beautiful page by the Ruma-nian novelist Virgil Gheorghiu in *De la vingt-cinquième heure à l'heure éternelle* [From the twenty-fifth hour to the eternal hour] describing the experience of a child who suddenly looks at the world and people with the eyes of faith:

> It was a Sunday, then. And it was after the Divine Liturgy. I was look-ing at the people of the village as they came out of the church.... The whole village was present, because on Sundays no one ever missed the Divine Liturgy.... Everyone seemed transfigured, divested of all earthly preoccupations, sanctified. And even more than sanctified: deified.... I knew why all their faces were beautiful and why all their eyes were lit up. For the ugly women were beautiful. The two for-estry workers wore on their cheeks and on their foreheads lights sim-ilar to the haloes of the saints. The children were like angels. As they went out after the Divine Liturgy, all the men and all the women of our village were *theophoroi*, that is, God-Bearers.... I have never seen skin or flesh more beautiful than on the faces of the Theophoroi, the people who carry within them the dazzling light of God. Their flesh was deified, without weight or volume, transfigured by the light of the divine Spirit.

Truly, the faith leads us to experience transfiguration. Of course this experience occurs every day in a form of obscurity that is often arid. Yet we already taste by anticipation what we will see in eternity by the actual vision of God.

We must live up to our Christian vocation. We must always remember the words of Pope Saint Leo: "Christian, recognize your dignity!" I would add: Do not deprive yourself of the treasure of the

---

[5] Hans Urs von Balthasar, *Cosmic Liturgy: The Universe according to Maximus the Confessor*, trans. Brian E. Daley, S.J. (Communio Books; San Francisco: Ignatius Press, 2003), 327.

faith. Christ came to open up full understanding for us, and we wish to return to the darkness? Some Christians seem to want to deprive themselves of this light. They force themselves to see the world from a secularized perspective. Why? Is it a desire to be accepted by the world? A desire to be like everyone else? I wonder whether, deep down, this attitude does not quite simply disguise the fear that makes us refuse to listen to what Jesus himself tells us: "You are the salt of the earth; you are the light of the world." What a responsibility! What a commission! To give up being the salt of the earth is to condemn the world to being insipid and flavorless; to give up being the light of the world is to condemn it to darkness. We must not be persuaded to do that. It even happens that some pastors, wishing to "meet the world", deliberately neglect this faith perspective in order to adopt a profane view. What a loss! In adopting categories that originated in an atheistic context, one chooses blindness and a blinkered view. Let us free ourselves from such a hang-up! Let us turn toward the world, but in order to bring to it the only light that does not deceive. "A turning of the Church toward the world, which would entail turning away from the cross, cannot lead to the Church's renewal, but [only] 'to her demise'. The purpose of the Church's turning toward the world cannot be to dispense with the scandal of the cross, but exclusively to render its nakedness accessible anew." Joseph Ratzinger spoke these serious words in 1966 in Bamberg at the *Katholikentag*.[6]

With many Christians, there is a reluctance to witness to the faith or to bring light to the world. Our faith has become lukewarm, like a memory that becomes blurred little by little. It becomes like a milky mist. Then we no longer dare to affirm that it is the only light of the world. Nevertheless, it is necessary to affirm with Cardinal Ratzinger in his book *Truth and Tolerance*:

> The Christian faith ... is not the product of our own experiences; rather, it is an event that comes to us from without. Faith is based on our meeting something (or someone) for which our capacity for experiencing things is inadequate.... Certainly, what touches us there effects an experience in us, but experience as the result of an event,

---

[6] As quoted by Eric Gaál in *The Theology of Pope Benedict XVI: The Christocentric Shift* (New York: Palgrave Macmillan, 2010), 50.

not of reaching deeper into ourselves. This is exactly what is meant by the concept of revelation: something not ours, not to be found in what we have, comes to me and takes me out of myself, above myself, creates something new.[7]

How could we bring to the world a strictly personal experience, an incommunicable illumination? We have to bear witness, not to ourselves, but to God, who came to meet us and revealed himself. God showed himself; he showed us his face in Jesus. He died to save us from sin and to offer us his beatitude: "In the revelation of God, he, the Living and True One, bursts into our world and also opens the prison of our theories", Cardinal Ratzinger said in Guadalajara in 1996.[8]

Faith is altogether an intimate, personal, interior act and an adherence to an objective content that we did not choose. Through faith, we personally make an act by which we decide to rely totally on God in full freedom. I believe: by this act, the heart, the authentic sanctuary of the person, opens up under the influence of grace to the objective content that God reveals, to which we give our assent. Then the faith blossoms into profession, in other words, into public witness. Our belief can never remain purely private. Faith, because it is an act of freedom, requires that the believer assume in the sight of everyone the responsibility that it involves. Therefore, the faith can be professed only in the Church, with the Church, which hands on to us the integral knowledge of the mystery, of the contents that are to be known and believed.

Making faith a purely personal feeling renders it incommunicable, cuts it off from the Church, and, above all, empties it of all content. It is therefore urgent to insist on the teaching of the catechism both to adults and to children. For that purpose, we have a marvelous tool available: the *Catechism of the Catholic Church* and the *Compendium* of it. Teaching the catechism is more than an intellectual knowledge of its contents. It promotes a true encounter with Jesus, who revealed

[7] Joseph Cardinal Ratzinger, *Truth and Tolerance: Christian Belief and World Religions*, trans. Henry Taylor (San Francisco: Ignatius Press, 2004), 87–89.

[8] Joseph Cardinal Ratzinger, Prefect of the Congregation for the Doctrine of the Faith, "The Current Situation of Faith and Theology", Meeting with the Doctrinal Commissions of Latin America (Guadalajara, Mexico, May 7, 1996).

these truths to us. As long as we have not encountered Jesus physically, we are not really Christians.

I think that bishops must rediscover the meaning of catechesis. We must learn again to become catechists, faithful teachers of the divine truths. After all, this is one of our primary missions. Look at the bishops of the early Church—Ambrose, Augustine, John Chrysostom, Basil, Gregory: they spent the greater part of their time teaching, catechizing in a way that was simple, humble, and direct. They did not give courses in theology; they did not comment on current events. The dared to teach the people of God because they knew that through their words the faithful would encounter Jesus. Today some contrast teaching and experience. The experience of God can be had only through teaching: "How are they to believe in him ... without a preacher?", Saint Paul asks (Rom 10:14–15).

This failure of catechesis leads a great many Christians to support a sort of vagueness concerning the faith. Some choose to believe one article of the Creed and reject another. Some go so far as to take surveys about the adherence of Catholics to the Christian faith ... The faith is not a merchant's stall where we go to select whatever fruits and vegetables we like. In receiving it, we receive God whole and entire. "Men of too familiar and too passive a faith, perhaps for us dogmas are no longer the Mystery on which we live, the Mystery which is to be accomplished in us",[9] said Father Henri de Lubac in *Paradoxes*. I solemnly call on Christians to love the dogmas, the articles of faith, and to cherish them. Let us love our catechism. If we receive it not only with our lips but with our heart, then, through the formulas of the faith, we will truly enter into communion with God.

It is time to snatch Christians from the surrounding relativism that anesthetizes hearts and puts love to sleep. Henri de Lubac added:

If heretics no longer horrify us today, as they once did our forefathers, is it certain that it is because there is more charity in our hearts? Or would it not too often be, perhaps, without our daring to say so, because the bone of contention, that is to say, the very substance of our faith, no longer interests us?... Consequently, then, heresy no

---

[9] Henri de Lubac, *Paradoxes of Faith*, trans. Paule Simon et al. (San Francisco: Ignatius Press), 226.

longer shocks us; at least, it no longer convulses us like something trying to tear the soul of our souls away from us.... It is not always charity, alas, which has grown greater, or which has become more enlightened: it is often faith, the taste for the things of eternity, which has grown less.[10]

It is time for the faith to become for Christians their most intimate, most precious treasure. Think of all the martyrs who died for the purity of their faith at the time of the Arian crisis: because they professed that the Son is not only similar to the Father but of one substance with him, how many bishops, priests, monks, and simple believers suffered torture and death! What is at stake is our relationship with God, not just some theological quarrels. You can gauge by our apathy regarding doctrinal deviations the lukewarmness that has set in among us. It is not uncommon to see serious errors being taught in the Catholic universities or in officially Christian publications. No one reacts! We bishops content ourselves with prudent, fearful clarifications. Beware, one day the faithful will demand an accounting of us. They will accuse us before God of having handed them over to the wolves, of having deserted our post as pastor defending the sheepfold. I am not calling here for a reinstatement of the Inquisition! My cry is a cry of love! Our faith affects our love for God. To defend the faith is to defend the weakest, the simplest, and to help them to love God in truth.

Dear brother bishops, priests, and all you baptized persons: we must burn with love for our faith. We must not tarnish it or dilute it in worldly compromises. We must not falsify or corrupt it. It is a matter of the salvation of souls: ours and those of our brethren! "The day when you no longer burn with love, others will die of cold", François Mauriac wrote. The day when we no longer burn with love for our faith, the world will die of cold, deprived of its most precious good. It is up to us to defend and to proclaim the faith!

What a grace for me, a child of Africa, to have seen French missionaries arrive in my remote village: their faith was so ardent that they left their fatherland, their families, and came to die in my homeland. Many died very young, having offered themselves as holocausts for the glory of God and the salvation of souls. Father Firmin Montels,

---

[10] Ibid., 226–27.

founder of my parish, Sainte-Rose d'Ourous, died six months after his arrival in the village while singing, "O Salutaris hostia". Who will rise up today to proclaim to the cities of the West the faith for which they are waiting? Who will rise up to proclaim the true faith to the Muslims? They seek it without knowing that they do. Who will be the missionaries whom the world needs? Who will be the missionaries who will teach the faith in its fullness to so many Catholics who do not know what they believe?

Let us stop putting the light of the faith under a bushel basket; let us stop hiding this treasure that was given to us gratuitously! Let us dare to proclaim, to witness, to catechize! We can no longer call ourselves believers and live in practice like atheists. The faith enlightens our whole life, not only our spiritual life.

In identifying with tolerance or secularism, one imposes upon oneself a kind of schizophrenia between private life and public life. Faith has its place in the public debate. We must speak about God, not to impose him, but to propose him. God is an indispensable light for man. In 2007, the Congregation for the Doctrine of the Faith had to remind everyone of the legitimacy of evangelizing and proclaiming the faith. Indeed, when religious questions are at stake, any attempt to convince may be perceived as an obstacle to freedom. Some declare that it is enough to help men be more human, and they refer them to their conscience. Now conscience needs to be enlightened. We live by each other's witness. Vatican Council II reminded us that "the truth cannot impose itself except by virtue of its own truth."[11] But it also explains in *Gaudium et spes* that respect for this liberty "must in no way render us indifferent to truth and goodness. Indeed, love itself impels the disciples of Christ to speak the saving truth to all men."[12]

As for the *Doctrinal Note on Some Aspects of Evangelization* by the Congregation for the Doctrine of the Faith, it recalled that:

> The truth which saves one's life inflames the heart of the one who has received it with a love of neighbor that motivates him to pass on to others in freedom what he has freely been given.

[11] Vatican Council II, Declaration on Religious Freedom *Dignitatis humanae* on the Right of the Person and of Communities to Social and Civil Freedom in Matters Religious (December 7, 1965), 1.

[12] Vatican Council II, Pastoral Constitution on the Church in the Modern World *Gaudium et spes* (December 7, 1965), 28.

Although non-Christians can be saved through the grace which God bestows in "ways known to him", the Church cannot fail to recognize that such persons are lacking a tremendous benefit in this world: to know the true face of God and the friendship of Jesus Christ, God-with-us. Indeed "there is nothing more beautiful than to be surprised by the Gospel, by the encounter with Christ. There is nothing more beautiful than to know him and to speak to others of our friendship with him". The revelation of the fundamental truths about God, about the human person and the world, is a great good for every human person, while living in darkness without the truths about ultimate questions is an evil and is often at the root of suffering and slavery which can at times be grievous. This is why Saint Paul does not hesitate to describe conversion to the Christian faith as liberation "from the power of darkness" and entrance into "the kingdom of his beloved Son in whom we have redemption and the forgiveness of our sins" (Col 1:13–14). Therefore, fully belonging to Christ, who is the Truth, and entering the Church do not lessen human freedom, but rather exalt it and direct it towards its fulfilment, in a love that is freely given and which overflows with care for the good of all people. It is an inestimable benefit to live within the universal embrace of the friends of God which flows from communion in the life-giving flesh of his Son, to receive from him the certainty of forgiveness of sins and to live in the love that is born of faith. The Church wants everyone to share in these goods so that they may possess the fullness of truth and the fullness of the means of salvation, in order "to enter into the freedom of the glory of the children of God" (Rom 8:21)....

However, the Church's "missionary proclamation is endangered today by relativistic theories which seek to justify religious pluralism, not only *de facto* but also *de iure* (or in principle)." For a long time, the reason for evangelization has not been clear to many among the Catholic faithful. It is even stated that the claim to have received the gift of the fullness of God's revelation masks an attitude of intolerance and a danger to peace.

Those who make such claims are overlooking the fact that the fullness of the gift of truth, which God makes by revealing himself to man, respects the freedom which he himself created as an indelible mark of human nature: a freedom which is not indifference, but which is rather directed towards truth. This kind of respect is a requirement of the Catholic faith itself and of the love of Christ; it is a constitutive element of evangelization and, therefore, a good which is to be promoted inseparably with the commitment to making the fullness of salvation, which God offers to the human race in the Church, known and freely embraced....

It is a love which lives in the heart of the Church and from there, as burning charity, radiates out to the ends of the earth, as far as the heart of every human being. The entire heart of man awaits the encounter with Jesus Christ.

Thus one understands the urgency of Christ's invitation to evangelization and why it is that the mission entrusted by the Lord to the Apostles involves all the baptized. The words of Jesus, "go therefore and teach all nations, baptizing them in the name of the Father, the Son and the Holy Spirit, teaching them to observe all that I have commanded you" (Mt 28:19–20), are directed to everyone in the Church, each according to his own vocation.[13]

Saint Augustine wrote: "In this life, virtue consists of loving what must be loved. Knowing how to choose it is prudence, not letting oneself be distracted by seductive powers is temperance, not letting oneself be led astray by pride is justice" (Letter 155). Basically, all virtues boil down to love and charity, do they not?

Indeed, charity is the virtue by which we love God more than everything, as well as our brethren, for the love of God. It is the perfect form of all the other Christian virtues. For a Christian, as Saint Augustine puts it in *De moribus ecclesiae*: "Temperance is love giving itself entirely to that which is loved; fortitude is love readily bearing all things for the sake of the loved object; justice is love serving only the loved object, and therefore ruling rightly; prudence is love distinguishing with sagacity between what hinders it and what helps it."[14]

Charity sums up and orients the whole life of the virtues. Unfortunately, many of our contemporaries think that it is a nice feeling. Far from it; it is a theological virtue that puts us in contact with God. It comes from God. To understand charity is, in the first place, to look toward God himself, because God is love, God is charity.

---

[13] Congregation for the Doctrine of the Faith, *Doctrinal Note on Some Aspects of Evangelization* (October 6, 2007), nos. 7, 10.

[14] St. Augustine, *Of the Morals of the Catholic Church*, trans. Richard Stothert, in *Nicene and Post-Nicene Fathers*, First Series, ed. Philip Schaff, vol. 4 (1887; Peabody, Mass.: Hendrickson, 1994), 48.

In *Deus caritas est*, Benedict XVI wrote:

When Jesus speaks in his parables of the shepherd who goes after the lost sheep, of the woman who looks for the lost coin, of the father who goes to meet and embrace his prodigal son, these are no mere words: they constitute an explanation of his very being and activity. His death on the Cross is the culmination of that turning of God against himself in which he gives himself in order to raise man up and save him. This is love in its most radical form. By contemplating the pierced side of Christ (cf. Jn 19:37), we can understand the starting-point of this Encyclical Letter: "God is love" (1 Jn 4:8). It is there that this truth can be contemplated. It is from there that our definition of love must begin. [*DCE* 12]

We cannot speak about charity unless we start with the heart of Jesus. Charity is not an emotion. Charity is a participation in the love with which God loves us, in the love that is manifested in the Sacrifice of the Mass. When Christians hear the word charity, they think of giving a little money to the poor or to a charitable organization. It is about much more than that. Charity is the blood that courses through the heart of Jesus. Charity is the love that gives itself to the point of death. Love causes us to embrace God himself; it makes us enter into his Trinitarian communion where everything is love. Charity manifests the presence of God in the soul. Saint Augustine said it clearly: "If you see charity, you see the Trinity" [*DCE* 19], because God is charity. Charity is God's gift and God himself. It draws us ever farther into union with God. Love is never finished or complete. It grows ceaselessly to become a communion of will with God. Through charity, little by little, God's will is no longer strange, "it is now my own will, based on the realization that God is in fact more deeply present to me than I am to myself. Then self-abandonment to God increases and God becomes our joy", as Benedict XVI remarked in *Deus caritas est* [*DCE* 17].

At the heart of our religion is this discovery of charity that gives the saints such a disconcerting countenance. A saint is someone who, fascinated by the beauty of God, gives up everything, even himself, and enters into the great movement of return to the Father that was initiated by Christ. We are all called to it. I want to repeat to all Christians: we are called to renounce everything, even ourselves, out of love for God. In this, consecrated religious show us the way. The monks and the nuns leave everything, renouncing themselves. They concretely take all the necessary means. Let us not think that their vocation does not concern us. We have to live out this radical renunciation, each one in his state of life. We all have to experience the truth that God's love is enough.

But charity concerns our neighbor, too, does it not?

Certainly, with one and the same love we love God and those whom God loves: our brethren. Communion with God draws me out of myself toward him and toward my brethren. "Union with Christ is also union with all those to whom he gives himself. I cannot possess Christ just for myself; I can belong to him only in union with all those who have become, or who will become, his own", Benedict XVI wrote in *Deus caritas est* [*DCE* 14].

I want to insist on this point. Christian charity makes me love my brethren for God and in God. When Mother Teresa held the hand of a dying person, she loved Christ in agony in that person. Mother Teresa, and the community of nuns that follows in her footsteps, have given us the example. She always set as the first condition for establishing her foundations the presence of a tabernacle. Without the presence of the love of God who gives himself, it would not have been possible to carry out that apostolate, it would not have been possible to live in such self-abandonment; only by entering into this abandonment in God, into this adventure of God, into this humility of God, could she accomplish, with her sisters, this great act of love, this openness to everyone.

I would like to make an appeal to all Christians. Does our charity really draw from its source in the tabernacle? The hours spent in adoring the Blessed Sacrament should lead me to the poorest of the poor, the ones most ignorant of God, those who suffer most; otherwise they are sterile. It is urgent and vital to ask ourselves how much time we spend before the Eucharistic Jesus present in the tabernacle. A parish in which there is no adoration of the Blessed Sacrament is a dead parish or a sick one. The humble, silent presence of Jesus in our midst calls for our humble, silent presence. Even cloistered religious are led by adoration to live in spiritual compassion with the souls who are in the world. But the active religious, all those who are at the forefront of the missions, of the struggle against poverty or for the relief of suffering, must ask themselves the question: Is their commitment rooted in a taste for action? If so, their works will be sterile and harmful. If adoration is present among them, if loving knowledge of the heart of Jesus is present among them, then they will be for the world like the hand of Jesus that comes to alleviate suffering.

I wish to turn to my brother priests. A little while ago, Pope Francis reminded us that charity is at the center of the life of the Church, that it is its heart. Can we adopt as our own these words of the Supreme Pastor? Do we live by the same love with which Christ has loved us? He left the glory of heaven to come and load us onto his shoulders—us, lost humanity! Let us not forget these magnificent words of Benedict XVI to all the priests gathered on Saint Peter's Square in April 2005.

> When the shepherd of all humanity, the living God, himself became a lamb, he stood on the side of the lambs, with those who are downtrodden and killed.... It is not power, but love that redeems us! This is God's sign: he himself is love.... God, who became a lamb, tells us that the world is saved by the Crucified One, not by those who crucified him. The world is redeemed by the patience of God. It is destroyed by the impatience of man.... [To be a shepherd means to love,] and loving also means being ready to suffer.[15]

Dear brother priests, do we love with that love which crucifies?

Archbishop Raymond-Marie Tchidimbo, my predecessor in the episcopal see of Conakry, after being arrested on December 24, 1970, and then imprisoned and tortured under the Marxist dictatorship of Sékou Touré, wrote these words upon his liberation:

> It was in prison that I understood better why the people of God loved to discover in the life of the priest this Passion of Christ, as the apostle Paul described it in his forceful letter to the Galatians. I understood better also why this same people of God desired and still desires to

---

[15] Pope Benedict XVI, Homily at the Mass, Imposition of the Pallium and Conferral of the Fisherman's Ring for the Beginning of the Petrine Ministry of the Bishop of Rome (April 24, 2005).

discover in the priest—not "as something extra", but as an integral part of his priestly being, along with this absolute thirst that is summed up in the Cross—all the qualities that are appreciated so much in human relations.

Our life must have a "sacrificial form". It must go so far as the love that is expressed in sacrifice. It must therefore be nourished by the Sacrifice of the altar and of the Mass.

Thérèse of Lisieux understood that the heart of the Church is love. She understood that the apostles would no longer proclaim the Gospel, that the martyrs could no longer shed their blood, if this heart stopped burning. She understood that she herself, the little nun behind the grilles of the Carmel in a little town in a French province, could be present everywhere, since in loving with Christ she was at the heart of the Church. This center, which Thérèse simply calls heart and love, is the Eucharist. Indeed, it is not only the permanent presence of the divine and human love of Jesus Christ, which is always the source of the Church, without which she would be doomed to sink and to be swallowed up by the gates of hell. As the presence of the divine and human love of Christ, the Eucharist is [also] the continual passage of the man Jesus to the human beings who are his members and who themselves become Eucharist and therefore the heart and the love of the Church. The heart must remain a heart so that, thanks to it, the other organs may be capable of serving as they should.

You have drawn the portrait of the Christian of our time, in which each virtue is a feature. Do you want to add a few lines to this portrait?

I wish to insist on the virtue of religion because it in particular is forgotten today. Religion is the virtue that makes us offer worship to God, that makes us pray to him and adore him. It culminates in the sacrifice of praise that we offer him through the Mass, which is prolonged by the recitation of the Divine Office.

We often forget that this worship is owed to God. We do not generously make to him a present of our time. It is justice to offer him the interior homage of our devotion and the exterior homage of our acts of adoration. The virtue of religion is founded on the transcendence of the Divine Majesty, on the one hand, and the dependence of our created littleness, on the other hand. We see today some priests and Christian faithful handling divine things with such disrespect and carelessness that its stirs up the heart against them. There is a veritable loss of the sense of the sacred and of God's infinite transcendence. Is modern man proud to the point of being reluctant to adore?

This too often forgotten virtue colors the acts of the three theological virtues, for which it prepares the ground, and they in turn nourish it. Every act of faith and love of God relies on adoration. In a nice metaphor, Cardinal Journet said that "charity comes from worship like fragrance from a flower." Already, in all human love, there is a sort of bow to the dignity conferred by God on the other person, who is created in the image of God. Already at the human level, genuine love cannot mean that we seize and possess the other. Love includes acknowledging, respectfully, the greatness and the uniqueness of the other person, of whom one must never take possession. In *God Is Near Us*, Cardinal Ratzinger wrote:

> In our Communion with Jesus Christ this attains a new level, since it inevitably goes beyond any human partnership. The Word of the Lord as our "partner" explains a great deal but leaves much else undisclosed. We are not on the same footing. He is the wholly other; it is the majesty of the living God that comes to us with him. Uniting ourselves with him means submitting and opening ourselves up to his greatness. That has found expression in the devotional approach to Communion in every age. Augustine says in one place, in a sermon to his new communicants: No one can receive Communion without first adoring.... What we are told about the monks of Cluny, around the year one thousand, is particularly striking. Whenever they went to receive Communion, they took their shoes off. They knew that the burning bush was here, the mystery before which Moses, in the desert, sank to his knees. The form may change, but what has to remain is the spirit of adoration.[16]

It seems to me that sometimes we try to create with the Lord God a familiarity that is misplaced and artificial. On the contrary, I am struck to see how the old Carthusian Fathers who have spent their

---

[16] Joseph Cardinal Ratzinger, *God Is Near Us: The Eucharist, the Heart of Life*, trans. Henry Taylor (San Francisco: Ignatius Press, 2003), 83.

whole life in intimacy with God insist on prostrating themselves on the ground before his Eucharistic Presence as a sign of adoration and love. At the Grande Chartreuse, I was personally impressed by the half-hour of prostration and adoration of the monks before the tabernacle, in preparation for the celebration of Mass. The more spiritual a man is, the more he has the sense of reverence before the Divine Majesty. Acts of adoration are not reserved to simple souls or to beginners. It is important not to despise this sense of the sacred, this joyful, simple fear before everything that concerns God. Yes, we have to kneel down before him. Yes, we should tremble with that "chaste fear, completely filled with love", to repeat the words of Saint Augustine, at the moment when we enter the sanctuary of a church or approach the altar. Yes, let us relearn to kneel in silence and to adore the Divine Majesty, let us learn to rediscover the joy of our littleness before God.

Some Christians, with a certain snobbishness, flaunt their casualness with the sacred, as though that category were pagan or reflected a primitive mentality. "Christ . . . did not abolish the sacred but brought it to fulfillment, inaugurating a new form of worship, which is indeed fully spiritual but which, however, as long as we are journeying in time, still makes use of signs and rites. . . . Thanks to Christ, the sacred is truer, more intense and, as happens with the Commandments, also more demanding!" Benedict XVI declared in his homily on the Feast of Corpus Christi, June 7, 2012. It would be arrogant to claim to go to God without getting rid of a profane attitude.

If Christians are deprived of the beautiful virtue of religion, which gives us this sense of adoration and worship, they are deprived of full communion with God. Such contempt for worship springs from pride. Our whole attitude must become religious, in other words, marked by veneration for God. It should be possible to offer him all our gestures, our interior movements, as worship. I love to see the monks bow profoundly each time their lips pronounce the concluding formula, "Gloria Patri et Filio et Spiritui Sancto." Nevertheless, they do this dozens of times each day. What a lesson in radical humility! What an expression of humble, filial love! The monks' humility reveals God's grandeur. I think that we would all gain from rediscovering this sense of religion. It is the signature of a particularly delicate, refined, and sensitive form of Christianity. I dare to say that it is one of the hallmarks of Christian civilization. It is the politeness, the distinction of the creature before his Creator. If you want to rediscover the virtue of religion, there is a school for you: the monasteries. Do not hesitate to visit them. You, too, will become *Theodidactoi*: pupils of God and adorers in spirit and in truth (Jn 4:24–25).

Not only monks, but all men and women religious, too, have a major role to play in the Church. By their lives, they must ceaselessly recall what it is to be offered, consecrated to the glory of God. The life of consecrated religious is like a great offertory. It teaches Christians an essential aspect: every baptized person must live in a state of oblation and offering. Our life must become a great liturgy, a spiritual sacrifice, as Saint Peter put it (1 Pet 2:5).

With what final message would you like to leave us to conclude this book?

I would like to confide something to you. I think that our time is experiencing the temptation to atheism. Not the hard, militant atheism we have seen aping Christianity through Marxist or Nazi pseudo-liturgies. That sort of atheism, a kind of religion in reverse, has become discreet. I mean, rather, a subtle, dangerous state of mind: fluid atheism. Now that is an insidious, dangerous sickness, even though its first symptoms seem benign.

In his book *Notre coeur contre l'athéisme* [Our heart versus atheism], Father Jérôme, a Cistercian monk at the Abbey of Sept-Fons, describes it as follows:

> Fluid atheism, which is never professed as such, mixes in seamlessly with other philosophies, with our personal problems, with our religion. Without our being aware of it, it can imbue our judgment as Christians. In any one of us, fluid atheism can infiltrate into all the nooks and crannies that are not occupied by the theological virtue of faith and grace....
>
> We think we are immune, and yet we foolishly applaud all sorts of hypotheses, postulates, slogans, and realizations that undermine our beliefs. We spread ideas without noticing the brand names on the labels. The worst thing is that some materialist ideas can remain in our mind without colliding violently with Christian ideas, which ought to be there, too. This suggests that our Christian convictions are not very firm or substantial. That is the beginning of defeat: fluid materialism

lives in our mind next door to our Christianity, which is probably fluid, too.

We must realize that this fluid atheism runs through our veins. It never says its name, but it infiltrates everywhere. And nevertheless, Saint Paul vehemently recommends: "Do not be mismated with unbelievers. For what partnership have righteousness and iniquity? Or what fellowship has light with darkness? What accord has Christ with Belial? Or what has a believer in common with an unbeliever? What agreement has the temple of God with idols?" (2 Cor 6:14–16). Despite the warnings of Saint Paul, we coexist fraternally and peacefully with fluid atheism; in our tolerance, we sympathize with it. Its first effect is a sort of lethargic faith. It anesthetizes our ability to react, to recognize error. This has spread in the Church. Pope Francis, in the homily that he gave on November 29, 2018, spoke terrible words. He commented on the destruction of Babylon, a city "of luxuriousness, of self-sufficiency, of worldly power, a lair of demons, the den of all impure spirits". This destruction starts from within, the pope explains, and ends when the Lord says: "Enough." There will be a day when the Lord says: "Enough with the appearances of this world." This is the crisis of a civilization that sees itself as proud, self-sufficient, dictatorial, and it ends in this manner. And the pope denounced "the paganization of life".

> Do we live as Christians? It seems like we do. But really our life is pagan, when these things happen: when we are seduced by Babylon and Jerusalem lives like Babylon. The two seek a synthesis which cannot be effected. And both are condemned. Are you a Christian man? Are you a Christian woman? Live like a Christian. Water and oil do not mix. They are always distinct. A contradictory society that professes Christianity but lives like a pagan shall end. . . .
>
> This teaches us to live the trials of the world, not in a compromise with worldliness or paganism which brings about our destruction, but in hope, separating ourselves from this worldly and pagan seduction by looking to the horizon and hoping in Christ the Lord. Hope is our strength for moving forward.

In conclusion he invited the congregation to think of the modern-day Babylons: "The great cities of today will also end this way, and so will our lives, if we continue along this road towards paganism. . . . Let us open our hearts with hope and distance ourselves from the paganization of Christian life."[17]

What is to be done? You may tell me that this is the way of the world. You may tell me that the Church has to adapt or die. You may tell me that if the essentials are intact, it is necessary to be flexible about the details. You may tell me that truth is theoretical but that the particular cases escape it. So many statements that seriously confirm the illness! Instead, I would like to invite you to reason differently. In the autobiographical novel by Solzhenitsyn, *The First Circle*, the hero hesitates to keep the privileges bestowed on him by the totalitarian system in order to buy his silence. A discovery tips the scale for him. He comes across the notebook of his elderly mother, now deceased, and in it reads these words: "What is the most precious thing in the world? I see now that it is the knowledge that you have no part in injustice. Injustice is stronger than you, it always was and always will be, but let it not be done through you."[18]

We Christians, too, must let ourselves be upset by these words. One does not compromise with falsehood! The distinctive feature of fluid atheism is its compromise with falsehood. This is the greatest temptation of our time.

Make no mistake: no one ever fights with that enemy and wins. It is possible to fight hard atheism head-on and to deal it decisive blows, to denounce and refute it. But fluid atheism is elusive and sticky. If you attack it, if you engage in a physical battle, fight hand-to-hand with fluid atheism, it will catch you in its subtle compromises. It is like a spider's web; the more you struggle, the tighter its hold on you. Fluid atheism is the ultimate snare of the Tempter. It draws you onto his own turf. If you follow him there, you will be led to use his weapons: falsehood and compromise. All around him he foments division, resentment, bitterness, and a partisan spirit. Just look at the state of the Church! Everywhere there is nothing but dissension, hostility, and suspicion.

[17] As reported in the article "Pope at Mass: 'So-Called Christian Societies Will End If Pagan'", *Vatican News*, November 29, 2018, https://www.vaticannews.va/en/pope-francis/mass-casa-santa-marta/2018-11/pope-francis-mass-christian-societies-end-if-pagan.html.

[18] Aleksandr Solzhenitsyn, *In the First Circle*, trans. Harry Willets (New York: Harper Collins, 2009), 438–39.

With all my heart as a pastor, I want to invite Christians today to act. We do not have to create parties within the Church. We do not have to proclaim ourselves the saviors of this or that institution. All that would play into the adversary's hands. Instead, each of us can make this resolution: the falsehood of atheism will no longer pass through me. I no longer want to renounce the light of faith; I no longer want, out of convenience, laziness, or conformism, to make light and darkness cohabit within me. This is a very simple decision, at the same time interior and concrete. It will change our lives in their most minute details. It is not about going off to war. It is not about denouncing enemies. It is not about attacking or criticizing. It is about remaining steadfastly faithful to Jesus Christ. If someone cannot change the world, he can change himself. If each one decided humbly to do that, then the system of falsehood would collapse by itself, because its only strength is the room that we make for it in ourselves: fluid atheism feeds only on my compromises with its falsehood.

Does that frighten you? Maybe your assurance is not steadfast enough? If that is the case, remember with Father Jérôme that

> The certitude possessed by the believer comes to him, not from what he knows and from what he sees, but from what is known and seen by the one in whom he trusts. I entrust myself to God because of the lights that *he* possesses, not because of the lights that *I* possess. I can be blind with respect to matters related to salvation, but my faith does not care, because it relies on the absolute knowledge of God.... This is why the believer experiences a sense of security, peace of mind, and intellectual courage. He is sure that he possesses the truth because he knows that he is taking the hand of Someone who is the Truth itself.

Dear Christians, in offering us the faith, God opens his hand so that we can put ours into it and let him lead us. What could we possibly fear? The essential thing is to keep our hand firmly in his! Our faith is this profound tie with God himself. "I know whom I have believed", Saint Paul says (2 Tim 1:12). He is the One in whom we have put our faith.

Father Jérôme's conclusion is brilliant: "In Christianity, there is nothing but the faith. However, confronted with atheism, whether hard or fluid, the faith acquires an essential importance. It is at the same time the treasure that we want to defend and the strength that enables us to defend it."

To keep the spirit of faith is to renounce all compromises; it is to refuse to see things in any other way than through faith. It is to keep our hand in God's hand. I profoundly believe that this is the only possible source of peace and kindness. Keeping our hand in God's is the pledge of true benevolence without complicity, true kindness without cowardice, true strength without violence. Faith is more than ever a relevant virtue!

I want to emphasize, too, how much joy the faith brings. How can we not be joyful when we commend ourselves to the one who is the source of joy! An attitude of faith is demanding, but it is not rigid or strained. Let us be happy since we are taking his hand. Faith gives rise to fortitude and joy together: "The LORD is the stronghold of my life; of whom shall I be afraid?" (Ps 27:1). The Church is dying, overrun by bitterness and a partisan spirit. Only the spirit of faith can establish an authentic fraternal benevolence. The world is dying, consumed by falsehood and rivalry. Only the spirit of faith can bring it peace.

Dear friends, I would like to repeat to you the strong, prophetic words of Father de Lubac, written in 1942, in the middle of the war, in his book *The Drama of Atheist Humanism*:

> In the present state of the world, a virile, strong Christianity must become a heroic Christianity.... It will consist, *above all*, in resisting with courage, in the face of the world and perhaps against one's own self, the lures and seductions of a false ideal and in proudly maintaining, in their paradoxical intransigence, the Christian values that are threatened and derided. Maintaining them with humble pride.... The Christian who would remain faithful is bound to reject with a categorical No a neopaganism that has set itself up against Christ. Gentleness and goodness, considerateness toward the lowly, pity for those who suffer, rejection of perverse methods, protection of the oppressed, unostentatious self-sacrifice, resistance to lies, the courage to call evil by its proper name, love of justice, the spirit of peace and concord, open-heartedness, mindfulness of heaven; those are the things that Christian heroism will rescue.... Christians have not been promised that they will always be in the majority. (Rather the

reverse.) Nor that they will always seem the strongest and that men will never be conquered by another ideal than theirs. But, whatever happens, Christianity will never have any real efficacy, it will never have any real existence or make any real conquests, except by the strength of its own spirit, *by the strength of charity.*[19]

Yes, more than ever we are called to be strong, vigorous, and unshakable in our faith! We are like the disciples. After the crucifixion, they no longer understand. Their faith is eroded. Sadness overcomes them. They think that everything is lost. We, too, see the world delivered over to the greed of the powerful. The Church seems to be overcome by the spirit of atheism. Now some shepherds are even abandoning their sheep. The sheepfold is devastated. We too, like the disciples, flee the city, disappointed, desperate, and set out for Emmaus, toward nothingness. Ahead of us lies a road that seems to lead nowhere. We walk without understanding and without knowing where to go. Only the wind comes to haunt our bitterness.

Nevertheless, here is a man walking with us. What are you conversing about as you walk, he asks us. And we tell him about our sadness, our anguish, our disappointment. Then he speaks again, reproaching us for our lack of faith: "O foolish men, and slow of heart to believe all that the prophets have spoken! Was it not necessary that the Christ should suffer these things and enter into his glory? Was it not necessary that the Church should suffer in order to be faithful to her Master?" He explains the Scriptures to us. His words strengthen us. He rekindles our faith. Our solitude is suddenly broken by the strength of his certitude and the kind benevolence of his glance.

And while, in the distance, the sun seems to fade away behind the mountains, while the shadows lengthen on the road and the cold spreads in our bodies, our courage is revived and we beg him: Our hearts burn within us when you speak to us. Stay with us, Lord, for it is toward evening and the day is now far spent.

---

[19] Henri de Lubac, *The Drama of Atheist Humanism*, trans. Edith M. Riley et al. (San Francisco: Ignatius Press, 1995), 129.

LET NOTHING TROUBLE ME

It is not enough always to follow the gleam: it is necessary sometimes to rest in the glow; to feel something sacred in the glow of the camp fire as well as the gleam of the polar star. And that same mysterious and to some divided voice, which alone tells that we have here no abiding city, is the only voice which within the limits of this world can build up cities that abide.

—G. K. Chesterton
The Outline of Sanity

The book that is coming to an end has roots that are deep and old. It is the final volume of a triptych—an adventure that began in December 2013.

With Robert Cardinal Sarah, we started then the conversations that would be the writing material for *God or Nothing*. In the Spring of 2015, the publication of these discussions about the faith was an event of unexpected magnitude. For ten days, the cardinal came to the French capital to speak about his book. The cold that prevailed in Paris hardly expressed the warmth, the fervor, and the enthusiasm that accompanied the publication of *God or Nothing*. I remember evenings at the Church of Saint Francis Xavier, at Trinity Church, at Saint Leo, at the Collège des Bernardins, or at the bookstore La Procure. Each time, people crowded to hear him.

Far from Paris, in the Abbey of Lagrasse, on his sickbed, suffering from a severe case of multiple sclerosis, Brother Vincent kept vigil and prayed. He was the cardinal's mysterious protector. For *God or Nothing* was a kind of miracle. How else can we understand the formidable success of such a radical and, therefore, incomprehensible book by a man who had always avoided the spotlight? For a long time, Robert Cardinal Sarah, a close friend of Benedict XVI and a collaborator with Pope Francis, preferred the radiant shadow of prayer. The real reason for this success lies in the simplicity, humility, and holiness of the cardinal.

A few months later, while traveling to Lagrasse, we thought about writing a book on the importance of silence in our world, which is overcome by noise, images, and passions. This was *The Power of Silence*, the second book in this triptych. Our conversation with Dom Dysmas de Lassus, prior of Grande Chartreuse monastery, with which these mystical, poetic pages conclude, remains the ardent heart of our literary adventure.

I will never be able to forget the three days that we spent in Chartreuse. It was early February 2016, but time seemed to stand still. In the presence of those expanses of snow, side by side with the solitary, secluded, contemplative monks, we were in heaven.

Today I can admit that I was afraid that *The Power of Silence* would not have a large readership. The subject was difficult, arid, far removed from facile polemics. But soon the book was a great success.

In November 2016, at the Cathedral of Versailles, an immense crowd listened attentively and respectfully to the cardinal. Several months later, at the Basilica in Fourvière, the citizens of Lyon had standing room only in the immense edifice. In Kraków, Avila, Washington, and Brussels, this experience was repeated. A man of God drew the people of God.

When I think back to those four years, the abbatial mottoes of the recent Father-Abbots of Fontgombault come to mind: *Unum necessarium* (The one thing necessary); *Donec dies elucescat* (Until the eternal day dawns); *Ad superna semper intenti* (Ever aiming at celestial things); *Modo geniti infantes* (Like newborn infants): they express the monastic ideal of a place where God is the one served first. They express the ideal of Cardinal Sarah.

The Day Is Now Far Spent is a prophetic cry. Will these distressing statements meet with a response, or will they fade away into the dark night? Hope is the cement that holds Cardinal Sarah's life together. Despite the poverty into which he was born, the violence of the dictatorship, the jolts of being uprooted repeatedly, the fatigue of exhausting responsibilities, he has never doubted. He has never feared. He has never retreated. For God is with him. The cardinal knows that he can constantly find him behind the doors of his little private chapel.

This is not to give the impression that everything went smoothly in this adventure. How many times I thought of the remark by Jules Barbey d'Aurevilly in his collection of short stories, *Disjecta membra*: "Great men are like the most beautiful flowers. They grow beneath the manure and through the dung thrown on them by the envious and the imbeciles." Which, of course, is putting it too strongly.

Georges Bernanos wrote in his *Diary of a Country Priest*: "When has any man of prayer told us that prayer had failed him?"[1] The cardinal always took his risks because prayer never disappointed him. Asceticism, fasting, and daily reading of Sacred Scripture helped him.

Eight months before his death, Brother Vincent had to be hospitalized in order to undergo a difficult surgical procedure. His community, his relatives, and friends were worried. The operation could be fatal. I had the difficult task of informing the cardinal about developments in the young patient's health. On the morning of the operation, when the prognosis was guarded, I shared with him the intense anxieties of Father Abbot and of the doctors. To my great surprise, the cardinal was serene. In his view, the operation would be a success; he had no doubt that the Brother would manage to get out of this crisis. Several days later, I learned that the cardinal had prayed in his private chapel the whole night before the operation. He had not rested. But he knew. He knew that Brother Vincent's hour had not yet come. He knew God's will.

Saint John Bosco liked to repeat: "Let nothing trouble you; always be joyful!" In the company of Cardinal Sarah, this poor earthly life often has the color of the hereafter. The reason for this is simple: Robert Cardinal Sarah has many friends in heaven. *Ut cooperatores simus veritatis* (We must serve in such a way that we are co-workers of the truth). This is the motto of Benedict XVI; Cardinal Sarah, his best disciple, can adopt it as his own. He is assuredly a great co-worker of the truth.

Nicolas Diat
Paris, Monday, February 25, 2019

[1] Georges Bernanos, *Diary of a Country Priest*, trans. Pamela Morris (New York: Carroll & Graf, 2002), 105.

BIBLIOGRAPHY

Augustine, Saint. *Essential Sermons*. Translated by Edmund Hill, O.P. Works of Saint Augustine: A Translation for the 21st Century, pt. 3. New York: New City Press, 2007.

——. *Homilies on the Gospel of John 1–40*. Translated by Edmund Hill, O.P. Works of Saint Augustine, A Translation for the 21st Century, pt. 3, vol. 12. New York: New City Press, 2009.

——. *Of the Morals of the Catholic Church*. Translated by Richard Stothert. In *Nicene and Post-Nicene Fathers*, First Series, ed. Philip Schaff, vol. 4. 1887; Peabody, Mass.: Hendrickson, 1994.

——. *Sermon 355*. In *Sermons 341–400 on Various Themes*. Hyde Park, N.Y.: New City Press, 1996.

Baudelaire, Charles. *Les Fleurs du mal*. Selections in English translation by Roy Campbell: *Poems of Baudelaire*. New York: Pantheon Books, 1952.

Bednarski, Piotr. *Les Neiges bleues*. Paris: Autrement, 2004.

Benedict XVI, Pope (Joseph Ratzinger). "Catholicism after the Council". Translated by Fr. Patrick Russell. *The Furrow* 18/1 (January 1967): 3–23.

——. *Church, Ecumenism, and Politics: New Endeavors in Ecclesiology*. Translated by Michael J. Miller et al. San Francisco: Ignatius Press, 2008.

——. *Collected Works*. Vol. 11: *Theology of the Liturgy*. Edited by Michael J. Miller. Translated by Kenneth Baker, S.J., et al. San Francisco: Ignatius Press, 2014.

——. *Europe Today and Tomorrow: Addressing the Fundamental Issues*. Translated by Michael J. Miller. San Francisco: Ignatius Press, 2007. Republished in 2019 under the title *Western Culture Today and Tomorrow: Addressing the Fundamental Issues*. San Francisco: Ignatius Press, 2019.

——. *Faith and Politics*. Selected Writings. Translated by Michael J. Miller et al. San Francisco: Ignatius Press, 2018.

——. *God Is Near Us: The Eucharist, the Heart of Life*. Translated by Henry Taylor. San Francisco: Ignatius Press, 2003.

——. *Introduction to Christianity*. Translated by J. R. Foster. Revised edition. San Francisco: Ignatius Press, 2004.

————. *Jesus of Nazareth: Holy Week: From the Entrance into Jerusalem to the Resurrection.* Translated by the Vatican Secretariat of State. San Francisco: Ignatius Press, 2011.

————. *Light of the World: The Pope, the Church, and the Signs of the Times.* Translated by Michael J. Miller and Adrian J. Walker. San Francisco: Ignatius Press, 2010.

————. *Ministers of Your Joy: Scriptural Meditations on Priesthood.* Translated by Robert Nowell. Ann Arbor: Redeemer Books, 1989.

————. *Principles of Catholic Theology: Building Stones for a Fundamental Theology.* Translated by Sister Mary Frances McCarthy, S.N.D. San Francisco: Ignatius Press, 1987.

————. *The Spirit of the Liturgy.* Translated by John Saward. San Francisco: Ignatius Press, 2000.

————. *Truth and Tolerance: Christian Belief and World Religions.* Translated by Henry Taylor. San Francisco: Ignatius Press, 2004.

————. *A Turning Point for Europe? The Church in the Modern World—Assessment and Forecast.* Translated by Brian McNeil, C.R.V. San Francisco: Ignatius Press, 1994.

————. *Values in a Time of Upheaval.* Translated by Brian McNeil. San Francisco: Ignatius Press, 2006.

————. "Why I Am Still in the Church". In *Fundamental Speeches from Five Decades*, translated by Michael J. Miller et al., 133–53. San Francisco: Ignatius Press, 2012.

————, with Vittorio Messori. *The Ratzinger Report: An Exclusive Interview on the State of the Church.* Translated by Salvator Attanasio and Graham Harrison. San Francisco: Ignatius Press, 1985.

Bernanos, Georges. "Brother Martin". Translated by Erwin W. Geissman. *Cross Currents* 2/4 (Summer 1952): 1–9.

————. *La France contre les robots.* FV Éditions, 2019.

————. *Jeanne relapse et sainte.* Paris: Desclée de Brouwer, 1994.

————. *Journal d'un curé de campagne.* Paris: Le Livre de Poche, 2015. Translated by Pamela Morris as *Diary of a Country Priest.* New York: Carroll & Graf, 2002.

Bernard of Clairvaux, Saint. *Some Letters of Saint Bernard, Abbot of Clairvaux.* London: John Hodges, 1904.

Bouyer, Louis. *Le Métier de théologien: entretiens avec Georges Daix.* Paris: Ad Solem, 2005.

Chesterton, G.K. *The Well and the Shallows.* In *Collected Works*, vol. 3. San Francisco: Ignatius Press, 1990.

Delsol, Chantal. *La Haine du monde: totalitarisme et postmodernité.* Paris: Cerf, 2016.

Diat, Nicolas. *Un temps pour mourir: Derniers jours de la vie des moines.* Paris: Fayard, 2018.

Francis, Pope (Jorge Mario Bergoglio). *Amour service et humilité: exercices spirituels donnés à ses frères évêques à la manière de saint Ignace de Loyola.* Paris: Magnificat, 2013.

Garonne, Gabriel-Marie. *L'Église: Lumen gentium: constitution dogmatique du 21 novembre 1964.* Paris: Le Centurion, 1972; Paris: Téqui, 2011.

Gheorghiu, Virgil. *De la vingt-cinquième heure à l'heure éternelle.* Paris: Pocket, 1977.

Guardini, Romano. *Meditations before Mass.* Translated by Elinor Castendyk Briefs. Westminster, Md.: Newman Press, 1956.

———. *The Spirit of the Liturgy.* Translated by Ada Lane. In Joseph Cardinal Ratzinger, *The Spirit of the Liturgy,* with Romano Guardini, *The Spirit of the Liturgy,* commemorative ed. San Francisco: Ignatius Press, 2018.

Ignatius Loyola, Saint. *Spiritual Exercises.* Translated by Thomas Corbishley. New York: Kennedy, 1963.

Ionesco, Eugène. *Antidotes.* Paris: Gallimard, 1977.

Irenaeus of Lyons, Saint. *Against Heresies.* In *Ante-Nicene Fathers,* edited by Alexander Roberts and James Donaldson, 1:315–567. 1885; Peabody, Mass.: Hendrickson, 1995.

Jérôme (Père). *Oeuvres spirituelles.* Vol. 6: *Notre coeur contre l'athéisme.* Paris: Ad Solem, 2014.

Jerome, Saint. *Commentary on Ezekiel.* Translated by W. H. Fremantle et al. In *Nicene and Post-Nicene Fathers,* Second Series, ed. Philip Schaff and Henry Wace. 1893; Peabody, Mass.: Hendrickson, 1995.

John of the Cross, Saint. *The Spiritual Canticle.* In *The Collected Works of St. John of the Cross,* translated by Kieran Kavanaugh, O.C.D., and Otilio Rodriguez, O.C.D. Washington, D.C.: Institute of Carmelite Studies, 1979.

Kierkegaard, Søren. *The Sickness unto Death: A Christian Psychological Exposition for Upbuilding and Awakening.* Translated by Howard V. Hong and Edna H. Hong. Princeton: Princeton University Press, 1988.

Lubac, Henri de. *De Lubac: A Theologian Speaks.* Los Angeles: Twin Circle Publishing Co., 1985.

———. *The Drama of Atheist Humanism.* Translated by Anne Englund Nash et al. San Francisco: Ignatius Press, 1995.

———. *More Paradoxes.* Translated by Anne Englund Nash. San Francisco: Ignatius Press, 2002.

———. *Paradoxes of Faith.* Translated by Paule Simon et al. San Francisco: Ignatius Press, 1987.

———. *Theology in History.* Translated by Anne Englund Nash. San Francisco: Ignatius Press, 1996.

Maritain, Jacques. *The Peasant of Garonne: An Old Catholic Layman Questions Himself about Modern Times.* Translated by Michael Cuddihy and Elizabeth Hughes. New York: Holt, Rinehart and Winston, 1968.

Mounier, Emmanuel. *L'Affrontement chrétien.* Les Plans-sur-Bex: Parole et Silence, 2017.

Nault, Jean-Charles. *The Noonday Devil: Acedia, the Unnamed Evil of our Times.* Translated by Michael J. Miller. San Francisco: Ignatius Press, 2015.

———. *La Saveur de Dieu, l'acédie dans le dynamisme de l'agir.* Paris: Cerf, 2006.

Newman, Blessed John Henry. *An Essay on the Development of Doctrine.* Westminster, Md.: Christian Classics, 1968.

Nietzsche, Friedrich. *The Gay Science.* In *The Portable Nietzsche,* translated by Walter Kaufmann. New York: Viking Press, 1954.

Pascal, Blaise. *Pensées.* Translated by W. F. Trotter. Mineola, N.Y.: Dover, 2018.

———. *Pour un traité du vide.* Paris: Nathan, 1999.

Péguy, Charles. *Une Éthique sans compromise.* Coll. "Agora". Paris: Pocket, 2011.

———. *Note conjointe.* Paris: Gallimard, 1935.

———. *Oeuvres en prose completes.* Vol. 1: *Articles antérieurs à la période des Cahiers, articles contenus dans les* Cahiers de la quinzaine *jusqu'en 1905.* Paris: Gallimard, 1987.

Puppinck, Grégor. *Les Droits de l'homme dénaturé.* Paris: Cerf, 2018.

Renard, Alexandre. *Où va l'Église?* Paris: Desclée de Brouwer, 1976.

———. *Riches et pauvres dans l'Église ancienne.* Coll. "Ictys", no. 6. Paris: Grasset, 1962.

Salles, Catherine de. *Saint Augustin, un destin africain.* Paris: Desclée de Brouwer, 2009.

Sartre, Jean-Paul. *Nausea.* Translated by Lloyd Alexander. Norfolk, Conn.: New Directions, 1949.

Schönborn, Christoph. *Loving the Church: Spiritual Exercises Preached in the Presence of Pope John Paul II.* Translated by John Saward. San Francisco: Ignatius Press, 1998.

Solzhenitsyn, Aleksandr. *L'Erreur de l'Occident.* Paris: Grasset, 1980.

———. *In the First Circle.* Translated by Harry Willets. New York: Harper Collins, 2009.

————. *The Solzhenitsyn Reader: New and Essential Writings, 1947–2005*. Edited and translated by Edward Ericson, Jr., and Daniel J. Mahoney. Wilmington, Del.: Intercollegiate Studies Institute, 2006.

Vincent of Lerins, *A Commonitory for the Antiquity and Universality of the Catholic Faith*. In *Nicene and Post-Nicene Fathers*, Second Series, edited by Philip Schaff and Henry Wace, 11:131–56. 1894; Peabody, Mass.: Hendrickson, 1995.

Von Balthasar, Hans Urs. *Cosmic Liturgy: The Universe according to Maximus the Confessor*. Translated by Brian E. Daley, S.J. Communio Books; San Francisco: Ignatius Press, 2003.

————. *A Short Primer for Unsettled Laymen*. Translated by Mary Theresilde Skerry. San Francisco: Ignatius Press, 1985.

Yourcenar, Marguerite. *Les Yeux ouverts: Entretiens avec Matthieu Galey*. Paris: Éditions du Centurion, 1980.